ANNUAL EDITIONS

Physical Anthropology 13/14

Twenty-Second Edition

EDITOR

Elvio Angeloni
Pasadena City College

Elvio Angeloni received his BA from UCLA in 1963, his MA in anthropology from UCLA in 1965, and his MA in communication arts from Loyola Marymount University in 1976. He has produced several films, including *Little Warrior,* winner of the Cinemedia VI Best Bicentennial Theme, and *Broken Bottles,* shown on PBS. He served as an academic adviser on the instructional television series *Faces of Culture.* He received the Pasadena City College Outstanding Teacher Award in 2006. He is also the academic editor of *Annual Editions: Anthropology, Classic Edition Sources: Anthropology,* co-editor of *Rountable Viewpoints Physical Anthropology,* and co-editor of *Annual Editions: Archaeology.* His primary area of interest has been indigenous peoples of the American Southwest.

Connect
Learn
Succeed™

ANNUAL EDITIONS: PHYSICAL ANTHROPOLOGY, TWENTY-SECOND EDITION

Published by McGraw-Hill, a business unit of The McGraw-Hill Companies, Inc., 1221 Avenue of the Americas, New York, NY 10020. Copyright © 2013 by The McGraw-Hill Companies, Inc. All rights reserved. Printed in the United States of America. Previous editions © 2012, 2011, and 2010. No part of this publication may be reproduced or distributed in any form or by any means, or stored in a database or retrieval system, without the prior written consent of The McGraw-Hill Companies, Inc., including, but not limited to, in any network or other electronic storage or transmission, or broadcast for distance learning.

Some ancillaries, including electronic and print components, may not be available to customers outside the United States.

This book is printed on acid-free paper.

Annual Editions® is a registered trademark of the McGraw-Hill Companies, Inc.
Annual Editions is published by the **Contemporary Learning Series** group within the McGraw-Hill Higher Education division.

1 2 3 4 5 6 7 8 9 0 QDB/QDB 1 0 9 8 7 6 5 4 3 2

MHID: 0-07-813590-7
ISBN: 978-0-07-813590-3
ISSN: 1074-1844 (print)
ISSN: 2162-5646 (online)

Managing Editor: *Larry Loeppke*
Marketing Director: *Adam Kloza*
Marketing Manager: *Nathan Edwards*
Senior Developmental Editor: *Debra A. Henricks*
Senior Project Manager: *Joyce Watters*
Buyer: *Nichole Birkenholz*
Cover Designer: *Studio Montage, St. Louis, MO.*
Content Licensing Specialist: *DeAnna Dausener*
Media Project Manger: *Sridevi Palani*

Compositor: Laserwords Private Limited
Cover Image: © Creatas/PunchStock (inset); © Digital Vision/PunchStock (background)

www.mhhe.com

Editors/Academic Advisory Board

Members of the Academic Advisory Board are instrumental in the final selection of articles for each edition of ANNUAL EDITIONS. Their review of articles for content, level, and appropriateness provides critical direction to the editors and staff. We think that you will find their careful consideration well reflected in this volume.

ANNUAL EDITIONS: Physical Anthropology 13/14
22nd Edition

EDITOR

Elvio Angeloni
Pasadena City College

ACADEMIC ADVISORY BOARD MEMBERS

Preface

In publishing ANNUAL EDITIONS we recognize the enormous role played by the magazines, newspapers, and journals of the public press in providing current, first-rate educational information in a broad spectrum of interest areas. Many of these articles are appropriate for students, researchers, and professionals seeking accurate, current material to help bridge the gap between principles and theories and the real world. These articles, however, become more useful for study when those of lasting value are carefully collected, organized, indexed, and reproduced in a low-cost format, which provides easy and permanent access when the material is needed. That is the role played by ANNUAL EDITIONS.

This twenty-second edition of *Annual Editions: Physical Anthropology* contains a variety of articles relating to human evolution. The writings were selected for their timeliness, relevance to issues not easily treated in the standard physical anthropology textbooks, and clarity of presentation.

Whereas textbooks tend to reflect the consensus within the field, *Annual Editions: Physical Anthropology 13/14* provides a forum for the controversial. We do this in order to convey to the student that the study of human development is an evolving entity in which each discovery encourages further research and each added piece of the puzzle raises new questions about the total picture.

Our final criterion for selecting articles is readability. All too often, the excitement of a new discovery or a fresh idea is deadened by the weight of a ponderous presentation. We seek to avoid that by incorporating essays written with enthusiasm and with the desire to communicate some very special ideas to the general public.

Included in this volume are a number of features that are designed to be useful for students, researchers, and professionals in the field of anthropology. While the articles are arranged along the lines of broadly unifying subject areas, the *Topic Guide* can be used to establish specific reading assignments tailored to the needs of a particular course of study. Other useful features include the *Contents* abstracts, which summarize each article and present key concepts in bold italics. In addition, each unit is preceded by an overview that provides a background for informed reading of the articles, emphasizes critical issues, and presents *Learning Outcomes* that are tied to *Critical Thinking* questions at the end of each article. The *Internet References* section can be used to further explore the topics online.

Finally, instructors will appreciate a password-protected online Instructor's Resource Guide, and students will find online quizzing to further test their understanding of the material. These tools are available at www.mhhe.com/cls via the Online Learning Center for this book.

Elvio Angeloni

Elvio Angeloni
Editor
evangeloni@gmail.com

The Annual Editions Series

VOLUMES AVAILABLE

Adolescent Psychology

Aging

American Foreign Policy

American Government

Anthropology

Archaeology

Assessment and Evaluation

Business Ethics

Child Growth and Development

Comparative Politics

Criminal Justice

Developing World

Drugs, Society, and Behavior

Dying, Death, and Bereavement

Early Childhood Education

Economics

Educating Children with Exceptionalities

Education

Educational Psychology

Entrepreneurship

Environment

The Family

Gender

Geography

Global Issues

Health

Homeland Security

Human Development

Human Resources

Human Sexualities

International Business

Management

Marketing

Mass Media

Microbiology

Multicultural Education

Nursing

Nutrition

Physical Anthropology

Psychology

Race and Ethnic Relations

Social Problems

Sociology

State and Local Government

Sustainability

Technologies, Social Media, and Society

United States History, Volume 1

United States History, Volume 2

Urban Society

Violence and Terrorism

Western Civilization, Volume 1

Western Civilization, Volume 2

World History, Volume 1

World History, Volume 2

World Politics

Contents

UNIT 1
Evolutionary Perspectives

The concepts in bold italics are developed in the article. For further expansion, please refer to the Topic Guide.

UNIT 2
Primates

UNIT 3
Sex and Gender

The concepts in bold italics are developed in the article. For further expansion, please refer to the Topic Guide.

UNIT 4
The Fossil Evidence

UNIT 5
Late Hominid Evolution

The concepts in bold italics are developed in the article. For further expansion, please refer to the Topic Guide.

UNIT 6
Human Diversity

The concepts in bold italics are developed in the article. For further expansion, please refer to the Topic Guide.

UNIT 7
Living with the Past

The concepts in bold italics are developed in the article. For further expansion, please refer to the Topic Guide.

The concepts in bold italics are developed in the article. For further expansion, please refer to the Topic Guide.

Correlation Guide

The *Annual Editions* series provides students with convenient, inexpensive access to current, carefully selected articles from the public press. **Annual Editions: Physical Anthropology 13/14** is an easy-to-use reader that presents articles on important topics such as *evolution, natural selection, primates,* and many more. For more information on *Annual Editions* and other *McGraw-Hill Contemporary Learning Series* titles, visit www.mhhe.com/cls.

This convenient guide matches the units in **Annual Editions: Physical Anthropology 13/14** with the corresponding chapters in four of our best-selling McGraw-Hill Anthropology textbooks by Fuentes, Relethford, Park, and Stein/Rowe.

Annual Editions: Physical Anthropology 13/14	Biological Anthropology: Concepts and Connections, 2/e by Fuentes	The Human Species: An Introduction to Biological Anthropology, 9/e by Relethford	Biological Anthropology, 7/e by Park	Physical Anthropology, 11/e by Stein/Rowe
Unit 1: Evolutionary Perspectives	**Chapter 1:** Introduction to Evolutionary Fact and Theory **Chapter 3:** Introduction to Genetics and Genomics **Chapter 4:** Modern Evolutionary Theory	**Chapter 1:** Science and Evolution **Chapter 2:** Human Genetics **Chapter 3:** The Forces of Evolution **Chapter 4:** The Evolution and Classification of Species	**Chapter 1:** Biological Anthropology **Chapter 2:** The Evolution of Evolution **Chapter 3:** Evolutionary Genetics **Chapter 4:** The Processes of Evolution **Chapter 5:** The Origin of Species and the Shape of Evolution **Chapter 6:** A Brief Evolutionary Timetable	**Chapter 1:** Investigating the Nature of Humankind **Chapter 2:** The Study of Heredity **Chapter 3:** The Modern Study of Human Genetics **Chapter 5:** Natural Selection and the Origin of Species
Unit 2: Primates	**Chapter 5:** Primate Behavioral Ecology **Chapter 6:** Early Primate Evolution	**Chapter 5:** The Primates **Chapter 6:** Primate Behavior and Ecology	**Chapter 5:** The Origin of Species and the Shape of Evolution **Chapter 7:** The Primates **Chapter 8:** Primate Behavior and Human Evolution	**Chapter 7:** The Living Primates **Chapter 9:** Nonhuman Primate Behavior **Chapter 12:** The Early Primate Fossil Record and the Origin of the Hominins **Chapter 13:** The Early Hominids
Unit 3: Sex and Gender	**Chapter 2:** The Basics of Human Biology **Chapter 10:** Human Biological Diversity in Context	**Chapter 7:** The Human Species	**Chapter 14:** Biological Anthropology and Today's World	**Chapter 16:** The Biology of Modern *Homo Sapiens*
Unit 4: The Fossil Evidence	**Chapter 7:** Early Hominin Evolution **Chapter 8:** Plio-Pleistocene Hominins and the Genus Homo **Chapter 9:** The Rise of Modern Humans	**Chapter 8:** The Fossil Record **Chapter 9:** Primate Origins and Evolution **Chapter 10:** The First Hominins **Chapter 11:** The Origin of the Genus Homo **Chapter 12:** The Evolution of Archaic Humans **Chapter 13:** The Origin of Modern Humans	**Chapter 9:** Studying the Human Past **Chapter 10:** Evolution of the Early Hominins **Chapter 11:** The Evolution of Genus Homo **Chapter 12:** Evolution and Adaptation in Human Populations	**Chapter 11:** The Record Of The Past **Chapter 12:** The Early Primate Fossil Record and the Origin of the Hominins **Chapter 14:** Early Species of The Genus *Homo*
Unit 5: Late Hominid Evolution	**Chapter 9:** The Rise of Modern Humans	**Chapter 13:** The Origin of Modern Humans	**Chapter 11:** The Evolution of Genus Homo	**Chapter 14:** Early Species of The Genus *Homo* **Chapter 15:** The Evolution Of *Homo Sapiens*
Unit 6: Human Diversity	**Chapter 2:** The Basics of Human Biology **Chapter 3:** Introduction to Genetics and Genomics **Chapter 10:** Human Biological Diversity in Context	**Chapter 14:** Race and Human Variation **Chapter 15:** Recent Human Evolution **Chapter 16:** Human Biocultural Adaptation	**Chapter 13:** Human Biological Diversity **Chapter 14:** Biological Anthropology and Today's World	**Chapter 8:** Comparative Studies: Anatomy and **Genetics** **Chapter 16:** The Biology of Modern *Homo Sapiens* **Chapter 17:** The Analysis of Human Variation
Unit 7: Living with the Past	**Chapter 4:** Modern Evolutionary Theory **Chapter 11:** The Present and Future of Human Evolution	**Chapter 17:** The Biological Impact of Agriculture and Civilization	**Chapter 14:** Biological Anthropology and Today's World	**Chapter 18:** The Modern World

Topic Guide

This topic guide suggests how the selections in this book relate to the subjects covered in your course. You may want to use the topics listed on these pages to search the Web more easily.

On the following pages a number of websites have been gathered specifically for this book. They are arranged to reflect the units of this Annual Editions reader. You can link to these sites by going to www.mhhe.com/cls.

All the articles that relate to each topic are listed below the bold-faced term.

Aggression
- 7. First, Kill the Babies
- 11. Dim Forest, Bright Chimps
- 12. Peace Among Primates

Anatomy
- 1. Was Darwin Wrong?
- 2. The Facts of Evolution
- 17. The Human Family's Earliest Ancestors
- 18. First of Our Kind
- 19. Rethinking Neanderthals
- 21. A New View of the Birth of *Homo sapiens*
- 22. Meet the New Human Family
- 23. Refuting a Myth About Human Origins
- 24. The Birth of Childhood
- 26. A Bigger, Better Brain
- 27. The Limits of Intelligence
- 28. Top Ten Myths About the Brain
- 29. The Naked Truth
- 30. Can White Men Jump?: Ethnicity, Genes, Culture, and Success
- 32. How Real Is Race?: Using Anthropology to Make Sense of Human Diversity
- 34. Dead Men Do Tell Tales

Archaeology
- 19. Rethinking Neanderthals
- 23. Refuting a Myth About Human Origins

Bipedalism
- 14. What's Love Got to Do with It?: Sex Among Our Closest Relatives Is a Rather Open Affair
- 17. The Human Family's Earliest Ancestors
- 18. First of Our Kind
- 29. The Naked Truth

Burials
- 19. Rethinking Neanderthals

Culture
- 10. Got Culture?
- 12. Peace Among Primates
- 19. Rethinking Neanderthals
- 23. Refuting a Myth About Human Origins
- 25. The Evolution of Grandparents
- 26. A Bigger, Better Brain
- 30. Can White Men Jump?: Ethnicity, Genes, Culture, and Success
- 32. How Real Is Race?: Using Anthropology to Make Sense of Human Diversity
- 39. The Inuit Paradox

Darwin, Charles
- 1. Was Darwin Wrong?
- 2. The Facts of Evolution
- 3. Evolution in Action
- 4. Darwin and His Disciples

Disease
- 6. Why Should Students Learn Evolution?
- 35. Different Minds
- 36. The Viral Superhighway
- 37. The Perfect Plague
- 38. The Human Vector
- 40. Curse and Blessing of the Ghetto
- 41. Ironing It Out

DNA (deoxyribonucleic acid)
- 6. Why Should Students Learn Evolution?
- 8. The 2% Difference
- 21. A New View of the Birth of *Homo sapiens*
- 40. Curse and Blessing of the Ghetto

Dominance hierarchy
- 7. First, Kill the Babies
- 12. Peace Among Primates
- 13. What Are Friends For?
- 14. What's Love Got to Do with It?: Sex Among Our Closest Relatives Is a Rather Open Affair

Ethnicity
- 30. Can White Men Jump?: Ethnicity, Genes, Culture, and Success
- 39. The Inuit Paradox
- 40. Curse and Blessing of the Ghetto

Evolution
- 1. Was Darwin Wrong?
- 2. The Facts of Evolution
- 3. Evolution in Action
- 4. Darwin and His Disciples
- 6. Why Should Students Learn Evolution?
- 8. The 2% Difference
- 17. The Human Family's Earliest Ancestors
- 18. First of Our Kind
- 25. The Evolution of Grandparents
- 29. The Naked Truth
- 31. Skin Deep
- 37. The Perfect Plague
- 38. The Human Vector
- 41. Ironing It Out

Evolutionary perspective
- 1. Was Darwin Wrong?
- 2. The Facts of Evolution
- 3. Evolution in Action
- 4. Darwin and His Disciples
- 5. The Latest Face of Creationism
- 6. Why Should Students Learn Evolution?
- 15. The Double Life of Women
- 31. Skin Deep
- 35. Different Minds
- 38. The Human Vector
- 39. The Inuit Paradox
- 41. Ironing It Out

Internet References

The following Internet sites have been selected to support the articles found in this reader. These sites were available at the time of publication. However, because websites often change their structure and content, the information listed may no longer be available. We invite you to visit www.mhhe.com/cls for easy access to these sites.

Annual Editions: Physical Anthropology 13/14

General Sources

American Anthropological Association (AAA)
www.aaanet.org

Maintained by the AAA, this site provides links to AAAs publications (including tables of contents of recent issues, style guides, and others) and to other anthropology sites.

Anthropology Resources on the Internet
www.socsciresearch.com/r7.html

Links to Internet resources of anthropological relevance, including Web servers in different fields, are available here. The Education Index rated it "one of the best education-related sites on the Web."

Anthropology Resources Page
www.usd.edu/anth

Many topics can be accessed from this University of South Dakota site. South Dakota archaeology, American Indian issues, and paleopathology resources are just a few examples.

Library of Congress
www.loc.gov

Examine this extensive website to learn about resource tools, library services/resources, exhibitions, and databases in many different subfields of anthropology.

The New York Times
www.nytimes.com

Browsing through the archives of *The New York Times* will provide a wide array of articles and information related to the different subfields of anthropology.

Smithsonian Institution Web Home Page
www.si.edu

Access to the vast anthropological and archaeological resources of the Smithsonian Institution.

UNIT 1: Evolutionary Perspectives

American Institute of Biological Sciences
www.actionbioscience.org

An education resource promoting bioscience literacy.

Charles Darwin on Human Origins
www.literature.org/Works/Charles-Darwin

This website contains the text of Charles Darwin's classic writing, *On the Origin of Species,* which presents his scientific theory of natural selection.

Clinical Epigenetics
www.clinicalepigeneticsjournal.com

Clinical Epigenetics is the official journal of the Clinical Epigenetics Society. It is an open access, peer-reviewed journal that encompasses all aspects of epigenetic principles and mechanisms.

Enter Evolution: Theory and History
www.ucmp.berkeley.edu/history/evolution.html

Find information related to Charles Darwin and other important scientists at this website. It addresses preludes to evolution, natural selection, and more. Topics cover systematics, dinosaur discoveries, and vertebrate flight.

Harvard Dept. of MCB—Biology Links
http://mcb.harvard.edu/BioLinks.html

This site features sources on evolution and links to anthropology departments and laboratories, taxonomy, paleontology, natural history, journals, books, museums, meetings, and many other related areas.

National Center for Science Education
www.natcenscied.org

A nationally recognized clearinghouse for information on how to defend the teaching of evolution in public schools.

UNIT 2: Primates

African Primates at Home
www.indiana.edu/~primate/primates.html

Don't miss this unusual and compelling site describing African primates on their home turf. "See" and "hear" features provide samples of vocalizations and beautiful photographs of various types of primates.

The Dian Fossey Gorilla Fund International
www.gorillafund.org

This site is dedicated to the conservation of gorillas and their habitats in Africa through anti-poaching, regular monitoring, research, education, and support of local communities. The DFGFI uniquely continues to promote the ideals and vision of Dr. Dian Fossey.

Electronic Zoo/NetVet-Primate Page
http://netvet.wustl.edu/primates.htm

This site touches on every kind of primate from A to Z and related information. The long list includes Darwinian theories and the *Descent of Man,* the Ebola virus, fossil hominids, the nonhuman Primate Genetics Lab, the Simian Retrovirus Laboratory, and zoonotic diseases, with many links in between.

Great Ape Survival Project: United Nations
www.unep.org/grasp/ABOUT_GRASP/index.asp

GRASP complements existing great ape conservation efforts by means of intergovernmental dialogue and policy making, conservation planning initiatives, technical and scientific support to great ape range state governments, flagship field projects and fund and awareness raising in donor countries.

Jane Goodall Institute for Wildlife Research, Education, and Conservation
www.janegoodall.org

This organization is devoted to wildlife research, education, and conservation.

Laboratory Primate Newsletter
www.brown.edu/Research/Primate/other.html

This series of websites on primates includes links to a large number of primate sites.

Internet References

Living Links
www.emory.edu/LIVING_LINKS/dewaal.html

An Emory University website consisting of a compendium of Frans de Waal's research and publications along with links to other related primate websites.

National Primate Research Center
http://pin.primate.wisc.edu/factsheets

A series of factsheets as a starting point to find information about the various primate species.

Orangutan Foundation International
www.orangutan.org

This organization promotes the dissemination of information about the orangutan and its plight in order to galvanize the public and policy makers toward an appreciation of the ape's value and current dilemma so that it might be saved from extinction.

Wellcome Trust Sanger Institute
www.sanger.ac.uk/research/projects/humanevolution

The human evolution team uses information on genetic variation in modern humans and apes to answer questions about our species' past. This allows us to understand more about the genetic influences on our current health and disease. This site provides links relevant to human genetics, human diseases, and human evolution.

UNIT 3: Sex and Gender

American Scientist
www.americanscientist.org

Investigating this site will help students of physical anthropology to explore issues related to sex and society.

The Kinsey Institute
www.kinseyinstitute.org/about

The Kinsey Institute at Indiana University works toward advancing sexual health and knowledge worldwide. For over 60 years, the institute has been a trusted source for investigating and informing the world about critical issues in sex, gender, and reproduction.

Sexuality Studies
https://sxs.sfsu.edu

The mission of the Department of Sexuality Studies at San Francisco State University is to "advance multidisciplinary teaching, research, and advocacy in sexuality studies, sexual literacy, well-being, and social justice."

Sexuality Studies.net
http://sexualitystudies.net/programs

This site provides a list of academic programs offered within the field of sexuality studies along with links to their parent institutions.

UNIT 4: The Fossil Evidence

Fossil Hominids FAQ
www.talkorigins.org/faqs/homs

Some links to materials related to hominid species and hominid fossils are provided on this site. The purpose of the site is to refute creationist claims that there is no evidence for human evolution.

Institute of Human Origins
http://iho.asu.edu/node/27

An important source for news, events, and current research into the hominid origins in Africa.

Long Foreground: Human Prehistory
www.wsu.edu/gened/learn-modules/top_longfor/lfopen-index.html

This Washington State University site presents a learning module covering three major topics in human evolution: Overview, Hominid Species Timeline, and Human Physical Characteristics. It also provides a helpful glossary of terms and links to other websites.

UNIT 5: Late Hominid Evolution

Human Prehistory
http://users.hol.gr/~dilos/prehis.htm

The evolution of the human species, beginning with the *Australopithecus* and continuing with *Homo habilis, Homo erectus,* and *Homo sapiens,* is examined on this site. Also included are data on the people who lived in the Paleolithic and Neolithic Age and are the immediate ancestors of modern man.

Max Planck Institute for Evolutionary Anthropology
www.eva.mpg.de/english/index.htm

This is the home page of one of the world's most important research centers for the study of human evolution. Its mission is to understand the human past through the study of genes, cultures, cognitive abilities, languages, social systems, and our closest primate relatives. You will also find publication references as well as links to other related sites.

UNIT 6: Human Diversity

Forensic Science Reference Page
www.lab.fws.gov

Look over this site from the U.S. Fish and Wildlife Forensics Lab to explore topics related to forensic anthropology.

Human Genome Project Information
www.ornl.gov/TechResources/Human_Genome/home.html

Obtain answers about the U.S. Human Genome Project from this site, which details progress, goals, support groups, ethical, legal, and social issues, and genetics information.

OMIM Home Page-Online Mendelian Inheritance in Man
www.ncbi.nlm.nih.gov

This database from the National Center for Biotechnology Information is a catalog of human genes and genetic disorders. It contains text, pictures, and reference information of great interest to students of physical anthropology.

Zeno's Forensic Page
www.forensic.to/forensic.html

A complete list of resources on forensics is presented on this website. It includes general information sources, DNA/serology sources and databases, forensic medicine anthropology sites, and related areas.

UNIT 7: Living with the Past

Evolution and Medicine Network
http://evmedreview.com

A resource for scientists and medical professionals working at the interface of evolutionary biology and medicine.

The Paleolithic Diet Page
www.paleodiet.com

A good source for research results on the paleolithic diet and its implications for living in the modern world.

UNIT 1

Evolutionary Perspectives

Unit Selections

1. **Was Darwin Wrong?,** David Quammen
2. **The Facts of Evolution,** Michael Shermer
3. **Evolution in Action,** Jonathan Weiner
4. **Darwin and His Disciples,** Jean-Andre Prager
5. **The Latest Face of Creationism,** Glenn Branch and Eugenie C. Scott
6. **Why Should Students Learn Evolution?,** Brian J. Alters and Sandra M. Alters

Learning Outcomes

After reading this Unit, you will be able to:

• Define "natural selection."

• Summarize Darwin's evidence for evolution.

• Explain the ways in which human ecological pressure is bringing about "evolution in action" in wildlife.

• Discuss the ways in which Darwin's ideas shaped the politics of the twentieth century.

• Discuss Eugenics as a social movement and as a misreading of Darwin's theory of evolution.

• Discuss why "creationism" should not be taught in the classroom.

• Give some examples of why students should learn about evolution.

Student Website

www.mhhe.com/cls

Internet References

American Institute of Biological Sciences
    www.actionbioscience.org
Charles Darwin on Human Origins
    www.literature.org/Works/Charles-Darwin
Enter Evolution: Theory and History
    www.ucmp.berkeley.edu/history/evolution.html
Harvard Dept. of MCB—Biology Links
    http://mcb.harvard.edu/BioLinks.html
National Center for Science Education
    www.natcenscied.org

As we reflect upon where the biological sciences have taken us over the past 300 years, we can see that we have been swept along a path of insight into the human condition, as well as into a heightened controversy on how to handle this potentially dangerous and/or unwanted knowledge of ourselves.

Certainly, Gregor Mendel, in the late nineteenth century, could not have anticipated that his study of pea plants would ultimately lead to the better understanding of over 3,000 genetically caused diseases, such as sickle-cell anemia, Huntington's chorea, Tay-Sachs, and hemophilia. Nor could he have foreseen the present-day controversies over matters such as cloning and genetic engineering. The significance of Mendel's work, of course, was his discovery that hereditary traits are conveyed by particular units that we now call "genes," a then-revolutionary notion that was later followed by a better understanding of how and why such units change. It is the knowledge of the process of "mutation," or alteration of the chemical structure of the gene, that is now providing us with the potential to control the genetic fate of individuals. This does not mean, however, that we should not continue to look at the role the environment plays in the development of what might be better termed as "genetically influenced conditions," such as alcoholism.

The other side of the evolutionary coin, as discussed in "The Facts of Evolution," is natural selection, a concept provided by Charles Darwin and Alfred Wallace. Natural selection refers to the "weeding out" of unfavorable mutations and the perpetuation of favorable ones (see "Was Darwin Wrong?").

As our understanding of evolutionary processes becomes more refined, the theory of natural selection, unfortunately, continues to be poorly understood by the general public. Ever since Darwin published *On the Origin of Species* in 1859, for instance, there have been those who have embraced it as supportive of everything from communism to laissez-faire capitalism. But, as Jean-Andre Prager shows in "Darwin and His Disciples," these interpretations say more about the theorists and their socioeconomic agenda than it does about the actual facts of human nature or even the social context in which human beings evolved. If the battle with "Social Darwinism" isn't enough, scientists throughout the same period of history have had to confront creationists with fallacies in their thinking (as in "The Latest Face of Creationism"), as well as remind the rest of us why this battle is important (see "Why Should Students Learn Evolution?").

There is something to be learned from these conflicts. Consider the claim of the "intelligent design theory" that nature is too orderly to have come about by a random process. What

© Courtesy of the National Library of Medicine

is missing from this view is the fact that natural selection is not a theory of chance, but is instead a process that results in the *appearance* of intentional design. In fact, what we see in nature is not the absolute perfection that one might expect from a purposeful god, but, rather, the somewhat orderly but less than ideal adaptation on the part of creatures that must make do with what they have. As we survey the articles in this section, we must keep in mind that science is not simply an established and agreed-upon body of knowledge. Rather, it is a way of thinking and a method of investigation in which we seek understanding for its own sake and not for some comforting, preconceived ideas.

Was Darwin Wrong?

DAVID QUAMMEN

Evolution by natural selection, the central concept of the life's work of Charles Darwin, is a theory. It's a theory about the origin of adaptation, complexity, and diversity among Earth's living creatures. If you are skeptical by nature, unfamiliar with the terminology of science, and unaware of the overwhelming evidence, you might even be tempted to say that it's "just" a theory. In the same sense, relativity as described by Albert Einstein is "just" a theory. The notion that Earth orbits around the sun rather than vice versa, offered by Copernicus in 1543, is a theory. Continental drift is a theory. The existence, structure, and dynamics of atoms? Atomic theory. Even electricity is a theoretical construct, involving electrons, which are tiny units of charged mass that no one has ever seen. Each of these theories is an explanation that has been confirmed to such a degree, by observation and experiment, that knowledgeable experts accept it as fact. That's what scientists mean when they talk about a theory: not a dreamy and unreliable speculation, but an explanatory statement that fits the evidence. They embrace such an explanation confidently but provisionally—taking it as their best available view of reality, at least until some severely conflicting data or some better explanation might come along.

The rest of us generally agree. We plug our televisions into little wall sockets, measure a year by the length of Earth's orbit, and in many other ways live our lives based on the trusted reality of those theories.

Evolutionary theory, though, is a bit different. It's such a dangerously wonderful and far-reaching view of life that some people find it unacceptable, despite the vast body of supporting evidence. As applied to our own species, *Homo sapiens,* it can seem more threatening still. Many fundamentalist Christians and ultraorthodox Jews take alarm at the thought that human descent from earlier primates contradicts a strict reading of the Book of Genesis. Their discomfort is paralleled by Islamic creationists such as Harun Yahya, author of a recent volume titled *The Evolution Deceit,* who points to the six-day creation story in the Koran as literal truth and calls the theory of evolution "nothing but a deception imposed on us by the dominators of the world system." The late Srila Prabhupada, of the Hare Krishna movement, explained that God created "the 8,400,000 species of life from the very beginning," in order to establish multiple tiers of reincarnation for rising souls. Although souls ascend, the species themselves don't change, he insisted, dismissing "Darwin's nonsensical theory."

Other people too, not just scriptural literalists, remain unpersuaded about evolution. According to a Gallup poll drawn from more than a thousand telephone interviews conducted in February 2001, no less than 45 percent of responding U.S. adults agreed that "God created human beings pretty much in their present form at one time within the last 10,000 years or so." Evolution, by their lights, played no role in shaping us.

Only 37 percent of the polled Americans were satisfied with allowing room for both God and Darwin—that is, divine initiative to get things started, evolution as the creative means. (This view, according to more than one papal pronouncement, is compatible with Roman Catholic dogma.) Still fewer Americans, only 12 percent, believed that humans evolved from other life-forms without any involvement of a god.

The most startling thing about these poll numbers is not that so many Americans reject evolution, but that the statistical breakdown hasn't changed much in two decades. Gallup interviewers posed exactly the same choices in 1982, 1993, 1997, and 1999. The creationist conviction—that God alone, and not evolution, produced humans—has never drawn less than 44 percent. In other words, nearly half the American populace prefers to believe that Charles Darwin was wrong where it mattered most.

Why are there so many antievolutionists? Scriptural literalism can only be part of the answer. The American public certainly includes a large segment of scriptural literalists—but not *that* large, not 44 percent. Creationist proselytizers and political activists, working hard to interfere with the teaching of evolutionary biology in public schools, are another part. Honest confusion and ignorance, among millions of adult Americans, must be still another. Many people have never taken a biology course that dealt with evolution nor read a book in which the theory was lucidly explained. Sure, we've all heard of Charles Darwin, and of a vague, somber notion about struggle and survival that sometimes goes by the catchall label "Darwinism." But the main sources of information from which most Americans have drawn their awareness of this subject, it seems, are haphazard ones at best: cultural osmosis, newspaper and magazine references, half-baked nature documentaries on the tube, and hearsay.

Evolution is both a beautiful concept and an important one, more crucial nowadays to human welfare, to medical science, and to our understanding of the world than ever before. It's also deeply persuasive—a theory you can take to the bank. The essential points are slightly more complicated than most people assume, but not so complicated that they can't be comprehended by any attentive person. Furthermore, the supporting evidence is abundant, various, ever increasing, solidly interconnected, and easily available in museums, popular books, textbooks, and a mountainous accumulation of peer-reviewed scientific studies. No one needs to, and no one should, accept evolution merely as a matter of faith.

Two big ideas, not just one, are at issue: the evolution of all species, as a historical phenomenon, and natural selection, as the main mechanism causing that phenomenon. The first is a question of what happened. The second is a question of how. The idea that all species are descended from common ancestors had been suggested by other thinkers, including Jean-Baptiste Lamarck, long before Darwin published *The Origin of Species* in 1859. What made Darwin's book so remarkable when it appeared, and so influential in the long run, was that it offered a rational explanation of how evolution must occur. The same insight came independently to Alfred Russel Wallace, a young naturalist doing fieldwork in the Malay Archipelago during the late 1850s. In historical annals, if not in the popular awareness, Wallace and Darwin share the kudos for having discovered natural selection.

The gist of the concept is that small, random, heritable differences among individuals result in different chances of survival and reproduction—success for some, death without offspring for others—and that this natural culling leads to significant changes in shape, size, strength, armament, color, biochemistry, and behavior among the descendants. Excess population growth drives the competitive struggle. Because less successful competitors produce fewer surviving offspring, the useless or negative variations tend to disappear, whereas the useful variations tend to be perpetuated and gradually magnified throughout a population.

So much for one part of the evolutionary process, known as anagenesis, during which a single species is transformed. But there's also a second part, known as speciation. Genetic changes sometimes accumulate within an isolated segment of a species, but not throughout the whole, as that isolated population adapts to its local conditions. Gradually it goes its own way, seizing a new ecological niche. At a certain point it becomes irreversibly distinct—that is, so different that its members can't interbreed with the rest. Two species now exist where formerly there was one. Darwin called that splitting-and-specializing phenomenon the "principle of divergence." It was an important part of his theory, explaining the overall diversity of life as well as the adaptation of individual species.

This thrilling and radical assemblage of concepts came from an unlikely source. Charles Darwin was shy and meticulous, a wealthy landowner with close friends among the Anglican clergy. He had a gentle, unassuming manner, a strong need for privacy, and an extraordinary commitment to intellectual honesty. As an undergraduate at Cambridge, he had studied halfheartedly toward becoming a clergyman himself, before he discovered his real vocation as a scientist. Later, having established a good but conventional reputation in natural history, he spent 22 years secretly gathering evidence and pondering arguments—both for and against his theory—because he didn't want to flame out in a burst of unpersuasive notoriety. He may have delayed, too, because of his anxiety about announcing a theory that seemed to challenge conventional religious beliefs—in particular, the Christian beliefs of his wife, Emma. Darwin himself quietly renounced Christianity during his middle age, and later described himself as an agnostic. He continued to believe in a distant, impersonal deity of some sort, a greater entity that had set the universe and its laws into motion, but not in a personal God who had chosen humanity as a specially favored species. Darwin avoided flaunting his lack of religious faith, at least partly in deference to Emma. And she prayed for his soul.

In 1859 he finally delivered his revolutionary book. Although it was hefty and substantive at 490 pages, he considered *The Origin of Species* just a quick-and-dirty "abstract" of the huge volume he had been working on until interrupted by an alarming event. (In fact, he'd wanted to title it *An Abstract of an Essay on the Origin of Species and Varieties Through Natural Selection,* but his publisher found that insufficiently catchy.) The alarming event was his receiving a letter and an enclosed manuscript from Alfred Wallace, whom he knew only as a distant pen pal. Wallace's manuscript sketched out the same great idea—evolution by natural selection—that Darwin considered his own. Wallace had scribbled this paper and (unaware of Darwin's own evolutionary thinking, which so far had been kept private) mailed it to him from the Malay Archipelago, along with a request for reaction and help. Darwin was horrified. After two decades of pains-taking effort, now he'd be scooped. Or maybe not quite. He forwarded Wallace's paper toward publication, though managing also to assert his own prior claim by releasing two excerpts from his unpublished work. Then he dashed off *The Origin,* his "abstract" on the subject. Unlike Wallace, who was younger and less meticulous, Darwin recognized the importance of providing an edifice of sup-porting evidence and logic.

The evidence, as he presented it, mostly fell within four categories: biogeography, paleontology, embryology, and morphology. Biogeography is the study of the geo-graphical distribution of living creatures—that is, which species inhabit which parts of the planet and why. Pale-ontology investigates extinct life-forms, as revealed in the fossil record. Embryology examines the revealing stages of development (echoing earlier stages of evolutionary history) that embryos pass through before birth or hatch-ing; at a stretch, embryology also concerns the immature forms of animals that metamorphose, such as the larvae of insects. Morphology is the science of anatomical shape and design. Darwin devoted sizable sections of *The Origin of Species* to these categories.

Biogeography, for instance, offered a great pageant of peculiar facts and patterns. Anyone who considers the biogeographical data, Darwin wrote, must be struck by the mysterious clustering pattern among what he called "closely allied" species—that is, similar creatures sharing roughly the same body plan. Such closely allied species tend to be found on the same continent (several species of zebras in Africa) or within the same group of oceanic islands (dozens of species of honeycreepers in Hawaii, 13 species of Galápagos finch), despite their species-by-species preferences for different habitats, food sources, or conditions of climate. Adjacent areas of South Amer-ica, Darwin noted, are occupied by two similar species of large, flightless birds (the rheas, *Rhea americana* and *Pterocnemia pennata*), not by ostriches as in Africa or emus as in Australia. South America also has agoutis and viscachas (small rodents) in terrestrial habitats, plus coypus and capybaras in the wetlands, not—as Darwin wrote—hares and rabbits in terrestrial habitats or beavers and muskrats in the wetlands. During his own youthful visit to the Galápagos, aboard the survey ship *Beagle,* Darwin himself had discovered three very similar forms of mockingbird, each on a different island.

Why should "closely allied" species inhabit neighbor-ing patches of habitat? And why should similar habitat on different continents be occupied by species that aren't so closely allied? "We see in these facts some deep organic bond, prevailing throughout space and time," Darwin wrote. "This bond, on my theory, is simply inheritance." Similar species occur nearby in space because they have descended from common ancestors.

Paleontology reveals a similar clustering pattern in the dimension of time. The vertical column of geologic strata, laid down by sedimentary processes over the eons, lightly peppered with fossils, represents a tangible record show-ing which species lived when. Less ancient layers of rock lie atop more ancient ones (except where geologic forces have tipped or shuffled them), and likewise with the ani-mal and plant fossils that the strata contain. What Darwin noticed about this record is that closely allied species tend to be found adjacent to one another in successive strata. One species endures for millions of years and then makes its last appearance in, say, the middle Eocene epoch; just above, a similar but not identical species replaces it. In North America, for example, a vaguely horselike creature known as *Hyracotherium* was succeeded by *Orohippus,* then *Epihippus,* then *Mesohippus,* which in turn were succeeded by a variety of horsey American critters. Some of them even galloped across the Bering land bridge into Asia, then onward to Europe and Africa. By five mil-lion years ago they had nearly all disappeared, leaving behind *Dinohippus,* which was succeeded by *Equus,* the modern genus of horse. Not all these fossil links had been unearthed in Darwin's day, but he captured the essence of the matter anyway. Again, were such sequences just coin-cidental? No, Darwin argued. Closely allied species suc-ceed one another in time, as well as living nearby in space, because they're related through evolutionary descent.

Embryology too involved patterns that couldn't be explained by coincidence. Why does the embryo of a mammal pass through stages resembling stages of the embryo of a reptile? Why is one of the larval forms of a barnacle, before metamorphosis, so similar to the lar-val form of a shrimp? Why do the larvae of moths, flies, and beetles resemble one another more than any of them resemble their respective adults? Because, Darwin wrote, "the embryo is the animal in its less modified state" and that state "reveals the structure of its progenitor."

Morphology, his fourth category of evidence, was the "very soul" of natural history, according to Darwin. Even today it's on display in the layout and organization of any zoo. Here are the monkeys, there are the big cats, and in that building are the alligators and crocodiles. Birds in the aviary, fish in the aquarium. Living creatures can be eas-ily sorted into a hierarchy of categories—not just species but genera, families, orders, whole kingdoms—based on which anatomical characters they share and which they don't.

All vertebrate animals have backbones. Among vertebrates, birds have feathers, whereas reptiles have scales. Mammals have fur and mammary glands, not feathers or scales. Among mammals, some have pouches in which they nurse their tiny young. Among these species, the marsupials, some have huge rear legs and strong tails by which they go hopping across miles of arid outback; we call them kangaroos. Bring in modern microscopic and molecular evidence, and you can trace the similarities still further back. All plants and fungi, as well as animals, have nuclei within their cells. All living organisms contain DNA and RNA (except some viruses with RNA only), two related forms of information-coding molecules.

Such a pattern of tiered resemblances—groups of similar species nested within broader groupings, and all descending from a single source—isn't naturally present among other collections of items. You won't find anything equivalent if you try to categorize rocks, or musical instruments, or jewelry. Why not? Because rock types and styles of jewelry don't reflect unbroken descent from common ancestors. Biological diversity does. The number of shared characteristics between any one species and another indicates how recently those two species have diverged from a shared lineage.

That insight gave new meaning to the task of taxonomic classification, which had been founded in its modern form back in 1735 by the Swedish naturalist Carolus Linnaeus. Linnaeus showed how species could be systematically classified, according to their shared similarities, but he worked from creationist assumptions that offered no material explanation for the nested pattern he found. In the early and middle 19th century, morphologists such as Georges Cuvier and Étienne Geoffroy Saint-Hilaire in France and Richard Owen in England improved classification with their meticulous studies of internal as well as external anatomies, and tried to make sense of what the ultimate source of these patterned similarities could be. Not even Owen, a contemporary and onetime friend of Darwin's (later in life they had a bitter falling out), took the full step to an evolutionary vision before *The Origin of Species* was published. Owen made a major contribution, though, by advancing the concept of homologues—that is, superficially different but fundamentally similar versions of a single organ or trait, shared by dissimilar species.

For instance, the five-digit skeletal structure of the vertebrate hand appears not just in humans and apes and raccoons and bears but also, variously modified, in cats and bats and porpoises and lizards and turtles. The paired bones of our lower leg, the tibia and the fibula, are also represented by homologous bones in other mammals and in reptiles, and even in the long-extinct bird-reptile *Archaeopteryx*. What's the reason behind such varied recurrence of a few basic designs? Darwin, with a nod to Owen's "most interesting work," supplied the answer: common descent, as shaped by natural selection, modifying the inherited basics for different circumstances.

Vestigial characteristics are still another form of morphological evidence, illuminating to contemplate because they show that the living world is full of small, tolerable imperfections. Why do male mammals (including human males) have nipples? Why do some snakes (notably boa constrictors) carry the rudiments of a pelvis and tiny legs buried inside their sleek profiles? Why do certain species of flightless beetles have wings, sealed beneath wing covers that never open? Darwin raised all these questions, and answered them, in *The Origin of Species*. Vestigial structures stand as remnants of the evolutionary history of a lineage.

Today the same four branches of biological science from which Darwin drew—biogeography, paleontology, embryology, morphology—embrace an ever growing body of supporting data. In addition to those categories we now have others: population genetics, biochemistry, molecular biology, and, most recently, the whiz-bang field of machine-driven genetic sequencing known as genomics. These new forms of knowledge overlap one another seamlessly and intersect with the older forms, strengthening the whole edifice, contributing further to the certainty that Darwin was right.

He was right about evolution, that is. He wasn't right about *everything*. Being a restless explainer, Darwin floated a number of theoretical notions during his long working life, some of which were mistaken and illusory. He was wrong about what causes variation within a species. He was wrong about a famous geologic mystery, the parallel shelves along a Scottish valley called Glen Roy. Most notably, his theory of inheritance—which he labeled pangenesis and cherished despite its poor reception among his biologist colleagues—turned out to be dead wrong. Fortunately for Darwin, the correctness of his most famous good idea stood independent of that particular bad idea. Evolution by natural selection represented Darwin at his best—which is to say, scientific observation and careful thinking at its best.

Douglas Futuyma is a highly respected evolutionary biologist, author of textbooks as well as influential research papers. His office, at the University of Michigan, is a long narrow room in the natural sciences building, well stocked with journals and books, including volumes about the conflict between creationism and evolution. I arrived carrying a well-thumbed copy of his own book on that subject, *Science on Trial: The Case for Evolution*. Killing time in the corridor before our appointment, I noticed a blue flyer on a departmental bulletin board, seeming oddly placed there amid the announcements of career opportunities for graduate students. "Creation vs. evolution," it said. "A series of messages challenging popular thought with Biblical truth and scientific evidences." A traveling lecturer from something called the Origins Research Association would deliver these messages at a local Baptist church. Beside the lecturer's photo was a drawing of a dinosaur. "Free pizza following the evening service," said a small line at the bottom. Dinosaurs, biblical truth, and pizza: something for everybody.

In response to my questions about evidence, Dr. Futuyma moved quickly through the traditional categories—paleontology, biogeography—and talked mostly about modern genetics. He pulled out his heavily marked copy of the journal *Nature* for February 15, 2001, a historic issue, fat with articles reporting and analyzing the results of the Human Genome Project. Beside it he slapped down a more recent issue of *Nature*, this one devoted to the sequenced genome of the house mouse, *Mus musculus*. The headline of the lead editorial announced: "HUMAN BIOLOGY BY PROXY." The mouse genome effort, according to *Nature*'s editors, had revealed "about 30,000 genes, with 99% having direct counterparts in humans."

The resemblance between our 30,000 human genes and those 30,000 mousy counterparts, Futuyma explained, represents another form of homology, like the resemblance between a five-fingered hand and a five-toed paw. Such genetic homology is what gives meaning to biomedical research using mice and other animals, including chimpanzees, which (to their sad misfortune) are our closest living relatives.

No aspect of biomedical research seems more urgent today than the study of microbial diseases. And the dynamics of those microbes within human bodies, within human populations, can only be understood in terms of evolution.

Nightmarish illnesses caused by microbes include both the infectious sort (AIDS, Ebola, SARS) that spread directly from person to person and the sort (malaria, West Nile fever) delivered to us by biting insects or other intermediaries. The capacity for quick change among disease-causing microbes is what makes them so dangerous to large numbers of people and so difficult and expensive to treat. They leap from wildlife or domestic animals into humans, adapting to new circumstances as they go. Their inherent variability allows them to find new ways of evading and defeating human immune systems. By natural selection they acquire resistance to drugs that should kill them. They evolve. There's no better or more immediate evidence supporting the Darwinian theory than this process of forced transformation among our inimical germs.

Take the common bacterium *Staphylococcus aureus*, which lurks in hospitals and causes serious infections, especially among surgery patients. Penicillin, becoming available in 1943, proved almost miraculously effective in fighting staphylococcus infections. Its deployment marked a new phase in the old war between humans and disease microbes, a phase in which humans invent new killer drugs and microbes find new ways to be unkillable. The supreme potency of penicillin didn't last long. The first resistant strains of *Staphylococcus aureus* were reported in 1947. A newer staph-killing drug, methicillin, came into use during the 1960s, but methicillin-resistant strains appeared soon, and by the 1980s those strains were widespread. Vancomycin became the next great weapon against staph, and the first vancomycin-resistant strain emerged in 2002. These antibiotic-resistant strains represent an evolutionary series, not much different in principle from the fossil series tracing horse evolution from *Hyracotherium* to *Equus*. They make evolution a very practical problem by adding expense, as well as misery and danger, to the challenge of coping with staph.

The biologist Stephen Palumbi has calculated the cost of treating penicillin-resistant and methicillin-resistant staph infections, just in the United States, at 30 billion dollars a year. "Antibiotics exert a powerful evolutionary force," he wrote last year, "driving infectious bacteria to evolve powerful defenses against all but the most recently invented drugs." As reflected in their DNA, which uses the same genetic code found in humans and horses and hagfish and honeysuckle, bacteria are part of the continuum of life, all shaped and diversified by evolutionary forces.

Even viruses belong to that continuum. Some viruses evolve quickly, some slowly. Among the fastest is HIV, because its method of replicating itself involves a high rate of mutation, and those mutations allow the virus to assume new forms. After just a few years of infection and drug treatment, each HIV patient carries a unique version of the virus. Isolation within one infected person, plus differing conditions and the struggle to survive, forces each version of HIV to evolve independently. It's nothing but a speeded up and microscopic case of what Darwin saw in the Galápagos—except that each human body is an island, and the newly evolved forms aren't so charming as finches or mockingbirds.

Understanding how quickly HIV acquires resistance to antiviral drugs, such as AZT, has been crucial to improving treatment by way of multiple drug cocktails. "This approach has reduced deaths due to HIV by severalfold since 1996," according to Palumbi, "and it has greatly slowed the evolution of this disease within patients."

Insects and weeds acquire resistance to our insecticides and herbicides through the same process. As we humans try to poison them, evolution by natural selection transforms the population of a mosquito or thistle into a new sort of creature, less vulnerable to that particular poison.

So we invent another poison, then another. It's a futile effort. Even DDT, with its ferocious and long-lasting effects throughout ecosystems, produced resistant house flies within a decade of its discovery in 1939. By 1990 more than 500 species (including 114 kinds of mosquitoes) had acquired resistance to at least one pesticide. Based on these undesired results, Stephen Palumbi has commented glumly, "humans may be the world's dominant evolutionary force."

Among most forms of living creatures, evolution proceeds slowly—too slowly to be observed by a single scientist within a research lifetime. But science functions by inference, not just by direct observation, and the inferential sorts of evidence such as paleontology and biogeography are no less cogent simply because they're indirect. Still, skeptics of evolutionary theory ask: Can we see evolution in action? Can it be observed in the wild? Can it be measured in the laboratory?

The answer is yes. Peter and Rosemary Grant, two British-born researchers who have spent decades where Charles Darwin spent weeks, have captured a glimpse of evolution with their long-term studies of beak size among Galápagos finches. William R. Rice and George W. Salt achieved something similar in their lab, through an experiment involving 35 generations of the fruit fly *Drosophila melanogaster.* Richard E. Lenski and his colleagues at Michigan State University have done it too, tracking 20,000 generations of evolution in the bacterium *Escherichia coli.* Such field studies and lab experiments document anagenesis—that is, slow evolutionary change within a single, unsplit lineage. With patience it can be seen, like the movement of a minute hand on a clock.

Speciation, when a lineage splits into two species, is the other major phase of evolutionary change, making possible the divergence between lineages about which Darwin wrote. It's rarer and more elusive even than anagenesis. Many individual mutations must accumulate (in most cases, anyway, with certain exceptions among plants) before two populations become irrevocabldy separated. The process is spread across thousands of generations, yet it may finish abruptly—like a door going slam!—when the last critical changes occur. Therefore it's much harder to witness. Despite the difficulties, Rice and Salt seem to have recorded a speciation event, or very nearly so, in their extended experiment on fruit flies. From a small stock of mated females they eventually produced two distinct fly populations adapted to different habitat conditions, which the researchers judged "incipient species."

After my visit with Douglas Futuyma in Ann Arbor, I spent two hours at the university museum there with Philip D. Gingerich, a paleontologist well-known for his work on the ancestry of whales. As we talked, Gingerich guided me through an exhibit of ancient cetaceans on the museum's second floor. Amid weird skeletal shapes that seemed almost chimerical (some hanging overhead, some in glass cases) he pointed out significant features and described the progress of thinking about whale evolution. A burly man with a broad open face and the gentle manner of a scoutmaster, Gingerich combines intellectual passion and solid expertise with one other trait that's valuable in a scientist: a willingness to admit when he's wrong.

Since the late 1970s Gingerich has collected fossil specimens of early whales from remote digs in Egypt and Pakistan. Working with Pakistani colleagues, he discovered *Pakicetus,* a terrestrial mammal dating from 50 million years ago, whose ear bones reflect its membership in the whale lineage but whose skull looks almost doglike. A former student of Gingerich's, Hans Thewissen, found a slightly more recent form with webbed feet, legs suitable for either walking or swimming, and a long toothy snout. Thewissen called it *Ambulocetus natans,* or the "walking-and-swimming whale." Gingerich and his team turned up several more, including *Rodhocetus balochistanensis,* which was fully a sea creature, its legs more like flippers, its nostrils shifted backward on the snout, halfway to the blowhole position on a modern whale. The sequence of known forms was becoming more and more complete. And all along, Gingerich told me, he leaned toward believing that whales had descended from a group of carnivorous Eocene mammals known as mesonychids, with cheek teeth useful for chewing meat and bone. Just a bit more evidence, he thought, would confirm that relationship. By the end of the 1990s most paleontologists agreed.

Meanwhile, molecular biologists had explored the same question and arrived at a different answer. No, the match to those Eocene carnivores might be close, but not close enough. DNA hybridization and other tests suggested that whales had descended from artiodactyls (that is, even-toed herbivores, such as antelopes and hippos), not from meat-eating mesonychids.

In the year 2000 Gingerich chose a new field site in Pakistan, where one of his students found a single piece of fossil that changed the prevailing view in paleontology. It was half of a pulley-shaped anklebone, known as an astragalus, belonging to another new species of whale.

A Pakistani colleague found the fragment's other half. When Gingerich fitted the two pieces together, he had a moment of humbling recognition: The molecular biologists were right. Here was an anklebone, from a four-legged whale dating back 47 million years, that closely resembled the homologus anklebone in an artiodactyl. Suddenly he realized how closely whales are related to antelopes.

This is how science is supposed to work. Ideas come and go, but the fittest survive. Downstairs in his office

Phil Gingerich opened a specimen drawer, showing me some of the actual fossils from which the display skeletons upstairs were modeled. He put a small lump of petrified bone, no longer than a lug nut, into my hand. It was the famous astragalus, from the species he had eventually named *Artiocetus clavis*. It felt solid and heavy as truth.

Seeing me to the door, Gingerich volunteered something personal: "I grew up in a conservative church in the Midwest and was not taught anything about evolution. The subject was clearly skirted. That helps me understand the people who are skeptical about it. Because I come from that tradition myself." He shares the same skeptical instinct. Tell him that there's an ancestral connection between land animals and whales, and his reaction is: Fine, maybe. But show me the intermediate stages. Like Charles Darwin, the onetime divinity student, who joined that round-the-world voyage aboard the *Beagle* instead of becoming a country parson, and whose grand view of life on Earth was shaped by attention to small facts, Phil Gingerich is a reverant empiricist. He's not satisfied until he sees solid data. That's what excites him so much about pulling shale fossils out of the ground. In 30 years he has seen enough to be satisfied. For him, Gingerich said, it's "a spiritual experience."

"The evidence is there," he added. "It's buried in the rocks of ages."

Critical Thinking

1. What is wrong with the argument that evolution is "just a theory"? What examples of scientific theories does the author provide?

2. What, approximately, are the current poll numbers on Americans' acceptance of evolution? How have these changed over time?

3. What reasons does the author suspect are behind American antievolutionism?

4. What is Darwin's theory of natural selection?

5. What is anagenesis? Speciation? How does speciation occur?

6. Describe Darwin's life. What was his most important work? When was it published?

7. What were the four categories of evidence presented by Darwin? List each and provide examples discussed by the author.

8. What is taxonomic classification? Who founded it (and when) in its modern form?

9. What is a homologue? Give an example and an explanation.

10. Complete and explain this statement: "There is no better or more immediate evidence supporting Darwinian theory than _____." What examples are given and discussed by the author?

11. Can evolution be observed in the wild? What examples does the author give?

12. Describe the debate (and the outcome) scientists have had about the evolution of modern day whales.

The Facts of Evolution

Michael Shermer

> The affinities of all the beings of the same class have sometimes been represented by a great tree. I believe this simile largely speaks the truth. As buds give rise by growth to fresh buds, and these, if vigorous, branch out and overtop on all sides many a feebler branch, so by generation I believe it has been with the great Tree of Life, which fills with its dead and broken branches the crust of the earth, and covers the surface with its ever branching and beautiful ramifications.
>
> —Charles Darwin,
> *On the Origin of Species,* 1859

The theory of evolution has been under attack since Charles Darwin first published *On the Origin of Species* in 1859. From the start, its critics have seized on the *theory* of evolution to try to undermine its facts. But all great works of science are written in support of some particular view. In 1861, shortly after he published his new theory, Darwin wrote a letter to his colleague, Henry Fawcett, who had just attended a special meeting of the British Association for the Advancement of Science during which Darwin's book was debated. One of the naturalists had argued that *On the Origin of Species* was too theoretical, that Darwin should have just "put his facts before us and let them rest." In response, Darwin reflected that science, to be of any service, required more than list-making; it needed larger ideas that could make sense of piles of data. Otherwise, Darwin said, a geologist "might as well go into a gravelpit and count the pebbles and describe the colours." Data without generalizations are useless; facts without explanatory principles are meaningless. A "theory" is not just someone's opinion or a wild guess made by some scientist. A theory is a well-supported and well-tested generalization that explains a set of observations. Science without theory is useless.

The process of science is fueled by what I call *Darwin's Dictum,* defined by Darwin himself in his letter to Fawcett: "all observation must be for or against some view if it is to be of any service."

Darwin's casual comment nearly a hundred and fifty years ago encapsulates a serious debate about the relative roles of data and theory, or observations and conclusions, in science. In a science like evolution, in which inferences about the past must be made from scant data in the present, this debate has been exploded to encompass a fight between religion and science.

Prediction and Observation

Most essentially, *evolution is a historical science.* Darwin valued above all else prediction and verification by subsequent observation. In an act of brilliant historical science, for example, Darwin correctly developed a theory of coral reef evolution years before he developed his theory of biological evolution. He had never seen a coral reef, but during the *Beagle*'s famous voyage to the Galápagos, he had studied the types of coral reefs Charles Lyell described in *Principles of Geology.* Darwin reasoned that the different examples of coral reefs did not represent different types, each of which needed a different causal explanation; rather, the different examples represented different stages of development of coral reefs, for which only a single cause was needed. Darwin considered this a triumph of theory in driving scientific investigation: Theoretical prediction was followed by observational verification, whereby "I had therefore only to verify and extend my views by a careful examination of coral reefs." In this case, the theory came first, then the data.

The publication of the *Origin of Species* triggered a roaring debate about the relative roles of data and theory in science. Darwin's "bulldog" defender, Thomas Henry Huxley, erupted in a paroxysm against those who pontificated on science but had never practiced it themselves: "There cannot be a doubt that the method of inquiry which Mr. Darwin has adopted is not only rigorously in accord with the canons of scientific logic, but that it is the only adequate method," Huxley wrote. Those "critics exclusively trained in classics or in mathematics, who have never determined a scientific fact in their lives by induction from experiment or observation, prate learnedly about Mr. Darwin's method," he bellowed, "which is not inductive enough, not Baconian enough, forsooth for them."

Darwin insisted that theory comes to and from the facts, not from political or philosophical beliefs, whether from God or the godfather of scientific empiricism. It is a point he voiced succinctly in his cautions to a young scientist. The facts speak for themselves, he said, advising "the advantage, at present, of being very sparing in introducing theory in your papers; let theory guide your observations, but till your reputation is well established, be sparing of publishing theory. It makes persons doubt your observations." Once Darwin's reputation was well established, he published his book that so well demonstrated the power of theory. As he noted in his autobiography, "some of my critics have said, 'Oh, he is a good observer, but has no power of reasoning.' I do not think that this can be true, for the *Origin of Species* is one long argument from the beginning to the end, and it has convinced not a few able men."

Against Some View

Darwin's "one long argument" was with the theologian William Paley and the theory Paley posited in his 1802 book, *Natural Theology: or, Evidences of the Existence and Attributes of the Deity, Collected from the Appearances of Nature.* Sound eerily familiar? The scholarly agenda of this first brand of Intelligent Design was to correlate the works of God (nature) with the words of God (the Bible). Natural theology kicked off with John Ray's 1691 *Wisdom of God Manifested in Works of the Creation,* which itself was inspired by Psalms 19:11: "The Heavens declare the Glory of the Lord and the Firmament sheweth his handy work." John Ray, in what still stands as a playbook for creationism, explains the analogy between human and divine creations: If a "curious Edifice or machine" leads us to "infer the being and operation of some intelligent Architect or Engineer," shouldn't the same be said of "the Works of nature, that Grandeur and magnificence, that excellent contrivance for Beauty, Order, use, &c. which is observable in them, wherein they do as much transcend the Efforts of human Art and infinite Power and Wisdom exceeds finite" to make us "infer the existence and efficiency of an Omnipotent and All-wise Creator"?

Paley advanced Ray's work through the accumulated knowledge of a century of scientific exploration. The opening passage of Paley's *Natural Theology* has become annealed into our culture as the winningly accessible and thus appealing "watch-maker" argument:

In crossing a heath, suppose I pitched my foot against a stone, and were asked how the stone came to be

there. I might possibly answer, that, for any thing I knew to the contrary, it had lain there forever. But suppose I had found a watch upon the ground, and it should be enquired how the watch happened to be in that place. The inference, we think, is inevitable; that the watch must have had a maker; that there must have existed, at some time and in some place or other, an artificer or artificers who formed it for the purpose which we find it actually to answer; who comprehended its construction, and designed its use.

But life is far more complex than a watch—so the design inference is even stronger!

There cannot be design without a designer; contrivance without a contriver . . . The marks of design are too strong to be got over. Design must have had a designer. That designer must have been a person. That person is GOD.

For longer than we have had the theory of evolution, we have had theologians arguing for Intelligent Design.

From Natural Theology to Natural Selection

After abandoning medical studies at Edinburgh University, Charles Darwin entered the University of Cambridge to study theology with the goal of becoming a Church of England cleric. Natural theology provided him with a socially acceptable excuse to study natural history, his true passion. It also educated Darwin in the arguments on design popularized by Paley and others. His intimacy with their ideas was respectful, not combative. For example, in November 1859, the same month that the *Origin of Species* was published, Darwin wrote his friend John Lubbock, "I do not think I hardly ever admired a book more than Paley's 'Natural Theology.' I could almost formerly have said it by heart." Both Paley and Darwin addressed a problem in nature: the origin of the design of life. Paley's answer was to posit a top-down designer—God. Darwin's answer was to posit a bottom-up designer—natural selection. Natural theologians took this to mean that evolution was an attack on God, without giving much thought to what evolution is.

Ever since Darwin, much has been written about what, exactly, evolution is. Ernst Mayr, arguably the greatest evolutionary theorist since Darwin, offers a subtly technical definition: "evolution is change in the adaptation and in the diversity of populations of organisms." He notes that evolution has a dual nature, a "'vertical' phenomenon of adaptive change," which describes how a species responds to its environment over time, and a "'horizontal' phenomenon of populations, incipient species, and new species," which describes adaptations that break through the genetic divide. And I'll never forget Mayr's definition of a species, because I had to memorize it in my first course on evolutionary biology: "A species is a group of actually or potentially interbreeding natural populations reproductively isolated from other such populations."

Mayr outlines five general tenets of evolutionary theory that have been discovered in the years since Darwin published his revolutionary book:

1. *Evolution:* Organisms change through time. Both the fossil record of life's history and nature today document and reveal this change.

2. *Descent with modification:* Evolution proceeds through the branching of common descent. As every parent and child knows, offspring are similar to but not exact replicas of their parents, producing the necessary variation that allows adaptation to the ever-changing environment.

3. *Gradualism:* All this change is slow, steady, and stately. Given enough time, small changes within a species can accumulate into large changes that create new species; that is, macro-evolution is the cumulative effect of microevolution.

4. *Multiplication:* Evolution does not just produce new species; it produces an increasing number of new species.

And, of course,

5. *Natural selection:* Evolutionary change is not haphazard and random; it follows a selective process. Codiscovered by Darwin and the naturalist Alfred Russel Wallace, natural selection operates under five rules:

   A. Populations tend to increase indefinitely in a geometric ratio: 2, 4, 8, 16, 32, 64, 128, 256, 512, 1024 . . .

   B. In a natural environment, however, population numbers must stabilize at a certain level. The population cannot increase to infinity—the earth is just not big enough.

   C. Therefore, there must be a "struggle for existence." Not all of the organisms produced can survive.

   D. There is variation in every species.

   E. Therefore, in the struggle for existence, those individuals with variations that are better adapted to the environment leave behind more offspring than individuals that are less well adapted. This is known as *differential reproductive success.*

As Darwin said, "as more individuals are produced than can possibly survive, there must in every case be a struggle for existence, either one individual with another of the same species, or with the individuals of distinct species, or with the physical conditions of life."

The process of natural selection, when carried out over countless generations, gradually leads varieties of species to develop into new species. Darwin explained:

It may be said that natural selection is daily and hourly scrutinising, throughout the world, every variation, even the slightest; rejecting that which is bad, preserving and adding up all that is good; silently and insensibly working, whenever and wherever opportunity offers, at the improvement of each organic being in relation to its organic and inorganic conditions of life. We see nothing of these slow changes in progress, until the hand of time has marked the long lapses of ages, and then so imperfect is our view into long past geological ages, that we only see that the forms of life are now different from what they formerly were.

The time frame is long and the changes from generation to generation are subtle. This may be one of the most important and difficult points to grasp about the theory of evolution. It is tempting to see species as they exist today as a living monument to evolution, to condense evolution into the incorrect but provocative shorthand that humans descended from chimpanzees—a shorthand that undercuts the facts of evolution.

Natural selection is the process of organisms struggling to survive and reproduce, with the result of propagating their genes into the next generation. As such, it operates primarily at the local level. The Oxford evolutionary biologist Richard Dawkins elegantly described the process as "random mutation plus non-random cumulative selection," emphasizing the non-random. Evolution is not the equivalent of a warehouse full of parts randomly assorting themselves into a jumbo jet, as the creationists like to argue. If evolution were truly random there would be no biological jumbo jets. Genetic mutations and the mixing of parental genes in offspring may be random, but the selection of genes through the survival of their hosts is anything but random. Out of this process of self-organized directional selection emerge complexity and diversity.

Natural selection is a description of a process, not a force. No one is "selecting" organisms for survival or extinction, in the benign sense of dog breeders selecting for desirable traits in show breeds, or in the malignant sense of Nazis selecting prisoners at Auschwitz-Birkenau. Natural selection, and thus evolution, is unconscious and nonprescient—it cannot look forward to anticipate what changes are going to be needed for survival. The evolutionary watchmaker is blind, says Dawkins, *pace* Paley.

By way of example, once when my young daughter asked how evolution works, I used the polar bear as an example of a "transitional species" between land mammals and marine mammals, because although they are land mammals they spend so much time in the water that they have acquired many adaptations to an aquatic life. But this is not correct. It implies that polar bears are *on their way* (in transition) to becoming marine mammals. They aren't. Polar bears are not "becoming" anything. Polar bears are well adapted for their lifestyle. That's all. If global warming continues, perhaps polar bears will adapt to a full-time aquatic existence, or perhaps they will move south and become smaller brown bears, or perhaps they will go extinct. Who knows? No one.

Where Are All the Fossils?

Evolution is a historical science, and historical data—fossils—are often the evidence most cited for and against it. In the creationist textbook, *Of Pandas and People*—one of the bones of contention in the 2005 Intelligent Design trial of *Kitzmiller et al. v. Dover Area School District,* in Dover, Pennsylvania—the authors state: "Design theories suggest that various forms of life began with their distinctive features already intact: fish with fins and scales, birds with feathers and wings, mammals with fur and mammary glands . . . Might not gaps exist . . . not because large numbers of transitional forms mysteriously failed to fossilize, but because they never existed?"

Darwin himself commented on this lack of transitional fossils, asking, "Why then is not every geological formation and every stratum full of such intermediate links?" In contemplating the answer, he turned to the data and noted that "geology assuredly does not reveal any such finely graduated organic chain; and this, perhaps, is the gravest objection which can be urged against my theory." So where *are* all the fossils?

One answer to Darwin's dilemma is the exceptionally low probability of any dead animal's escaping the jaws and stomachs of predators, scavengers, and detritus feeders, reaching the stage of fossilization, and then somehow finding its way back to the surface through geological forces and unpredictable events to be discovered millions of years later by the handful of paleontologists looking for its traces. Given this reality, it is remarkable that we have as many fossils as we do.

There is another explanation for the missing fossils. Ernst Mayr outlines the most common way that a species gives rise to a new species: when a small group (the "founder" population) breaks away and becomes geographically—and thus reproductively—isolated from its ancestral group. As long as it remains small and detached, the founder group can experience fairly rapid genetic changes, especially relative to large populations, which tend to sustain their genetic homogeneity through diverse interbreeding. Mayr's theory, called *allopatric speciation,* helps to explain why so few fossils would exist for these animals.

The evolutionary theorists Niles Eldredge and Stephen Jay Gould took Mayr's observations about how new species emerge and applied them to the fossil record, finding that gaps in the fossil record are not missing evidence of gradual changes; they are extant evidence of punctuated changes. They called this theory *punctuated equilibrium.* Species are so static and enduring that they leave plenty of fossils in the strata while they are in their stable state (equilibrium). The change from one species to another, however, happens relatively quickly on a geological time scale, and in these smaller, geographically isolated population groups (punctuated). In fact, species change happens so rapidly that few "transitional" carcasses create fossils to record the change. Eldredge and Gould conclude that "breaks in the fossil record are real; they express the way in which evolution occurs, not the fragments of an imperfect record." Of course, the small group will also be reproducing, following the geometric increases that are observed in all species, and will eventually form a relatively large population of individuals that retain their phenotype for a considerable time—and leave behind many well-preserved fossils. Millions of years later this process results in a fossil record that records mostly the equilibrium. The punctuation is in the blanks.

The Evidence of Evolution

In August 1996, NASA announced that it discovered life on Mars. The evidence was the Allan Hills 84001 rock, believed to have been ejected out of Mars by a meteor impact millions of years ago, which then fell into an orbit that brought it to Earth. On the panel of NASA experts was paleobiologist William Schopf, a specialist in ancient microbial life. Schopf was skeptical of NASA's claim because, he said, the four "lines of evidence" claimed to support the find did not converge toward a single conclusion. Instead, they pointed to several possible conclusions.

Schopf's analysis of "lines of evidence" reflects a method of science first described by the nineteenth-century philosopher of science William Whewell. To prove a theory, Whewell believed, one must have more than one induction, more than a single generalization drawn from specific facts. One must have multiple inductions that converge upon one another, independently but in conjunction.

Whewell said that if these inductions "jump together" it strengthens the plausibility of a theory: "Accordingly the cases in which inductions from classes of facts altogether different have thus jumped together, belong only to the best established theories which the history of science contains. And, as I shall have occasion to refer to this particular feature in their evidence, I will take the liberty of describing it by a particular phrase; and will term it the Consilience of Inductions." I call it a *convergence of evidence*.

Just as detectives employ the convergence of evidence technique to deduce who most likely committed a crime, scientists employ the method to deduce the likeliest explanation for a particular phenomenon. Cosmologists reconstruct the history of the universe through a convergence of evidence from astronomy, planetary geology, and physics. Geologists reconstruct the history of the planet through a convergence of evidence from geology, physics, and chemistry. Archaeologists piece together the history of civilization through a convergence of evidence from biology (pollen grains), chemistry (kitchen middens), physics (potsherds, tools), history (works of art, written sources), and other site-specific artifacts.

As a historical science, evolution is confirmed by the fact that so many independent lines of evidence converge to its single conclusion. Independent sets of data from geology, paleontology, botany, zoology, herpetology, entomology, biogeography, comparative anatomy and physiology, genetics and population genetics, and many other sciences each point to the conclusion that life evolved. This is a convergence of evidence. Creationists can demand "just one fossil transitional form" that shows evolution. But evolution is not proved through a single fossil. It is proved through a convergence of fossils, along with a convergence of genetic comparisons between species, and a convergence of anatomical and physiological comparisons between species, and many other lines of inquiry. For creationists to disprove evolution, they need to unravel all these independent lines of evidence, as well as construct a rival theory that can explain them better than the theory of evolution. They have yet to do so.

The Tests of Evolution

Creationists like to argue that evolution is not a science because no one was there to observe it and there are no experiments to run today to test it. The inability to observe past events or set up controlled experiments is no obstacle to a sound science of cosmology, geology, or archaeology, so why should it be for a sound science of evolution? The key is the ability to test one's hypothesis. There are a number of ways to do so, starting with the broadest method of how we know evolution happened.

Consider the evolution of our best friend, the dog. With so many breeds of dogs popular for so many thousands of years, one would think that there would be an abundance of transitional fossils providing paleontologists with copious data from which to reconstruct their evolutionary ancestry. Not so. In fact, according to Jennifer A. Leonard of the National Museum of Natural History in Washington, D.C., "the fossil record from wolves to dogs is pretty sparse." Then how do we know the origin of dogs? In a 2002 issue of *Science,* Leonard and her colleagues report that mitochrondrial DNA (mtDNA) data from early dog remains "strongly support the hypothesis that ancient American and Eurasian domestic dogs share a common origin from Old World gray wolves." In the same issue of *Science,* Peter Savolainen from the Royal Institute of Technology in Stockholm and his colleagues note that the fossil record is problematic "because of the difficulty in discriminating between small wolves and domestic dogs," but their study of mtDNA sequence variation among 654 domestic dogs from around the world "points to an origin of the domestic dog in East Asia ~15,000 yr B.P." from a single gene pool of wolves. Finally, Brian Hare from Harvard and his colleagues describe the results of their study in which they found that domestic dogs are more skillful than wolves at using human communicative signals indicating the location of hidden food, but that "dogs and wolves do not perform differently in a non-social memory task, ruling out the possibility that dogs outperform wolves in all human-guided tasks." Therefore, "dogs' social-communicative skills with humans were acquired during the process of domestication." Although no single fossil proves that dogs came from wolves, the convergence of evidence from archaeological, morphological, genetic, and behavioral "fossils" reveals the ancestor of all dogs to be the East Asian wolf.

The tale of human evolution is revealed in a similar manner (although here we do have an abundance of transitional fossil riches), as it is for all ancestors in the history of life. One of the finest compilations of evolutionary convergence is Richard Dawkins's magnum opus, *The Ancestor's Tale,* 673 pages of convergent science recounted with literary elegance. Dawkins traces innumerable "transitional fossils" (what he calls "concestors"— the "point of rendezvous" of the last common ancestor shared by a set of species) from *Homo sapiens* back four billion years to the origin of replicating molecules and the emergence of evolution. No one concestor proves that evolution happened, but together they reveal a majestic story of a process over time. We know human evolution happened because innumerable bits of data from myriad fields of science conjoin to paint a rich portrait of life's pilgrimage.

But the convergence of evidence is just the start. The *comparative method* allows us to infer evolutionary relationships using data from a wide variety of fields. Luigi Luca Cavalli-Sforza and his colleagues, for example, compared fifty years of data from population genetics, geography, ecology, archaeology, physical anthropology, and linguistics to trace the evolution of the human races. Using both the convergence and comparative methods led them to conclude that "the major stereotypes, all based on skin color, hair color and form, and facial traits, reflect superficial differences that are not confirmed by deeper analysis with more reliable genetic traits." By comparing surface (physical) traits—the phenotype of individuals—with genetic traits—the genotype—they teased out the relationship between different groups of people. Most interesting, they found that the genetic traits disclosed "recent evolution mostly under the effect of climate and perhaps sexual selection." For example, they discovered that Australian aborigines are genetically more closely related to southeast Asians than they are to African blacks, which makes sense from the perspective of the evolutionary timeline: The migration pattern of humans out of Africa would have led them first to Asia and then to Australia.

Dating techniques provide evidence of the timeline of evolution. The dating of fossils, along with the earth, moon, sun, solar system, and universe, are all tests of evolutionary theory, and so far they have passed all the tests. We know that the earth is approximately 4.6 billion years old because of the convergence of evidence from several methods of dating rocks: Uranium Lead, Rubidium Strontium, and Carbon-14. Further, the age of the earth, the age of the moon, the age of the sun, the age of the solar system, and the age of the universe are consistent, maintaining yet another consilience. If, say, the earth was dated at 4.6 billion years old but the solar system was dated at one million years old, the theory of evolution would be in trouble. But Uranium Lead, Rubidium Strontium, and Carbon-14 have not provided any good news for the so-called Young Earth creationists.

Better yet, the fossils and organisms speak for themselves. *Fossils do show intermediate stages,* despite their rarity. For example, there are now at least eight intermediate fossil stages identified in the evolution of whales. In human evolution, there are at least a dozen known intermediate fossil stages since hominids branched off from the great apes six million years ago. *And geological strata consistently reveal the same sequence of fossils.* A quick and simple way to debunk the theory of evolution would be to find a fossil horse in the same geological stratum as a trilobite. According to evolutionary theory, trilobites and mammals are separated by hundreds of millions of years.

If such a fossil juxtaposition occurred, and it was not the product of some geological anomaly (such as uplifted, broken, bent, or even flipped strata—all of which occur but are traceable), it would mean that there was something seriously wrong with the theory of evolution.

Evolution also posits that *modern organisms should show a variety of structures from simple to complex, reflecting an evolutionary history rather than an instantaneous creation.* The human eye, for example, is the result of a long and complex pathway that goes back hundreds of millions of years. Initially a simple eyespot with a handful of light-sensitive cells that provided information to the organism about an important source of the light, it developed into a recessed eyespot, where a small surface indentation filled with light-sensitive cells provided additional data on the direction of light; then into a deep recession eyespot, where additional cells at greater depth provide more accurate information about the environment; then into a pinhole camera eye that is able to focus an image on the back of a deeply recessed layer of light-sensitive cells; then into a pinhole lens eye that is able to focus the image; then into a complex eye found in such modern mammals as humans. All of these structures are expressed in modern eyes.

Further, *biological structures show signs of natural design.* The anatomy of the human eye, in fact, shows anything but "intelligence" in its design. It is built upside down and backwards, requiring photons of light to travel through the cornea, lens, aqueous fluid, blood vessels, ganglion cells, amacrine cells, horizontal cells, and bipolar cells before they reach the light-sensitive rods and cones that transduce the light signal into neural impulses—which are then sent to the visual cortex at the back of the brain for processing into meaningful patterns. For optimal vision, why would an intelligent designer have built an eye upside down and backwards? This "design" makes sense only if natural selection built eyes from available materials, and in the particular configuration of the ancestral organism's preexisting organic structures. The eye shows the pathways of evolutionary history, not of intelligent design.

Additionally, *vestigial structures stand as evidence of the mistakes, the misstarts, and, especially, the leftover traces of evolutionary history.* The cretaceous snake *Pachyrhachis problematicus,* for example, had small hind limbs used for locomotion that it inherited from its quadrupedal ancestors, gone in today's snakes. Modern whales retain a tiny pelvis for hind legs that existed in their land mammal ancestors but have disappeared today. Likewise, there are wings on flightless birds, and of course humans are replete with useless vestigial structures, a distinctive sign of our evolutionary ancestry. A short list of just ten vestigial structures in humans leaves one musing: Why would an Intelligent Designer have created these?

6. *Male nipples.* Men have nipples because females need them, and the overall architecture of the human body is more efficiently developed in the uterus from a single developmental structure.

2. *Male uterus.* Men have the remnant of an undeveloped female reproductive organ that hangs off the prostate gland for the same reason.

3. *Thirteenth rib.* Most modern humans have twelve sets of ribs, but 8 percent of us have a thirteenth set, just like chimpanzees and gorillas. This is a remnant of our primate ancestry: We share common ancestors with chimps and gorillas, and the thirteenth set of ribs has been retained from when our lineage branched off six million years ago.

4. *Coccyx.* The human tailbone is all that remains from our common ancestors' tails, which were used for grasping branches and maintaining balance.

5. *Wisdom teeth.* Before stone tools, weapons, and fire, hominids were primarily vegetarians, and as such we chewed a lot of plants, requiring an extra set of grinding molars. Many people still have them, despite the smaller size of our modern jaws.

6. *Appendix.* This muscular tube connected to the large intestine was once used for digesting cellulose in our largely vegetarian diet before we became meat eaters.

7. *Body hair.* We are sometimes called "the naked ape"; however, most humans have a layer of fine body hair, again left over from our evolutionary ancestry from thick-haired apes and hominids.

8. *Goose bumps.* Our body hair ancestry can also be inferred from the fact that we retain the ability of our ancestors to puff up their fur for heat insulation, or as a threat gesture to potential predators. Erector pili—"goose bumps"—are a telltale sign of our evolutionary ancestry.

9. *Extrinsic ear muscles.* If you can wiggle your ears you can thank our primate ancestors, who evolved the ability to move their ears independently of their heads as a more efficient means of discriminating precise sound directionality and location.

10. *Third eyelid.* Many animals have a nictitating membrane that covers the eye for added protection; we retain this "third eyelid" in the corner of our eye as a tiny fold of flesh.

Evolutionary scientists can provide dozens more examples of vestigial structures—let alone examples of how we know evolution happened from all of these other various lines of historical evidence. Yet as a science, evolution depends primarily on the ability to test a hypothesis. How can we ever test an evolutionary hypothesis if we cannot go into a lab and create a new species naturally?

I once had the opportunity to help dig up a dinosaur with Jack Horner, the curator of paleontology at the Museum of the Rockies in Bozeman, Montana. As Horner explains in his book *Digging Dinosaurs,* "paleontology is not an experimental science; it's a historical science. This means that paleontologists are seldom able to test their hypotheses by laboratory experiments, but they can still test them." Horner discusses this process of historical science at the famous dig in which he exposed the first dinosaur eggs ever found in North America. The initial stage of the dig was "getting the fossils out of the ground." Unsheathing the bones from the overlying and surrounding stone is backbreaking work. As you move from jackhammers and pickaxes to dental tools and small brushes, historical interpretation accelerates as a function of the rate of bone unearthed. Then, in the second phase of a dig, he gets "to look at the fossils, study them, make hypotheses based on what we saw and try to prove or disprove them."

When I arrived at Horner's camp I expected to find the busy director of a fully sponsored dig barking out orders to his staff. I was surprised to come upon a patient historical scientist, sitting cross-legged before a cervical vertebra from a 140-million-year-old *Apatosaurus* (formerly known as *Brontosaurus*), wondering what to make of it. Soon a reporter from a local paper arrived inquiring of Horner what this discovery meant for the history of dinosaurs. Did it change any of his theories? Where was the head? Was there more than one body at this site? Horner's answers were those of a cautious scientist: "I don't know yet." "Beats me." "We need more evidence." "We'll have to wait and see." It was historical science at its best.

After two long days of exposing nothing but solid rock and my own ineptness at seeing bone within stone, one of the pale-ontologists pointed out that the rock I was about to toss away was a piece of bone that appeared to be part of a rib. If it was a rib, then the bone should retain its rib-like shape as more of the overburden was chipped away. This it did for about a foot, until it suddenly flared to the right. Was it a rib, or something else? Horner moved in to check. "It could be part of the pelvis," he suggested. If it was part of the pelvis, then it should also flare out to the left when more was uncovered. Sure enough, Horner's prediction was verified by further digging.

In science, this process is called the *hypothetico-deductive method,* in which one forms a hypothesis based on existing data, deduces a prediction from the hypothesis, then tests the prediction against further data. For example, in 1981 Horner discovered a site in Montana that contained approximately thirty million fossil fragments of approximately ten thousand *Maiasaurs* in a bed measuring 1.25 miles by .25 miles. His hypothesizing began with a question: "What could such a deposit represent?" There was no evidence that predators had chewed the bones, yet many were broken in half lengthwise. Further, the bones were all arranged from east to west—the long dimension of the bone deposit. Small bones had been separated from bigger bones, and there were no bones of baby *Maiasaurs,* only those of individuals between nine and twenty-three feet long. What would cause the bones to splinter lengthwise? Why would the small bones be separated from the big bones? Was this one giant herd, all killed at the same time, or was it a dying ground over many years?

An early hypothesis—that a mud flow buried the herd alive—was rejected because "it didn't make sense that even the most powerful flow of mud could break bones lengthwise . . . nor did it make sense that a herd of living animals buried in mud would end up with all their skeletons disarticulated." Horner constructed another hypothesis. "It seemed that there had to be a twofold event," he reasoned, "the dinosaurs dying in one incident and the bones being swept away in another." Since there was a layer of volcanic ash 1.5 feet above the bone bed, volcanic activity was implicated in the death of the herd. Horner then deduced that only fossil bones would split lengthwise, and therefore the damage to the bones had occurred long after the dying event. His hypothesis and deduction led to his conclusion that the herd was "killed by the gases, smoke and ash of a volcanic eruption. And if a huge eruption killed them all at once, then it might have also killed everything else around." Then perhaps there was a flood, maybe from a breached lake, carrying the rotting bodies downstream, separating the big bones from the small, lighter bones, and giving the bones a uniform orientation.

A paleontological dig is a good example of how hypothetico-deductive reasoning and historical sciences can make predictions based on initial data that are then verified or rejected by later historical evidence. Evolutionary theory is rooted in a rich array of data from the past that, while nonreplicable in a laboratory, are nevertheless valid sources of information that can be used to piece together specific events and test general hypotheses. While the specifics of evolution—how quickly it happens, what triggers species change, at which level of the organism it occurs—are still being studied and unraveled, the general theory of evolution is the most tested in science over the past century and a half. Scientists agree: Evolution happened.

Critical Thinking

1. What is the point Shermer is trying to make in this article?
2. What was Darwin's contribution to our understanding of coral reefs?
3. Who was Darwin's "one long argument" with? What was his view? How was it different from the Darwinian one?
4. What did Ernst Mayr mean when he asserted that evolution has both "horizontal" and "vertical" dimensions?
5. What five tenets of evolution does Mayr outline? Describe each.
6. What, according to Shermer, is "one of the most important and difficult points to grasp about evolution?" Why do you think this is?
7. What are the random and non-random processes in evolution as identified by Richard Dawkins? What makes them random and non-random respectively?
8. What was wrong with Shermer's example of a "polar bear" as a transitional species when he was talking to his daughter?
9. Why are fossils so difficult to come by?
10. Why is it that genetic change can occur more quickly in small groups? Why is this important for the evolution of new species?
11. What does Shermer mean by the "convergence of evidence"?
12. How long ago did the domestic dog "evolve"? Why does Shermer use this as an example of the way science works?
13. What is the "comparative method"?
14. What other lines of evidence mentioned by Shermer support the evolution?
15. What human vestigial structures does he mention? What is the evolutionary reason for their existence? Discuss the likely original function of at least four of these supposedly meaningless features.

Evolution in Action

Finches, monkeyflowers, sockeye salmon, and bacteria are changing before our eyes.

JONATHAN WEINER

Charles Darwin's wife, Emma, was terrified that they would be separated for eternity, because she would go to heaven and he would not. Emma confessed her fears in a letter that Charles kept and treasured, with his reply to her scribbled in the margin: "When I am dead, know that many times, I have kissed and cryed over this."

Close as they were, the two could hardly bear to talk about Darwin's view of life. And today, those of us who live in the United States, by many measures the world's leading scientific nation, find ourselves in a house divided. Half of us accept Darwin's theory, half of us reject it, and many people are convinced that Darwin burns in hell. I find that old debate particularly strange, because I've spent some of the best years of my life as a science writer peering over the shoulders of biologists who actually watch Darwin's process in action. What they can see casts the whole debate in a new light—or it should.

Darwin himself never tried to watch evolution happen. "It may metaphorically be said," he wrote in the *Origin of Species,*

that natural selection is daily and hourly scrutinizing, throughout the world, the slightest variations; rejecting those that are bad, preserving and adding up all that are good; silently and insensibly working, whenever and wherever opportunity offers. . . . We see nothing of these slow changes in progress, until the hand of time has marked the lapse of ages.

Darwin was a modest man who thought of himself as a plodder (one of his favorite mottoes was, "It's dogged as does it"). He thought evolution plodded too. If so, it would be more boring to watch evolution than to watch drying paint. As a result, for several generations after Darwin's death, almost nobody tried. For most of the twentieth century the only well-known example of evolution in action was the case of peppered moths in industrial England. The moth had its picture in all the textbooks, as a kind of special case.

Then, in 1973, a married pair of evolutionary biologists, Peter and Rosemary Grant, now at Princeton University, began a study of Darwin's process in Darwin's islands, the Galápagos,

watching Darwin's finches. At first, they assumed that they would have to infer the history of evolution in the islands from the distribution of the various finch species, varieties, and populations across the archipelago. That is pretty much what Darwin had done, in broad strokes, after the *Beagle*'s five-week survey of the islands in 1835. But the Grants soon discovered that at their main study site, a tiny desert island called Daphne Major, near the center of the archipelago, the finches were evolving rapidly. Conditions on the island swung wildly back and forth from wet years to dry years, and finches on Daphne adapted to each swing, from generation to generation. With the help of a series of graduate students, the Grants began to spend a good part of every year on Daphne, watching evolution in action as it shaped and reshaped the finches' beaks.

At the same time, a few biologists began making similar discoveries elsewhere in the world. One of them was John A. Endler, an evolutionary biologist at the University of California, Santa Barbara, who studied Trinidadian guppies. In 1986 Endler published a little book called *Natural Selection in the Wild,* in which he collected and reviewed all of the studies of evolution in action that had been published to that date. Dozens of new field projects were in progress. Biologists finally began to realize that Darwin had been too modest. Evolution by natural selection can happen rapidly enough to watch.

Now the field is exploding. More than 250 people around the world are observing and documenting evolution, not only in finches and guppies, but also in aphids, flies, grayling, monkeyflowers, salmon, and sticklebacks. Some workers are even documenting pairs of species—symbiotic insects and plants—that have recently found each other, and observing the pairs as they drift off into their own world together like lovers in a novel by D.H. Lawrence.

The Grants' own study gets more sophisticated every year. A few years ago, a group of molecular biologists working with the Grants nailed down a gene that plays a key role in shaping the beaks of the finches. The gene codes for a signaling molecule called bone morphogenic protein 4 (BMP4). Finches with bigger beaks tend to have more BMP4, and finches with smaller beaks have less. In the laboratory, the biologists demonstrated that they could sculpt the beaks themselves by adding or subtracting BMP4. The same gene that shapes the beak of the finch in the egg also shapes the human face in the womb.

Some of the most dramatic stories of evolution in action result from the pressures that human beings are imposing on the planet. As Stephen Palumbi, an evolutionary biologist at Stanford University, points out, we are changing the course of evolution for virtually every living species everywhere, with consequences that are sometimes the opposite of what we might have predicted, or desired.

Take trophy hunting. Wild populations of bighorn mountain sheep are carefully managed in North America for hunters who want a chance to shoot a ram with a trophy set of horns. Hunting permits can cost well into the six figures. On Ram Mountain, in Alberta, Canada, hunters have shot the biggest of the bighorn rams for more than thirty years. And the result? Evolution has made the hunters' quarry scarce. The runts have had a better chance than the giants of passing on their genes. So on Ram Mountain the rams have gotten smaller, and their horns are proportionately smaller yet.

Or take fishing, which is economically much more consequential. The populations of Atlantic cod that swam for centuries off the coasts of Labrador and Newfoundland began a terrible crash in the late 1980s. In the years leading up to the crash, the cod had been evolving much like the sheep on Ram Mountain. Fish that matured relatively fast and reproduced relatively young had the better chance of passing on their genes; so did the fish that stayed small. So even before the population crashed, the average cod had been shrinking.

We often seem to lose out wherever we fight hardest to control nature. Antibiotics drive the evolution of drug-resistant bacteria at a frightening pace. Sulfonamides were introduced in the 1930s, and resistance to them was first observed a decade later. Penicillin was deployed in 1943, and the first penicillin resistance was observed in 1946. In the same way, pesticides and herbicides create resistant bugs and weeds.

Palumbi estimates that the annual bill for such unintended human-induced evolution runs to more than $100 billion in the U.S. alone. Worldwide, the pressure of global warming, fragmented habitats, heightened levels of carbon dioxide, acid rain, and the other myriad perturbations people impose on the chemistry and climate of the planet—all change the terms of the struggle for existence in the air, in the water, and on land. Biologists have begun to worry about those perturbations, but global change may be racing ahead of them.

To me, the most interesting news in the global evolution watch concerns what Darwin called "that mystery of mysteries, the origin of species."

The process whereby a population acquires small, inherited changes through natural selection is known as microevolution. Finches get bigger, fish gets smaller, but a finch is still a finch and a fish is still a fish. For people who reject Darwin's theory, that's the end of the story: no matter how many small, inherited changes accumulate, they believe, natural selection can never make a new kind of living thing. The kinds, the species, are eternal.

Darwin argued otherwise. He thought that many small changes could cause two lines of life to diverge. Whenever animals and plants find their way to a new home, for instance, they suffer, like emigres in new countries. Some individuals fail, others adapt and prosper. As the more successful individuals reproduce, Darwin maintained, the new population begins to differ from the ancestral one. If the two populations diverge widely enough, they become separate species. Change on that scale is known as macroevolution.

In *Origin,* Darwin estimated that a new species might take between ten thousand and fourteen thousand generations to arise. Until recently, most biologists assumed it would take at least that many, or maybe even millions of generations, before microevolutionary changes led to the origin of new species. So they assumed they could watch evolution by natural selection, but not the divergence of one species into separate, reproductively isolated species. Now that view is changing too.

Not long ago, a young evolution-watcher named Andrew Hendry, a biologist at McGill University in Montreal, reported the results of a striking study of sockeye salmon. Sockeye tend to reproduce either in streams or along lake beaches. When the glaciers of the last ice age melted and retreated, about ten thousand years ago, they left behind thousands of new lakes. Salmon from streams swam into the lakes and stayed. Today their descendants tend to breed among themselves rather than with sockeyes that live in the streams. The fish in the lakes and streams are reproductively isolated from each other. So how fast did that happen?

In the 1930s and 1940s, sockeye salmon were introduced into Lake Washington, in Washington State. Hundreds of thousands of their descendants now live and breed in Cedar River, which feeds the lake. By 1957 some of the introduced sockeye also colonized a beach along the lake called Pleasure Point, about four miles from the mouth of Cedar River.

Hendry could tell whether a full-grown, breeding salmon had been born in the river or at the beach by examining the rings on its otoliths, or ear stones. Otolith rings reflect variations in water temperature while a fish embryo is developing. Water temperatures at the beach are relatively constant compared with the river temperatures. Hendry and his colleagues checked the otoliths and collected DNA samples from the fish—and found that more than a third of the sockeye breeding at Pleasure Point had grown up in the river. They were immigrants.

With such a large number of immigrants, the two populations at Pleasure Point should have blended back together. But they hadn't. So at breeding time many of the river sockeye that swam over to the beach must have been relatively unsuccessful at passing on their genes.

Hendry could also tell the stream fish and the beach fish apart just by looking at them. Where the sockeye's breeding waters are swift-flowing, such as in Cedar River, the males tend to be slender. Their courtship ritual and competition with other males requires them to turn sideways in strong current—an awkward maneuver for a male with a deep, roundish body. So in strong current, slender males have the better chance of passing on their genes. But in still waters, males with the deepest bodies have the best chance of getting mates. So beach males tend to be rounder—their dimensions greater from the top of the back to the bottom of the belly—than river males.

What about females? In the river, where currents and floods are forever shifting and swirling the gravel, females have to dig deep nests for their eggs. So the females in the river tend to be bigger than their lake-dwelling counterparts, because bigger females can dig deeper nests. Where the water is calmer, the gravel stays put, and shallower nests will do.

So all of the beachgoers, male and female, have adapted to life at Pleasure Point. Their adaptations are strong enough that reproductive isolation has evolved. How long did the evolution take? Hendry began studying the salmon's reproductive isolation in 1992. At that time, the sockeyes in the stream and the ones at Pleasure Point had been breeding in their respective habitats for at most thirteen generations. That is so fast that, as Hendry and his colleagues point out, it may be possible someday soon to catch the next step, the origin of a new species.

And it's not just the sockeye salmon. Consider the three-spined stickleback. After the glaciers melted at the end of the last ice age, many sticklebacks swam out of the sea and into new glacial lakes—just as the salmon did. In the sea, sticklebacks wear heavy, bony body armor. In a lake they wear light armor. In a certain new pond in Bergen, Norway, during the past century, sticklebacks evolved toward the lighter armor in just thirty-one years. In Loberg Lake, Alaska, the same kind of change took only a dozen years. A generation for sticklebacks is two years. So that dramatic evolution took just six generations.

Dolph Schluter, a former finch-watcher from the Galápagos and currently a biologist at the University of British Columbia in Vancouver, has shown that, along with the evolution of new body types, sticklebacks also evolve a taste for mates with the new traits. In other words, the adaptive push of sexual selection is going hand-in-hand with natural selection. Schluter has built experimental ponds in Vancouver to observe the phenomenon under controlled conditions, and the same patterns he found in isolated lakes repeat themselves in his ponds. So adaptation can sometimes drive sexual selection and accelerate reproductive isolation.

There are other developments in the evolution watch, too, many to mention in this small space. Some of the fastest action is microscopic. Richard Lenski, a biologist at Michigan State University in East Lansing, watches the evolution of *Escherichia coli*. Because one generation takes only twenty minutes, and billions of *E. coli* can fit in a petri dish, the bacteria make ideal subjects for experimental evolution. Throw some *E. coli* into a new dish, for instance, with food they haven't encountered before, and they will evolve and adapt—quickly at first and then more slowly, as they refine their fit with their new environment.

And then there are the controversies. Science progresses and evolves by controversy, by internal debate and revision. In the United States these days one almost hates to mention that there are arguments among evolutionists. So often, they are taken out of context and hyperamplified to suggest that nothing about Darwinism is solid—that Darwin is dead. But research is messy

because nature is messy, and fieldwork is some of the messiest research of all. It is precisely here at its jagged cutting edge that Darwinism is most vigorously alive.

Not long ago, one of the most famous icons of the evolution watch toppled over: the story of the peppered moths, familiar to anyone who remembers biology 101. About half a century ago, the British evolutionist Bernard Kettlewell noted that certain moths in the British Isles had evolved into darker forms when the trunks of trees darkened with industrial pollution. When the trees lightened again, after clean air acts were passed, the moths had evolved into light forms again. Kettlewell claimed that dark moths resting on dark tree trunks were harder for birds to see; in each decade, moths of the right color were safer.

But in the past few years, workers have shown that Kettlewell's explanation was too simplistic. For one thing, the moths don't normally rest on tree trunks. In forty years of observation, only twice have moths been seen resting there. Nobody knows where they do rest. The moths did evolve rapidly, but no one can be certain why.

To me what remains most interesting is the light that studies such as Hendry's, or the Grants', may throw on the origin of species. It's extraordinary that scientists are now examining the very beginnings of the process, at the level of beaks and fins, at the level of the genes. The explosion of evolution-watchers is a remarkable development in Darwin's science. Even as the popular debate about evolution in America is reaching its most heated moment since the trial of John Scopes, evolutionary biologists are pursuing one of the most significant and surprising voyages of discovery since the young Darwin sailed into the Galápagos Archipelago aboard Her Majesty's ship *Beagle*.

Not long ago I asked Hendry if his studies have changed the way he thinks about the origin of species. "Yes," he replied without hesitation, "I think it's occurring all over the place."

Critical Thinking

1. Did Darwin ever see evolution in action? Why or why not?

2. Who are Rosemary and Peter Grant? What did they study? Where? How did they show that natural selection occurs?

3. How many people around the world are documenting evolution now?

4. What recent advance has been found in the Grants' research?

5. How have trophy hunting and fishing impacted the evolution of species according to the research presented by Weiner?

6. When was penicillin first deployed? How soon did resistance show up?

7. What is "microevolution"?

8. How many generations did Darwin think it would take for a new species to arise? Did more recent scholars agree with this? Was Darwin right, too optimistic, or too pessimistic?

9. What happened with the sockeye salmon? What did they show about the number of generations these changes took?

10. What selection pressure drove differences in morphology (body shape and size) between males and females of the river and lake types?

11. How do the stickleback findings show that "adaptations sometimes drive sexual selection and accelerate reproductive isolation"?

12. Why does Weiner say "in the United States these days one almost hates to mention that there are arguments among evolutionists"?

13. What is the classic story about the peppered moths? Why has this icon been "toppled"?

JONATHAN WEINER began writing about evolution in 1990, when he met Peter and Rosemary Grant, who observe evolution firsthand in finch populations in the Galápagos. Weiner's book *The Beak of the Finch* (Alfred A. Knopf) won a Pulitzer Prize in 1994. He is a professor in the Graduate School of Journalism at Columbia University, in New York City. He is also working on a book about human longevity for Ecco Press.

Darwin and His Disciples

JEAN-ANDRE PRAGER

By the time the acting secretary of the Committee of Clergymen, W. R. Freemantle, put his signature to the Oxford Declaration of 25 February 1864, the divisions between the defenders of the United Church of England and Ireland and the new prophets of scientific revolution were clear. No fewer than 11,000 clergymen signed the declaration, which asserted that the Bible was the indisputable word of God. Their motivation was a series of seven essays, from 1860, by liberal churchmen, dubbed the 'Seven against Christ', which had sought to accommodate advances in biology and geology with the prevailing theology in *Essays and Reviews*. The essays caused greater uproar than *On the Origin of Species by Means of Natural Selection* by Charles Darwin, published four months earlier, and reflected a growing distrust in the dogmatic literalism of the Church's orthodoxy.

Although Darwin, who had initially trained to join the church, was fearful of the reaction to his book by organised religion, he could not have expected that his work would be co-opted and interpreted by others and lead to fundamental changes in society. The political impact of Darwin's work would be to undermine the Church's creationist doctrine, puncture its veneer of omniscient authority, hasten the erosion of its power and position in English society and replace the laws of scripture with the laws of science. The profound political consequences of this shift in outlook were felt around the world and can be seen in the competing and paradoxical ideologies of Marxism and the Social Darwinist ideas of Libertarianism and Eugenics.

"The political impact of Darwin's work would be to undermine the Church's creationist doctrine, puncture its veneer of omniscient authority, hasten the erosion of its power and position in English society and replace the laws of scripture with the laws of science"

The Debate

In 1860, Oxford was a crossroad of power, the centre of religious orthodoxy and the home of the High Anglican Oxford Movement led by John Henry Newman, which sought to reassert the Catholic traditions into the Anglican Communion. It was fitting that Oxford should be the place for the most significant early debate over Darwin's thesis. Theories of evolutionary change had been discussed and advanced in Britain for nearly 75 years but none had gained widespread impact or popularity. The biologist Thomas Huxley, initially a sceptic, had become convinced by Darwin's theories in the preceding years. He had helped organise the first public pronouncement of Darwin's theories at the Linnean Society on 1 July 1858, and was a powerful advocate for both Darwin and *On the Origin of Species*.

Huxley was born in Ealing and had initially trained as a doctor. His interest in biology was matched by his dissent against the Church. Darwin's comprehensive work and evolutionist ideas of 'struggle for survival' and 'natural selection' gave him the platform to fashion a broadside against Church dogmas and literalism. Huxley's intention was plain: 'My screed was meant as a protest against Theology and Parsondom . . . both of which are in my mind the natural and irreconcilable enemies of science. Few see it but I believe we are on the Eve of a new Reformation, and if I have a wish to live thirty years it is that I may see the foot of science on the necks of her enemies'. Huxley was one of a number of outspoken academics who argued for the establishment, in 1858, of a Faculty of Science and BSc degree at University College London, which had been founded in 1826 as an alternative to the social and religious restrictions found at Oxford and Cambridge.

While controversy engulfed the liberal theologians who had dared to publish in *Essays and Reviews*, the British Association for the Advancement of Science convened a meeting in Oxford on 30 June 1860 at the newly built Museum of Natural History. The debate that ensued pitted Thomas Huxley, rapidly becoming known as Darwin's Bulldog, against the Bishop of Oxford, Samuel

Wilberforce, the third son of the abolitionist William Wilberforce, and an outspoken and intransigent anti-evolutionist. Although the ostensible argument centred on Darwin's theories, the underlying issue of the authority of the divinely inspired scriptures as enshrined by the Reformation and the possibility that these scriptures were false, was on the minds of those in attendance. This was a battle to preserve both the theological authority of the Church and its role at the centre of the political establishment.

Huxley was widely regarded as winning the argument, but the event was remembered for one exchange in particular. When asked by Wilberforce whether it was 'through his grandfather or his grandmother that he claimed descent from a monkey', Huxley responded: 'If the question is put to me "Would I rather have a miserable ape for a grandfather, or a man highly endowed by nature and possessed of great means and influence, and yet who employs these faculties and that great influence for the mere purpose of introducing ridicule into a grave scientific discussion", [then] I unhesitatingly affirm my preference for the ape'. The effect was to make Huxley, a man of science, appear more principled than the greatest orator of the Church.

Although the question would continue to be fiercely debated for years to come, the need for theology to accommodate the march of science in order to sustain its place at the centre of society was now plain. The Oxford Declaration, which came four years later, used 'fear of everlasting punishment to the cursed' as a stick to try to beat back the growth of evolutionary sentiment. While 11,000 members of the clergy signed the Oxford Declaration, 16,000 did not—a division that reflected the theological split in the Anglican Communion and revealed that Wilberforce's views had become those of the minority. The Church's accommodation of evolution accelerated and was completed when Frederick Temple, the author of the first essay in the demonised *Essays and Reviews,* was named Archbishop of Canterbury in 1896. The appointment meant that the church had made way for science, while its political relevance diminished as theological literalism was replaced by scientific investigation.

Darwin's evolutionary premise had changed the way the individual was seen, and the political consequences of this shift were soon to be felt. Man was no longer made in the image of God; he was now simply a member of a species battling for survival. This altered perspective was co-opted and used to serve agendas across the political spectrum, from the far left to the far right.

Marx

Darwin's alternative to the theological miracle of creation was admired by Karl Marx and sat easily with his social and political theories. Marx, who believed that Darwin's theories would help break the Church's opiate-like hold over the masses, was confident that Darwin's scientific writing supported the class struggle: the proletariat would prove to be the fittest and would overthrow the capitalist masters. In fact, Marx appropriated from Darwin only what served the purpose of class struggle. The 'struggle for existence' that Darwin described became, for Marx and his followers, a class struggle or a 'social struggle for existence'. Fredrick Engels was also an admirer, arguing at Marx's graveside in 1883: 'Just as Darwin discovered the law of development of organic nature, so Marx discovered the law of development of human history'.

Similarly, Darwin's ideas became inseparable from those of Marx in the Soviet ideology of the 1930s. Leading members of the Communist Party embraced Darwinism, and evolution was taught as part of the state dogma. There seemed an apparent contradiction, however, between Darwin's view of slow evolutionary change in nature and the Marxist concept of sudden revolutionary change. This was overcome by co-opting a competing theory by Dutch biologist Hugo DeVries, which described change as a 'gradual evolution with sudden revolutionary spurts'. Thus Darwin's ideas, when translated into political or social theory, were appropriated when convenient, modified as necessary and accommodated in much the same way the Church had tried to accommodate them at the end of the 19th century.

Spencer and Carnegie

Marx was not alone in seeing the attractiveness of Darwin's scientific work as a foundation for a political and social philosophy. One of the most important figures in the promulgation of Darwin's ideas was Hebert Spencer. He moved Darwin's scientific concepts into the sphere of politics and social thought in both Britain and America. Indeed many historians believe that 'Social Darwinism' should more appropriately be called 'Social Spencerism'. Spencer aimed to formulate a general concept informed by the principle of evolution, and he found in Darwin compelling evidence for belief in free enterprise, *laissez-faire* economics and competition. In 1852 he coined a phrase forever associated with Darwinism, 'the survival of the fittest', a form of words Darwin himself accepted and which became synonymous with 'Natural Selection'.

Spencer's philosophy crossed the Atlantic with Darwin's science and enjoyed great recognition. The 'survival of the fittest' imperative of Darwin's science and Spencer's philosophy was a match for the American rugged individualism that was at the heart of that nation's westward expansion.

Libertarian businessmen and American academics appropriated Darwin's ideas to advocate both freedom from government intervention and the exploitation of the fruits of the 'New World'. Those who had accumulated great wealth believed in a *laissez-faire* economic approach and felt that interference with the economy would only lead to the deterioration of America's economic success.

Andrew Carnegie, a Scottish immigrant who amassed his fortune in steel, was deeply disturbed by the 'collapse of Christian theology' until he had the opportunity to read the work of Darwin and Spencer: 'I remember that light came as in a flood and all was clear. Not only had I got rid of theology and the supernatural, but I found the truth of evolution. "All is well since all grows better" became my motto, my true source of comfort.' Carnegie believed that the 'law' of competition allowed 'the survival of the fittest in every department'. He adopted a similar approach to Spencer and, although believing there should be no state welfare for the poor, he thought that industrialists should return money to the community in the form of private charity. John D. Rockefeller, Chauncey Depew and James J. Hill also believed that they had achieved success because they were more evolved, with a greater ability to adapt. Distrust of government led both Carnegie and Rockefeller to become philanthropists, and they gave considerable amounts of their wealth to charities, believing that government could not rectify the social problems which plagued society.

"Man was no longer made in the image of God; he was now simply a member of a species battling for survival"

The idea that Social Darwinism was widely adopted by successful businessmen of the time is hotly debated by historians. Nonetheless, the idea of *laissez-faire* economics spread into academia where it was studied and sustained. Although the great universities of the United States had, like Oxford and Cambridge, traditionally been run by Churchmen, the appointment of Charles William Eliot, a chemist, to be President of Harvard in 1869 signalled the rise of the scientist in America. In the following decade, Johns Hopkins University was the first university to be dedicated to research and free of any religious requirements. At Yale, also in the 1870s, William Graham Summer, one of the most outspoken advocates of Social Darwinism, became a professor of Political and Social Science in 1872. Summer held that the human struggle to survive had two distinct parts. The first is the 'struggle for existence' with nature, and the second was the 'competition for life' with other men. He was an outspoken critic of government intervention, since this would interfere with these natural struggles. His work, and that of others, reflected a growing acceptance of *laissez-faire* economics and put considerable pressure on politicians to accept the tenets of Darwinism.

Eugenics

The Eugenics movement tested the moral conscience of civilised society throughout the 20th century and changed the way that governments viewed their relationship with citizens. Francis Galton, Darwin's cousin, coined the word Eugenics in 1883 and defined it as the 'science of improving the stock'. He wrote of Darwin's work that its effect 'was to demolish a multitude of dogmatic barriers by a single stroke and to arouse a spirit of rebellion against all ancient authorities whose positive and unauthenticated statements were contradicted by modern science'. He established the National Eugenics Society in 1907 and gained the support of Fellows of the Royal Society and Cambridge academics, including Sir Clifford Allbutt, the Regius Professor of Medicine. Their encouragement helped the movement to gain both credibility and access to British political circles. When Leonard Darwin, Charles Darwin's youngest son, became chairman of the organisation in 1911 it was beginning to establish a foothold in both left and right wing politics.

In 1910 the Eugenics Society wrote to all candidates in the British general election, advising them to implement measures to stop 'degenerates' from having offspring, while widespread public support resulted in a Private Member's Bill called 'The Feeble-Minded Persons Bill' the following year. Politicians from all political parties embraced Eugenics, including Home Secretary Winston Churchill, former Prime Minister Arthur Balfour and Will Crooks, the fourth elected MP of the Labour Party. The Bill was withdrawn, but the strength of feeling among the upper echelons of the Liberal party meant that the government decided to introduce a Mental Deficiency Bill in 1913. While this bill did not sanction compulsory sterilisation it did allow 'idiots', 'imbeciles', 'the feeble-minded' and 'moral defectives' to be segregated. 'The Idiots Act' gave nine hospitals and institutions the right to segregate the mentally disabled from society. Remaining in place until 1959, it is said to have segregated 60,000 people at its peak and placed another 43,000 under supervisory control orders in the community. Sterilisation was also attractive to all parties because it was a cost effective way of coping with an economic underclass and fitted in with Labour's idea of social planning.

"The Eugenics movement tested the moral conscience of civilised society throughout the 20th century"

The three key designers of Britain's post war welfare reforms—John Maynard Keynes, William Beveridge and Richard Titmuss—were all Eugenicists. They extrapolated the underlying concepts of Eugenics, improving the stock and social planning, into a means for social improvement. This culminated in legislation after the Second World War, which cemented in the mind of the British public the concepts of state intervention in the welfare of its citizens and universal healthcare. The principle that the State could intervene in the lives of its citizens, against their will if it felt it was in their best interests, was a natural extension of these concepts. Although Briton pulled away from a compulsory sterilisation policy America embraced it.

The concept of Eugenics was widely accepted in the United States with supporters in both the corridors of academia and political power. Harvard zoologist Charles Davenport, considered an intellectual disciple of Francis Galton, created the 'Eugenics Record Office' in 1910, which documented family trees and inherited defects. The office was led by Harry Laughlin and the records were used to try to identify those that were considered 'defective'. With this newly compiled data many States began to consider legislation which would sterilise their citizens. By 1917 sixteen states had enacted sterilisation statutes, though opposition elsewhere meant the constitutionality of sterilisation laws had to be tested in the courts. In 1924, Virginia adopted a law calling for the sterilisation of 'the mentally retarded, insane, criminal, epileptic, inebriated, diseased, blind, deaf, deformed, and economically dependent', and three years later the Supreme Court ruled that the legislation was not only constitutional but, in its opinion, wise. By 1940, this ruling had led to the sterilisation of 36,000 men and women across the United States. Nazi legislation, 'Preventing Hereditarily Ill Progeny', was almost identical, and the leap from these Social Darwinist inspired eugenics laws to the Wannsee Conference's Final Solution is not hard to imagine.

Conclusion

The appropriation of Darwin's biological findings by advocates of a wide range of political beliefs was responsible for a fundamental shift in the political constructs of Western society. Science became the new religion that guided political principles. The moral guidance of the Church was diminished and replaced by the presumed infallibility of scientific data. Frederick Temple's accommodation of Darwin in order to preserve the status of the Church against the onslaught of science was the first of many accommodations of Darwin's theories. Karl Marx co-opted Darwin to agitate against the Church's presence in a socialist society. Social Darwinist principles, which spawned the libertarianism advanced by Herbert Spencer and William Graham Sumner and embraced inequality as a fact of nature, became corrupted by the Eugenics movement which called for human intervention to 'improve the stock'. The secularism of our daily life, and the presumption by the modern State that it knows what is best for the welfare of its citizens, is a direct result of the political impact of Charles Darwin.

"The secularism of our daily life, and the presumption by the modern State that it knows what is best for the welfare of its citizens, is a direct result of the political impact of Charles Darwin"

Critical Thinking

1. How does the author assess the political impact of Darwin's work?

2. Why was it fitting that Oxford would be the place for the most significant early debate over Darwin's thesis and that Thomas Huxley would be a participant in that debate? How does the author describe this "battle"?

3. What were the indicators that theology did, in fact, accommodate the march of science?

4. How did Marx and the Communist Party of the Soviet Union each appropriate Darwin's theory and translate it into their political and social theories?

5. Why should "Social Darwinism" be more appropriately called "Social Spencerism"?

6. Why was Spencer's "survival of the fittest" imperative an easy match for the American rugged individualism? How did it come to be expressed in the views of Andrew Carnegie and John D. Rockefeller?

7. What events signaled the rise of the scientist in America?

8. Be familiar with the rise of the Eugenics movement and the ways in which it was put into effect.

9. Discuss the ways in which science became the "new religion".

Further Reading

J.W. Burrow, *Evolution and Society: A Study in Victorian Social Theory* (Cambridge University Press, 1966)

A. Desmond, *Huxley: From Devil's Disciple to Evolution's High Priest* (Perseus Books, 1999)

M. Hawkins, *Social Darwinism in European and American Thought, 1860–1945* (Cambridge University Press, 1997)

D.R. Oldroyd, *Darwinian Impacts* (Open University Press, 1980)

D. Sewell, *The Political Gene: How Darwin's Ideas Changed Politics* (Picador, 2009)

J.G. West, *Darwin's Day in America: How Our Politics and Culture Have Been Dehumanised in the Name of Science* (ISI Books, 2007)

The Latest Face of Creationism

Creationists who want religious ideas taught as scientific fact in public schools continue to adapt to courtroom defeats by hiding their true aims under ever changing guises.

GLENN BRANCH AND EUGENIE C. SCOTT

Professors routinely give advice to students but usually while their charges are still in school. Arthur Landy, a distinguished professor of molecular and cell biology and biochemistry at Brown University, recently decided, however, that he had to remind a former pre-med student of his that "without evolution, modern biology, including medicine and biotechnology, wouldn't make sense."

The sentiment was not original with Landy, of course. Thirty-six years ago geneticist Theodosius Dobzhansky, a major contributor to the foundations of modern evolutionary theory, famously told the readers of *The American Biology Teacher* that "nothing in biology makes sense, except in the light of evolution." Back then, Dobzhansky was encouraging biology teachers to present evolution to their pupils in spite of religiously motivated opposition. Now, however, Landy was addressing Bobby Jindal—the governor of the state of Louisiana—on whose desk the latest antievolution bill, the so-called Louisiana Science Education Act, was sitting, awaiting his signature.

Remembering Jindal as a good student in his genetics class, Landy hoped that the governor would recall the scientific importance of evolution to biology and medicine. Joining Landy in his opposition to the bill were the American Institute of Biological Sciences, which warned that "Louisiana will undoubtedly be thrust into the national spotlight as a state that pursues politics over science and education," and the American Association for the Advancement of Science, which told Jindal that the law would "unleash an assault against scientific integrity." Earlier, the National Association of Biology Teachers had urged the legislature to defeat the bill, pleading "that the state of Louisiana not allow its science curriculum to be weakened by encouraging the utilization of supplemental

Key Concepts

- Creationists continue to agitate against the teaching of evolution in public schools, adapting their tactics to match the roadblocks they encounter.
- Past strategies have included portraying creationism as a credible alternative to evolution and disguising it under the name "intelligent design."
- Other tactics misrepresent evolution as scientifically controversial and pretend that advocates for teaching creationism are defending academic freedom.

—The Editors

materials produced for the sole purpose of confusing students about the nature of science."

But all these protests were of no avail. On June 26, 2008, the governor's office announced that Jindal had signed the Louisiana Science Education Act into law. Why all the fuss? On its face, the law looks innocuous: it directs the state board of education to "allow and assist teachers, principals, and other school administrators to create and foster an environment within public elementary and secondary schools that promotes critical thinking skills, logical analysis, and open and objective discussion of scientific theories being studied," which includes providing "support and guidance for teachers regarding effective ways to help students understand, analyze, critique, and objectively review scientific theories being studied." What's not to like? Aren't critical thinking, logical analysis, and open and objective discussion exactly what science education aims to promote?

As always in the contentious history of evolution education in the U.S., the devil is in the details. The law explicitly targets evolution, which is unsurprising—for

It's Your Move

This time line notes some key events in the seesawing history of the battle between creationists and evolutionists. It highlights the way creationist tactics have shifted in response to evolution's advances in classrooms and to court rulings that have banned religious proselytizing in public schools.

Late 1910s and Early 1920s

As high school attendance rises, more American students become exposed to evolution.

1925

Butler Act in Tennessee outlaws teaching of human evolution. Teacher John T. Scopes is prosecuted and convicted under the law, although the conviction is later overturned on a technicality.

1958

Biological Sciences Curriculum Study (BSCS) is founded with funds from a federal government concerned about science education in the wake of Sputnik. BSCS's textbooks emphasize evolution, which was largely absent from textbooks after the Scopes trial; commercial publishers follow suit.

1968

Supreme Court rules in case of *Epperson v. Arkansas* that laws barring the teaching of evolution in public schools are unconstitutional.

1981

Louisiana passes the Balanced Treatment for Creation-Science and Evolution-Science in Public School Instruction Act. Also in the 1980s legislators in more than 25 states introduce bills calling for "creation science" to have equal time with evolution.

1987

Supreme Court rules in the case of *Edwards v. Aguillard* that the Louisiana Balanced Treatment Act violates the Establishment Clause of the First Amendment.

1989

Of *Pandas and People,* the first book systematically to use the term "intelligent design" is published; it touts the notion as an alternative to evolution.

2001

Passage of the No Child Left Behind Act cements the importance of state science standards, which have become a new battleground between creationism and evolution (because inclusion of evolution in science standards increases the likelihood that evolution will be taught).

2005

Decision in *Kitzmiller v. Dover Area School District* rules that teaching intelligent design in the public schools is unconstitutional. The photograph at the right captures plaintiff Tammy Kitzmiller during a break from the trial.

2008

Governor Bobby Jindal signs the Louisiana Science Education Act into law. Marketed as supporting critical thinking in classrooms, the law threatens to open the door for the teaching of creationism and for scientifically unwarranted critiques of evolution in public school science classes.

lurking in the background of the law is creationism, the rejection of a scientific explanation of the history of life in favor of a supernatural account involving a personal creator. Indeed, to mutate Dobzhansky's dictum, nothing about the Louisiana law makes sense except in the light of creationism.

Creationism's Evolution

Creationists have long battled against the teaching of evolution in U.S. public schools, and their strategies have evolved in reaction to legal setbacks. In the 1920s they attempted to ban the teaching of evolution outright, with laws such as Tennessee's Butler Act, under which teacher John T. Scopes was prosecuted in 1925. It was not until 1968 that such laws were ruled to be unconstitutional, in the Supreme Court case *Epperson v. Arkansas.* No longer able to keep evolution out of the science classrooms of the public schools, creationists began to portray creationism as a scientifically credible alternative, dubbing it creation science or scientific creationism. By the early 1980s legislation calling for equal time for creation science had been introduced in no fewer than 27 states, including Louisiana. There, in 1981, the legislature passed the Balanced Treatment for Creation-Science and Evolution-Science in Public School Instruction Act, which required teachers to teach creation science if they taught evolution.

The Louisiana Balanced Treatment Act was based on a model bill circulated across the country by creationists working at the grassroots level. Obviously inspired by a particular literal interpretation of the book of Genesis, the model bill defined creation science as including creation ex nihilo ("from nothing"), a worldwide flood, a "relatively recent inception" of the earth, and a rejection of the common ancestry of humans and apes. In Arkansas, such a bill was enacted earlier in 1981 and promptly challenged in court as unconstitutional. So when the Louisiana Balanced Treatment Act was still under consideration by the state legislature, supporters, anticipating a similar challenge, immediately purged the bill's definition of creation science of specifics, leaving only "the scientific evidences for creation and inferences from those scientific evidences." But this tactical vagueness failed to render the law constitutional, and in 1987 the Supreme Court ruled in *Edwards v. Aguillard* that the Balanced Treatment Act violated the Establishment Clause of the First Amendment to the Constitution, because the act "impermissibly endorses religion by advancing the religious belief that a supernatural being created humankind."

Creationism adapts quickly. Just two years later a new label for creationism—"intelligent design"—was introduced in the supplementary textbook *Of Pandas and People,* produced by the Foundation for Thought and Ethics, which styles itself a Christian think tank. Continuing the Louisiana Balanced Treatment Act's strategy of reducing overt religious content, intelligent design is advertised as not based on any sacred texts and as not requiring any appeal to the supernatural. The designer, the proponents say, might be God, but it might be space aliens or time-traveling cell biologists from the future. Mindful that teaching creationism in the public schools is unconstitutional, they vociferously reject any characterization of intelligent design as a form of creationism. Yet on careful inspection, intelligent design proves to be a rebranding of creationism—silent on a number of creation science's distinctive claims (such as the young age of the earth and the historicity of Noah's flood) but otherwise riddled with the same scientific errors and entangled with the same religious doctrines.

Such a careful inspection occurred in a federal courtroom in 2005, in the trial of *Kitzmiller vs. Dover Area School District.* At issue was a policy in a local school district in Pennsylvania requiring a disclaimer to be read aloud in the classroom alleging that evolution is a "Theory . . . not a fact," that "gaps in the Theory exist for which there is no evidence," and that intelligent design as presented in *Of Pandas and People* is a credible scientific alternative to evolution. Eleven local parents filed suit in federal district court, arguing that the policy was unconstitutional. After a trial that spanned a biblical 40 days, the judge agreed, ruling that the policy violated the Establishment Clause and writing, "In making this determination, we have addressed the seminal question of whether [intelligent design] is science. We have concluded that it is not, and moreover that [intelligent design] cannot uncouple itself from its creationist; and thus religious, antecedents."

The expert witness testimony presented in the *Kitzmiller* trial was devastating for intelligent design's scientific pretensions. Intelligent design was established to be creationism lite: at the trial philosopher Barbara Forrest,

co-author of *Creationism's Trojan Horse: The Wedge of Intelligent Design,* revealed that references to creationism in *Of Pandas and People* drafts were replaced with references to design shortly after the 1987 *Edwards* decision striking down Louisiana's Balanced Treatment Act was issued. She even found a transitional form, where the replacement of "creationists" by "design proponents" was incomplete—"cdesign proponentsists" was the awkward result. More important, intelligent design was also established to be scientifically bankrupt: one of the expert witnesses in the trial, biochemist Michael Behe, testified that no articles have been published in the scientific research literature that "provide detailed rigorous accounts of how intelligent design of any biological system occurred"—and he was testifying in *defense* of the school board's policy.

Donning a Fake Mustache

Failing to demonstrate the scientific credibility of their views, creationists are increasingly retreating to their standard fallback strategy for undermining the teaching of evolution: misrepresenting evolution as scientifically controversial while remaining silent about what they regard as the alternative. This move represents only a slight rhetorical shift. From the Scopes era onward, creationists have simultaneously employed three central rhetorical themes, sometimes called the three pillars of creationism, to attack evolution: that evolution is unsupported by or actually in conflict with the facts of science; that teaching evolution threatens religion, morality and society; and that fairness dictates the necessity of teaching creationism alongside evolution. The fallback strategy amounts to substituting for creationism the scientifically unwarranted claim that evolution is a theory in crisis.

Creationists are fond of asserting that evolution is a theory in crisis because they assume that there are only two alternatives: creationism (whether creation science or intelligent design) and evolution. Evidence against evolution is thus evidence for creationism; disproving evolution thus proves creationism. The judge in *McLean v. Arkansas,* the 1981 case in which Arkansas's Balanced Treatment Act was ruled to be unconstitutional, succinctly described the assumption as "a contrived dualism." Yet by criticizing evolution without mentioning creationism, proponents of the fallback strategy hope to encourage students to acquire or retain a belief in creationism without running afoul of the Establishment Clause. Creationism's latest face is just like its earlier face, only now thinly disguised with a fake mustache.

Underscoring the conscious decision to emphasize the supposed evidence against evolution, the Institute for Creation Research, which promotes creation science, candidly recommended immediately after the *Edwards* decision that "school boards and teachers should be strongly encouraged at least to stress the scientific evidences and arguments *against evolution* in their classes . . . even if they don't wish to recognize these as evidences and arguments *for creation.*" Similarly, the Discovery Institute, the de facto institutional headquarters of intelligent design, saw the writing on the wall even before the decision in the *Kitzmiller* ruling that teaching intelligent design in the public schools is unconstitutional. Although a widely discussed internal memorandum-"The Wedge Document"—had numbered among its goals the inclusion of intelligent design in the science curricula of 10 states,the Discovery Institute subsequently retreated to a strategy to undermine the teaching of evolution, introducing a flurry of labels and slogans—"teach the controversy," "critical analysis" and "academic freedom"—to promote its version of the fallback strategy.

"Academic freedom" was the creationist catchphrase of choice in 2008: the Louisiana Science Education Act was in fact born as the Louisiana Academic Freedom Act, and bills invoking the idea were introduced in Alabama, Florida, Michigan, Missouri and South Carolina, although, as of November, all were dead or stalled [*see box on Antievolution Bills of 2008*]. And academic freedom was a central theme of the first creationist movie to tarnish the silver screen: *Expelled: No Intelligence Allowed.* (Science columnist Michael Shermer eviscerated *Expelled* in his review in the June 2008 issue of *Scientific American,* and the magazine's staff added commentary on www.SciAm. com.) Portraying the scientific community as conspiring to persecute scientists for their views on creationism, *Expelled* was ostensibly concerned with academic freedom mainly at the college level, but it was used to lobby for the academic freedom legislation in Missouri and Florida aimed at the public schools. (The movie, by the way, was a critical failure and jam-packed with errors.)

The appeal of academic freedom as a slogan for the creationist fallback strategy is obvious: everybody approves of freedom, and plenty of people have a sense that academic freedom is desirable, even if they do not necessarily have a good understanding of what it is. The concept of academic freedom is primarily relevant to college teaching, and the main organization defending it, the American Association of University Professors, recently reaffirmed its opposition to antievolution laws such as Louisiana's, writing, "Such efforts run counter to the overwhelming scientific consensus regarding evolution and are inconsistent with a proper understanding of the meaning of academic freedom." In the public schools, even if there is no legal right to academic freedom, it is sound educational

Antievolution Bills of 2008

Several states aside from Louisiana entertained antievolution bills last year. Clearly, efforts to push such legislation continue unabated.

State (Bill)	Ostensible Aim	Status
Alabama (HB 923)	Support academic freedom	Died May 2008
Florida (HB 1483)	Foster critic, analysis	Died May 2008
Florida (SB 2692)	Support academic freedom	Died May 2008
Michigan (SB 1361)	Support academic freedom	In committee when this issue went to press
Michigan (HB 6027)	Support academic freedom	Identical to SB 1361; in committee when this issue went to press
Missouri (HB 2554)	Promote teaching of evolution's strengths and weaknesses	Died May 2008
South Carolina (SB 1386)	Promote teaching of evolution's strengths and weaknesses	Died June 2008

policy to allow teachers a degree of latitude to teach their subjects as they see fit—but there are limits. Allowing teachers to instill scientifically unwarranted doubts about evolution is clearly beyond the pale. Yet that is what the Louisiana Science Education Act was evidently created, or designed, to do.

The Worm in the Apple

The real purpose of the law—as opposed to its ostensible support for academic freedom—becomes evident on analysis. First, consider what the law seeks to accomplish. Aren't teachers in the public schools *already* exhorted to promote critical thinking, logical analysis and objective discussion of the scientific theories that they discuss? Yes, indeed: in Louisiana, policies established by the state board of education already encourage teachers to do so, as critics of the bill protested during a legislative hearing.

So what is the law's true intent? That only a handful of scientific topics—"biological evolution, the chemical origins of life, global warming, and human cloning"— are explicitly mentioned is a hint. So is the fact that the bill was introduced at the behest of the Louisiana Family Forum, which seeks to "persuasively present biblical principles in the centers of influence on issues affecting the family through research, communication and networking." And so is the fact that the group's executive director was vocally dismayed when those topics were temporarily deleted from the bill.

Second, was there in fact a special need for the Louisiana legislature to encourage teachers to promote critical thinking with respect to evolution in particular? No evidence seems to have been forthcoming. Patsye Peebles, a veteran science teacher in Baton Rouge, commented, "I was a biology teacher for 22 years, and I never needed the legislature to tell me how to present anything. This bill doesn't solve any of the problems classroom teachers face, and it will make it harder for us to keep the focus on accurate science in science classrooms." And of course, the National Association of Biology Teachers, representing more than 9,000 biology educators across the country, took a firm stand against the bill. In neighboring Florida, the sponsors of similar bills alleged that there were teachers who were prevented from or penalized for "teaching the 'holes'" in evolution. But no such teachers were ever produced, and the state department of education and local newspapers were unable to confirm that the claimed incidents of persecution ever occurred.

And, third, what are these "holes" in evolution, anyhow? The savvier supporters of bills such as Florida's and Louisiana's realize that it is crucial to disclaim any intention to promote creationism. But because there is no scientifically credible challenge to evolution, only long-ago-debunked creationist claptrap [see "15 Answers to Creationist Nonsense," by John Rennie; *Scientific American*, June 2002], the supporters of such bills are forced to be evasive when asked about what material would be covered.

In Florida, for example, a representative of the Discovery Institute dithered when asked whether intelligent design constituted "scientific information" in the sense of the bill, saying, "In my personal opinion, I think it does. But the intent of this bill is not to settle that question," and adding, unhelpfully, "The intent of this bill is . . . it protects the 'teaching of scientific information.'" Similarly, during debate on the Senate floor, the bill's sponsor was noticeably reluctant to address the question of whether it would license the teaching of creationism, preferring instead to simply recite its text.

Thus, despite the lofty language, the ulterior intent and likely effect of these bills are evident: undermining the teaching of evolution in public schools—a consequence only creationists regard as a blessing. Unfortunately, among their numbers are teachers. A recent national survey conducted by researchers at Pennsylvania State University reveals that one in eight U.S. high school biology

What to Do

If controversy over the teaching of evolution erupts in your area, here are some actions you can take:

- Resolving the controversy requires thinking politically, which means forming coalitions. Join with like-minded science educators, scientists, members of the clergy and other citizens to convince policymakers not to accede to creationist proposals.
- Keep in mind that the goal is not only to keep creationism out of the science classroom but also to ensure that evolution is taught properly—without qualifiers such as "only a theory" and unaccompanied by specious "evidence against evolution."
- Be ready to rebut assertions that evolution is a theory in crisis; that evolution is a threat to religion, morality and society; and that it is only fair to teach "both sides" of the issue.
- Arrange for defenders of evolution to write letters to the editor and op-eds, attend and speak at meetings of the board of education or legislature, and work to turn out the vote on Election Day.

Adapted from "Defending the Teaching of Evolution: Strategies and Tactics for Activists," by Glenn Branch, in *Not in Our Classrooms: Why Intelligent Design Is Wrong for Our Schools*. Edited by Eugenie C. Scott and Glenn Branch. Beacon, 2006.

teachers already presents creationism as a "valid scientific alternative to Darwinian explanations for the origin of species," with about the same percentage emphasizing that "many reputable scientists" view creationism as a scientifically valid alternative to evolution.

Not all creationist teachers are as extreme as John Freshwater, a Mount Vernon, Ohio, middle school teacher who became immersed in legal troubles over his religious advocacy in the classroom, which included not only teaching creationism but also, allegedly, using a high-voltage electrical apparatus to brand his students with a cross. But even the less zealous will probably take laws such as Louisiana's as a license to miseducate. Such laws are also likely to be used to bully teachers who are not creationists: nationally, 3 in 10 already report pressure to present creationism or downplay evolution.

These bills will also further encourage school districts where creationists are politically powerful to adopt anti-evolution policies. A statement by a member of the Livingston Parish School Board who supported the Louisiana bill is instructive. After saying "both sides—the creationism side and the evolution side—should be presented," he explained that the bill was needed because "teachers are scared to talk about" creation. How plausible is it, then, that the law's provision that it is not to be "construed to promote any religious doctrine" will be honored in practice? As conservative columnist John Derbyshire commented, "the Act will encourage Louisiana local school boards to unconstitutional behavior. That's what it's *meant* to do."

The Future of Steady Misrepresentation

What are the legal prospects of the creationist fallback strategy? A case in Georgia, *Selman v. Cobb County School District,* is suggestive, if not decisive. In 2002 the Cobb County board of education, bowing to the demands of local creationists, decided to require warning labels for biology textbooks. Using a phrase employed by creationists even before the Scopes trial in 1925, the labels described evolution as "a theory, not a fact," while remaining silent about creationism. Five parents in the county filed suit in federal district court, arguing that the policy requiring the labels was unconstitutional, and the trial judge agreed, citing the abundant history linking the warning labels with creationist activity in Cobb County in particular and linking the fallback strategy with creationism in general. The case was vacated on appeal because of concerns about the evidence submitted at trial, remanded to the trial court and settled on terms favorable to the parents. It remains to be seen whether the fallback strategy will survive constitutional scrutiny elsewhere—but it is likely that it will be challenged, whether in Louisiana or elsewhere.

In the meantime, it is clear why the Louisiana Science Education Act is pernicious: it tacitly encourages teachers and local school districts to miseducate students about evolution, whether by teaching creationism as a scientifically credible alternative or merely by misrepresenting evolution as scientifically controversial. Vast areas of evolutionary science are for all intents and purposes scientifically settled; textbooks and curricula used in the public schools present precisely such basic, uncomplicated, uncontroversial material. Telling students that evolution is a theory in crisis is—to be blunt—a lie.

Moreover, it is a dangerous lie, because Dobzhansky was right to say that nothing in biology makes sense except in the light of evolution: without evolution, it would be impossible to explain why the living world is the way it is rather than otherwise. Students who are not given the chance to acquire a proper understanding of evolution will not achieve a basic level of scientific literacy. And scientific literacy will be indispensable for workers, consumers and policymakers in a future dominated by medical, biotechnological and environmental concerns.

In the sesquicentennial year of *On the Origin of Species,* it seems fitting to end with a reference to Charles Darwin's seminal 1859 book. In the first edition of *Origin of Species,* Darwin was careful to acknowledge the limits to his project, writing, "I am convinced that natural selection has been the main but not the exclusive means of modification." Nevertheless, he was misinterpreted as claiming that natural selection was entirely responsible for evolution, provoking him to add a rueful comment to the sixth edition: "Great is the power of steady misrepresentation; but the history of science shows that fortunately this power does not long endure."

The enactment of the Louisiana Science Education Act, and the prospect of similar legislation in the future, confirms Darwin's assessment of the power of steady misrepresentation. But because the passage of such antievolution bills ultimately results from politics rather than science, it will not be the progress of science that ensures their failure to endure. Rather it will take the efforts of citizens who are willing to take a stand and defend the uncompromised teaching of evolution.

More to Explore

Analyzing Critical Analysis: The Fallback Antievolutionist Strategy. Nicholas J. Matzke and Paul R. Gross in *Not in Our Classrooms: Why Intelligent Design Is Wrong for Our Schools.* Edited by Eugenie C. Scott and Glenn Branch. Beacon, 2006.

Evolution: The Triumph of an Idea. Carl Zimmer. Harper Perennial, 2006.

Creationism's Trojan Horse: The Wedge of Intelligent Design. Revised edition. Barbara Forrest and Paul R. Gross. Oxford University Press, 2007.

The Devil in Dover: An Insider's Story of Dogma v. Darwin in Small-Town America. Lauri Lebo. New Press, 2008.

Evolution vs. Creationism: An introduction. Second edition. Eugenie C. Scott. Greenwood, 2009.

Critical Thinking

1. Why do the authors claim that the Louisiana Education Act is not promoting the aims of science education?

2. Describe how and why the creationist strategies against the teaching of evolution have evolved. How was the latest attempt involving "intelligent design" foiled?

3. Describe the standard fallback strategy involving the "three pillars of creationism." Describe the fallacy of "contrived dualism."

4. Why has this strategy included "academic freedom"? In what sense are there limits to academic freedom, according to the authors?

5. Why is the real purpose of the Louisiana law evident upon analysis? What are some of the possible negative effects of such a law?

6. Why is the Louisiana law "pernicious"? Why is it a "dangerous lie"?

GLENN BRANCH AND EUGENIE C. SCOTT are deputy director and executive director, respectively, of the National Center for Science Education (NCSE) in Oakland, Calif., where they work to defend the teaching of evolution in the public schools. Together they edited *Not in Our Classrooms: Why Intelligent Design Is Wrong for Our Schools.* Branch is trained in philosophy and is a longtime observer of pseudoscience of all kinds. Scott, a physical anthropologist by training and a former university professor, is internationally known as a leading authority on the antievolution movement and has received many awards and honorary degrees for her work at NCSE.

Why Should Students Learn Evolution?

BRIAN J. ALTERS AND SANDRA M. ALTERS

"When you combine the lack of emphasis on evolution in kindergarten through 12th grade, with the immense popularity of creationism among the public, and the industry discrediting evolution, it's easy to see why half of the population believes humans were created 10,000 years ago and lived with dinosaurs. It is by far the biggest failure of science education from top to bottom."

—Randy Moore, Editor, *The American Biology Teacher*

"This is an important area of science, with particular significance for a developmental psychologist like me. Unless one has some understanding of the key notions of species, variation, natural selection, adaptation, and the like (and how these "have been discovered"), unless one appreciates the perennial struggle among individuals (and populations) for survival in a particular ecological niche, one cannot understand the living world of which we are a part."

—Howard Gardner, Professor, Harvard Graduate School of Education

With all of the controversy over the teaching of evolution reported in the media, with parents confronting their children's science teachers on this issue, and with students themselves confronting their instructors in high schools and colleges, would it be best—and easiest—to just delete the teaching of evolution in the classroom? Can't students attain a well-rounded background in science without learning this controversial topic? The overwhelming consensus of biologists in the scientific community is "no." Why, then, should science students learn about evolution?

A simple answer is that evolution is the basic context of all the biological sciences. Take away this context, and all that is left is disparate facts without the thread that ties them all together. Put another way, evolution is the explanatory framework, the unifying theory. It is indispensable to the study of biology, just as the atomic theory is indispensable to the study of chemistry. The characteristics and behavior of atoms and their subatomic particles form the basis of this physical science. So, too, biology can be understood fully only in an evolutionary context. In explaining how the organisms of today got to be the way they are, evolution helps make sense out of the history of life and explains relationships among species. It is a useful and often essential framework within which scientists organize and interpret observations and make predictions about the living world.

But this simple answer is not the entire reason why students should learn evolution. There are other considerations as well. Evolutionary explanations answer key questions in the biological sciences such as why organisms across species have so many striking similarities yet are tremendously diverse. These key questions are the *why* questions of biology. Much of biology explains *how* organisms work . . . how we breathe, how fish swim, or how leopard frogs produce thousands of eggs at one time . . . but it is up to evolution to explain the why behind these mechanisms. In answering the key *why* questions of biology, evolutionary explanations become an important lens through which scientists interpret data, whether they are developmental biologists, plant physiologists, or biochemists, to mention just a few of the many foci of those who study life.

Understanding evolution also has practical considerations that affect day-to-day life. Without an understanding of natural selection, students cannot recognize and understand problems based on this process, such as insect resistance to pesticides or microbial resistance to antibiotics. In a report released in June, 2000, Dr. Gro Harlem Brunddand, Director-General of the World Health Organization, stated that the world is at risk of losing drugs that control many infectious diseases because of increasing antimicrobial resistance. The report goes on to give examples, stating that 98% of strains of gonorrhea in Southeast Asia are now resistant to penicillin. Additionally, 14,000 people die each year from drug-resistant infections acquired in hospitals in the United States. And in New Delhi, India, typhoid drugs are no longer effective against this disease. Such problems face every person on our planet, and an understanding of natural selection will help students realize how important their behavior is in either contributing to or helping stem this crisis in medical progress.

Evolution not only enriches and provides a conceptual foundation for biological sciences such as ecology, genetics, developmental biology, and systematics, it provides a framework for scientific disciplines with historical aspects, such as anthropology, astronomy, geology, and paleontology. Evolution is therefore a unifying theme among many sciences, providing students with a framework by which to understand the natural world from many perspectives.

As scientists search for evolutionary explanations to the many questions of life, they develop methods and formulate concepts that are being applied in other fields, such as molecular biology, medicine, and statistics. For example, scientists studying molecular evolutionary change have developed methods to distinguish variations in gene sequences within and among species. These methods not only add to the toolbox of the molecular biologist but also will have likely applications in medicine by helping to identify variations that cause genetic diseases. In characterizing and analyzing variation, evolutionary biologists have also developed statistical methods, such as analysis of variance and path analysis, which are widely used in other fields. Thus, methods and concepts developed by evolutionary biologists have wide relevance in other fields and influence us all daily in ways we cannot realize without an understanding of this important and central idea.

Evolution is not only a powerful and wide-reaching concept among the pure and applied sciences, it also permeates other disciplines such as philosophy, psychology, literature, and the arts. Evolution by means of natural selection, articulated amidst controversy in the mid-nineteenth century, has reached the twenty-first century having had an extensive and expansive impact on human thought. An important intellectual development in the history of ideas, evolution should hold a central place in science teaching and learning.

Why is evolution—the context of the biological sciences—a unifying theory?

First, how does evolution take place? A key idea is that some of the individuals within a population of organisms possess measurable changes in inheritable characteristics that favor their survival. (These characteristics can be morphological, physiological, behavioral, or biochemical.) These individuals are more likely to live to reproductive age than are individuals not possessing the favorable characteristics. These reproductively advantageous traits (called *adaptive traits* or *adaptations*) are passed on from

surviving individuals to their offspring. Over time, the individuals carrying these traits will increase in numbers within the population, and the nature of the population as a whole will gradually change. This process of survival of the most reproductively fit organisms is called *natural selection.*

The process of evolutionary change explains that the organisms of today got to be the way they are, at least in part, as the result of natural selection over billions of years and even billions more generations. Organisms are related to one another, some more distantly, branching from a common ancestor long ago, and some more recently, branching from a common ancestor closer to the present day. The fact that diverse organisms have descended from common ancestors accounts for the similarities exhibited among species. Since biology is the story of life, then evolution is the story of biology and the relatedness of all life.

How do evolutionary explanations answer key questions in the biological sciences?

Evolution answers the question of the unity and similarity of life by its relatedness and shared history. But what about its diversity? And how does evolution answer other key questions in the biological sciences? What are these questions and how does evolution answer the *why* question inherent in each?

Evolution explains the diversity of life in the same way that it explains its unity. As mentioned in the preceding paragraphs, some individuals within a population of organisms possess measurable changes in inheritable characteristics that favor their survival. These adaptive traits are passed on from surviving individuals to their offspring. Over time, as populations inhabit different ecological niches, the individuals carrying adaptive traits in each population increase in numbers, and the nature of each population gradually changes. Such divergent evolution, the splitting of single species into multiple, descendant species, accounts for variation. There are different modes, or patterns, of divergence, and various reproductive isolating mechanisms that contribute to divergent evolution. However, the result is the same: Populations split from common ancestral populations and their genetic differences accumulate.

What are some other key questions in biology that are answered by evolution? One key question asks why form is adapted to function. Evolutionary theory tells us that more organisms that have parts of their anatomy (a long, slender beak, for instance) better adapted to certain functions (such as capturing food that lives deep within holes in rotting tree trunks) will live to reproductive age in greater numbers than those with less-well-adapted beaks. Therefore, the organisms with better-adapted beaks will pass on the genes for these features to greater numbers of off-spring. Eventually, after numerous generations, natural selection will result in a population that has long slender beaks adapted to procuring food. Thus, anatomical, behavioral, or biochemical traits (the "forms") fit their functions because form fitting function is adaptive. But this idea leads us to yet another important question: Why do organisms have a variety of nonadaptive features that coexist amidst those that are adaptive?

During the course of evolution, traits that no longer confer a reproductive advantage do not disappear in the population unless they are reproductively disadvantageous. A population of beige beach birds that escaped predation because of protective coloration will not change coloration if this population becomes geographically isolated to a grasslands environment, unless the now useless beige coloration allows the birds to be hunted and killed more easily. In other words, if beige coloration is not a liability in the new environment, the genes that code for this trait will be passed on by all surviving birds in this grasslands niche. Even as the population of birds changes over generations, the genes for beige feathers will be retained in the population as long as this trait confers no reproductive disadvantage (and as long as mutation and genetic drift do not result in such a change).

These preceding examples do not cover all the key questions of biology (of course), but do show that such key questions are really questions about evolution and its mechanisms. Only evolutionary theory can answer the *why* questions inherent in these themes of life.

How does understanding evolution help us understand processes that affect our health and our day-to-day life? and How are evolutionary methods applied to other fields?

As mentioned earlier, without an understanding of natural selection, students cannot recognize and understand problems based on this process, such as insect resistance to pesticides or microbial resistance to antibiotics. Additionally, it is only through such understanding that scientists can hope to find solutions to these serious situations. Scientists know that the underlying cause of microbial resistance to antibiotics is improper use of these drugs. As explained in the World Health Organization report *Overcoming Antimicrobial Resistance,* in poor countries antibiotics are often used in ways that encourage the development of resistance. Unable to afford the full course of treatment, patients often take antibiotics only until their symptoms go away—killing the most susceptible microbes while allowing those more resistant to survive and reproduce. When these most resistant pathogens infect another host, antibiotics are less effective against the more resistant strains. In wealthy countries such as the United States, antibiotics are overused, being prescribed for viral diseases for which they are ineffective and being used in agriculture to treat sick animals and promote the growth of those that are well. Such misuse and overuse of antibiotics speeds the process whereby less resistant strains of bacteria are wiped out and more resistant strains flourish.

In addition to developing resistance to antibiotics and other therapies, pathogens can evolve resistance to the body's natural defenses. The virulence of pathogens (the ease with which they cause disease) can also evolve rapidly. Understanding the co-evolution of the human immune system and the pathogens that attack it help scientists track and predict disease outbreaks.

Understanding evolution also helps researchers understand the frequency, nature, and distribution of genetic disease. Gene frequencies in populations are affected by selection pressures, mutation, migration, and random genetic drift. Studying genetic diseases from an evolutionary standpoint helps us see that even lethal genes can remain in a population if there is a reproductive advantage in the heterozygote, as in the case of sickle-cell anemia and malaria.

Sickle-cell anemia is one of the most common genetic disorders among African Americans, having arisen in their African ancestors. It has been observed in persons whose ancestors came from the Mediterranean basin, the Indian subcontinent, the Caribbean, and parts of Central and South America (particularly Brazil). The sickle-cell gene has persisted in these populations, even though the disease eventually kills its victims, because carriers who inherit a single defective gene are resistant to malaria. Those with the sickle-cell gene have a survival advantage in regions of the world in which malaria is prevalent, which are the regions of the ancestral populations listed previously. Although many of these peoples have since migrated from these areas, this ancestral gene still persists within their populations.

Scientists are also working to identify gene variations that cause genetic diseases. Molecular evolutionary biologists have developed methods to distinguish between variations in gene sequences that affect reproductive fitness and variations that do not. To do this, scientists analyze human DNA sequences and DNA sequences among closely related species. The Human Genome Project, a worldwide effort to map the positions of all the genes and to sequence the over 3 billion DNA base pairs of the human genome, is providing much of the data for this effort and also is allowing scientists to study the relationships between the structure of genes and the proteins they produce. (On June 26, 2000, scientists announced the completion of the "working draft," of the human genome. The working draft covers 85% of the genome's coding regions in rough form.)

Some diseases are caused by interaction between genes and environment (lifestyle) factors. Genetic factors may predispose a person to a disease. For example, America's number one killers, cardiovascular disease and cancer, have both genetic and environmental causes. However, the complex interplay between genes and environmental factors in the development of these diseases makes it difficult for scientists to study the genetics of these diseases. Nevertheless, using evolutionary principles and approaches, scientists have developed a technique called *gene tree analysis* to discover genetic markers that are predictive of certain diseases. (Genetic markers are pairs of alleles whose inheritance can be traced through a pedigree [family tree].) Analyses of gene trees can help medical researchers identify the mutations in genes that cause certain diseases. This knowledge helps medical researchers understand the cause of the diseases to which these genes are linked and can help them develop treatments for such illnesses.

How is evolution indispensable to the subdisciplines of biology? and How does it enrich them?

Organizing life, for example, a process on which Linnaeus worked as he grouped organisms by morphological characteristics, continues today with processes that reflect evolutionary relationships. Systematics, the branch of biology that studies the classification of life, does so in the context of evolutionary relationships. Cladistics, the predominant method used in systematics today, classifies organisms with respect to their phylogenetic relationships—those based on their evolutionary history. Therefore, students who do not understand evolution cannot understand modern methods of classification.

Developmental biology is another example of a biological subdiscipline enriched by an evolutionary perspective. In fact, some embryological phenomena can be understood only in the light of evolutionary history. For example, why terrestrial salamanders go through a larval stage with gills and fins that are never used is a question answered by evolution. During evolution, as new species (e.g., terrestrial salamanders) evolve from ancestral forms (e.g., aquatic ancestors), their new developmental instructions are often added to developmental instructions already in place. Thus, patterns of development in groups of organisms were built over the evolutionary history of those groups, thus retaining ancestral instructions. This process results in the embryonic stages of particular vertebrates reflecting the embryonic stages of those vertebrates' ancestors.

The study of animal behavior is enriched by an evolutionary perspective as well. Behavioral traits also evolve, and like morphological traits they are often most similar among closely related species. Phylogenetic studies of behavior have provided examples of how complex behaviors such as the courtship displays of some birds have evolved from simpler ancestral behaviors. Likewise, the study of human behavior can be enhanced by an evolutionary perspective. Evolutionary psychologists seek to uncover evolutionary reasons for many human behaviors, searching through our ancestral programming to determine how natural selection has resulted in a species that behaves as it does.

There are many sciences with significant historical aspects, such as anthropology, astronomy, geology, and paleontology. Geology, for example, is the study of the history of the earth, especially as recorded in the rocks. Paleontology is the study of fossils. Inherent in the work of the geologist and the paleontologist are questions about the relationships of modern animals and plants to ancestral forms, and about the chronology of the history of the earth. Evolution provides the framework within which these questions can be answered.

What do science and education societies say about the study of evolution?

Instructors often look to scientific societies for answers to many questions regarding their teaching. There is one aspect of teaching on which the scientific societies agree and are emphatic. Evolution is key to scientific study, and should be taught in the science classroom. The National Research Council, part of the National Academy of Science, identified evolution as a major unifying idea in science that transcends disciplinary boundaries. Its publication *National Science Education Standards* lists biological evolution as one of the six content areas in the life sciences that are important for all high school students to study. Likewise, the American Association for the Advancement of Science identified the evolution of life as one of six major areas of study in the life sciences in its publication *Benchmarks for Scientific Literacy* . The National Science Teachers Association, the largest organization in the world committed to promoting excellence and innovation "in science teaching and learning," published a position statement on the teaching of evolution in 1997, which states that "evolution is a major unifying concept of science and should be included as part of K—College science frameworks and curricula." The National Association of Biology Teachers, a leading organization in life science education, also issued a position statement on the teaching of evolution in 1997, which states that evolution has a "central, unifying role . . . in nature, and therefore in biology. Teaching biology in an effective and scientifically honest manner requires classroom discussions and laboratory experiences on evolution." Evolution has been identified as the unifying theme of biology by almost all science organizations that focus on the biological sciences.

So why should students learn evolution? Eliminating evolution from the education of students removes the context and unifying theory that underpins and permeates the biological sciences. Students thus learn disparate facts in the science classroom without the thread that ties them together, and they miss the answers to its underlying *why* questions. Without an understanding of evolution, they cannot understand processes based on this science, such as insect resistance to pesticides and microbial resistance to antibiotics. Students will not come to understand evolutionary connections to other scientific fields, nor will they fully understand the world of which we are a part. Evolution is, in fact, one of the most important concepts in attaining scientific literacy.

Critical Thinking

1. Why does evolution provide the basic context of all the biological sciences?

2. Be aware of each of the following reasons students should learn evolution: answering the *why* questions; dealing with problems of everyday life; providing a conceptual foundation for the biological sciences; applications in medicine.

3. Why is evolution the context of the biological sciences—a unifying theory?

4. How do evolutionary explanations answer key questions in the biological sciences?

5. How does understanding evolution help us understand processes that affect our health and our day-to-day life? How are evolutionary methods applied to other fields?

6. How is evolution indispensable to the subdisciplines of biology and how does it enrich them?

7. What do science and education societies say about the study of evolution?

UNIT 2
Primates

Unit Selections

Learning Outcomes

After reading this Unit, you will be able to:

- Explain why infanticide is so widespread among primates.

- Explain why we humans are so different from chimpanzees even though we share 98% of our DNA with them.

- Explain how it is possible to objectively study and assess the emotional and mental states of nonhuman primates.

- Discuss the implications of tool use, social hunting, and food sharing by the Ivory Coast chimpanzees for human evolution.

- Determine if chimpanzees' behavioral patterns should be classified as "cultural."

- Decide whether or not primates are naturally aggressive.

- Discuss whether or not human beings are naturally cooperative or competitive.

- Describe the conditions in which primate species make peace in spite of violent traits that seem built into their natures.

Student Website
www.mhhe.com/cls

Internet References

African Primates at Home
www.indiana.edu/~primate/primates.html

The Dian Fossey Gorilla Fund International
www.gorillafund.org

Electronic Zoo/NetVet-Primate Page
http://netvet.wustl.edu/primates.htm

Great Ape Survival Project: United Nations
www.unep.org/grasp/ABOUT_GRASP/index.asp

Jane Goodall Institute for Wildlife Research, Education, and Conservation
www.janegoodall.org

Laboratory Primate Newsletter
www.brown.edu/Research/Primate/other.html

Living Links
www.emory.edu/LIVING_LINKS/dewaal.html

National Primate Research Center
http://pin.primate.wisc.edu/factsheets

Orangutan Foundation International
www.orangutan.org

Wellcome Trust Sanger Institute
www.sanger.ac.uk/research/projects/humanevolution

Primates are fun. They are active, intelligent, colorful, emotionally expressive, and unpredictable. Because, in some ways, they are very much like us (see "The 2% Difference"), observing them is like holding up an opaque mirror to ourselves. The image may not be crystal-clear or, indeed, what some would consider flattering, but it is certainly familiar enough to be illuminating.

Primates are, of course, one of the many orders of mammals that adaptively radiated into the variety of ecological niches, which were vacated at the end of the Age of Reptiles about 65 million years ago. Whereas some mammals took to the sea (cetaceans), and some took to the air (chiroptera, or bats), primates took to the land and are characterized by an arboreal or forested adaptation. While some mammals can be identified by their food-getting habits, such as the meat-eating carnivores, primates have a penchant for eating almost anything and are best described as omnivorous. In taking to the trees, primates did not simply develop a full-blown set of distinguishing characteristics that set them off easily from other orders of mammals, the way the rodent order can be readily identified by its gnawing set of front teeth. Rather, each primate seems to represent degrees of anatomical, biological, and behavioral characteristics on a continuum of change, in the direction of the particular traits in which we humans happen to be interested.

None of this is meant to imply, of course, that the living primates are our ancestors. Because the prosimians, monkeys, and apes are contemporaries, they are no more our ancestors than we are theirs, and, as living end-products of evolution, we have all descended from a common stock in the distant past. So, if we are interested primarily in our own evolutionary past, why study primates at all? Because, by the criteria we have set up as significant milestones in the evolution of humanity, an inherent reflection of our own bias, primates have not evolved as far as we have. They and their environments, therefore, may give a glimmer of the evolutionary stages and ecological circumstances through which our own ancestors may have gone. What we stand to gain, for instance, is an educated guess as to how our own ancestors might have appeared and behaved as semi-erect creatures before becoming bipedal. Aside from being a pleasure to observe, then, living primates can teach us something about our past.

This unit demonstrates that the kind of answers obtained depend upon the kind of questions asked, and that we have to be very careful in making inferences about the motivations of any given species of primate, including humans, based on limited study (see "First, Kill the Babies" by Carl Zimmer). This goes for theory as well. Ever since Darwin published *On the Origin of Species* in 1859, for instance, some prominent economists have embraced it as supportive of laissez-faire capitalism. This interpretation, however, says more about the theorists and their socioeconomic agenda than it does about the actual facts of human nature or even the social context in which human beings evolved (see "Peace Among Primates" by Robert Sapolsky).

Still another benefit of primate field research is that it provides us with perspectives that the bones and stones of the fossil hunters will never reveal: a sense of the richness and variety of social patterns that must have existed in the primate order for

© Digital Vision

many tens of millions of years (see "The Mind of the Chimpanzee" by Jane Goodall).

Even if we had the physical remains of the earliest hominids in front of us, which we do not, there is no way such evidence could thoroughly answer the questions that physical anthropologists care most deeply about: How did these creatures move about and get their food? Did they cooperate and share? At what levels did they think and communicate? Did they have a sense of family, let alone a sense of self? In one way or another, all of the previously mentioned articles on primates relate to these issues, as do some of the subsequent ones on fossil evidence. But what sets off this unit from others is how some of the authors attempt to deal with these matters head-on, even in the absence of direct fossil evidence. Christophe Boesch and Hedwige Boesch-Achermann, in "Dim Forest, Bright Chimps," indicate that some aspects of "hominization" (the acquisition of humanlike qualities such as cooperative hunting and food sharing) may have actually begun in the African rainforest rather than in the dry savanna, as has been proposed usually. They base their suggestions on some remarkable first-hand observations of forest-dwelling chimpanzees. As Craig Stanford shows in "Got Culture?" chimpanzee behavior may vary according to local circumstances, just as we know human behavior does. He makes a strong case for such differences to be classified as cultural.

Taken collectively, the articles in this section show how far anthropologists are willing to go to construct theoretical formulations based upon limited data. Although making so much out of so little may be seen as a fault and may generate irreconcilable differences among theorists, a readiness to entertain new ideas should be welcomed for what it is—a stimulus for more intensive and meticulous research.

First, Kill the Babies

CARL ZIMMER

Twenty-five years ago this summer a Harvard graduate student named Sarah Hrdy went to northwestern India and met the monkeys that would make her famous. The immediate impetus for the trip was a series of lectures by Stanford ecologist Paul Ehrlich on the dangers of overpopulation. Though Ehrlich was speaking about humans, what Hrdy thought of were the Indian monkeys known as Hanuman langurs. The langurs are considered sacred by many Indians and so are regularly fed by the people with whom they come into contact. Consequently, near towns, Hanuman langurs live in extremely dense populations, and apparently this unnatural density had led to unnatural, pathologically violent behavior. There had been several reports of adult males killing infants. "So there I was, listening to Ehrlich," says Hrdy, "with this adolescent desire to go do something relevant with my life, and I thought, 'I am going to go study the effects of crowding on behavior.'"

Hrdy traveled to dry, deforested Mount Abu and began to get acquainted with the sandy-bodied, dark-faced Hanumans. Before long she decided the assumption that had propelled her to India had been wrong. "It happened pretty fast. I was watching these very crowded animals, and here were these infants playing around, bouncing on these males like trampolines, pulling on their tails, and so forth. These guys were aloof but totally tolerant. They might show some annoyance occasionally, but there was nothing approaching pathological hostility toward offspring. The trouble seemed to be when males came into the troop from outside it."

The langurs of Abu are arranged into two kinds of groups. In the first, a single male—or, rarely, two—lives with a group of females and their infants. The infant females, when they grow up, stay put; the males leave to join the other kind of group, a small all-male band.

Eventually a grown male lucky enough to be in a troop of females will come under attack, either from the all-male bands or from the male of another mixed troop. Odds are that sooner or later the resident male will be chased out by a new one. Hrdy witnessed many such takeovers, and she noticed that afterward the new male would often chase after the babies in the troop, presumably all of which were offspring of the old male's. Before long some of these infants would disappear. She didn't actually see what happened to the infants, but townspeople around Abu told her that they had seen a male killing baby langurs. Soon after these takeovers, the new resident male would mate with the females.

"I realized I needed a new explanatory model," says Hrdy. Her new model would become one of modern biology's most famous—and in some circles, notorious—hypotheses about animal behavior. There was nothing pathological about langur infanticide, she suggested. On the contrary, it actually made a chilling kind of sense: While a langur mother nurses, she cannot conceive; when she stops nursing, she can. Thus if a male langur kills her infant—one that is not related to him—she can bear the infanticidal male's own offspring. In Hanuman langur society, in which a male's sojourn with a harem averages a little over two years, the time saved can be critical. After all, for any offspring to survive, they should ideally be weaned before a new, potentially infanticidal male shows up. Seen in this light, infanticide could actually be an "adaptive" evolutionary strategy for fathering as many offspring as possible.

In the quarter century since Hrdy first conceived this idea, naturalists have reported cases of infanticide among a wide range of animals. Some now argue that the threat of infanticide is such a pervasive and powerful influence that it can shape animal societies. A few theorists even claim that infanticide was an important factor in human evolution.

Yet when Hrdy first published her hypothesis, she was immediately attacked, most of all by other researchers studying langurs. They contended that Hanuman langurs living in natural conditions, in remote forests, had never been observed killing infants. At Abu, they said, human feeding had crowded the langurs into conditions evolution had never prepared them for, and as a result the transfer of males into new groups became drenched with aggression. In other words, the langurs of Abu were simply not normal.

Underlying this species-specific dustup, though, was a deeper conflict. Before the 1970s most researchers viewed animal societies as smooth-running systems in which each member knew its proper role and played it for the good of the many. Animal societies—and primate societies in particular—were often portrayed as utopias that we humans would do well to emulate. But then biologists such as E. O. Wilson and Robert Trivers (both mentors of Hrdy's at Harvard) argued that such a view didn't make sense in a world shaped by evolution. Just as a bird's wing is the product of natural selection, so are the ways the individual bird interacts with other birds. Its social behavior, like its body, is ultimately designed for one purpose: to get its own genes duplicated as much as possible. Rather than being a peaceful group of community-minded role players, an animal society was made up of individuals trying to maximize their reproductive gain, with cooperation always a compromise between competing genetic interests. As a biological explanation for society, this school of thought came to be known as sociobiology.

When Hrdy hypothesized about langur infanticide, then, she wasn't just explaining the odd behavior of a few monkeys. She was pushing sociobiology to its logical extreme, in which a male's drive to reproduce was so strong that it would resort to the decidedly antisocial act of killing the young of its own species.

Over time, Hrdy added some nuances to her stark hypothesis. For example, she noted that female langurs did not passively sit by as invading males tried to rob them of their genetic legacy. Rather, females banded together to help fend off males bent on infanticide. Once an infanticidal male was in charge, however, they might choose a different tack. Female langurs can continue to have sex even after they conceive, and by mating with an invading male, they might trick him into thinking the infant was his own.

Hrdy also began noting reports of infanticide among other animals. Her "outsider male" infanticide, she realized, was clearly not the only kind of adaptive strategy practiced in the animal world. A mother might resort to infanticide if she didn't have the resources to raise all her children. Adults might also kill the infants of strangers simply for food or to eliminate the competition for limited resources.

In the decade and a half since Hrdy's work first appeared, infanticide has been reported among mice and ground squirrels, bears and deer, prairie dogs and foxes, fish and dwarf mongooses and wasps and bumblebees and dung beetles. Although the evidence from the wild has often been sketchy, most of the strategies appear to fall into one of those that Hrdy sketched out. In a few cases researchers have been able to test the hypothesis by performing natural experiments. In 1987, for example, Cornell ornithologist Stephen Emlen was studying the jacana, a Panamanian bird in which the common sex roles are switched: males sit on the eggs and raise the young alone while the females rove around their territories, mating with many males and fighting off intruding females. Essentially, if you turn Hanuman langurs into birds and switch the sex roles, you get jacanas—and theoretically, under the right conditions, you should also see infanticide. Emlen needed to shoot some birds for DNA testing, and he chose two females with male partners caring for nests of babies.

"I shot a female one night, and the next morning was just awesome. By first light a new female was already on the turf. I saw terrible things—pecking and picking up and throwing down chicks until they were dead. Within hours she was soliciting the male, and he was mounting her the same day. The next night I shot the other female, then came out the next morning and saw the whole thing again."

Among mammals, one of the best documented killers of infants has proved to be the lion. Though actual killings have only rarely been witnessed (the total is about a dozen), massive indirect evidence for the phenomenon has been gathered by the husband-and-wife team of Craig Packer and Anne Pusey, both behavioral ecologists at the University of Minnesota. From their observations of lions in the Serengeti, they've found that whenever a new male comes into the pride, the death rate of nursing cubs—and nursing cubs only—shoots up. Within six months none of the cubs are left alive.

Other primates have also joined the ranks of the infanticidal. The first reports were of only a few species such as the red howlers of Venezuela, the gorillas of Rwanda, and the blue monkeys of Uganda. But in the past few years there have been more reported instances of primate infanticide, some of which demand some expansion of Hrdy's ideas. Lemurs in Madagascar, for example, breed once a year. If a male kills another male's nursing infant, he doesn't hasten his own fatherhood, since he still has to wait until the breeding season to mate. Nonetheless, researchers have seen male lemurs sinking their fangs into babies. One observer, Michael Pereira of Bucknell University, offers an idea as to why it happens. Madagascar has a harsh climate, with a long dry season that keeps female lemurs on a knife-edge of survival. Pregnancy and the first few months of nursing take place in the harshest time of the year, and, says Pereira, successfully raising an infant one year may reduce the chances a mother will be able to raise the next year's baby. "Females who lose their infants are much fatter than females whose infants survive," Pereira explains. "If by your killing the infant she's more likely to be successful during your reign, then it's to your advantage."

In Sumatra, Dutch researchers have been studying a relative of the Hanumans known as the Thomas langur. Thomas langurs were essentially a mystery when the Utrecht University primatologists began to observe them in 1988. Now, after eight years of relentlessly tracking the animals through the forest and painstakingly recording their daily habits, the researchers are finding the langurs to be all too revealing. "Infanticide does occur. I've seen the attacks," explains Romy Steenbeek, who ran the program for four years. "We saw the body of a baby with canine slices in its belly. I saw a male attack a baby, and the baby disappeared. One baby received big wounds in an attack by a neighboring male, and she died after two very bad weeks. The males run a few hundred meters to the troop, silently attack, and when they leave they loud-call."

Like lemurs, these langurs require yet one more variation on Hrdy's grisly theme. Thomas langurs have the same all-male bands and one-male/many-female troops of other langurs, but what distinguishes this species is that the males don't make hostile takeovers of groups of females—at least not directly. Instead outside males make harassing raids on a troop, chasing the infants and sometimes killing them. One by one the females abandon their male, the childless females first, the others as soon as their babies are weaned or die. Steenbeek suspects that the infanticidal male langurs are trying to discredit the harem male, demonstrating how incompetent he is by killing the troop's infants. The females are continually judging the contest, and if they sense that their male is getting weak, they abandon him. "Sometimes at the end of the tenure, a male stops protecting the troop," says Steenbeek. "It's like he's just given up."

If infanticide has long been a natural part of animal behavior, then so too, one would expect, has been the fight against it. Over evolutionary time, both currents would shape new behaviors and social organizations. Lionesses live in prides, according to Packer and Pusey, in large part to protect their young against murderous males. One result is that lionesses must tolerate cubs not their own stealing milk—something rarely seen in other carnivores. Female mice can somehow tell if a male approaching their litter is infanticidal or not; if he is, they leap into battle. And apparently even the babies have evolved a protection against infanticide: they call much more frequently in the presence of an infanticidal male.

Evidence is emerging that primates may face similar pressure. Female red howler monkeys in Venezuela, for example, tend to travel in small groups—generally under five members—and are hostile to new female howlers who want to join them. What determines their group size? In some animals the availability of food is the key: if the group is too big, the competition among individuals grows too intense. Yet evidently food competition isn't a problem for red howlers. What is a problem, it seems, is that the bigger a female group, the more likely it is to suffer an infanticidal attack by a male. The benefits for a male of taking over a big group make those groups good targets, and as a result females keep the groups small.

Carel Van Schaik, a primatologist with Duke University and the Wildlife Conservation Society, thinks infanticide's effects may reach even further into the core of primate life. He first began thinking seriously about Hrdy's ideas in the late 1980s, while studying gibbons with Robin Dunbar, who was then at University College, London. These Asian apes are for the most part monogamous, although it's hard to see why. It's not that gibbon babies need the extra parental care, because the fathers don't give any. And calculations suggested that males might do better, from a genetic viewpoint, if they tried to impregnate as many females as possible rather than just one. Van Schaik and Dunbar concluded that male gibbons were staying close to home to guard their infants from other males, and the females were choosing good protectors as mates. That would explain why on the one hand gibbon couples make calls together—advertising to neighboring males that the infant is well guarded—but why on the other hand a nursing mother who becomes widowed falls silent. It doesn't matter to Van Schaik that gibbon infanticide has never been reported—it's not seen, he thinks, because the animals do such a good job of preventing it.

Van Schaik now suspects that the ever-present threat of infanticide has a similar effect on all primates. Among mammals, primate males and females are far and away the most likely to form a long-term bond. "That raises the issue: Why primates?" says Van Schaik. The answer, he thinks, is that primate babies are particularly vulnerable to infanticide. They take a long time to mature, and compared with other young mammals, they are defenseless and exposed, more often than not clinging to their mother. Female primates also tend to stay in a given territory, thereby giving males an added incentive for disposing of unrelated infants. "If you do commit infanticide, there is a good probability that you will have a future opportunity for mating," says Van Schaik. Thus the incentive and opportunity for infanticide have driven primates more than other mammals into long-term bonds, in order that males can defend their young.

If Van Schaik is right, he will add considerable weight to speculations Hrdy made in the 1980s, that protection against infanticide may have had a profound impact on primates, including early humans. Nursing is a contraceptive among humans, as it is in langurs, and it can lower a woman's fertility for up to two or three years. That could make the incentive for infanticide on the part of a new mate enormous, as would the incentives to guard against it. Such a scenario would fly in the face of the conventional view that long-term bonds between men and women evolved so that extra parental care can help their babies survive. Instead, Van Schaik suggests that infanticide may have been the prime mover behind these bonds, and only later did the added advantage of help from a father come into play.

Not surprisingly, perhaps, such ideas are not easily accepted. Most anthropologists and psychologists still view humans much as biologists once viewed animals. "Anthropology has a long history of believing that everything is for the good of the social group," says anthropologist Kim Hill of the University of New Mexico, and in that context Hrdy's ideas about infanticide don't make sense; such instances as do occur among humans can only be explained as a result of a particular cultural bias (favoring male babies over females, say) or of individual pathology. But there are a few disturbing data points. Over the past 16 years Martin Daly and Margo Wilson, both psychologists at McMaster University in Hamilton, Ontario, have collected child abuse data from governments and humane associations. One of the most startling statistics they've uncovered is this: a preschool American stepchild is 60 times more likely than a biological child to be the victim of infanticide.

Hill himself, with his studies of the Ache people of Paraguay, has gathered some of the best infanticide data available on non-Western cultures. The Ache still go on long hunting-and-foraging expeditions, as their ancestors did for 10,000 years. When a man kills an animal, he gives it to another man, who then distributes the meat to the entire band. Congenial as this may seem, natural selection creates inevitable tension: by giving most of his food away, a man allows his efforts to be diverted from his own family. This cost is outweighed by the benefits of cooperation, but when a child's father dies, the tension reveals itself. If a child loses a father, his chances of becoming the victim of infanticide at the hands of another man increase fourfold. It's not uncommon for orphaned children to be thrown into their father's grave.

But Hill does not think that the pattern is purely a cultural tradition. "If you ask them why they're killing all these babies, their first answer is 'That's our custom,'" says Hill. "And then if you push them on that, they say, 'They don't have parents, and we have to take care of them, and that makes us mad.'"

The resistance to infanticide as a reproductive strategy is still shared by many researchers. In some cases they've tested some of the predictions and found them wanting. Agustin Fuentes of the University of California at Berkeley, for example, studies the Mentawai langur, which lives on the islands of the same name, off the west coast of Sumatra. Like the gibbon, the Mentawai langur is monogamous, but it doesn't behave as Van Schaik said it should. For example, when a bonded couple are close to a solitary (and supposedly infanticidal) male, they do not become hostile or even make calls to show they are together.

Deborah Overdorff of the University of Texas at Austin studies rufous lemurs, and among these primates, at least, doubts the reality of infanticide. While rufous lemurs travel in large groups, male and female pairs will often be seen staying close together. That might seem to fit the notion of males protecting their young. Not to Overdorff. "I've found that the male is not necessarily the one the females mated with. Sometimes they turn out to be brothers. Infanticide is probably not a good explanation for pair-bonding."

Others criticize the quality of the data. They complain that most reports are inferred from indirect evidence, such as the disappearance of a baby. And except for Hanuman langurs, the few witnessed infanticides have not been followed up to see how much reproductive success the killing males have had. Given the difficulty of observing monkeys in the wild, the scrappiness of the data shouldn't be surprising, and some primatologists—including some who think that infanticide is real—worry that the theory is getting too far ahead of the data.

The biggest opposition results from the application of Hrdy's ideas to humans. Popular accounts of the theory, Hrdy complains, are "very quick to jump from the langur case to cases of strange-male-in-the-household infanticide, but the underpinnings, the groundwork for that extrapolation, aren't there." After all, a step-father can't speed up his own reproduction through infanticide. Hrdy and Daly agree that this kind of abuse has more to do with resource competition—the resource being the mother. Moreover, they don't envision a stepfather consciously trying to eliminate that competition—rather, he may simply have a lower threshold of irritation toward the child. Such a threshold is suggested by a recent study by Daly and Wilson, in which they compared the ways in which biological fathers and stepfathers killed their children. In most cases, biological fathers shoot or suffocate their offspring (and then often kill themselves), while stepfathers kill by striking—hinting that a "lashing out" reflex is at work.

Another point of criticism is the matter of how infanticide can be carried down through the generations, and again confusion abounds. One magazine article Hrdy mentions, for example, contains a reference to an "infanticide gene." She scoffs, "I don't talk about genes." While it's true that Hrdy doesn't dabble in oversimplified genetic determinism, some of sociobiology's early pioneers did—and sometimes with great abandon. These days, however, a much suppler view exists. In any species, each individual keeps a Darwinian account book, and whenever it has to "choose" an action, it weighs the immediate and long-term costs and benefits. "Selection hasn't molded an animal that's altruistic or infanticidal," says Emlen. "It has molded an animal capable of showing a whole range of subtly different behaviors under different circumstances, but they're all predictable."

"Under one set of circumstances, a female might behave by abandoning a baby, but under another set of circumstances she would care for a baby," says Hrdy. "These are both maternal behaviors. In the first case, presumably selection has operated on her to postpone raising her young because there is the option that she might have a better chance of pulling a baby through at a future date. So it's not nonreproductive, it's not nonadaptive; it's simply a question of an animal over the course of a lifetime gauging herself." Infanticide is thus at one extreme in a spectrum of parental care. Hrdy herself has recently been exploring the ways in which European parents have historically lowered their investment in children, such as hiring a wet nurse or leaving a child at a monastery.

For animals, and to some degree ourselves, this "gauging" happens unconsciously. And while it might seem hard to believe that animals can make careful decisions, many experiments have revealed that they can. Few of these accounting experiments have been done on infanticide, though, and there isn't anywhere near enough data to test in primates, let alone humans. While almost 20 percent of Ache children fall victim to infanticide before age ten, the rate is zero among many other foraging cultures. Until researchers can explain the variation, all speculation on the role of infanticide in early human evolution must be put on hold. Our long, complex social lives and our dizzying array of cultures hide the effects of evolution as the high, obscuring leaves of the Sumatran forest hide the secrets of Thomas langurs.

Yet those who believe that infanticide is a Darwinian reality think that we need to keep looking through the foliage. "Sure, you can deny all these results—at your own peril," says Van Schaik. "What is it that makes males infanticidal, and what is it that stops males from being infanticidal? If you know these things better, you know what to do, take certain measures, counsel people. It arms us."

A look back at the infanticide hypothesis on its silver anniversary makes clear how long it takes to test and flesh out the shocking ideas of sociobiology. Hrdy herself sees this as the necessary pace of any science. She often describes her job as creating "imaginary worlds" that other scientists can then explore to see if they can help us understand the real one. "I see scientists working in different phases. Some people are better at one phase than another. Theoreticians think of other people as technicians; technicians think of theoreticians as people in outer space, not connected to the real world. But for the whole process, you need these phases, and in the initial phase, you're selecting a project, you're coming up with assumptions, you're trying to model what might be true and to generate the hypotheses that you want to look at. Then you have the actual collection of data and all the methodologies that go into that. Imaginary worlds have a place in science."

Critical Thinking

1. Describe langur social life and behavior that seems to lead to infanticide?

2. Why should langur infanticide not be seen as pathological?

3. Describe the school of sociobiology and how its principles might apply to langur society.

4. Describe a female langur's reaction to the prospect of her own infant being killed.

5. Discuss the other circumstances in which a mother or another adult might kill an infant.

6. Discuss the findings regarding infanticide in other species.

7. Discuss Carl Van Schaik's view as to why gibbons are monogamous.

8. Explain why primate infants are particularly vulnerable to attack and why the nursing of infants provides for further incentives in this regard.

9. Discuss the relevance of human data regarding child abuse and murder.

10. Be familiar with the criticisms regarding sociobiology and infanticide.

From *Discover*, September 1996, pp. 73–76, 78. Copyright © 1996 by Carl Zimmer. Reprinted by permission by the author.

The 2% Difference

Now that scientists have decoded the chimpanzee genome, we know that 98 percent of our DNA is the same. So how can we be so different?

ROBERT SAPOLSKY

If you find yourself sitting close to a chimpanzee, staring face to face and making sustained eye contact, something interesting happens, something that is alternately moving, bewildering, and kind of creepy. When you gaze at this beast, you suddenly realize that the face gazing back is that of a sentient individual, who is recognizably kin. You can't help but wonder, What's the matter with those intelligent design people?

Chimpanzees are close relatives to humans, but they're not identical to us. We are not chimps. Chimps excel at climbing trees, but we beat them hands down at balance-beam routines; they are covered in hair, while we have only the occasional guy with really hairy shoulders. The core differences, however, arise from how we use our brains. Chimps have complex social lives, play power politics, betray and murder each other, make tools, and teach tool use across generations in a way that qualifies as culture. They can even learn to do logic operations with symbols, and they have a relative sense of numbers. Yet those behaviors don't remotely approach the complexity and nuance of human behaviors, and in my opinion there's not the tiniest bit of scientific evidence that chimps have aesthetics, spirituality, or a capacity for irony or poignancy.

What makes the human species brainy are huge numbers of standard-issue neurons.

What accounts for those differences? A few years ago, the most ambitious project in the history of biology was carried out: the sequencing of the human genome. Then just four months ago, a team of researchers reported that they had likewise sequenced the complete chimpanzee genome. Scientists have long known that chimps and humans share about 98 percent of their DNA. At last, however, one can sit down with two scrolls of computer printout, march through the two genomes, and see exactly where our 2 percent difference lies.

Given the outward differences, it seems reasonable to expect to find fundamental differences in the portions of the genome that determine chimp and human brains—reasonable, at least, to a brainocentric neurobiologist like me. But as it turns out, the chimp brain and the human brain differ hardly at all in their genetic underpinnings. Indeed, a close look at the chimp genome reveals an important lesson in how genes and evolution work, and it suggests that chimps and humans are a lot more similar than even a neurobiologist might think.

DNA, or deoxyribonucleic acid, is made up of just four molecules, called nucleotides: adenine (A), cytosine (C), guanine (G), and thymine (T). The DNA codebook for every species consists of billions of these letters in a precise order. If, when DNA is being copied in a sperm or an egg, a nucleotide is mistakenly copied wrong, the result is a mutation. If the mutation persists from generation to generation, it becomes a DNA difference—one of the many genetic distinctions that separate one species (chimpanzees) from another (humans). In genomes involving billions of nucleotides, a tiny 2 percent difference translates into tens of millions of ACGT differences. And that 2 percent difference can be very broadly distributed. Humans and chimps each have somewhere between 20,000 and 30,000 genes, so there are likely to be nucleotide differences in every single gene.

To understand what distinguishes the DNA of chimps and humans, one must first ask: What is a gene? A gene is a string of nucleotides that specify how a single distinctive protein should be made. Even if the same gene in chimps and humans differs by an A here and a T there, the result may be of no consequence. Many nucleotide differences are neutral—both the mutation and the normal gene cause the same protein to be made. However, given the right nucleotide difference between the same gene in the two species, the resulting proteins may differ slightly in construction and function.

One might assume that the differences between chimp and human genes boil down to those sorts of typographical errors: one nucleotide being swapped for a different one and altering the gene it sits in. But a close look at the two codebooks reveals very few such instances. And the typos that do occasionally occur follow a compelling pattern. It's important to note that genes don't act alone. Yes, each gene regulates the construction of a specific protein. But what tells that gene *when* and *where* to build that protein? Regulation is everything: It's important not to start up genes related to puberty during, say, infancy, or to activate genes that are related to eye color in the bladder.

In the DNA code list, that critical information is contained in a short stretch of As and Cs and Gs and Ts that lie just before each gene and act as a switch that turns the gene on or off. The switch, in turn, is flicked on by proteins called transcription factors, which activate certain genes in response to certain stimuli. Naturally, every gene is not regulated by its own distinct transcription factor; otherwise, a codebook of as many as 30,000 genes would require 30,000 transcription factors—and 30,000 more genes to code for them. Instead, one transcription factor can flick on an array of functionally related genes. For example, a certain type of injury can activate one transcription factor that turns on a bunch of genes in your white blood cells, triggering inflammation.

Accurate switch flickers are essential. Imagine the consequences if some of those piddly nucleotide changes arose in a protein that happened to be a transcription factor: Suddenly, instead of activating 23 different genes, the protein might charge up 21 or 25 of them—or it might turn on the usual 23 but in different ratios than normal. Suddenly, one minor nucleotide difference would be amplified across a network of gene differences. (And imagine the ramifications if the altered proteins are transcription factors that activate the genes coding for still other transcription factors!) When the chimp and human genomes are compared, some of the clearest cases of nucleotide differences are found in genes coding for transcription factors. Those cases are few, but they have far-ranging implications.

The genomes of chimps and humans reveal a history of other kinds of differences as well. Instead of a simple mutation, in which a single nucleotide is copied incorrectly, consider an insertion mutation, where an extra A, C, G, or T is dropped in, or a deletion mutation, whereby a nucleotide drops out. Insertion or deletion mutations can have major consequences: Imagine the deletion mutation that turns the sentence "I'll have the mousse for dessert" into "I'll have the mouse for dessert," or the insertion mutation implicit in "She turned me down for a date after I asked her to go bowling with me." Sometimes, more than a single nucleotide is involved; whole stretches of a gene may be dropped or added. In extreme cases, entire genes may be deleted or added.

More important than how the genetic changes arise—by insertion, deletion, or straight mutation—is where in the genome they occur. Keep in mind that, for these genetic changes to persist from generation to generation, they must convey some evolutionary advantage. When one examines the 2 percent difference between humans and chimps, the genes in question turn out to be evolutionarily important, if banal. For example, chimps have a great many more genes related to olfaction than we do; they've got a better sense of smell because we've lost many of those genes. The 2 percent distinction also involves an unusually large fraction of genes related to the immune system, parasite vulnerability, and infectious diseases: Chimps are resistant to malaria, and we aren't; we handle tuberculosis better than they do. Another important fraction of that 2 percent involves genes related to reproduction—the sorts of anatomical differences that split a species in two and keep them from interbreeding.

That all makes sense. Still, chimps and humans have very different brains. So which are the brain-specific genes that have evolved in very different directions in the two species? It turns out that there are hardly any that fit that bill. This, too, makes a great deal of sense. Examine a neuron from a human brain under a microscope, then do the same with a neuron from the brain of a chimp, a rat, a frog, or a sea slug. The neurons all look the same: fibrous dendrites at one end, an axonal cable at the other. They all run on the same basic mechanism: channels and pumps that move sodium, potassium, and calcium around, triggering a wave of excitation called an action potential. They all have a similar complement of neurotransmitters: serotonin, dopamine, glutamate, and so on. They're all the same basic building blocks.

The main difference is in the sheer number of neurons. The human brain has 100 million times the number of neurons a sea slug's brain has. Where do those differences in quantity come from? At some point in their development, all embryos—whether human, chimp, rat, frog, or slug—must have a single first cell committed toward generating neurons. That cell divides and gives rise to 2 cells; those divide into 4, then 8, then 16. After a dozen rounds of cell division, you've got roughly enough neurons to run a slug. Go another 25 rounds or so and you've got a human brain. Stop a couple of rounds short of that and, at about one-third the size of a human brain, you've got one for a chimp. Vastly different outcomes, but relatively few genes regulate the number of rounds of cell division in the nervous system before calling a halt. And it's precisely some of those genes, the ones involved in neural development, that appear on the list of differences between the chimp and human genomes.

That's it; that's the 2 percent solution. What's shocking is the simplicity of it. Humans, to be human, don't need to have evolved unique genes that code for entirely novel types of neurons or neurotransmitters, or a more complex hippocampus (with resulting improvements in memory), or a more complex frontal cortex (from which we gain the ability to postpone gratification). Instead, our braininess as a species arises from having humongous numbers of just a few types of off-the-rack neurons and from the exponentially greater number of interactions between them. The difference is sheer quantity: Qualitative distinctions emerge from large numbers. Genes may have something to do with that quantity, and thus with the complexity of the quality that emerges. Yet no gene or genome can ever tell us what sorts of qualities those will be. Remember that when you and the chimp are eyeball to eyeball, trying to make sense of why the other seems vaguely familiar.

Critical Thinking

1. What are the similarities and differences between chimps and humans?

2. How much of our DNA differs from chimps? How do these differences come about?

3. What is the structure of DNA? How much of this material is different between chimps and humans, given the 2% overall difference between us?

4. What does Sapolsky mean when he says "genes don't act alone"?

5. What is a transcription factor? Is every gene regulated by its own transcription factor?

6. Where are "some of the clearest cases of nucleotide differences" between chimps and humans found?

7. What is the difference between a "simple mutation," an "insertion mutation," and a "deletion mutation"?

8. What type of genes do chimps have more of than we do? What other types of genes are disproportionately impacted by the 2% difference? What are four areas of difference?

9. How are chimp brains and human brains similar and how are they different?

10. What is shocking about the "2% solution"?

The Mind of the Chimpanzee

JANE GOODALL

Often I have gazed into a chimpanzee's eyes and wondered what was going on behind them. I used to look into Flo's, she so old, so wise. What did she remember of her young days? David Greybeard had the most beautiful eyes of them all, large and lustrous, set wide apart. They somehow expressed his whole personality, his serene self-assurance, his inherent dignity—and, from time to time, his utter determination to get his way. For a long time I never liked to look a chimpanzee straight in the eye—I assumed that, as is the case with most primates, this would be interpreted as a threat or at least as a breach of good manners. No so. As long as one looks with gentleness, without arrogance, a chimpanzee will understand, and may even return the look. And then—or such is my fantasy—it is as though the eyes are windows into the mind. Only the glass is opaque so that the mystery can never be fully revealed.

I shall never forget my meeting with Lucy, an eight-year-old home-raised chimpanzee. She came and sat beside me on the sofa and, with her face very close to mine, searched in my eyes—for what? Perhaps she was looking for signs of mistrust, dislike, or fear, since many people must have been somewhat disconcerted when, for the first time, they came face to face with a grown chimpanzee. Whatever Lucy read in my eyes clearly satisfied her for she suddenly put one arm round my neck and gave me a generous and very chimp-like kiss, her mouth wide open and laid over mine. I was accepted.

For a long time after that encounter I was profoundly disturbed. I had been at Gombe for about fifteen years then and I was quite familiar with chimpanzees in the wild. But Lucy, having grown up as a human child, was like a changeling, her essential chimpanzeeness overlaid by the various human behaviours she had acquired over the years. No longer purely chimp yet eons away from humanity, she was man-made, some other kind of being. I watched, amazed, as she opened the refrigerator and various cupboards, found bottles and a glass, then poured herself a gin and tonic. She took the drink to the TV, turned the set on, flipped from one channel to another then, as though in disgust, turned it off again. She selected a glossy magazine from the table and, still carrying her drink, settled in a comfortable chair. Occasionally, as she leafed through the magazine she identified something she saw, using the signs of ASL, the American Sign Language used by the deaf. I, of course, did not understand, but my hostess, Jane Temerlin (who was also Lucy's 'mother'),

translated: 'That dog,' Lucy commented, pausing at a photo of a small white poodle. She turned the page. 'Blue,' she declared, pointing then signing as she gazed at a picture of a lady advertising some kind of soap powder and wearing a brilliant blue dress. And finally, after some vague hand movements—perhaps signed mutterings—'This Lucy's, this mine,' as she closed the magazine and laid it on her lap. She had just been taught, Jane told me, the use of the possessive pronouns during the thrice weekly ASL lessons she was receiving at the time.

The book written by Lucy's human 'father,' Maury Temerlin, was entitled *Lucy, Growing Up Human.* And in fact, the chimpanzee is more like us than is any other living creature. There is close resemblance in the physiology of our two species and genetically, in the structure of the DNA, chimpanzees and humans differ by only just over one percent. This is why medical research uses chimpanzees as experimental animals when they need substitutes for humans in the testing of some drug or vaccine. Chimpanzees can be infected with just about all known human infectious diseases including those, such as hepatitis B and AIDS, to which other non-human animals (except gorillas, orangutans and gibbons) are immune. There are equally striking similarities between humans and chimpanzees in the anatomy and wiring of the brain and nervous system, and—although many scientists have been reluctant to admit to this—in social behaviour, intellectual ability, and the emotions. The notion of an evolutionary continuity in physical structure from pre-human ape to modern man has long been morally acceptable to most scientists. That the same might hold good for mind was generally considered an absurd hypothesis—particularly by those who used, and often misused, animals in their laboratories. It is, after all, convenient to believe that the creature you are using, while it may react in disturbingly human-like ways, is, in fact, merely a mindless and, above all, unfeeling, 'dumb' animal.

When I began my study at Gombe in 1960 it was not permissible—at least not in ethological circles—to talk about an animal's mind. Only humans had minds. Nor was it quite proper to talk about animal personality. Of course everyone knew that they *did* have their own unique characters—everyone who had ever owned a dog or other pet was aware of that. But ethologists, striving to make theirs a 'hard' science, shied away from the task of trying to explain such things objectively. One respected ethologist, while acknowledging that there was 'variability between individual animals,' wrote that it was best that this fact be 'swept under the carpet.' At that time ethological carpets fairly bulged with all that was hidden beneath them.

How naïve I was. As I had not had an undergraduate science education I didn't realize that animals were not supposed to have personalities, or to think, or to feel emotions or pain. I had no idea that it would have been more appropriate to assign each of the chimpanzees a number rather than a name when I got to know him or her. I didn't realize that it was not scientific to discuss behaviour in terms of motivation or purpose. And no one had told me that terms such as *childhood* and *adolescence* were uniquely human phases of the life cycle, culturally determined, not to be used when referring to young chimpanzees. Not knowing, I freely made use of all those forbidden terms and concepts in my initial attempt to describe, to the best of my ability, the amazing things I had observed at Gombe.

I shall never forget the response of a group of ethologists to some remarks I made at an erudite seminar. I described how Figan, as an adolescent, had learned to stay behind in camp after senior males had left, so that we could give him a few bananas for himself. On the first occasion he had, upon seeing the fruits, uttered loud, delighted food calls: whereupon a couple of the older males had charged back, chased after Figan, and taken his bananas. And then, coming to the point of the story, I explained how, on the next occasion, Figan had actually suppressed his calls. We could hear little sounds, in his throat, but so quiet that none of the others could have heard them. Other young chimps, to whom we tried to smuggle fruit without the knowledge of their elders, never learned such self-control. With shrieks of glee they would fall to, only to be robbed of their booty when the big males charged back. I had expected my audience to be as fascinated and impressed as I was. I had hoped for an exchange of views about the chimpanzee's undoubted intelligence. Instead there was a chill silence, after which the chairman hastily changed the subject. Needless to say, after being thus snubbed, I was very reluctant to contribute any comments, at any scientific gatherings, for a very long time. Looking back, I suspect that everyone was interested, but it was, of course, not permissible to present a mere 'anecdote' as evidence for anything.

The editorial comments on the first paper I wrote for publication demanded that every *he* or *she* be replaced with *it,* and every *who* be replaced with *which.* Incensed, I, in my turn, crossed out the *its* and *whichs* and scrawled back the original pronouns. As I had no desire to carve a niche for myself in the world of science, but simply wanted to go on living among and learning about chimpanzees, the possible reaction of the editor of the learned journal did not trouble me. In fact I won that round: the paper when finally published did confer upon the chimpanzees the dignity of their appropriate genders and properly upgraded them from the status of mere 'things' to essential Beingness.

However, despite my somewhat truculent attitude, I did want to learn, and I was sensible of my incredible good fortune in being admitted to Cambridge. I wanted to get my PhD, if only for the sake of Louis Leakey and the other people who had written letters in support of my admission. And how lucky I was to have, as my supervisor, Robert Hinde. Not only because I

thereby benefitted from his brilliant mind and clear thinking, but also because I doubt that I could have found a teacher more suited to my particular needs and personality. Gradually he was able to cloak me with at least some of the trappings of a scientist. Thus although I continued to hold to most of my convictions—that animals had personalities; that they could feel happy or sad or fearful; that they could feel pain; that they could strive towards planned goals and achieve greater success if they were highly motivated—I soon realized that these personal convictions were, indeed, difficult to prove. It was best to be circumspect—at least until I had gained some credentials and credibility. And Robert gave me wonderful advice on how best to tie up some of my more rebellious ideas with scientific ribbon. 'You can't *know* that Fifi was jealous,' he had admonished on one occasion. We argued a little. And then: 'Why don't you just say *If Fifi were a human child we would say she was jealous*?' I did.

It is not easy to study emotions even when the subjects are human. I know how I feel if I am sad or happy or angry, and if a friend tells me that he is feeling sad, happy or angry, I assume that his feelings are similar to mine. But of course I cannot know. As we try to come to grips with the emotions of beings progressively more different from ourselves the task, obviously, becomes increasingly difficult. If we ascribe human emotions to non-human animals we are accused of being anthropomorphic—a cardinal sin in ethology. But is it so terrible? If we test the effect of drugs on chimpanzees because they are biologically so similar to ourselves, if we accept that there are dramatic similarities in chimpanzee and human brain and nervous system, is it not logical to assume that there will be similarities also in at least the more basic feelings, emotions, moods of the two species?

In fact, all those who have worked long and closely with chimpanzees have no hesitation in asserting that chimps experience emotions similar to those which in ourselves we label pleasure, joy, sorrow, anger, boredom and so on. Some of the emotional states of the chimpanzee are so obviously similar to ours that even an inexperienced observer can understand what is going on. An infant who hurls himself screaming to the ground, face contorted, hitting out with his arms at any nearby object, banging his head, is clearly having a tantrum. Another youngster, who gambols around his mother, turning somersaults, pirouetting and, every so often, rushing up to her and tumbling into her lap, patting her or pulling her hand towards him in a request for tickling, is obviously filled with *joie de vivre.* There are few observers who would not unhesitatingly ascribe his behaviour to a happy, carefree state of well-being. And one cannot watch chimpanzee infants for long without realizing that they have the same emotional need for affection and reassurance as human children. An adult male, reclining in the shade after a good meal, reaching benignly to play with an infant or idly groom an adult female, is clearly in a good mood. When he sits with bristling hair, glaring at his subordinates and threatening them with irritated gestures if they come too close, he is clearly feeling cross and grumpy. We make these judgements because the similarity of so much of a chimpanzee's behaviour to our own permits us to empathize.

It is hard to empathize with emotions we have not experienced. I can image, to some extent, the pleasure of a female chimpanzee during the act of procreation. The feelings of her male partner are beyond my knowledge—as are those of the human male in the same context. I have spent countless hours watching mother chimpanzees interacting with their infants. But not until I had an infant of my own did I begin to understand the basic, powerful instinct of mother-love. If someone accidentally did something to frighten Grub, or threaten his well-being in any way, I felt a surge of quite irrational anger. How much more easily could I then understand the feelings of the chimpanzee mother who furiously waves her arm and barks in threat at an individual who approaches her infant too closely, or at a playmate who inadvertently hurts her child. And it was not until I knew the numbing grief that gripped me after the death of my second husband that I could even begin to appreciate the despair and sense of loss that can cause young chimps to pine away and die when they lose their mothers.

Empathy and intuition can be of tremendous value as we attempt to understand certain complex behavioral interactions, provided that the behaviour, as it occurs, is recorded precisely and objectively. Fortunately I have seldom found it difficult to record facts in an orderly manner even during times of powerful emotional involvement. And "knowing" intuitively how a chimpanzee is feeling—after an attack, for example—may help one to understand what happens next. We should not be afraid at least to try to make use of our close evolutionary relationship with the chimpanzees in our attempts to interpret complex behaviour.

Today, as in Darwin's time, it is once again fashionable to speak of and study the animal mind. This change came about gradually, and was, at least in part, due to the information collected during careful studies of animal societies in the field. As these observations became widely known, it was impossible to brush aside the complexities of social behaviour that were revealed in species after species. The untidy clutter under the ethological carpets was brought out and examined, piece by piece. Gradually it was realized that parsimonious explanations of apparently intelligent behaviours were often misleading. This led to a succession of experiments that, taken together, clearly prove that many intellectual abilities that had been thought unique to humans were actually present, though in a less highly developed form, in other, non-human beings. Particularly, of course, in the non-human primates and especially in chimpanzees.

When first I began to read about human evolution, I learned that one of the hallmarks of our own species was that we, and only we, were capable of making tools. *Man the Toolmaker* was an oft-cited definition—and this despite the careful and exhaustive research of Wolfgang Kohler and Robert Yerkes on the tool-using and tool-making abilities of chimpanzees. Those studies, carried out independently in the early twenties, were received with scepticism. Yet both Kohler and Yerkes were respected scientists, and both had a profound understanding of chimpanzee behaviour. Indeed, Kohler's descriptions of the personalities and behaviour of the various individuals in his colony, published in his book *The Mentality of Apes,* remain some of the most vivid and colourful ever written. And his experiments, showing how chimpanzees could stack boxes, then climb the unstable constructions to reach fruit suspended from the ceiling, or join two short sticks to make a pole long enough to rake in fruit otherwise out of reach, have become classic, appearing in almost all textbooks dealing with intelligent behaviour in non-human animals.

By the time systematic observations of tool-using came from Gombe those pioneering studies had been largely forgotten. Moreover, it was one thing to know that humanized chimpanzees in the lab could use implements: it was quite another to find that this was a naturally occurring skill in the wild. I well remember writing to Louis about my first observations, describing how David Greybeard not only used bits of straw to fish for termites but actually stripped leaves from a stem and thus *made* a tool. And I remember too receiving the now oft-quoted telegram he sent in response to my letter: "Now we must redefine *tool,* redefine *Man,* or accept chimpanzees as humans."

There were initially, a few scientists who attempted to write off the termiting observations, even suggesting that I had taught the chimps! By and large, though, people were fascinated by the information and by the subsequent observations of the other contexts in which the Gombe chimpanzees used objects as tools. And there were only a few anthropologists who objected when I suggested that the chimpanzees probably passed their tool-using traditions from one generation to the next, through observations, imitation and practice, so that each population might be expected to have its own unique tool-using culture. Which, incidentally, turns out to be quite true. And when I described how one chimpanzee, Mike, spontaneously solved a new problem by using a tool (he broke off a stick to knock a banana to the ground when he was too nervous to actually take it from my hand) I don't believe there were any raised eyebrows in the scientific community. Certainly I was not attacked viciously, as were Kohler and Yerkes, for suggesting that humans were not the only beings capable of reasoning and insight.

The mid-sixties saw the start of a project that, along with other similar research, was to teach us a great deal about the chimpanzee mind. This was Project Washoe, conceived by Trixie and Allen Gardner. They purchased an infant chimpanzee and began to teach her the signs of ASL, the American Sign Language used by the deaf. Twenty years earlier another husband and wife team, Richard and Cathy Hayes, had tried, with an almost total lack of success, to teach a young chimp, Vikki, to talk. The Hayes's undertaking taught us a lot about the chimpanzee mind, but Vikki, although she did well in IQ tests, and was clearly an intelligent youngster, could not learn human speech. The Gardners, however, achieved spectacular success with their pupil, Washoe. Not only did she learn signs easily, but she quickly began to string them together in meaningful ways. It was clear that each sign evoked, in her mind, a mental image of the object it represented. If, for example, she was asked, in sign language, to fetch an apple, she would go and locate an apple that was out of sight in another room.

Other chimps entered the project, some starting their lives in deaf signing families before joining Washoe. And finally Washoe adopted an infant, Loulis. He came from a lab where no thought of teaching signs had ever penetrated. When he was with Washoe he was given no lessons in language acquisition—not by humans, anyway. Yet by the time he was eight years old he had made fifty-eight signs in their correct contexts. How did he learn them? Mostly, it seems, by imitating the behaviour of Washoe and the other three signing chimps, Dar, Moja and Tatu. Sometimes, though, he received tuition from Washoe herself. One day, for example, she began to swagger about bipedally, hair bristling, signing *food! food! food!* in great excitement. She had seen a human approaching with a bar of chocolate. Loulis, only eighteen months old, watched passively. Suddenly Washoe stopped her swaggering, went over to him, took his hand, and moulded the sign for *food* (fingers pointing towards mouth). Another time, in a similar context, she made the sign for *chewing gum*—but with *her* hand on *his* body. On a third occasion Washoe, apropos of nothing, picked up a small chair, took it over to Loulis, set it down in front of him, and very distinctly made the *chair* sign three times, watching him closely as she did so. The two food signs became incorporated into Loulis's vocabulary but the sign for chair did not. Obviously the priorities of a young chimp are similar to those of a human child!

When news of Washoe's accomplishments first hit the scientific community it immediately provoked a storm of bitter protest. It implied that chimpanzees were capable of mastering a human language, and this, in turn, indicated mental powers of generalization, abstraction and concept-formation as well as an ability to understand and use abstract symbols. And these intellectual skills were surely the prerogatives of *Homo sapiens*. Although there were many who were fascinated and excited by the Gardners' findings, there were many more who denounced the whole project, holding that the data was suspect, the methodology sloppy, and the conclusions not only misleading, but quite preposterous. The controversy inspired all sorts of other language projects. And, whether the investigators were sceptical to start with and hoped to disprove the Gardners' work, or whether they were attempting to demonstrate the same thing in a new way, their research provided additional information about the chimpanzee's mind.

And so, with new incentive, psychologists began to test the mental abilities of chimpanzees in a variety of different ways; again and again the results confirmed that their minds are uncannily like our own. It had long been held that only humans were capable of what is called 'cross-modal transfer of information'—in other words, if you shut your eyes and someone allows you to feel a strangely shaped potato, you will subsequently be able to pick it out from other differently shaped potatoes simply by looking at them. And vice versa. It turned out that chimpanzees can 'know' with their eyes what they 'feel' with their fingers in just the same way. In fact, we now know that some other non-human primates can do the same thing. I expect all kinds of creatures have the same ability.

Then it was proved, experimentally and beyond doubt, that chimpanzees could recognize themselves in mirrors—that they had, therefore, some kind of self-concept. In fact, Washoe, some years previously, had already demonstrated the ability when she spontaneously identified herself in the mirror, staring at her image and making her name sign. But that observation was merely anecdotal. The proof came when chimpanzees who had been allowed to play with mirrors were, while anaesthetized, dabbed with spots of odourless paint in places, such as the ears or the top of the head, that they could see only in the mirror. When they woke they were not only fascinated by their spotted images, but immediately investigated, with their fingers, the dabs of paint.

The fact that chimpanzees have excellent memories surprised no one. Everyone, after all, has been brought up to believe that 'an elephant never forgets' so why should a chimpanzee be any different? The fact that Washoe spontaneously gave the name-sign of Beatrice Gardner, her surrogate mother, when she saw her after a separation of eleven years was no greater an accomplishment than the amazing memory shown by dogs who recognize their owners after separations of almost as long—and the chimpanzee has a much longer life span than a dog. Chimpanzees can plan ahead, too, at least as regards the immediate future. This, in fact, is well illustrated at Gombe, during the termiting season: often an individual prepares a tool for use on a termite mound that is several hundred yards away and absolutely out of sight.

This is not the place to describe in detail the other cognitive abilities that have been studied in laboratory chimpanzees. Among other accomplishments chimpanzees possess pre-mathematical skills: they can, for example, readily differentiate between *more* and *less*. They can classify things into specific categories according to a given criterion—thus they have no difficulty in separating a pile of food into *fruits* and *vegetables* on one occasion, and, on another, dividing the same pile of food into *large* versus *small* items, even though this requires putting some vegetables with some fruits. Chimpanzees who have been taught a language can combine signs creatively in order to describe objects for which they have no symbol. Washoe, for example, puzzled her caretakers by asking, repeatedly, for a *rock berry*. Eventually it transpired that she was referring to Brazil nuts which she had encountered for the first time a while before. Another language-trained chimp described a cucumber as a *green banana,* and another referred to an Alka-Seltzer as a *listen drink.* They can even invent signs. Lucy, as she got older, had to be put on a leash for her outings. One day, eager to set off but having no sign for *leash,* she signalled her wishes by holding a crooked index finger to the ring on her collar. This sign became part of her vocabulary. Some chimpanzees love to draw, and especially to paint. Those who have learned sign language sometimes spontaneously label their works, 'This [is] apple'—or bird, or sweetcorn, or whatever. The fact that the paintings often look, to our eyes, remarkably unlike the objects depicted by the artists either means that the chimpanzees are poor draughtsmen or that we have much to learn regarding ape-style representational art!

People sometimes ask why chimpanzees have evolved such complex intellectual powers when their lives in the wild are so simple. The answer is, of course, that their lives in the wild are not so simple! They use—and need—all their mental skills during normal day-to-day life in their complex society. They are always having to make choices—where to go, or with whom to travel. They need highly developed social skills—particularly those males who are ambitious to attain high positions in the dominance hierarchy. Low-ranking chimpanzees must learn deception—to conceal their intentions or to do things in secret—if they are to get their way in the presence of their superiors. Indeed, the study of chimpanzees in the wild suggests that their intellectual abilities evolved, over the millennia, to help them cope with daily life. And now, the solid core of data concerning chimpanzee intellect collected so carefully in the lab setting provides a background against which to evaluate the many examples of intelligent, rational behaviour that we see in the wild.

It is easier to study intellectual prowess in the lab where, through carefully devised tests and judicious use of rewards, the chimpanzees can be encouraged to exert themselves, to stretch their minds to the limit. It is more meaningful to study the subject in the wild, but much harder. It is more meaningful because we can better understand the environmental pressures that led to the evolution of intellectual skills in chimpanzee societies. It is harder because, in the wild, almost all behaviours are confounded by countless variables; years of observing, recording and analysing take the place of contrived testing; sample size can often be counted on the fingers of one hand; the only experiments are nature's own, and only time—eventually—may replicate them.

In the wild a single observation may prove of utmost significance, providing a clue to some hitherto puzzling aspect of behaviour, a key to the understanding of, for example, a changed relationship. Obviously it is crucial to see as many incidents of this sort as possible. During the early years of my study at Gombe it became apparent that one person alone could never learn more than a fraction of what was going on in a chimpanzee community at any given time. And so, from 1964 onwards, I gradually built up a research team to help in the gathering of information about the behaviour of our closest living relatives.

Critical Thinking

1. Describe Lucy's "human" behavior.
2. What is the physiological evidence that chimpanzees resemble us?
3. Why has it been, for some scientists, more absurd to accept a similarity of mind than a similarity in physical structure?
4. What were considered inappropriate descriptions of chimpanzees when Jane Goodall began her study at Gombe?
5. What is a "cardinal sin" in ethology? What is Jane Goodall's answer to such a view?
6. Why did it eventually become impossible to brush aside observations regarding animal minds?
7. What was considered one of the "hallmarks of our species"? What did Kohler's study show?
8. Why were Jane Goodall's observations significant?
9. What did Washoe and Loulis show regarding chimpanzee abilities? What was the "bitter protest" about?
10. Be familiar with chimpanzee abilities with respect to "cross-modal transfer of information," "self-concept," memory, planning ahead, pre-mathematical skills, classifying ability, combining signs creatively, and labeling their own art.
11. How does Jane Goodall answer the question of why chimpanzees have evolved such complex intellectual powers?
12. How does Jane Goodall characterize the differences between lab studies versus studies in the wild?

Got Culture?

CRAIG STANFORD

On my first trip to east Africa in the early 1990s, I stood by a dusty, dirt road hitchhiking. I had waited hours in rural Tanzania for an expected lift from a friend who had never shown up, leaving me with few options other than the kindness of strangers. I stood with my thumb out, but the cars and trucks roared by me, leaving me caked in paprika-red dust. I switched to a palm-down gesture I had seen local people using to get lifts. Voilà; on the first try a truck pulled over and I hopped in. A conversation in Kiswahili with the truck driver ensued and I learned my mistake. Hitchhiking with your thumb upturned may work in the United States, but in Africa the gesture can be translated in the way that Americans understand the meaning of an extended, declarative middle finger. Not exactly the best way to persuade a passing vehicle to stop. The universally recognized symbol for needing a lift is not so universal.

Much of culture is the accumulation of thousands of such small differences. Put a suite of traditions together—religion, language, ways of dress, cuisine and a thousand other features—and you have a culture. Of course cultures can be much simpler too. A group of toddlers in a day care center possesses its own culture, as does a multi-national corporation, suburban gardeners, inner-city gang members. Many elements of a culture are functional and hinged to individual survival: thatched roof homes from the tropics would work poorly in Canada, nor would harpoons made for catching seals be very useful in the Sahara. But other features are purely symbolic. Brides in Western culture wear white to symbolize sexual purity. Brides in Hindu weddings wear crimson, to symbolize sexual purity. Whether white or red is more pure is nothing more than a product of the long-term memory and mindset of the two cultures. And the most symbolic of cultural traditions, the one that has always been considered the bailiwick of humanity only, is language. The words "white" and "red" have an entirely arbitrary relationship to the colors themselves. They are simply code names.

Arguing about how to define culture has long been a growth industry among anthropologists. We argue about culture the way the Joint Chiefs of Staff argue about national security: as though our lives depended on it. But given that culture requires symbolism and some linguistic features, can we even talk about culture in other animals?

In 1996 I was attending a conference near Rio de Janeiro when the topic turned to culture.[1] As a biological anthropologist with a decade of field research on African great apes, I offered my perspective on the concept of culture. Chimpanzees, I said with confidence, display a rich cultural diversity. Recent years have shown that each wild chimpanzee population is more than just a gene pool. It is also a distinct culture, comprising a unique assortment of learned traditions in tool use, styles of grooming and hunting, and other features of the sort that can only be seen in the most socially sophisticated primates. Go from one forest to another and you will run into a new culture, just as walking between two human villages may introduce you to tribes who have different ways of building boats or celebrating marriages.

At least that's what I meant to say. But I had barely gotten the word "culture" past my lips when I was made to feel the full weight of my blissful ignorance. The cultural anthropologists practically leaped across the seminar table to berate me for using the words "culture" and "chimpanzee" in the same sentence. I had apparently set off a silent security alarm, and the culture-theory guards came running. How dare you, they said, use a human term like "cultural diversity" to describe what chimpanzees do? Say "behavioral variation," they demanded. "Apes are mere animals, and culture is something that only the human animal can claim. Furthermore, not only can humans alone claim culture, culture alone can explain humanity." It became clear to me that culture, as understood by most anthropologists, is a human concept, and many passionately want it to stay that way. When I asked if this was not just a semantic difference—what are cultural traditions if not learned behavioral variations?—they replied that culture is symbolic, and what animals do lacks symbolism.

When Jane Goodall first watched chimpanzees make simple stick tools to probe into termite mounds, it became clear that tool cultures are not unique to human societies. Of course many animals use tools. Sea otters on the California coast forage for abalones, which they place on their chests and hammer open with stones. Egyptian vultures use stones to break the eggs of ostriches. But these are simple, relatively inflexible lone behaviors. Only among chimpanzees do we see elaborate forms of tools made and used in variable ways, and also see distinct chimp tool cultures across Africa. In

Gombe National Park in Tanzania, termite mounds of red earth rise 2 meters high and shelter millions of the almond-colored insects. Chimpanzees pore over the mounds, scratching at plugged tunnels until they find portals into the mound's interior. They will gently insert a twig or blade of grass into a tunnel until the soldier termites latch onto the tools with their powerful mandibles, then they'll withdraw the probe from the mound. With dozens of soldier and worker termites clinging ferociously to the twig, the chimpanzee draws the stick between her lips and reaps a nutritious bounty.

Less than 100 kilometers away from Gombe's termite-fishing apes is another culture. Chimpanzees in Mahale National Park live in a forest that is home to most of the same species of termites, but they practically never use sticks to eat them. If Mahale chimpanzees forage for termites at all, they use their fingers to crumble apart soil and pick out their insect snacks. However, Mahale chimpanzees love to eat ants. They climb up the straight-sided trunks of great trees and poke Gombe-like probes into holes to obtain woodboring species. As adept as Gombe chimpanzees are at fishing for termites, they practically never fish for these ants, even though both the ants and termites occur in both Gombe and Mahale.[2]

Segue 2,000 kilometers westward, to a rainforest in Côte d'Ivoire. In a forest filled with twigs, chimpanzees do not use stick tools. Instead, chimpanzees in Taï National Park and other forests in western Africa use hammers made of rock and wood. Swiss primatologists Christophe and Hedwige Boesch and their colleagues first reported the use of stone tools by chimpanzees twenty years ago.[3] Their subsequent research showed that Taï chimpanzees collect hammers when certain species of nut-bearing trees are in fruit. These hammers are not modified in any way as the stone tools made by early humans were; they are hefted, however, and appraised for weight and smashing value before being carried back to the nut tree. A nut is carefully positioned in a depression in the tree's aboveground root buttresses (the anvil) and struck with precision by the tool-user. The researchers have seen mothers instructing their children on the art of tool use, by assisting them in placing the nut in the anvil in the proper way.

So chimpanzees in East Africa use termite- and ant-fishing tools, and West African counterparts use hammers, but not vice versa. These are subsistence tools; they were almost certainly invented for food-getting. Primatologist William McGrew of Miami University of Ohio has compared the tool technologies of wild chimpanzees with those of traditional human hunter-gatherer societies. He found that in at least some instances, the gap between chimpanzee technology and human technology is not wide. The now-extinct aboriginal Tasmanians, for example, possessed no complex tools or weapons of any kind. Though they are an extreme example, the Tasmanians illustrate that human culture need not be technologically complex.[4]

As McGrew first pointed out, there are three likeliest explanations for the differences we see among the chimpanzee tool industries across Africa.[5] The first is genetic: perhaps there are mutations that arise in one population but not others that

govern tool making. This seems extremely unlikely, just as we would never argue that Hindu brides wear red while Western brides wear white due to a genetic difference between Indians and Westerners. The second explanation is ecological: maybe the environment in which the chimpanzee population lives dictates patterns of tool use. Maybe termite-fishing sticks will be invented in places where there are termites and sticks but not rocks and nuts, and hammers invented in the opposite situation. But a consideration of each habitat raises doubts. Gombe is a rugged, rock-strewn place where it is hard to find a spot to sit that is not within arm's reach of a few stones, but Gombe chimpanzees do not use stone tools. The West African chimpanzees who use stone tools live, by contrast, in low-land rainforests that are nearly devoid of rocks. Yet they purposely forage to find them. The tool-use pattern is exactly the opposite of what we would expect if environment and local availability accounted for differences among chimpanzee communities in tool use.

British psychologist Andrew Whiten and his colleagues recently conducted the first systematic survey of cultural differences in tool use among the seven longest-term field studies, representing more than a century and a half of total observation time. They found thirty-nine behaviors that could not be explained by environmental factors at the various sites.[6] Alone with humans in the richness of their behavior repertoire, chimpanzee cultures show variations that can only be ascribed to learned traditions. These traditions, passed from one generation to the next through observation and imitation, are a simple version of human culture.

But wait. I said earlier that human culture must have a symbolic element. Tools that differ in form and function, from sticks to hammers to sponges made of crushed leaves, are all utterly utilitarian. They tell us much about the environment in which they are useful but little about the learned traditions that led to their creation. Human artifacts, on the other hand, nearly always contain some purely symbolic element, be it the designs carved into a piece of ancient pottery or the "Stanley" logo on my new claw hammer. Is there anything truly symbolic in chimpanzee culture, in the human sense of an object or behavior that is completely detached from its use?

Male chimpanzees have various ways of indicating to a female that they would like to mate. At Gombe, one such courtship behavior involves rapidly shaking a small bush or branch several times, after which a female in proximity will usually approach the male and present her swelling to him. But in Mahale, males have learned to use leaves in their courtship gesture. A male plucks a leafy stem from a nearby plant and noisily uses his teeth and fingers to tear off its leaves. Leaf-clipping is done mainly in the context of wanting to mate with a particular female, and appears to function as a purely symbolic signal of sexual desire (it could also be a gesture of frustration). A second leafy symbol is leaf-grooming. Chimpanzees pick leaves and intently groom them with their fingers, as seriously as though they were grooming another chimpanzee. And this may be the function; leaf-grooming may signal a desire for real grooming from a social partner. Since the signal for grooming involves grooming, albeit of another object, this gesture is not symbolic in the sense that leaf-clipping is. But its distribution across Africa is equally spotty; leaf-grooming is commonly practiced in East African chimpanzee cultures but is largely absent in western Africa.[7]

These two cases of potentially symbolic behavior may not seem very impressive. After all, the briefest consideration of human culture turns up a rich array of symbolism, from language to the arts. But are all human cultures highly symbolic? If we use language and other forms of symbolic expression as the criterion for culture, then how about a classroom full of two-year-old toddlers in a day care center? They communicate by a very simple combination of gestures and half-formed sentences. Toddlers have little symbolic communication or appreciation for art and are very little different from chimpanzees in their cultural output. We grant them human qualities because we know they will mature into symbol-using, linguistically expert adults, leaving chimpanzees in the dust. But this is no reason to consider them on a different plane from the apes when both are fifteen months old.

Chimpanzee societies are based on learned traditions passed from mother to child and from adult males to eager wannabe males. These traditions vary from place to place. This is culture. Culture is not limited, however, to those few apes that are genetically 99 percent human. Many primates show traditions. These are usually innovations by younger members of a group, which sweep rapidly through the society and leave it just slightly different than before. Japanese primatologists have long observed such traditions among the macaques native to their island nation. Researchers long ago noticed that a new behavior had arisen in one population of Japanese macaque monkeys living on Koshima Island just offshore the mainland. The monkeys were regularly tossed sweet potatoes, rice and other local treats by the locals. One day Imo, a young female in the group, took her potato and carried it to the sea, where she washed it with salty brine before eating it. This behavior rapidly spread throughout the group, a nice example of innovation happening in real time so that researchers could observe the diffusion. Later, other monkeys invented the practice of scooping up rice offered them with the beach sand it was scattered on, throwing both onto the surf and then scraping up the grains that floated while the sand sank.

At a supremely larger scale, such innovations are what human cultural differences are all about. Of course, only in human cultures do objects such as sweet potatoes take on the kind of symbolic meaning that permits them to stand for other objects and thus become a currency. Chimpanzees lack the top-drawer cognitive capacity needed to invent such a currency. Or do they? Wild chimpanzees hunt for a part of their living. All across equatorial Africa, meat-eating is a regular feature of chimpanzee life, but its style and technique vary from one forest to another. In Taï National Park in western Africa, hunters are highly cooperative; Christophe Boesch has reported specific roles such as ambushers and

drivers as part of the apes' effort to corral colobus monkeys in the forest canopy.[8] At Gombe in East Africa, meanwhile, hunting is like a baseball game; a group sport performed on an individual basis. This difference may be environmentally influenced; perhaps the high canopy rain forest at Taï requires cooperation more than the broken, low canopy forest at Gombe. There is a culture of hunting in each forest as well, in which young and eager male wannabes copy the predatory skills of their elders. At Gombe, for instance, chimpanzees relish wild pigs and piglets in addition to monkeys and small antelope. At Taï, wild pigs are ignored even when they stroll in front of a hunting party.

There is also a culture of sharing the kill. Sharing of meat is highly nepotistic at Gombe; sons who make the kill share with their mothers and brothers but snub rival males. They also share preferentially with females who have sexual swellings, and with high-ranking females. At Taï, the captor shares with the other members of the hunting party whether or not they are allies or relatives; a system of reciprocity seems to be in place in which the golden rule works. I have argued that since the energy and time that chimpanzees spend hunting is rarely paid back by the calories, protein and fat gotten from a kill, we should consider hunting a social behavior done at least partly for its own sake.[9] When chimpanzees barter a limited commodity such as meat for other services—alliances, sex, grooming—they are engaging in a very simple and primitive form of a currency exchange. Such an exchange relies on the ability of the participants to remember the web of credits and debts owed one another and to act accordingly. It may be that the two chimpanzee cultures 2,000 kilometers apart have developed their distinct uses of meat as a social currency. In one place meat is used as a reward for cooperation, in the other as a manipulative tool of nepotism. Such systems are commonplace in all human societies, and their roots may be seen in chimpanzees' market economy, too.[10]

I have not yet considered one obvious question. If tool use and other cultural innovations can be so valuable to chimpanzees, why have they not arisen more widely among primates and other big-brained animals? Although chimpanzees are adept tool-users, their very close relatives the bonobos are not. Bonobos do a number of very clever things—dragging their hands beside them as they wade through streams to catch fish is one notable example—but they are not accomplished technicians. Gorillas don't use tools at all, and orangutans have only recently been observed to occasionally use sticks as probing tools in their rainforest canopy world.[11]

Other big-brained animals fare even worse. Wild elephants don't use their wonderfully dexterous trunks to manipulate tools in any major way, although when you're strong enough to uproot trees you may not have much use for a pokey little probe. Dolphins and whales, cognitively gifted though they may be, lack the essential anatomical ingredient for tool manufacture—a pair of nimble hands. Wild bottlenose dolphins have been observed to carry natural sponges about on their snouts to ferret food from the sea bottom, the only known form of cetacean tool use.[12] But that may be the limit of how much a creature that lacks any grasping appendages can manipulate its surroundings.

So to be a cultural animal, it is not enough to be big-brained. You must have the anatomical prerequisites for tool cultures to develop. Even if these are in place, there is no guarantee that a species will generate a subsistence culture in the form of tools. Perhaps environmental necessity dictates which ape species use tools and which don't, except it is hard to imagine that bonobos have much less use for tools than chimpanzees do. There is probably a strong element of chance involved. The chance that a cultural tradition—tool use, hunting style or grooming technique—will develop may be very small in any given century or millennium. Once innovated, the chance that the cultural trait will disappear—perhaps due to the death of the main practitioners from whom everyone learned the behavior—may conversely be great. Instead of a close fit between the environment and the cultural traditions that evolve in it—which many scholars believe explains cultural diversity in human societies—the roots of cultural variation may be much more random. A single influential individual who figures out how to make a better mousetrap, so to speak, can through imitation spread his mousetrap through the group and slowly into other groups.

We tend to think of cultural traditions as highly plastic and unstable compared to biological innovation. It takes hundreds of generations for natural selection to bring about biological change, whereas cultural change can happen in one lifetime, even in a few minutes. Because we live in a culture in which we buy the newest cell phone and the niftiest handheld computer—we fail to appreciate how conservative traditions like tool use can be. *Homo erectus*, with a brain nearly the size of our own, invented a teardrop-shaped stone tool called a hand axe 1.5 million years ago. It was presumably used for butchering carcasses, though some archaeologists think it may have also been a weapon. Whatever its purpose, more than a million years later those same stone axes were still being manufactured and used. Fifty thousand generations passed without a significant change in the major piece of material culture in a very big-brained and intelligent human species. *That's* conservatism and it offers us two lessons. First, if it ain't broke don't fix it: when a traditional way of making a tool works and the environment is not throwing any curves your way, there may be no pressure for a change. Second, we see a human species vastly more intelligent than an ape (*Homo erectus'* neocortical brain volume was a third smaller than a modern human's, but two and a half times larger than a chimpanzee's) whose technology didn't change at all. This tells us that innovations, once made, may last a very long time without being either extinguished or improved upon. It suggests that chimpanzee tool cultures may have been in place for all of the 5 million years since their divergence from our shared ancestor.

The very word *culture,* as William McGrew has pointed out, was invented for humans, and this has long blinded cultural theorists to a more expansive appreciation of the concept.

Whether apes have culture or not is not really the issue. The heart of the debate is whether scholars who study culture and consider it their intellectual territory will accept a more expansive definition. In purely academic arguments like this one, the power lies with the party who owns the key concepts of the discipline. They define concepts however they choose, and the choice is usually aimed at fencing off their intellectual turf from all others.

Primatologists are latecomers to the table of culture, and they have had to wait their turn before being allowed to sit. We should be most interested in what the continuum of intelligence tells us about the roots of human behavior, not whether what apes do or don't do fits any particular, rigid definition of culture. When it comes to human practices, from building boats to weddings to choosing mates, we should look at the intersections of our biology and our culture for clues about what has made us who we are.

Notes

1. *Changing Views of Primate Societies: The Role of Gender and Nationality,* June 1996, sponsored by the Wenner-Gren Foundation for Anthropological Research.

2. For an enlightening discussion of cross-cultural differences in chimpanzee tool use, see almost anything William McGrew has written, but especially McGrew (1992).

3. See Boesch and Boesch (1989).

4. Again, see McGrew (1992).

5. McGrew (1979).

6. Whiten *et al.* (1999) combined data from seven long-term chimpanzees studies to produce the most systematic examination of cultural variation in these apes.

7. For further discussion of chimpanzee symbolic behavior in the wild, see Goodall (1986), Wrangham *et al.* (1994), and McGrew et al. (1996).

8. See Boesch and Boesch (1989).

9. See Stanford (1999, 2001).

10. See de Waal (1996) and Stanford (2001).

11. For the first report of systematic tool use by wild orangutans, see van Schaik *et al.* (1996).

12. See Smolker *et al.* (1997).

Critical Thinking

1. Be aware of the fact that a culture may consist of a suite of traditions and it may be simple, symbolic, or even arbitrary, as with language.

2. What were the cultural anthropologists' objections to the author's use of culture to describe chimpanzee behavior?

3. How does the author distinguish chimpanzee tool behavior from that of otters and Egyptian vultures?

4. What is the difference between Gombe chimps and Mahale chimps with regard to tool use and ant/termite eating?

5. What kinds of tools do the Taï chimps use and for what purpose? What kind of instruction is involved?

6. Why does McGrew conclude that, at least in some instances, the gap between chimpanzee technology and human technology is not wide?

7. How does the author assess the three likeliest explanations for the differences among chimpanzee tool industries across Africa in light of the evidence?

8. Do other primates show traditions that vary from place to place? How do the Japanese macaques serve as an example?

9. How does hunting and meat sharing vary among chimps? In what sense do they engage in a form of currency exchange?

10. Why does the author think that chimpanzee tool cultures may have existed for all the 5 million years since our shared ancestry?

11. What is really the issue, according to the author? In what should we be most interested?

Dim Forest, Bright Chimps

In the rain forest of Ivory Coast, chimpanzees meet the challenge of life by hunting cooperatively and using crude tools.

CHRISTOPHE BOESCH AND HEDWIGE BOESCH-ACHERMANN

Taï National Park, Ivory Coast, December 3, 1985. Drumming, barking, and screaming, chimps rush through the undergrowth, little more than black shadows. Their goal is to join a group of other chimps noisily clustering around Brutus, the dominant male of this seventy-member chimpanzee community. For a few moments, Brutus, proud and self-confident, stands fairly still, holding a shocked, barely moving red colobus monkey in his hand. Then he begins to move through the group, followed closely by his favorite females and most of the adult males. He seems to savor this moment of uncontested superiority, the culmination of a hunt high up in the canopy. But the victory is not his alone. Cooperation is essential to capturing one of these monkeys, and Brutus will break apart and share this highly prized delicacy with most of the main participants of the hunt and with the females. Recipients of large portions will, in turn, share more or less generously with their offspring, relatives, and friends.

In 1979, we began a long-term study of the previously unknown chimpanzees of Taï National Park, 1,600 square miles of tropical rain forest in the Republic of the Ivory Coast (Côte d'Ivoire). Early on, we were most interested in the chimps' use of natural hammers—branches and stones—to crack open the five species of hard-shelled nuts that are abundant here. A sea otter lying on its back, cracking an abalone shell with a rock, is a familiar picture, but no primate had ever before been observed in the wild using stones as hammers. East Africa's savanna chimps, studied for decades by Jane Goodall in Gombe, Tanzania, use twigs to extract ants and termites from their nests or honey from a bees' nest, but they have never been seen using hammerstones.

As our work progressed, we were surprised by the many ways in which the life of the Taï forest chimpanzees differs from that of their savanna counterparts, and as evidence accumulated, differences in how the two populations hunt proved the most intriguing. Jane Goodall had found that chimpanzees hunt monkeys, antelope, and wild pigs, findings confirmed by Japanese biologist Toshida Nishida, who conducted a long-term study 120 miles south of Gombe, in the Mahale Mountains. So we were not surprised to discover that the Taï chimps eat meat. What

intrigued us was the degree to which they hunt cooperatively. In 1953 Raymond Dart proposed that group hunting and cooperation were key ingredients in the evolution of *Homo sapiens*. The argument has been modified considerably since Dart first put it forward, and group hunting has also been observed in some social carnivores (lions and African wild dogs, for instance), and even some birds of prey. Nevertheless, many anthropologists still hold that hunting cooperatively and sharing food played a central role in the drama that enabled early hominids, some 1.8 million years ago, to develop the social systems that are so typically human.

We hoped that what we learned about the behavior of forest chimpanzees would shed new light on prevailing theories of human evolution. Before we could even begin, however, we had to habituate a community of chimps to our presence. Five long years passed before we were able to move with them on their daily trips through the forest, of which "our" group appeared to claim some twelve square miles. Chimpanzees are alert and shy animals, and the limited field of view in the rain forest—about sixty-five feet at best—made finding them more difficult. We had to rely on sound, mostly their vocalizations and drumming on trees. Males often drum regularly while moving through the forest: pant-hooting, they draw near a big buttress tree; then, at full speed they fly over the buttress, hitting it repeatedly with their hands and feet. Such drumming may resound more than half a mile in the forest. In the beginning, our ignorance about how they moved and who was drumming led to failure more often than not, but eventually we learned that the dominant males drummed during the day to let other group members know the direction of travel. On some days, however, intermittent drumming about dawn was the only signal for the whole day. If we were out of earshot at the time, we were often reduced to guessing.

During these difficult early days, one feature of the chimps' routine proved to be our salvation: nut cracking is a noisy business. So noisy, in fact, that in the early days of French colonial rule, one officer apparently even proposed the theory that some unknown tribe was forging iron in the impenetrable and dangerous jungle.

Guided by the sounds made by the chimps as they cracked open nuts, which they often did for hours at a time, we were gradually able to get within sixty feet of the animals. We still seldom saw the chimps themselves (they fled if we came too close), but even so, the evidence left after a session of nut cracking taught us a great deal about what types of nuts they were eating, what sorts of hammer and anvil tools they were using, and—thanks to the very distinctive noise a nut makes when it finally splits open—how many hits were needed to crack a nut and how many nuts could be opened per minute.

After some months, we began catching glimpses of the chimpanzees before they fled, and after a little more time, we were able to draw close enough to watch them at work. The chimps gather nuts from the ground. Some nuts are tougher to crack than others. Nuts of the *Panda oleosa* tree are the most demanding, harder than any of the foods processed by present-day hunter-gatherers and breaking open only when a force of 3,500 pounds is applied. The stone hammers used by the Taï chimps range from stones of ten ounces to granite blocks of four to forty-five pounds. Stones of any size, however, are a rarity in the forest and are seldom conveniently placed near a nut-bearing tree. By observing closely, and in some cases imitating the way the chimps handle hammerstones, we learned that they have an impressive ability to find just the right tool for the job at hand. Taï chimps could remember the positions of many of the stones scattered, often out of sight, around a panda tree. Without having to run around rechecking the stones, they would select one of appropriate size that was closest to the tree. These mental abilities in spatial representation compare with some of those of nine-year-old humans.

To extract the four kernels from inside a panda nut, a chimp must use a hammer with extreme precision. Time and time again, we have been impressed to see a chimpanzee raise a twenty-pound stone above its head, strike a nut with ten or more powerful blows, and then, using the same hammer, switch to delicate little taps from a height of only four inches. To finish the job, the chimps often break off a small piece of twig and use it to extract the last tiny fragments of kernel from the shell. Intriguingly, females crack panda nuts more often than males, a gender difference in tool use that seems to be more pronounced in the forest chimps than in their savanna counterparts.

After five years of fieldwork, we were finally able to follow the chimpanzees at close range, and gradually, we gained insights into their way of hunting. One morning, for example, we followed a group of six male chimps on a three-hour patrol that had taken them into foreign territory to the north. (Our study group is one of five chimpanzee groups more or less evenly distributed in the Taï forest.) As always during these approximately monthly incursions, which seem to be for the purpose of territorial defense, the chimps were totally silent, clearly on edge and on the lookout for trouble. Once the patrol was over, however, and they were back within their own borders, the chimps shifted their attention to hunting. They were after monkeys, the most abundant mammals in the forest. Traveling in large, multi-species groups, some of the forest's ten species of monkeys are more apt than others to wind up as a meal for the chimps. The relatively sluggish and large (almost thirty pounds) red colobus monkeys are the chimps' usual fare. (Antelope also live in the forest, but in our ten years at Taï, we have never seen a chimp catch, or even pursue, one. In contrast, Gombe chimps at times do come across fawns, and when they do, they seize the opportunity—and the fawn.)

The six males moved on silently, peering up into the vegetation and stopping from time to time to listen for the sound of monkeys. None fed or groomed; all focused on the hunt. We followed one old male, Falstaff, closely, for he tolerates us completely and is one of the keenest and most experienced hunters. Even from the rear, Falstaff set the pace; whenever he stopped, the others paused to wait for him. After thirty minutes, we heard the unmistakable noises of monkeys jumping from branch to branch. Silently, the chimps turned in the direction of the sounds, scanning the canopy. Just then, a diana monkey spotted them and gave an alarm call. Dianas are very alert and fast; they are also about half the weight of colobus monkeys. The chimps quickly gave up and continued their search for easier, meatier prey.

Shortly after, we heard the characteristic cough of a red colobus monkey. Suddenly Rousseau and Macho, two twenty-year-olds, burst into action, running toward the cough. Falstaff seemed surprised by their precipitousness, but after a moment's hesitation, he also ran. Now the hunting barks of the chimps mixed with the sharp alarm calls of the monkeys. Hurrying behind Falstaff, we saw him climb up a conveniently situated tree. His position, combined with those of Schubert and Ulysse, two mature chimps in their prime, effectively blocked off three of the monkeys' possible escape routes. But in another tree, nowhere near any escape route and thus useless, waited the last of the hunters, Kendo, eighteen years old and the least experienced of the group. The monkeys, taking advantage of Falstaff's delay and Kendo's error, escaped.

The six males moved on and within five minutes picked up the sounds of another group of red colobus. This time, the chimps approached cautiously, nobody hurrying. They screened the canopy intently to locate the monkeys, which were still unaware of the approaching danger. Macho and Schubert chose two adjacent trees, both full of monkeys, and started climbing very quietly, taking care not to move any branches. Meanwhile, the other four chimps blocked off anticipated escape routes. When Schubert was halfway up, the monkeys finally detected the two chimps. As we watched the colobus monkeys take off in literal panic, the appropriateness of the chimpanzees' scientific name—*Pan* came to mind: with a certain stretch of the imagination, the fleeing monkeys could be shepherds and shepherdesses frightened at the sudden appearance of Pan, the wild Greek god of the woods, shepherds, and their flocks.

Taking off in the expected direction, the monkeys were trailed by Macho and Schubert. The chimps let go with loud hunting barks. Trying to escape, two colobus monkeys jumped into smaller trees lower in the canopy. With this, Rousseau and Kendo, who had been watching from the ground, sped up into the trees and tried to grab them. Only a third of the weight of the chimps, however, the monkeys managed to make it to the next tree along branches too small for their pursuers. But Falstaff had anticipated this move and was waiting for them. In the following confusion, Falstaff seized a juvenile and killed it with a bite to the neck. As the chimps met in a rush on the ground, Falstaff began to eat, sharing with Schubert and Rousseau. A juvenile colobus does not provide much meat, however, and this time, not all the chimps got a share. Frustrated individuals soon started off on another hunt, and relative calm returned fairly quickly: this sort of hunt, by a small band of chimps acting on their own at the edge of their territory, does not generate the kind of high excitement that prevails when more members of the community are involved.

So far we have observed some 200 monkey hunts and have concluded that success requires a minimum of three motivated hunters acting cooperatively. Alone or in pairs, chimps succeed less than 15 percent of the time, but when three or four act as a group, more than half the hunts result in a kill. The chimps seem well aware of the odds; 92 percent of all the hunts we observed were group affairs.

Gombe chimps also hunt red colobus monkeys, but the percentage of group hunts is much lower: only 36 percent. In addition, we learned from Jane Goodall that even when Gombe chimps do hunt in groups, their strategies are different. When Taï chimps arrive under a group of monkeys, the hunters scatter, often silently, usually out of sight of one another but each aware of the others' positions. As the hunt progresses, they gradually close in, encircling the quarry. Such movements require that each chimp coordinate his movements with those of the other hunters, as well as with those of the prey, at all times.

Coordinated hunts account for 63 percent of all those observed at Taï but only 7 percent of those at Gombe. Jane Goodall says that in a Gombe group hunt, the chimpanzees typically travel together until they arrive at a tree with monkeys. Then, as the chimps begin climbing nearby trees, they scatter as each pursues a different target. Goodall gained the impression that Gombe chimps boost their success by hunting independently but simultaneously, thereby disorganizing their prey; our impression is that the Taï chimps owe their success to being organized themselves.

Just why the Gombe and Taï chimps have developed such different hunting strategies is difficult to explain, and we plan to spend some time at Gombe in the hope of finding out. In the meantime, the mere existence of differences is interesting enough and may perhaps force changes in our understanding of human evolution. Most currently accepted theories propose that some three million years ago, a dramatic climate change in Africa east of the Rift Valley turned dense forest into open, drier habitat. Adapting to the difficulties of life under these new conditions, our ancestors supposedly evolved into cooperative hunters and began sharing food they caught. Supporters of this idea point out that plant and animal remains indicative of dry, open environments have been found at all early hominid excavation sites in Tanzania, Kenya, South Africa, and Ethiopia. That the large majority of apes in Africa today live west of the Rift Valley appears to many anthropologists to lend further support to the idea that a change in environment caused the common ancestor of apes and humans to evolve along a different line from those remaining in the forest.

Our observations, however, suggest quite another line of thought. Life in dense, dim forest may require more sophisticated behavior than is commonly assumed: compared with their savanna relatives, Taï chimps show greater complexity in both hunting and tool use. Taï chimps use tools in nineteen different ways and have six different ways of making them, compared with sixteen uses and three methods of manufacture at Gombe.

Anthropologist colleagues of mine have told me that the discovery that some chimpanzees are accomplished users of hammerstones forces them to look with a fresh eye at stone tools turned up at excavation sites. The important role played by female Taï chimps in tool use also raises the possibility that in the course of human evolution, women may have been decisive in the development of many of the sophisticated manipulative skills characteristic of our species. Taï mothers also appear to pass on their skills by actively teaching their offspring. We have observed mothers providing their young with hammers and then stepping in to help when the inexperienced youngsters encounter difficulty. This help may include carefully showing how to position the nut or hold the hammer properly. Such behavior has never been observed at Gombe.

Similarly, food sharing, for a long time said to be unique to humans, seems more general in forest than in savanna chimpanzees. Taï chimp mothers share with their young up to 60 percent of the nuts they open, at least until the latter become sufficiently adept, generally at about six years old. They also share other foods acquired with tools, including honey, ants, and bone marrow. Gombe mothers share such foods much less often, even with their infants. Taï chimps also share meat more frequently than do their Gombe relatives, sometimes dividing a chunk up and giving portions away, sometimes simply allowing beggars to grab pieces.

Any comparison between chimpanzees and our hominid ancestors can only be suggestive, not definitive. But our studies lead us to believe that the process of hominization may have begun independently of the drying of the environment. Savanna life could even have delayed the process; many anthropologists have been struck by how slowly hominid-associated remains, such as the hand ax, changed after their first appearance in the Olduvai age.

Will we have the time to discover more about the hunting strategies or other, perhaps as yet undiscovered abilities of these forest chimpanzees? Africa's tropical rain forests, and their inhabitants, are threatened with extinction by extensive logging, largely to provide the Western world with tropical timber and such products as coffee, cocoa, and rubber. Ivory Coast has lost 90 percent of its original forest, and less than 5 percent of the remainder can be considered pristine. The climate has changed dramatically. The harmattan, a cold, dry wind from the Sahara previously unknown in the forest, has now swept through the Taï forest every year since 1986. Rainfall has diminished; all the rivulets in our study region are now dry for several months of the year.

In addition, the chimpanzee, biologically very close to humans, is in demand for research on AIDS and hepatitis vaccines. Captive-bred chimps are available, but they cost about twenty times more than wild-caught animals. Chimps taken from the wild for these purposes are generally young, their mothers having been shot during capture. For every chimp arriving at its sad destination, nine others may well have died in the forest or on the way. Such priorities—cheap coffee and cocoa and chimpanzees—do not do the economies of Third World countries any good in the long run, and they bring suffering and death to innocent victims in the forest. Our hope is that Brutus, Falstaff, and their families will survive, and that we and others will have the opportunity to learn about them well into the future. But there is no denying that modern times work against them and us.

Critical Thinking

1. To what extent does cooperation and sharing of food exist among the Ivory Coast chimpanzees?

2. What were the researchers interested in at first? What was unique about it? What did they find that was not surprising? What was surprising?

3. What is the purpose of drumming?

4. How do the authors describe the chimps' mental abilities with regard to hammerstones? What manual skills are required? In what respect is there a gender difference in tool use?

5. What is the purpose of the "patrol" into foreign territories?

6. What is their favorite hunting target and why?

7. Describe the hunting strategies. What is the minimum number for success? In what ways do these chimps contrast with the Gombe chimps and what is the partial explanation given?

8. How did chimps and humans diverge, according to most currently accepted theories?

9. How do comparisons between forest-dwelling chimps and the savanna-dwelling Gombe chimps lead the authors to different conclusions from the above? (Include in this the important role of females in tool use and food sharing.)

10. In what ways are chimpanzee populations threatened?

Peace Among Primates

Robert Sapolsky

It used to be thought that humans were the only savagely violent primate. "We are the only species that kills its own," narrators intoned portentously in nature films several decades ago. That view fell by the wayside in the 1960s as it became clear that some other primates kill their fellows aplenty. Males kill; females kill. Some use their tool making skills to fashion bigger and better cudgels. Other primates even engage in what can only be called warfare—organized, proactive group violence directed at other populations.

Yet as field studies of primates expanded, what became most striking was the variation in social practices across species. Yes, some primate species have lives filled with violence, frequent and varied. But life among others is filled with communitarianism, egalitarianism, and cooperative child rearing. Patterns emerged. In less aggressive species, such as gibbons or marmosets, groups tend to live in lush rain forests where food is plentiful and life is easy. Females and males tend to be the same size, and the males lack secondary sexual markers such as long, sharp canines or garish coloring. Couples mate for life, and males help substantially with child care. In violent species, such as baboons and rhesus monkeys, the opposite conditions prevail.

The most disquieting fact about the violent species was the apparent inevitability of their behavior. Certain species seemed simply to be the way they were, fixed products of the interplay of evolution and ecology, and that was that. And although human males might not be inflexibly polygamous or outfitted with bright red butts and six-inch canines designed for tooth-to-tooth combat, it was clear that our species had at least as much in common with the violent primates as with the gentle ones. "In their nature" thus became "in our nature." This was the humans-as-killer-apes theory popularized by the writer Robert Ardrey, according to which humans have as much chance of becoming intrinsically peaceful as they have of growing prehensile tails.

That view always had little more scientific rigor than a Planet of the Apes movie, but it took a great deal of field research to figure out just what should supplant it. After decades' more work, the picture has become quite interesting. Some primate species, it turns out, are indeed simply violent or peaceful, with their behavior driven by their social structures and ecological settings. More importantly, however, some primate species can make peace despite violent traits that seem built into their natures. The challenge now is to figure out under what conditions that can happen, and whether we humans can manage the trick ourselves.

Old Primates and New Tricks

To an overwhelming extent, the age-old "nature versus nurture" debate is silly. The action of genes is completely intertwined with the environment in which they function; in a sense, it is pointless to even discuss what gene X does, and we should consider instead only what gene X does in environment Y. Nonetheless, if one had to predict the behavior of some organism on the basis of only one fact, one might still want to know whether the most useful fact would be about genetics or about the environment.

Two classic studies have shown that primates are somewhat independent from their "natures." In the early 1970s, a highly respected primatologist named Hans Kummer was working in a region of Ethiopia containing two species of baboons with markedly different social systems. Savanna baboons live in large troops, with plenty of adult females and males. Hamadryas baboons, in contrast, have a more complex and quite different multilevel society. When confronted with a threatening male, the females of the two species react differently: A hamadryas baboon placates the male by approaching him, whereas a savanna baboon can only run away if she wants to avoid injury.

Kummer conducted a simple experiment, trapping an adult female savanna baboon and releasing her into a hamadryas troop and trapping an adult female hamadryas and releasing her into a savanna troop. The females who were dropped in among a different species initially carried out their species-typical behavior, a major faux pas in the new neighborhood. But gradually, they absorbed the new rules. How long did this learning take? About an hour. In other words, millennia of genetic differences separating the two species, a lifetime of experience with a crucial social rule for each female—and a miniscule amount of time to reverse course completely.

The second experiment was set up by Frans de Waal of Emory University and his student Denise Johanowicz in the early 1990s, working with two macaque monkey species. By any human standards, male rhesus macaques are unappealing animals. Their hierarchies are rigid, those at the top seize a disproportionate share of the spoils, they enforce this inequity with ferocious aggression, and they rarely reconcile after fights. In contrast, male stump tail macaques, which share almost all of their genes with their rhesus macaque cousins, display much less aggression, looser hierarchies, more egalitarianism, and more behaviors that promote group cohesion.

Working with captive primates, de Waal and Johanowicz created a mixed-sex social group of juvenile macaques, combining rhesus and stump tails together. Remarkably, instead of the rhesus macaques bullying the stump tails, over the course of a few months the rhesus males adopted the stump tails' social style, eventually even matching the stump tails' high rates of reconciliatory behavior. It so happens, moreover, that stump tails and rhesus macaques use different gestures when reconciling. The rhesus macaques in the study did not start using the stump tails' reconciliatory gestures, but rather increased the incidence of their own species-typical gestures. In other words, they were not merely imitating the stump tails' behavior; they were incorporating the concept of frequent reconciliation into their own social practices. Finally, when the newly warm-and-fuzzy rhesus macaques were returned to a larger, all-rhesus group, their new behavioral style persisted.

This is nothing short of extraordinary. But it brings up one further question: When those rhesus macaques were transferred back into the all-rhesus world, did they spread their insights and behaviors to the others? Alas, they did not—at least not within the relatively short time they were studied. For that, we need to move on to a final case.

In the early 1980s, "Forest Troop," a group of savanna baboons I had been studying—virtually living with—for years, was going about its business in a national park in Kenya when a neighboring baboon group had a stroke of luck: Its territory encompassed a tourist lodge that expanded its operations and, consequently, so did the amount of food tossed into its garbage dump. Baboons are omnivorous, and this "Garbage Dump Troop" was delighted to feast on leftover drumsticks, half-eaten hamburgers, remnants of chocolate cake, and anything else that wound up there. Soon they had shifted to sleeping in the trees immediately above the pit, descending each morning just in time for the day's dumping of garbage. (They soon got quite obese from the rich diet and lack of exercise, but that is another story.) The development produced nearly as dramatic a shift in the social behavior of Forest Troop. Each morning, approximately half of its adult males would infiltrate Garbage Dump Troop's territory, descending on the pit in time for the day's dumping and battling the resident males for access to the garbage. The particular Forest Troop males who did this shared two traits: They were especially combative (which was necessary to get the food away from the other baboons), and they were not very interested in socializing (the raids took place early in the morning, during the hours when the bulk of a savanna baboon's daily communal grooming occurs).

Soon afterward, tuberculosis, a disease that moves with devastating speed and severity in nonhuman primates, broke out in Garbage Dump Troop. Over the next year, most of its members died, as did all of the males from Forest Troop who had foraged at the dump. (Considerable sleuthing ultimately revealed that the disease had come from tainted meat in the garbage dump. There was little animal-to-animal transmission of the tuberculosis, and so the disease did not spread in Forest Troop beyond the garbage eaters.) The results were that Forest Troop was left with males who were less aggressive and more social than average, and the troop now had double its previous female-to-male ratio.

The social consequences of these changes were dramatic. There remained a hierarchy among the Forest Troop males, but it was far looser than before. Compared with other, more typical savanna baboon groups, high-ranking males rarely harassed subordinates and occasionally even relinquished contested resources to them. Aggression was less frequent, particularly against third parties. And rates of affiliative behaviors, such as males and females grooming each other or sitting together, soared. There were even instances, now and then, of adult males grooming each other—a behavior nearly as unprecedented as baboons sprouting wings.

This unique social milieu did not arise merely as a function of the skewed sex ratio (with half the males having died); other primatologists have occasionally reported on troops with similar ratios but without a comparable social atmosphere. What was key was not just the predominance of females but the type of male who remained. The demographic disaster—what evolutionary biologists term a "selective bottleneck"—had produced a savanna baboon troop quite different from what most experts would have anticipated. But the largest surprise did not come until some years later. Female savanna baboons spend their lives in the troop into which they are born, whereas males leave their birth troop around puberty; a troop's adult males have thus all grown up elsewhere and immigrated as adolescents. By the early 1990s, none of the original low aggression/high affiliation males of Forest Troop's tuberculosis period was still alive; all of the group's adult males had joined after the epidemic. Despite this, the troop's unique social milieu persisted—as it does to this day, some 20 years after the selective bottleneck. In other words, adolescent males that enter Forest Troop after having grown up elsewhere wind up adopting the unique behavioral style of the resident males. As defined by both anthropologists and animal behaviorists, "culture" consists of local behavioral variations, occurring for nongenetic and nonecological reasons that last beyond the time of their originators. Forest Troop's low aggression/high affiliation society constitutes nothing less than a multigenerational benign culture.

Continuous study of the troop has yielded some insights into how its culture is transmitted to newcomers. Genetics obviously plays no role, nor apparently does self-selection: Adolescent males that transfer into the troop are no different from those that transfer into other troops, displaying on arrival similarly high rates of aggression and low rates of affiliation. Nor is there evidence that new males are taught to act in benign ways by the residents. One cannot rule out the possibility that some observational learning is occurring, but it is difficult to detect, given that the distinctive feature of this culture is not the performance of a unique behavior but the performance of typical behaviors at atypically extreme rates.

To date, the most interesting hint about the mechanism of transmission is the way recently transferred males are treated by Forest Troop's resident females. In a typical savanna baboon troop, newly transferred adolescent males spend years slowly working their way into the social fabric; they are extremely low ranking—ignored by females and noted by adult males only as convenient targets for aggression. In Forest Troop, by contrast, new male transfers are inundated with female attention soon after their arrival. Resident females first present themselves sexually to new males an average of 18 days after the males arrive, and they first groom the new males an average of 20 days after they arrive, whereas normal savanna baboons introduce such behaviors after 63 and 78 days, respectively. Furthermore, these welcoming gestures occur more frequently in Forest Troop during the early post-transfer period, and there is four times as much grooming of males by females in Forest Troop as elsewhere. From almost the moment they arrive, in other words, new males find out that in Forest Troop, things are done differently.

At present, I think the most plausible explanation is that this troop's special culture is not passed on actively but simply emerges, facilitated by the actions of the resident members. Living in a group with half the typical number of males, and with the males being nice guys to boot, Forest Troop's females become more relaxed and less wary. (This is so, in part, because in a typical baboon troop, a male who loses a dominance interaction with another male will often attack a female in frustration.) As a result, they are more willing to take a chance and reach out socially to new arrivals, even if the new guys are typical jerky adolescents at first. The new males, in turn, finding themselves treated so well, eventually relax and adopt the behaviors of the troop's distinctive social milieu.

Natural Born Killers?

Are there any lessons to be learned here that can be applied to human-on-human violence apart, that is, from the possible desirability of giving fatal cases of tuberculosis to aggressive people? Can human behavior be as malleable and as peaceful as Forest Troops? Any biological anthropologist opining about human behavior is required by long-established tradition to note that for 99 percent of human history, humans lived in small, stable bands of related hunter-gatherers. Game theorists have shown that a small, cohesive group is the perfect setting for the emergence of cooperation: The identities of the other participants are known, there are opportunities to play games together repeatedly (and thus the ability to punish cheaters), and there is open-book play (players can acquire reputations). And so, those hunter-gatherer bands were highly egalitarian. Empirical and experimental data have also shown the cooperative advantages of small groups at the opposite human extreme, namely in the corporate world.

But the lack of violence within small groups can come at a heavy price. Small homogeneous groups with shared values can be a nightmare of conformity. They can also be dangerous

for outsiders. Unconsciously emulating the murderous border patrols of closely related male chimps, militaries throughout history have sought to form small, stable units; inculcate them with rituals of pseudo kinship; and thereby produce efficient, cooperative killing machines.

Is it possible to achieve the cooperative advantages of a small group without having the group reflexively view outsiders as the Other? One often encounters pessimism in response to this question, based on the notion that humans, as primates, are hard-wired for xenophobia. Some brain-imaging studies have appeared to support this view in a particularly discouraging way. There is a structure deep inside the brain called the amygdala, which plays a key role in fear and aggression, and experiments have shown that when subjects are presented with a face of someone from a different race, the amygdala gets metabolically active, aroused, alert, ready for action. This happens even when the face is presented subliminally, which is to say, so rapidly that the subject does not consciously see it.

More recent studies, however, should mitigate this pessimism. Test a person who has a lot of experience with people of different races, and the amygdala does not activate. Or, as in a wonderful experiment by Susan Fiske, of Princeton University, subtly bias the subject beforehand to think of people as individuals rather than as members of a group, and the amygdala does not budge. Humans may be hard-wired to get edgy around the Other, but our views on who falls into that category are decidedly malleable. In the early 1960s, a rising star of primatology, Irven DeVore of Harvard University, published the first general overview of the subject. Discussing his own specialty, savanna baboons, he wrote that they "have acquired an aggressive temperament as a defense against predators, and aggressiveness cannot be turned on and off like a faucet. It is an integral part of the monkeys' personalities, so deeply rooted that it makes them potential aggressors in every situation. Thus the savanna baboon became, literally, a textbook example of life in an aggressive, highly stratified, male-dominated society. Yet in my observation of Forest Troop, I saw members of that same species demonstrate enough behavioral plasticity to transform their society into a baboon utopia.

The first half of the twentieth century was drenched in the blood spilled by German and Japanese aggression, yet only a few decades later it is hard to think of two countries more pacific. Sweden spent the 17th century rampaging through Europe, yet it is now an icon of nurturing tranquility. Humans have invented the small nomadic band and the continental mega state, and have demonstrated flexibility whereby uprooted descendants of the former can function effectively in the latter. We lack the type of physiology or anatomy that in other mammals determine their mating system, and have come up with societies based on monogamy, polygyny, and polyandry. And we have fashioned some religions in which violent acts are the entrance to paradise and other religions in which the same acts consign one to hell. Is a world of peacefully coexisting human Forest Troops possible? Anyone who says, "No, it is beyond our nature," knows too little about primates, including ourselves.

Critical Thinking

1. What have we found out about primates killing their own kind?

2. How have our views with respect to violence among humans and primates changed over the years?

3. What has been the most disquieting fact about violent species? How have decades of field research made the picture "quiet interesting"?

4. Why does the author call the "nature versus nurture" debate "silly"?

5. Be familiar with the lessons learned from the two classic studies cited regarding primate violence.

6. How and why did the "Forest Troop" baboons develop a low aggression/high affiliation society?

7. How did the continuous study of the Forest Troop yield insights into the culture transmission of low aggression/high affiliation behavior?

8. What evidence is there that human behavior is as malleable and as peaceful as that of the Forest Troop?

ROBERT M. SAPOLSKY, PhD, is the John A. and Cynthia Fry Gunn Professor of Biological Sciences and a professor of neurology and neurological sciences at Stanford University. He wrote the classic *Why Zebras Don't Get Ulcers: An Updated Guide to Stress, Stress Related Diseases and Coping.* His most recent book is *Monkeyluv: And Other Essays on Our Lives as Animals.*

Originally appeared in *Greater Good,* April 5, 12, 19, 2008. Copyright © 2008 by Greater Good Science Center at the University of California, Berkeley. Reprinted by permission. http://greatergood.berkeley.edu.

UNIT 3

Sex and Gender

Unit Selections

Learning Outcomes

After reading this Unit, you will be able to:

- Explain why friendship is important to olive baboons and determine the implications for the origin of pair-bonding.

- Discuss the circumstances in which long-term male-female bonds form.

- Discuss how the study of bonobo sexual behavior helps us understand human evolution.

- Discuss the pros and cons of the theory of "hidden heat."

- Explain how social bonds help provide protection against abusive male apes for female apes.

- Discuss the ways in which women's reproductive cycles shape the everyday behavior between men and women.

- Explain how and why a woman's reproductive cycle affects her preferences, perceptions, and behavior with respect to men.

Student Website

www.mhhe.com/cls

Internet References

American Scientist
www.americanscientist.org
The Kinsey Institute
www.kinseyinstitute.org/about
Sexuality Studies
https://sxs.sfsu.edu
Sexuality Studies.net
http://sexualitystudies.net/programs

Any account of hominid evolution would be remiss if it did not attempt to explain that which is the most mystifying of all human experiences—our sexuality. No other aspect of humanity—whether it be upright posture, tool-making ability, or intelligence in general—seems to elude our intellectual grasp at least as much as it dominates our subjective consciousness. While we are a long way from reaching a consensus as to why it arose and what it is all about, there is widespread agreement that our very preoccupation with sex is, in itself, one of the hallmarks of being human. Even as we experience it and analyze it, we exalt it and condemn it. Beyond seemingly irrational fixations, however, there is the further tendency to project our own values onto the observations we make and the data we collect.

There are many who argue, quite reasonably, that the human bias has been more male-oriented than otherwise and that the recent "feminization" of anthropology has resulted in new kinds of research and refreshingly new, theoretical perspectives. Not only should we consider the source when evaluating the old theories, but we should also welcome the source when considering the new.

One reason for studying the sexual and social lives of primates is that they allow us to test certain notions too often taken for granted. For instance, Barbara Smuts, in "What Are Friends For?" reveals that friendship bonds, as illustrated by the olive baboons of East Africa, have little if anything to do with a sex-based division of labor or with sexual exclusivity between a pair-bonded male and female. Smuts challenges the traditional male-oriented idea that primate societies are dominated solely by males and for males.

With the understanding of primate social and sexual lives as a backdrop, we are better able to understand ourselves. As Annie Murphy Paul (in "The Double Life of Women") shows us, women do in fact provide clues as to the timing of ovulation, the moment when an egg is released and ready to be fertilized. Moreover, when she shops for a mate, she is searching for the best genes possible, but after she has had offspring, her preference shifts to males who are willing and able to share resources and protection for her and her offspring.

© Brand X Pictures/Punchstock

Finally, there is the question of the social significance of sexuality in humans. In "Mothers and Others," Sarah Blaffer Hrdy points out that reproductive success often depends upon how much assistance the mother gets from others, including males. In "What's Love Got to Do with It?: Sex Among Our Closest Relatives Is a Rather Open Affair," Meredith Small shows that the chimp-like bonobos of Zaire use sex to reduce tensions and cement social relations and, in so doing, have achieved a high degree of equality between the sexes. Whether we see parallels in the human species, says Small, depends on our willingness to interpret bonobo behavior as a "modern version of our own ancestors' sex play," and this, in turn, may depend on our prior theoretical beliefs.

What Are Friends For?

Among East African baboons, friendship means companions, health, safety . . . and, sometimes, sex.

BARBARA SMUTS

Virgil, a burly adult male olive baboon, closely followed Zizi, a middle-aged female easily distinguished by her grizzled coat and square muzzle. On her rump Zizi sported a bright pink swelling, indicating that she was sexually receptive and probably fertile. Virgil's extreme attentiveness to Zizi suggested to me—and all rival males in the troop—that he was her current and exclusive mate.

Zizi, however, apparently had something else in mind. She broke away from Virgil, moved rapidly through the troop, and presented her alluring sexual swelling to one male after another. Before Virgil caught up with her, she had managed to announce her receptive condition to several of his rivals. When Virgil tried to grab her, Zizi screamed and dashed into the bushes with Virgil in hot pursuit. I heard sounds of chasing and fighting coming from the thicket. Moments later Zizi emerged from the bushes with an older male named Cyclops. They remained together for several days, copulating often. In Cyclops's presence, Zizi no longer approached or even glanced at other males.

Primatologists describe Zizi and other olive baboons (*Papio cynocephalus anubis*) as promiscuous, meaning that both males and females usually mate with several members of the opposite sex within a short period of time. Promiscuous mating behavior characterizes many of the larger, more familiar primates, including chimpanzees, rhesus macaques, and gray langurs, as well as olive, yellow, and chacma baboons, the three subspecies of savanna baboon. In colloquial usage, promiscuity often connotes wanton and random sex, and several early studies of primates supported this stereotype. However, after years of laboriously recording thousands of copulations under natural conditions, the Peeping Toms of primate fieldwork have shown that, even in promiscuous species, sexual pairings are far from random.

Some adult males, for example, typically copulate much more often than others. Primatologists have explained these differences in terms of competition: the most dominant males monopolize females and prevent lower-ranking rivals from mating. But exceptions are frequent. Among baboons, the exceptions often involve scruffy, older males who mate in full view of younger, more dominant rivals.

A clue to the reason for these puzzling exceptions emerged when primatologists began to question an implicit assumption of the dominance hypothesis—that females were merely passive objects of male competition. But what if females were active arbiters in this system? If females preferred some males over others and were able to express these preferences, then models of mating activity based on male dominance alone would be far too simple.

Once researchers recognized the possibility of female choice, evidence for it turned up in species after species. The story of Zizi, Virgil, and Cyclops is one of hundreds of examples of female primates rejecting the sexual advances of particular males and enthusiastically cooperating with others. But what is the basis for female choice? Why might they prefer some males over others?

This question guided my research on the Eburru Cliffs troop of olive baboons, named after one of their favorite sleeping sites, a sheer rocky outcrop rising several hundred feet above the floor of the Great Rift Valley, about 100 miles northwest of Nairobi, Kenya. The 120 members of Eburru Cliffs spent their days wandering through open grassland studded with occasional acacia thorn trees. Each night they retired to one of a dozen sets of cliffs that provided protection from nocturnal predators such as leopards.

Most previous studies of baboon sexuality had focused on females who, like Zizi, were at the peak of sexual receptivity. A female baboon does not mate when she is pregnant or lactating, a period of abstinence lasting about eighteen months. The female then goes into estrus, and for about two weeks out of every thirty-five-day cycle, she mates. Toward the end of this two-week period she may ovulate, but usually the female undergoes four or five estrous cycles before she conceives. During pregnancy, she once again resumes a chaste existence. As a result, the typical female baboon is sexually active for less than 10 percent of her adult life. I thought that by focusing on the other 90 percent, I might learn something new. In particular, I suspected that routine, day-to-day relationships between males and pregnant or lactating (nonestrous) females might provide clues to female mating preferences.

Nearly every day for sixteen months, I joined the Eburru Cliffs baboons at their sleeping cliffs at dawn and traveled several miles with them while they foraged for roots, seeds, grass, and occasionally, small prey items, such as baby gazelles or hares (see "Predatory Baboons of Kekopey," *Natural History,* March 1976). Like all savanna baboon troops, Eburru Cliffs functioned as a cohesive unit organized around a core of related females, all of whom were born in the troop. Unlike the females, male savanna baboons leave their natal troop to join another where they may remain for many years, so most of the Eburru Cliffs adult males were immigrants. Since membership in the troop remained relatively constant during the period of my study, I learned to identify each individual. I relied on differences in size, posture, gait, and especially, facial features. To the practiced observer, baboons look as different from one another as human beings do.

As soon as I could recognize individuals, I noticed that particular females tended to turn up near particular males again and again. I came to think of these pairs as friends. Friendship among animals is not a well-documented phenomenon, so to convince skeptical colleagues that baboon friendship was real, I needed to develop objective criteria for distinguishing friendly pairs.

I began by investigating grooming, the amiable simian habit of picking through a companion's fur to remove dead skin and ectoparasites (see "Little Things That Tick Off Baboons," *Natural History,* February 1984). Baboons spend much more time grooming than is necessary for hygiene, and previous research had indicated that it is a good measure of social bonds.

Although eighteen adult males lived in the troop, each nonestrous female performed most of her grooming with just one, two, or occasionally, three males. For example, of Zizi's twenty-four grooming bouts with males, Cyclops accounted for thirteen, and a second male, Sherlock, accounted for all the rest. Different females tended to favor different males as grooming partners.

Another measure of social bonds was simply who was observed near whom. When foraging, traveling, or resting, each pregnant or lactating female spent a lot of time near a few males and associated with the others no more often than expected by chance. When I compared the identities of favorite grooming partners and frequent companions, they overlapped almost completely. This enabled me to develop a formal definition of friendship: any male that scored high on both grooming and proximity measures was considered a friend.

Virtually all baboons made friends; only one female and three males who had most recently joined the troop lacked such companions. Out of more than 600 possible adult female–adult male pairs in the troop, however, only about one in ten qualified as friends; these really were special relationships.

Several factors seemed to influence which baboons paired up. In most cases, friends were unrelated to each other, since the male had immigrated from another troop. (Four friendships, however, involved a female and an adolescent son who had not yet emigrated. Unlike other friends, these related pairs never mated.) Older females tended to be friends with older males; younger females with younger males. I witnessed occasional May–December romances, usually involving older females and young adult males. Adolescent males and females were strongly rule-bound, and with the exception of mother-son pairs, they formed friendships only with one another.

Regardless of age or dominance rank, most females had just one or two male friends. But among males, the number of female friends varied greatly from none to eight. Although high-ranking males enjoyed priority of access to food and sometimes mates, dominant males did not have more female friends than low-ranking males. Instead it was the older males who had lived in the troop for many years who had the most friends. When a male had several female friends, the females were often closely related to one another. Since female baboons spend a lot of time near their kin, it is probably easier for a male to maintain bonds with several related females at once.

When collecting data, I focused on one nonestrous female at a time and kept track of her every movement toward or away from any male; similarly, I noted every male who moved toward or away from her. Whenever the female and male moved close enough to exchange intimacies, I wrote down exactly what happened. When foraging together, friends tended to remain a few yards apart. Males more often wandered away from females than the reverse, and females, more often than males, closed the gap. The female behaved as if she wanted to keep the male within calling distance, in case she needed his protection. The male, however, was more likely to make approaches that brought them within actual touching distance. Often, he would plunk himself down right next to his friend and ask her to groom him by holding a pose with exaggerated stillness. The female sometimes responded by grooming, but more often, she exhibited the most reliable sign of true intimacy: she ignored her friend and simply continued whatever she was doing.

In sharp contrast, when a male who was not a friend moved close to a female, she dared not ignore him. She stopped whatever she was doing and held still, often glancing surreptitiously at the intruder. If he did not move away, she sometimes lifted her tail and presented her rump. When a female is not in estrus, this is a gesture of appeasement, not sexual enticement. Immediately after this respectful acknowledgement of his presence, the female would slip away. But such tense interactions with nonfriend males were rare, because females usually moved away before the males came too close.

These observations suggest that females were afraid of most of the males in their troop, which is not surprising: male baboons are twice the size of females, and their canines are longer and sharper than those of a lion. All Eburru Cliffs males directed both mild and severe aggression toward females. Mild aggression, which usually involved threats and chases but no body contact, occurred most often during feeding competition or when the male redirected aggression toward a female after losing a fight with another male. Females and juveniles showed aggression toward other females and juveniles in similar circumstances and occasionally inflicted superficial wounds. Severe aggression by males, which involved body contact and sometimes biting, was less common and also more puzzling, since there was no apparent cause.

An explanation for at least some of these attacks emerged one day when I was watching Pegasus, a young adult male, and his friend Cicily, sitting together in the middle of a small clearing. Cicily moved to the edge of the clearing to feed, and a higher-ranking female, Zora, suddenly attacked her. Pegasus stood up and looked as if he were about to intervene when both females disappeared into the bushes. He sat back down, and I remained with him. A full ten minutes later, Zora appeared at the edge of the clearing; this was the first time she had come into view since her attack on Cicily. Pegasus instantly pounced on Zora, repeatedly grabbed her neck in his mouth and lifted her off the ground, shook her whole body, and then dropped her. Zora screamed continuously and tried to escape. Each time, Pegasus caught her and continued his brutal attack. When he finally released her five minutes later she had a deep canine gash on the palm of her hand that made her limp for several days.

This attack was similar in form and intensity to those I had seen before and labeled "unprovoked." Certainly, had I come upon the scene after Zora's aggression toward Cicily, I would not have understood why Pegasus attacked Zora. This suggested that some, perhaps many, severe attacks by males actually represented punishment for actions that had occurred some time before.

Whatever the reasons for male attacks on females, they represent a serious threat. Records of fresh injuries indicated that Eburru Cliffs adult females received canine slash wounds from males at the rate of one for every female each year, and during my study, one female died of her injuries. Males probably pose an even greater threat to infants. Although only one infant was killed during my study, observers in Botswana and Tanzania have seen recent male immigrants kill several young infants.

Protection from male aggression, and from the less injurious but more frequent aggression of other females and juveniles, seems to be one of the main advantages of friendship for a female baboon. Seventy times I observed an adult male defend a female or her offspring against aggression by another troop member, not infrequently a high-ranking male. In all but six of these cases, the defender was a friend. Very few of these confrontations involved actual fighting; no male baboon, subordinate or dominant, is anxious to risk injury by the sharp canines of another.

Males are particularly solicitous guardians of their friends' youngest infants. If another male gets too close to an infant or if a juvenile female plays with it too roughly, the friend may intervene. Other troop members soon learn to be cautious when the mother's friend is nearby, and his presence provides the mother with a welcome respite from the annoying pokes and prods of curious females and juveniles obsessed with the new baby. Male baboons at Gombe Park in Tanzania and Amboseli Park in Kenya have also been seen rescuing infants from chimpanzees and lions. These several forms of male protection help to explain why females in Eburru Cliffs stuck closer to their friends in the first few months after giving birth than at any other time.

The male–infant relationship develops out of the male's friendship with the mother, but as the infant matures, this new bond takes on a life of its own. My co-worker Nancy Nicolson found that by about nine months of age, infants actively sought out their male friends when the mother was a few yards away, suggesting that the male may function as an alternative care-giver. This seemed to be especially true for infants undergoing unusually early or severe weaning. (Weaning is generally a gradual, prolonged process, but there is tremendous variation among mothers in the timing and intensity of weaning. See "Mother Baboons," *Natural History*, September 1980). After being rejected by the mother, the crying infant often approached the male friend and sat huddled against him until its whimpers subsided.

Two of the infants in Eburru Cliffs lost their mothers when they were still quite young. In each case, their bond with the mother's friend subsequently intensified, and—perhaps as a result—both infants survived.

A close bond with a male may also improve the infant's nutrition. Larger than all other troop members, adult males monopolize the best feeding sites. In general, the personal space surrounding a feeding male is inviolate, but he usually tolerates intrusions by the infants of his female friends, giving them access to choice feeding spots.

Although infants follow their male friends around rather than the reverse, the males seem genuinely attached to their tiny companions. During feeding, the male and infant express their pleasure in each other's company by sharing spirited, antiphonal grunting duets. If the infant whimpers in distress, the male friend is likely to cease feeding, look at the infant, and grunt softly, as if in sympathy, until the whimpers cease. When the male rests, the infants of his female friends may huddle behind him, one after the other, forming a "train," or, if feeling energetic, they may use his body as a trampoline.

When I returned to Eburru Cliffs four years after my initial study ended, several of the bonds formed between males and the infants of their female friends were still intact (in other cases, either the male or the infant or both had disappeared). When these bonds involved recently matured females, their long-time male associates showed no sexual interest in them, even though the females mated with other adult males. Mothers and sons, and usually maternal siblings, show similar sexual inhibitions in baboons and many other primate species.

The development of an intimate relationship between a male and the infant of his female friend raises an obvious question: Is the male the infant's father? To answer this question definitely we would need to conduct genetic analysis, which was not possible for these baboons. Instead, I estimated paternity probabilities from observations of the temporary (a few hours or days) exclusive mating relationships, or consortships, that estrous females form with a series of different males. These estimates were apt to be fairly accurate, since changes in the female's sexual swelling allow one to pinpoint the timing of conception to within a few days. Most females consorted with only two or three males during this period, and these males were termed likely fathers.

In about half the friendships, the male was indeed likely to be the father of his friend's most recent infant, but in the other half he was not—in fact, he had never been seen mating with the female. Interestingly, males who were friends with the mother but not likely fathers nearly always developed a relationship with her infant, while males who had mated with the female but were not her friend usually did not. Thus friendship with the mother, rather than paternity, seems to mediate the development of male–infant bonds. Recently, a similar pattern was documented for South American capuchin monkeys in a laboratory study in which paternity was determined genetically.

These results fly in the face of a prominent theory that claims males will invest in infants only when they are closely related. If males are not fostering the survival of their own genes by caring for the infant, then why do they do so? I suspected that the key was female choice. If females preferred to mate with males who had already demonstrated friendly behavior, then friendships with mothers and their infants might pay off in the future when the mothers were ready to mate again.

To find out if this was the case, I examined each male's sexual behavior with females he had befriended before they resumed estrus. In most cases, males consorted considerably more often with their friends than with other females. Baboon females typically mate with several different males, including both friends and nonfriends, but prior friendship increased a male's probability of mating with a female above what it would have been otherwise.

This increased probability seemed to reflect female preferences. Females occasionally overtly advertised their disdain for certain males and their desire for others. Zizi's behavior, described above, is a good example. Virgil was not one of her friends, but Cyclops was. Usually, however, females expressed preferences and aversions more subtly. For example, Delphi, a petite adolescent female, found herself pursued by Hector, a middle-aged adult male. She did not run away or refuse to mate with him, but whenever he wasn't watching, she looked around for her friend Homer, an adolescent male. When she succeeded in catching Homer's eye, she narrowed her eyes and flattened her ears against her skull, the friendliest face one baboon can send another. This told Homer she would rather be with him. Females expressed satisfaction with a current consort partner by staying close to him, initiating copulations, and not making advances toward other males. Baboons are very sensitive to such cues, as indicated by an experimental study in which rival hamadryas baboons rarely challenged a male–female pair if the female strongly preferred her current partner. Similarly, in Eburru Cliffs, males were less apt to challenge consorts involving a pair that shared a long-term friendship.

Even though females usually consorted with their friends, they also mated with other males, so it is not surprising that friendships were most vulnerable during periods of sexual activity. In a few cases, the female consorted with another male more often than with her friend, but the friendship survived nevertheless. One female, however, formed a strong sexual bond with a new male. This bond persisted after conception, replacing her previous friendship. My observations suggest that adolescent and young adult females tend to have shorter, less stable friendships than do older females. Some friendships, however, last a very long time. When I returned to Eburru Cliffs six years after my study began, five couples were still together. It is possible that friendships occasionally last for life (baboons probably live twenty to thirty years in the wild), but it will require longer studies, and some very patient scientists to find out.

By increasing both the male's chances of mating in the future and the likelihood that a female's infant will survive, friendship contributes to the reproductive success of both partners. This clarifies the evolutionary basis of friendship-forming tendencies in baboons, but what does friendship mean to a baboon? To answer this question we need to view baboons as sentient beings with feelings and goals not unlike our own in similar circumstances. Consider, for example, the friendship between Thalia and Alexander.

The affair began one evening as Alex and Thalia sat about fifteen feet apart on the sleeping cliffs. It was like watching two novices in a singles bar. Alex stared at Thalia until she turned and almost caught him looking at her. He glanced away immediately, and then she stared at him until his head began to turn toward her. She suddenly became engrossed in grooming her toes. But as soon as Alex looked away, her gaze returned to him. They went on like this for more than fifteen minutes, always with split-second timing. Finally, Alex managed to catch Thalia looking at him. He made the friendly eyes-narrowed, ears-back face and smacked his lips together rhythmically. Thalia froze, and for a second she looked into his eyes. Alex approached, and Thalia, still nervous, groomed him. Soon she calmed down, and I found them still together on the cliffs the next morning. Looking back on this event months later, I realized that it marked the beginning of their friendship. Six years later, when I returned to Eburru Cliffs, they were still friends.

If flirtation forms an integral part of baboon friendship, so does jealousy. Overt displays of jealousy, such as chasing a friend away from a potential rival, occur occasionally, but like humans, baboons often express their emotions in more subtle ways. One evening a colleague and I climbed the cliffs and settled down near Sherlock, who was friends with Cybelle, a middle-aged female still foraging on the ground below the cliffs. I observed Cybelle while my colleague watched Sherlock, and we kept up a running commentary. As long as Cybelle was feeding or interacting with females, Sherlock was relaxed, but each time she approached another male, his body would stiffen, and he would stare intently at the scene below. When Cybelle presented politely to a male who had recently tried to befriend her, Sherlock even made threatening sounds under his breath. Cybelle was not in estrus at the time, indicating that male baboon jealousy extends beyond the sexual arena to include affiliative interactions between a female friend and other males.

Because baboon friendships are embedded in a network of friendly and antagonistic relationships, they inevitably lead to repercussions extending beyond the pair. For example, Virgil once provoked his weaker rival Cyclops into a fight by first attacking Cyclops's friend Phoebe. On another occasion, Sherlock chased Circe, Hector's best friend, just after Hector had chased Antigone, Sherlock's friend.

In another incident, the prime adult male Triton challenged Cyclops's possession of meat. Cyclops grew increasingly tense and seemed about to abandon the prey to the younger male. Then Cyclops's friend Phoebe appeared with her infant Phyllis. Phyllis wandered over to Cyclops. He immediately grabbed her, held her close, and threatened Triton away from the prey. Because any challenge to Cyclops now involved a threat to Phyllis as well, Triton risked being mobbed by Phoebe and her relatives and friends. For this reason, he backed down. Males frequently use the infants of their female friends as buffers in this way. Thus, friendship involves costs as well as benefits because it makes the participants vulnerable to social manipulation or redirected aggression by others.

Finally, as with humans, friendship seems to mean something different to each baboon. Several females in Eburru Cliffs had only one friend. They were devoted companions. Louise and Pandora, for example, groomed their friend Virgil and no other male. Then there was Leda, who, with five friends, spread herself more thinly than any other female. These contrasting patterns of friendship were associated with striking personality differences. Louise and Pandora were unobtrusive females who hung around quietly with Virgil and their close relatives. Leda seemed to be everywhere at once, playing with infants, fighting with juveniles, and making friends with males. Similar differences were apparent among the males. Some devoted a great deal of time and energy to cultivating friendships with females, while others focused more on challenging other males. Although we probably will never fully understand the basis of these individual differences, they contribute immeasurably to the richness and complexity of baboon society.

Male–female friendships may be widespread among primates. They have been reported for many other groups of savanna baboons, and they also occur in rhesus and Japanese Macaques, capuchin monkeys, and perhaps in bonobos (pygmy chimpanzees). These relationships should give us pause when considering popular scenarios for the evolution of male–female relationships in humans. Most of these scenarios assume that, except for mating, males and females had little to do with one another until the development of a sexual division of labor, when, the story goes, females began to rely on males to provide meat in exchange for gathered food. This, it has been argued, set up new selection pressures favoring the development of long-term bonds between individual males and females, female sexual fidelity, and as paternity certainty increased, greater male investment in the offspring of these unions. In other words, once women began to gather and men to hunt, presto—we had the nuclear family.

This scenario may have more to do with cultural biases about women's economic dependence on men and idealized views of the nuclear family than with the actual behavior of our hominid ancestors. The nonhuman primate evidence challenges this story in at least three ways.

First, long-term bonds between the sexes can evolve in the absence of a sexual division of labor of food sharing. In our primate relatives, such relationships rest on exchanges of social, not economic, benefits.

Second, primate research shows that highly differentiated, emotionally intense male–female relationships can occur without sexual exclusivity. Ancestral men and women may have experienced intimate friendships long before they invented marriage and norms of sexual fidelity.

Third, among our closest primate relatives, males clearly provide mothers and infants with social benefits even when they are unlikely to be the fathers of those infants. In return, females provide a variety of benefits to the friendly males, including acceptance into the group and, at least in baboons, increased mating opportunities in the future. This suggests that efforts to reconstruct the evolution of hominid societies may have overemphasized what the female must supposedly do (restrict her mating to just one male) in order to obtain male parental investment.

Maybe it is time to pay more attention to what the male must do (provide benefits to females and young) in order to obtain female cooperation. Perhaps among our ancestors, as in baboons today, sex and friendship went hand in hand. As for marriage—well, that's another story.

Critical Thinking

1. How have primatologists typically described the sexual behavior of olive baboons? In what sense is this description a stereotype?

2. How have primatologists explained the fact that some males copulate more than others? What has been the explicit assumption? How does the alternative view help to explain the apparent exceptions?

3. Why did the author choose not to focus simply upon females in estrus?

4. How does the author describe the typical baboon troop? How does she measure friendship? What proportion of the possible relationships actually constituted friendship?

5. What factors influenced friendship?

6. Describe the behavior patterns of friends.

7. Why are females afraid of most males in their troop?

8. What advantages does friendship bring to females and to their infants?

9. Does paternity have anything to do with a male's relationship with his female friend's infant? Explain.

10. According to Smuts, why do males care for the infants of their female friends?

11. In what ways do females express preference for certain male friends? Do other males tend to honor this preference?

12. Which baboons tend to have shorter, less stable friendships?

13. How does friendship increase the reproductive success of both partners?

14. Discuss flirtation and jealousy among baboons.

15. Why does the author say that friendship involves a network of relationships that result in repercussions extending beyond the pair?

16. To what extent is friendship something different to each baboon?

17. What has been the assumption of popular scenarios regarding the evolution of male–female relationships? In what ways does the author challenge this story?

What's Love Got to Do with It?

Sex Among Our Closest Relatives Is a Rather Open Affair

MEREDITH F. SMALL

Maiko and Lana are having sex. Maiko is on top, and Lana's arms and legs are wrapped tightly around his waist. Lina, a friend of Lana's, approaches from the right and taps Maiko on the back, nudging him to finish. As he moves away, Lina enfolds Lana in her arms, and they roll over so that Lana is now on top. The two females rub their genitals together, grinning and screaming in pleasure.

This is no orgy staged for an X-rated movie. It doesn't even involve people—or rather, it involves them only as observers. Lana, Maiko, and Lina are bonobos, a rare species of chimplike ape in which frequent couplings and casual sex play characterize every social relationship—between males and females, members of the same sex, closely related animals, and total strangers. Primatologists are beginning to study the bonobos' unrestrained sexual behavior for tantalizing clues to the origins of our own sexuality.

In reconstructing how early man and woman behaved, researchers have generally looked not to bonobos but to common chimpanzees. Only about 5 million years ago human beings and chimps shared a common ancestor, and we still have much behavior in common: namely, a long period of infant dependency, a reliance on learning what to eat and how to obtain food, social bonds that persist over generations, and the need to deal as a group with many everyday conflicts. The assumption has been that chimp behavior today may be similar to the behavior of human ancestors.

Bonobo behavior, however, offers another window on the past because they, too, shared our 5-million-year-old ancestor, diverging from chimps just 2 million years ago. Bonobos have been less studied than chimps for the simple reason that they are difficult to find. They live only on a small patch of land in Zaire, in central Africa. They were first identified, on the basis of skeletal material, in the 1920s, but it wasn't until the 1970s that their behavior in the wild was studied, and then only sporadically.

Bonobos, also known as pygmy chimpanzees, are not really pygmies but welterweights. The largest males are as big as chimps, and the females of the two species are the same size. But bonobos are more delicate in build, and their arms and legs are long and slender.

On the ground, moving from fruit tree to fruit tree, bonobos often stand and walk on two legs—behavior that makes them seem more like humans than chimps. In some ways their sexual behavior seems more human as well, suggesting that in the sexual arena, at least, bonobos are the more appropriate ancestral model. Males and females frequently copulate face-to-face, which is an uncommon position in animals other than humans. Males usually mount females from behind, but females seem to prefer sex face-to-face. "Sometimes the female will let a male start to mount from behind," says Amy Parish, a graduate student at the University of California at Davis who's been watching female bonobo sexual behavior in several zoo colonies around the world. "And then she'll stop, and of course he's really excited, and then she continues face-to-face." Primatologists assume the female preference is dictated by her anatomy: her enlarged clitoris and sexual swellings are oriented far forward. Females presumably prefer face-to-face contact because it feels better.

Like humans but unlike chimps and most other animals, bonobos separate sex from reproduction. They seem to treat sex as a pleasurable activity, and they rely on it as a sort of social glue, to make or break all sorts of relationships. "Ancestral humans behaved like this," proposes Frans de Waal, an ethologist at the Yerkes Regional Primate Research Center at Emory University. "Later, when we developed the family system, the use of sex for this sort of purpose became more limited, mainly occurring within families. A lot of the things we see, like pedophilia and homosexuality, may be leftovers that some now consider unacceptable in our particular society."

Depending on your morals, watching bonobo sex play may be like watching humans at their most extreme and perverse. Bonobos seem to have sex more often and in more combinations than the average person in any culture, and most of the time bonobo sex has nothing to do with making babies. Males mount females and females sometimes mount them back; females rub against other females just for fun; males stand rump to rump and press their scrotal areas together. Even juveniles participate by rubbing their genital areas against adults, although ethologists don't think that males actually insert their penises into juvenile females. Very young animals also have sex with each other: little males suck on each other's penises or French-kiss. When two animals initiate sex, others freely join in by poking their fingers and toes into the moving parts.

One thing sex does for bonobos is decrease tensions caused by potential competition, often competition for food. Japanese primatologists observing bonobos in Zaire were the first to notice that when bonobos come across a large fruiting tree or encounter piles of provisioned sugarcane, the sight of food triggers a binge of sex. The atmosphere of this sexual free-for-all is decidedly friendly, and it eventually calms the group down. "What's striking is how rapidly the sex drops off," says Nancy Thompson-Handler of the State University of New York at Stony Brook, who has observed bonobos at a site in Zaire called Lomako. "After ten minutes, sexual behavior decreases by fifty percent." Soon the group turns from sex to feeding.

But it's tension rather than food that causes the sexual excitement. "I'm sure the more food you give them, the more sex you'll get," says de Waal. "But it's not really the food, it's competition that triggers this. You can throw in a cardboard box and you'll get sexual behavior." Sex is just the way bonobos deal with competition over limited resources and with the normal tensions caused by living in a group. Anthropologist Frances White of Duke University, a bonobo observer at Lomako since 1983, puts it simply: "Sex is fun. Sex makes them feel good and therefore keeps the group together."

Sex is fun. Sex makes them feel good and keeps the group together.

Sexual behavior also occurs after aggressive encounters, especially among males. After two males fight, one may reconcile with his opponent by presenting his rump and backing up against the other's testicles. He might grab the penis of the other male and stroke it. It's the male bonobo's way of shaking hands and letting everyone know that the conflict has ended amicably.

Researchers also note that female bonobo sexuality, like the sexuality of female humans, isn't locked into a monthly cycle. In most other animals, including chimps, the female's interest in sex is tied to her ovulation cycle. Chimp females sport pink swellings on their hind ends for about two weeks, signaling their fertility, and they're only approachable for sex during that time. That's not the case with humans, who show no outward signs that they are ovulating, and can mate at all phases of the cycle. Female bonobos take the reverse tack, but with similar results. Their large swellings are visible for weeks before and after their fertile periods, and there is never any discernibly wrong time to mate. Like humans, they have sex whether or not they are ovulating.

What's fascinating is that female bonobos use this boundless sexuality in all their relationships. "Females rule the business—sex and food," says de Waal. "It's a good species for feminists, I think." For instance, females regularly use sex to cement relationships with other females. A genital-genital rub, better known as GG-rubbing by observers, is the most frequent behavior used by bonobo females to reinforce social ties

or relieve tension. GG-rubbing takes a variety of forms. Often one female rolls on her back and extends her arms and legs. The other female mounts her and they rub their swellings right and left for several seconds, massaging their clitorises against each other. GG-rubbing occurs in the presence of food because food causes tension and excitement, but the intimate contact has the effect of making close friends.

Females rule the business. It's a good species for feminists, I think.

Sometimes females would rather GG-rub with each other than copulate with a male. Parish filmed a 15-minute scene at a bonobo colony at the San Diego Wild Animal Park in which a male, Vernon, repeatedly solicited two females, Lisa and Loretta. Again and again he arched his back and displayed his erect penis—the bonobo request for sex. The females moved away from him, tactfully turning him down until they crept behind a tree and GG-rubbed with each other.

Unlike most primate species, in which males usually take on the dangerous task of leaving home, among bonobos females are the ones who leave the group when they reach sexual maturity, around the age of eight, and work their way into unfamiliar groups. To aid in their assimilation into a new community, the female bonobos make good use of their endless sexual favors. While watching a bonobo group at a feeding tree, White saw a young female systematically have sex with each member before feeding. "An adolescent female, presumably a recent transfer female, came up to the tree, mated with all five males, went into the tree, and solicited GG-rubbing from all the females present," says White.

Once inside the new group, a female bonobo must build a sister-hood from scratch. In groups of humans or chimps, unrelated females construct friendships through the rituals of shopping together or grooming. Bonobos do it sexually. Although pleasure may be the motivation behind a female-female assignation, the function is to form an alliance.

These alliances are serious business, because they determine the pecking order at food sites. Females with powerful friends eat first, and subordinate females may not get any food at all if the resource is small. When times are rough, then, it pays to have close female friends. White describes a scene at Lomako in which an adolescent female, Blanche, benefited from her established friendship with Freda. "I was following Freda and her boyfriend, and they found a tree that they didn't expect to be there. It was a small tree, heavily in fruit with one of their favorites. Freda went straight up the tree and made a food call to Blanche. Blanche came tearing over—she was quite far away—and went tearing up the tree to join Freda, and they GG-rubbed like crazy."

Alliances also give females leverage over larger, stronger males who otherwise would push them around. Females have discovered there is strength in numbers. Unlike other species of primates, such as chimpanzees or baboons (or, all too often, humans), where tensions run high between males and females, bonobo females are not afraid of males, and the sexes mingle

Hidden Heat

Standing upright is not a position usually—or easily—associated with sex. Among people, at least, anatomy and gravity prove to be forbidding obstacles. Yet our two-legged stance may be the key to a distinctive aspect of human sexuality: the independence of women's sexual desires from a monthly calendar.

Males in the two species most closely related to us, chimpanzees and bonobos, don't spend a lot of time worrying, "Is she interested or not?" The answer is obvious. When ovulatory hormones reach a monthly peak in female chimps and bonobos, and their eggs are primed for fertilization, their genital area swells up, and both sexes appear to have just one thing on their mind. "These animals really turn on when this happens. Everything else is dropped," says primatologist Frederick Szalay of Hunter College in New York.

Women, however, don't go into heat. And this departure from our relatives' sexual behavior has long puzzled researchers. Clear signals of fertility and the willingness to do something about it bring major evolutionary advantages: ripe eggs lead to healthier pregnancies, which leads to more of your genes in succeeding generations, which is what evolution is all about. In addition, male chimps give females that are waving these red flags of fertility first chance at high-protein food such as meat.

So why would our ancestors give this up? Szalay and graduate student Robert Costello have a simple explanation. Women gave heat up, they say, because our ancestors stood up. Fossil footprints indicate that somewhere around 3.5 million years ago hominids—non-ape primates—began walking on two legs. "In hominids, something dictated getting up. We don't know what it was," Szalay says. "But once it did, there was a problem with the signaling system." The problem was that it didn't work. Swollen genital areas that were visible when their owners were down on all fours became hidden between the legs. The mating signal was lost.

"Uprightness meant very tough times for females working with the old ovarian cycle," Szalay says. Males wouldn't notice them, and the swellings themselves, which get quite large, must have made it hard for two-legged creatures to walk around.

Those who found a way out of this quandary, Szalay suggests, were females with small swellings but with a little less hair on their rears and a little extra fat. It would have looked a bit like the time-honored mating signal. They got more attention, and produced more offspring. "You don't start a completely new trend in signaling," Szalay says. "You have a little extra fat, a little nakedness to mimic the ancestors. If there was an ever-so-little advantage because, quite simply, you look good, it would be selected for."

And if a little nakedness and a little fat worked well, Szalay speculates, then a lot of both would work even better. "Once you start a trend in sexual signaling, crazy things happen," he notes. "It's almost like: let's escalate, let's add more. That's what happens in horns with sheep. It's a particular part of the body that brings an advantage." In a few million years human ancestors were more naked than ever, with fleshy rears not found in any other primate. Since these features were permanent, unlike the monthly ups and downs of swellings, sex was free to become a part of daily life.

It's a provocative notion, say Szalay's colleagues, but like any attempt to conjure up the past from the present, there's no real proof of cause and effect. Anthropologist Helen Fisher of the American Museum of Natural History notes that Szalay is merely assuming that fleshy buttocks evolved because they were sex signals. Yet their mass really comes from muscles, which chimps don't have, that are associated with walking. And anthropologist Sarah Blaffer Hrdy of the University of California at Davis points to a more fundamental problem: our ancestors may not have had chimplike swellings that they needed to dispense with. Chimps and bonobos are only two of about 200 primate species, and the vast majority of those species don't have big swellings. Though they are our closest relatives, chimps and bonobos have been evolving during the last 5 million years just as we have, and swollen genitals may be a recent development. The current unswollen human pattern may be the ancestral one.

"Nobody really knows what happened," says Fisher. "Everybody has an idea. You pays your money and you takes your choice."

—Joshua Fischman

peacefully. "What is consistently different from chimps," says Thompson-Handler, "is the composition of parties. The vast majority are mixed, so there are males and females of all different ages."

Female bonobos cannot be coerced into anything, including sex. Parish recounts an interaction between Lana and a male called Akili at the San Diego Wild Animal Park. "Lana had just been introduced into the group. For a long time she lay on the grass with a huge swelling. Akili would approach her with a big erection and hover over her. It would have been easy for him to do a mount. But he wouldn't. He just kept trying to catch her eye, hovering around her, and she would scoot around the ground, avoiding him. And then he'd try again. She went around

full circle." Akili was big enough to force himself on her. Yet he refrained.

In another encounter, a male bonobo was carrying a large clump of branches. He moved up to a female and presented his erect penis by spreading his legs and arching his back. She rolled onto her back and they copulated. In the midst of their joint ecstasy, she reached out and grabbed a branch from the male. When he pulled back, finished and satisfied, she moved away, clutching the branch to her chest. There was no tension between them, and she essentially traded copulation for food. But the key here is that the male allowed her to move away with the branch—it didn't occur to him to threaten her, because their status was virtually equal.

Although the results of sexual liberation are clear among bonobos, no one is sure why sex has been elevated to such a high position in this species and why it is restricted merely to reproduction among chimpanzees. "The puzzle for me," says de Waal, "is that chimps do all this bonding with kissing and embracing, with body contact. Why do bonobos do it in a sexual manner?" He speculates that the use of sex as a standard way to underscore relationships began between adult males and adult females as an extension of the mating process and later spread to all members of the group. But no one is sure exactly how this happened.

It is also unclear whether bonobo sexually became exaggerated only after their split from the human lineage or whether the behavior they exhibit today is the modern version of our common ancestor's sex play. Anthropologist Adrienne Zihlman of the University of California at Santa Cruz, who has used the evidence of fossil bones to argue that our earliest known non-ape ancestors, the australopithecines, had body proportions similar to those of bonobos, says, "The path of evolution is not a straight line from either species, but what I think is important is that the bonobo information gives us more possibilities for looking at human origins."

Some anthropologists, however, are reluctant to include the details of bonobo life, such as wide-ranging sexuality and a strong sisterhood, into scenarios of human evolution. "The researchers have all these commitments to male dominance [as in chimpanzees], and yet bonobos have egalitarian relationships," says de Waal. "They also want to see humans as unique, yet bonobos fit very nicely into many of the scenarios, making humans appear less unique."

Our divergent, non-ape path has led us away from sex and toward a culture that denies the connection between sex and social cohesion. But bonobos, with their versatile sexuality, are here to remind us that our heritage may very well include a primordial urge to make love, not war.

Critical Thinking

1. How long ago did humans and chimps share a common ancestor? What kinds of behavior do we still have in common?

2. When did Bonobos diverge from chimps? How do they differ from chimps? How do primatologists explain the female preference for face-to-face sex?

3. In what respects do bonobos, like humans, separate sex from reproduction?

4. How does Bonobo sexual behavior contrast with that of most humans?

5. What is the "one thing" that sex does for bonobos? Why is this not just connected with food?

6. How is sexual behavior related to aggression?

7. In what way is female bonobo sexuality similar to that of female humans and different from that of chimps? How is it also different from humans?

8. How do females use sex? How is "GG-rubbing" related to the fact that females are the ones to leave the group? What are the parallels in humans and chimps? Why are such alliances "serious business"? How does this affect the relationship between the sexes and how is this different from chimps?

9. Can female bonobos be coerced into sex?

10. How do the methods of bonding contrast between chimps and bonobos? Do we know why this is so?

11. Do we know if bonobo sexuality became exaggerated before or after their split from the human lineage? Why are some anthropologists reluctant to include the details of bonobo life in scenarios of human evolution, according to de Waal?

12. Discuss the pros and cons of Szalay and Costello's theory of "hidden heat."

The Double Life of Women

The invisible turns of the reproductive cycle shape the everyday behavior of women and men. A woman's cycle influences not just her preference in a partner, but her personality as well.

ANNIE MURPHY PAUL

Step into any bar or party and it won't take you long to spot her. She's the woman with the ringing laugh, the daring clothes, the magnetic appeal that has drawn a circle of admirers around her. If the room were a solar system, she would be the sun—and at the outer reaches, you notice, are several other women seated quietly in her shadow.

Why does this woman command all the attention? Psychologists, image experts, and dating advisers propose a host of explanations: It's her extraverted personality, her come-hither look, her approachable persona. But an evolutionary biologist observing the scene would offer a more surprising interpretation, one that may help explain barroom dynamics and much more: It's her "real" time of the month. The belle of the bar is likely reaching peak fertility, while her drabber companions are slogging through a non-fertile phase.

Not long ago, such an explanation would have been intellectual heresy. Sure, biologists could tell when chimpanzees were ready to mate: Once every 28 days, the genitalia of female chimps swell and turn a dramatic shade of pink. And estrus, as the state of sexual receptivity is known, is also readily apparent in less exotic animals, as anyone who's seen a house cat in heat can attest. Every female mammal on earth, it was believed, advertises her period of greatest fertility—except the female human. In woman, estrus was "lost" somewhere in the long meander of evolution. "That's the conventional, traditional view of human estrus," says Randy Thornhill, professor of biology at the University of New Mexico. "But it turns out to be wrong."

Over the past decade, evolutionary biologists and psychologists have uncovered abundant evidence that women do, in fact, provide clues to the timing of ovulation, the moment when an egg is released and ready to be fertilized. Though these changes are far subtler than those in other species, they have a powerful effect on women's perceptions, preferences, and behavior—and the reaction of others to her. Monthly shifts even affect *men's* feelings and actions. Indeed, the invisible but influential turns of the reproductive cycle shape the everyday behavior of us all. "Human ovulation is not an observable event, and men and women have no explicit awareness of it," says Martie Haselton, associate professor of communication studies and psychology at UCLA. "But the effects of the menstrual cycle on human behavior are surprisingly strong."

Take, for example, women's preferences in male partners. We may think that each woman has an unchanging "type"— but it turns out that women prefer quite different kinds of men depending on whether or not they are fertile. In the two days or so of the ovulatory phase—the time when women are most likely to become pregnant—they gravitate toward men with more "masculine" traits. That means a man who sports a leaner, V-shaped body, and a face with a squarer chin, straighter, heavier eyebrows, and thinner lips; one who speaks in a lower-pitched voice, and displays more aggressive, dominant behavior. When a woman is in the follicular or luteal phases—during which the uterus sheds its lining and then builds it up again, and in which she generally cannot become pregnant—she prefers men with softer features, less-defined bodies, higher voices, and a gentler manner.

So pronounced are these preferences that Thornhill and his University of New Mexico colleague Steven Gangestad have proposed that women actually have two sexualities: one when they're ovulating, and another during the rest of the month. These distinct modes emerge out of two competing reproductive goals. "Women want to get the highest-quality genes for their children," says Thornhill, and high genetic quality in a man is indicated by his degree of testosteronization—the extent to which the male hormone testosterone has affected his brain, his face, and the rest of his body.

Women actually have two sexualities: One when they're ovulating, and another during the rest of the month.

Once she is pregnant or in the non-fertile part of her cycle, however, a woman's aims do an abrupt about-face: She wants

to secure the most generous and stable source of goods for herself and her offspring. Now the nice-guy provider starts to look appealing. "When women are in what we call the extended-sexuality phase, their preferences shift towards men who appear to have a willingness to share resources like food and protection with her and her children," says Thornhill.

The influence of the menstrual cycle on women is apparent not only in whom they desire but in how they act. Women who are in the ovulatory phase show more interest in erotic materials than women in the luteal or follicular phases; given a choice of movies to watch, they select ones with more romantic or sexual themes. They take more care with their appearance, and they choose more revealing clothes to wear. In 2004, a group of researchers from the University of Vienna digitally analyzed pictures of 351 women going out to Austrian nightclubs and collected a saliva sample from each. Women whose clothes were tight or showed a lot of skin had higher levels of estradiol, a female hormone that is elevated around the time of ovulation.

It even appears that ovulating women are more receptive to the advances of men—handsome French men at least. In a study led by psychologist Nicolas Guéguen of the University of South Brittany, 22 percent of women in their fertile phase accepted an attractive man's invitation for a date, while only 8 percent of women who were not ovulating said yes. Perhaps the fertile women were open to a stranger's overtures because they were feeling especially good about themselves; studies by Martie Haselton and others have found that women judge themselves as sexier and more attractive when they are in the ovulatory phase than at other times of the month.

And they may actually *be* more attractive. Women's faces and bodies undergo subtle changes over the course of the menstrual cycle, research reveals. On fertile days, their voices go up in pitch, their breasts become more symmetrical, and their waist-hip ratio is accentuated (the ratio of the circumference of a woman's waist to that of her hips is a marker of general health and fertility). Subjects shown pictures of the same woman taken over the course of a month pick the one from her fertile period as the most attractive, and men offered T-shirts worn by women in different phases say that the one worn during ovulation smells best.

Whether they're responding to biochemical cues like body odor, to changes in women's appearance, or to women's altered attitudes and behaviors, research shows that men act differently according to the menstrual phase of the women they encounter. A study by Thornhill and Gangestad reported that a man with an ovulating female partner is more likely to engage in mate-guarding behaviors, such as paying close attention to her whereabouts and calling her cell phone at random times to see what she's up to. He is also more agreeable in his interactions with her, and more likely to give her gifts.

One of the most arresting studies of male responses to female fertility cues was conducted by Geoffrey Miller, an associate professor of psychology at the University of New Mexico. Miller found that 18 "lap dancers"—strip club workers who perform provocative dances for male customers—who were menstruating earned an average of about $184 per five-hour shift, while those who were ovulating earned about $354—almost twice as much money, offered by clients who were told nothing about the dancers' cycles.

Moreover, dancers taking birth control pills earned about $193 per shift—more than menstruating women, but much less than women in estrus—and their tips showed no variation across the month. "Hormonal contraception places the female body in a state of pseudo-pregnancy, and it seems that on some level the male customers recognized the women's biological status and responded to it in economic terms," says Miller. Other studies have demonstrated that the pill effectively eliminates the biological and psychological changes associated with estrus, with unexplored effects on women's long-term mate choices.

Modern contraception, then, maybe disrupting an adaptation forged over many thousands of years of evolution. But the precise nature of that adaptation remains to be figured out. There are three principal theories, the first of which is known as the "signaling hypothesis": With her tight clothes, alluring scent, and seductive waist-hip ratio, a woman in estrus is sending out a signal not unlike the chimp or the cat in heat. "Obviously, women who didn't attract mates and have sex when they were fertile were not going to leave behind any offspring at all," notes Kim Wallen, a professor of psychology and behavioral neuroendocrinology at Emory University.

Yet there's reason to think that matters are more complicated than that. Rather than a simple exchange of information between the sexes—the woman communicates that she's ready to mate, and the man obliges—something altogether more shrewd and devious seems to be afoot. According to this hypothesis, men and women are engaged in an eons-old co-evolutionary race, in which one sex makes a move and the other matches it.

By identifying a female's fertile phase, a male can maximize his efforts to impregnate her and to keep other males from doing the same. Women, meanwhile, are strongly motivated to conceal the timing of ovulation. If a man isn't sure when his partner is fertile, he can't restrict her movements or limit her interactions. Hidden ovulation also allows females to discreetly mate with different partners, since none of the potential fathers can be sure of the paternity of the offspring. Her efforts at subterfuge, however, are always incomplete. "It's difficult for women to fully conceal all signs of fertility—some of them inevitably leak out," says Martie Haselton. "We call this the 'leaky cues hypothesis.'"

In another spin of the evolutionary wheel, men have evolved to recognize the signs women let slip. "Human males can detect estrus—not as well as male wombats, but at rates reliably higher than chance," says Thornhill. Research published earlier this year by psychologists Saul Miller and Jon Maner of Florida State University reported that men's testosterone levels spiked after smelling a T-shirt worn by an ovulating woman.

A third hypothesis is trickiest of all. It proposes that the pattern of changes in women that accompany the menstrual cycle is itself a marker of youth and reproductive health (in addition to a sign of transitory fertility), so women have evolved to display cyclical changes, whether they are truly fertile or not.

The effects of the menstrual cycle aren't confined to dating and mating. Female gonadal hormones "not only influence ovulation and reproductive behavior but also affect cognitive

A Pregnant Pause

Forget Decorating the Nursery. Gestating a Fetus Brings out Far More Adaptive Concerns and Behaviors in Women.

If the phases of the menstrual cycle produce distinctive behaviors in women, so too do the nine months of pregnancy. During gestation, evolution's aim is to protect mother and fetus from disease, infection, and contamination. A pregnant woman is vulnerable to such dangers, especially during her first trimester, because her immune system is suppressed to prevent it from attacking the fetus as a foreign body.

Daniel Fessler, an anthropologist at the University of California, Los Angeles, has studied a suite of such protective behaviors that accompany pregnancy. Women in the critical first trimester report more intense feelings of disgust than do women who are farther along in their pregnancies. Such sensitivity likely "compensates" for women's increased vulnerability by prompting them to avoid potential sources of illness.

For the same reason, Fessler has found, women make different dietary choices when they are pregnant. The food cravings and aversions, odor sensitivity, and nausea that many women develop during pregnancy all help protect the fetus from dietary pathogens. Meat is a principal source of such dangerous organisms, Fessler notes, so it's no surprise that it's high on pregnant women's list of foods to avoid.

Women may even spurn meat during some phases of their menstrual cycle, leading Fessler to a bold theory: Our male ancestors ate more meat than their female counterparts, leading them to become our species' principal hunters, leading in turn to the gender-based division of labor that we still largely practice today.

There is evidence that pregnancy leads women to treat people, and not just nutrients, in particular ways. Benedict Jones, a professor of psychology at the University of Aberdeen in Scotland, showed pictures to 115 pregnant women and 857 nonpregnant controls. The women were asked to pick which of two faces they preferred in the photographs; one set had been digitally manipulated to look healthy, the other to look diseased. Women who were pregnant showed a stronger preference for the healthy-looking faces—evidence Jones argues, that pregnant women are unconsciously motivated to avoid people who may be carrying infectious diseases that could disrupt fetal development.

In our ancestral past, the individuals bearing illnesses to which we lack immunity were more likely to be strangers, people outside our clan or tribe. In a 2007 experiment, Fessler found that "ethnocentrism"—the tendency to prefer the members of one's own group—peaked among women in their first trimester of pregnancy. Shown an essay by an American praising the United States, and an essay critical of the U.S. written by a foreigner, women early in their pregnancies reported stronger pro-American feelings.

---

functions, affective state, vulnerability to drugs of abuse, and pain sensitivity," notes psychiatrist and neuroscientist Karen Berman of the National Institute of Mental Health. Women who take stimulants such as amphetamine and cocaine, for example, will be more strongly affected by the drugs if they're in the follicular (pre-ovulatory) phase of their menstrual cycle. Women tend to consume more calories, especially from sweets, when they're in the luteal phase. And women seem to take more risks, and experience more pleasure when those risks pay off, during fertile days of the month.

Female hormones affect cognitive functions, affective state, vulnerability to drugs of abuse, and pain sensitivity.

An unpublished study by economists Matthew Pearson and Burkhard Schipper found that in a series of sealed-bid auctions set up by the experimenters, women bid significantly higher amounts at times when they were more likely to conceive. Pearson and Schipper, both professors at the University of California, Davis, speculate that women are "predisposed by hormones to generally behave more riskily during the fertile phase of their menstrual cycle"—a tendency that originally

functioned "to increase the probability of conception, quality of offspring, and genetic variety," but which now extends into other domains of life.

Even as these monthly shifts affect women's everyday experience, they may also have larger consequences—for the conduct of scientific investigations, for example. For decades scientists have been puzzled over inconsistencies in the reports of research on gender differences. A review of experimental pain studies, for instance, found that women felt more intense pain, at lower thresholds, than men—but only about two-thirds of the time. Psychologists Jeffrey Sherman and Linda LeResche of the University of Washington suggest that this may be because experimenters were ignoring a crucial variable. "Few studies on sex differences before 1995 recorded the time in the menstrual cycle when experimental manipulations took place, or accounted for the variability associated with female reproductive hormones during the cycle," write Sherman and LeResche. More recent investigations have begun taking the menstrual cycle into account when evaluating women's perceptions and responses, and have found that women are more sensitive to pain during phases when estrogen levels are low.

The monthly revolutions of women's reproductive cycles may also help account for their heightened vulnerability to psychological disorders like depression and anxiety. Before puberty, psychiatric conditions are far more common in boys than in

girls. But once the reproductive years begin, women become the more susceptible sex, and it's believed that sex hormones account for much of this difference. Estrogen and progesterone, which rise to their highest levels when women are ovulating, have anxiety-reducing effects, and the subsequent drop in the levels of these hormones may leave women more sensitive to stress than men. Although higher levels of estrogen and progesterone generally give reproductive-age women some protection against psychotic illnesses like schizophrenia, the monthly hormonal "withdrawal" they experience seems to make them more vulnerable to mood disorders such as anxiety and depression.

All this talk of shifting moods and monthly changes may well raise a concern: Will such research reinforce old stereotypes of women as hysterical, irrational, at the mercy of their hormones? Quite the opposite, says Geoffrey Miller. "The traditional and rather patronizing male view was that women are fickle, that their preferences are random and arbitrary," he says. "Now it turns out that what looked like fickleness is actually deeply adaptive, and is shared with the females of most animal species. There is a deep logic to the shifts in female desire."

This logic operates below our conscious awareness, of course: Many generations of humans have faithfully followed it without knowing a thing about evolutionary theory. But once we do learn about the effects of the menstrual cycle on our perceptions and behavior, we can put that knowledge to good use. Women can keep a journal of their fluctuating moods and desires over the course of a month, matching up the entries with their cycles to identify a pattern; according to Miller, many female evolutionary biologists keep such diaries.

Gordon Gallup, an evolutionary psychologist at SUNY Albany, suggests that women use knowledge of their monthly cycles to plan important events. "If you have a first date coming up, or even a job interview, try to time it to coincide with your most fertile period," he advises. "The initial impression you make may be affected by the stage of your menstrual cycle." By the same token, says Gallup, if you're in a line of work in which your income depends on snap evaluations by others—a waitress, say, or a lap dancer—taking birth control pills "is like shooting yourself in the foot," since you miss out on the bountiful tips garnered by women in estrus.

A young woman should try to time a first date or job interview to coincide with her most fertile phase.

Psychologist Kim Wallen notes that women can also use knowledge of their menstrual cycles to manage their sexuality. "Research shows that women are more likely to take social risks around the time of ovulation," he says. "Women who know that's the case can choose not to put themselves in risky situations, such as drinking too much at a bar or party, at that time of the month." And if a woman should feel attracted to a man who would make an inappropriate partner, says Wallen, she can restrain her impulse, knowing that soon enough her preferences will shift and her desire will wane. "The adolescent male doesn't have that option," he points out. "If he lusts after someone today, he'll still be lusting after her next week and next month."

A familiarity with the changes associated with estrus can even help us make sense of our feelings about long-term romantic partners. Women who experience an attraction to men other than their husbands or boyfriends need not conclude that there's anything amiss in their relationships, says Martie Haselton. "If a woman understands the evolutionary underpinnings of these impulses, she can reassure herself that these feelings don't mean that she doesn't love her partner or isn't 'meant' to be with him," she says. "The goal she's trying to achieve—to have a stable, loving, monogamous relationship—is not the goal that evolution has built her to act upon."

Although we can consciously choose to resist evolution's dictates, says Haselton, "the fingerprints of evolution are all over the behavior we engage in today."

Critical Thinking

1. What evidence is there that a woman's reproductive cycle affects her preferences, perceptions of self, and behavior with respect to men?

2. In what ways do men respond to women's fertility cycles?

3. How and why does the author think that modern contraception disrupts an adaptation forged many thousands of years ago?

4. Be familiar with the three principle theories regarding ovulation: the "signaling hypothesis," the notion of "hidden ovulation," and the idea that the menstrual cycle is a marker of youth and reproductive health.

5. What evidence is there that women are more likely to take risks when ovulating? Why would this be so?

6. In what ways can an understanding of women's shifting moods during the menstrual cycle be used for their benefit?

ANNIE MURPHY PAUL is the author of *Origins: How the Nine Months Before Birth Shape the Rest of Our Lives*, published in 2010.

Mothers and Others

Sarah Blaffer Hrdy

Mother apes—chimpanzees, gorillas, orangutans, humans—dote on their babies. And why not? They give birth to an infant after a long gestation and, in most cases, suckle it for years. With humans, however, the job of providing for a juvenile goes on and on. Unlike all other ape babies, ours mature slowly and reach independence late. A mother in a foraging society may give birth every four years or so, and her first few children remain dependent long after each new baby arrives; among nomadic foragers, grown-ups may provide food to children for eighteen or more years. To come up with the 10–13 million calories that anthropologists such as Hillard Kaplan calculate are needed to rear a young human to independence, a mother needs help.

So how did our prehuman and early human ancestresses living in the Pleistocene Epoch (from 1.6 million until roughly 10,000 years ago) manage to get those calories? And under what conditions would natural selection allow a female ape to produce babies so large and slow to develop that they are beyond her means to rear on her own?

The old answer was that fathers helped out by hunting. And so they do. But hunting is a risky occupation, and fathers may die or defect or take up with other females. And when they do, what then? New evidence from surviving traditional cultures suggests that mothers in the Pleistocene may have had a significant degree of help—from men who thought they just might have been the fathers, from grandmothers and great-aunts, from older children.

These helpers other than the mother, called allomothers by sociobiologists, do not just protect and provision youngsters. In groups such as the Efe and Aka Pygmies of central Africa, allomothers actually hold children and carry them about. In these tight-knit communities of communal foragers—within which men, women, and children still hunt with nets, much as humans are thought to have done tens of thousands of years ago—siblings, aunts, uncles, fathers, and grandmothers hold newborns on the first day of life. When University of New Mexico anthropologist Paula Ivey asked an Efe woman, "Who cares for babies?" the immediate answer was, "We all do!" By three weeks of age, the babies are in contact with allomothers 40 percent of the time. By eighteen weeks, infants actually spend more time with allomothers than with their gestational mothers. On average, Efe babies have fourteen different caretakers, most of whom are close kin. According to Washington State University anthropologist Barry Hewlett, Aka babies are within arm's reach of their fathers for more than half of every day.

Accustomed to celebrating the antiquity and naturalness of mother-centered models of child care, as well as the nuclear family in which the mother nurtures while the father provides, we Westerners tend to regard the practices of the Efe and the Aka as exotic. But to sociobiologists, whose stock in trade is comparisons across species, all this helping has a familiar ring. It's called cooperative breeding. During the past quarter century, as anthropologists and sociobiologists started to compare notes, one of the spectacular surprises has been how much allomaternal care goes on, not just within various human societies but among animals generally. Evidently, diverse organisms have converged on cooperative breeding for the best of evolutionary reasons.

A broad look at the most recent evidence has convinced me that cooperative breeding was the strategy that permitted our own ancestors to produce costly, slow-maturing infants at shorter intervals, to take advantage of new kinds of resources in habitats other than the mixed savanna-woodland of tropical Africa, and to spread more widely and swiftly than any primate had before. We already know that animal mothers who delegate some of the costs of infant care to others are thereby freed to produce more or larger young or to breed more frequently. Consider the case of silver-backed jackals. Patricia Moehlman, of the World Conservation Union, has shown that for every extra helper bringing back food, jackal parents rear one extra pup per litter. Cooperative breeding also helps various species expand into habitats in which they would normally not be able to rear any young at all. Florida scrub-jays, for example, breed in an exposed landscape where unrelenting predation from hawks and snakes usually precludes the fledging of young; survival in this habitat is possible only because older siblings help guard and feed the young. Such cooperative arrangements permit animals as different as naked mole rats (the social insects of the mammal world) and wolves to move into new habitats and sometimes to spread over vast areas.

When animal mothers delegate some infant-care costs to others, they can produce more or larger young and raise them in less-than-ideal habitats.

What does it take to become a cooperative breeder? Obviously, this lifestyle is an option only for creatures capable of living in groups. It is facilitated when young but fully mature individuals (such as young Florida scrub-jays) do not or cannot immediately leave their natal group to breed on their own and instead remain among kin in their natal location. As with delayed maturation, delayed dispersal of young means that teenagers, "spinster" aunts, real and honorary uncles will be on hand to help their kin rear young. Flexibility is another criterion for cooperative breeders. Helpers must be ready to shift to breeding mode should the opportunity arise. In marmosets and tamarins—the little South American monkeys that are, besides us, the only full-fledged cooperative breeders among primates—a female has to be ready to be a helper this year and a mother the next. She may have one mate or several. In canids such as wolves or wild dogs, usually only the dominant, or alpha, male and female in a pack reproduce, but younger group members hunt with the mother and return to the den to regurgitate predigested meat into the mouths of her pups. In a fascinating instance of physiological flexibility, a subordinate female may actually undergo hormonal transformations similar to those of a real pregnancy: her belly swells, and she begins to manufacture milk and may help nurse the pups of the alpha pair. Vestiges of cooperative breeding crop up as well in domestic dogs, the distant descendants of wolves. After undergoing a pseudopregnancy, my neighbors' Jack Russell terrier chased away the family's cat and adopted and suckled her kittens. To suckle the young of another species is hardly what Darwinians call an adaptive trait (because it does not contribute to the surrogate's own survival). But in the environment in which the dog family evolved, a female's tendency to respond when infants signaled their need—combined with her capacity for pseudopregnancy—would have increased the survival chances for large litters born to the dominant female.

According to the late W.D. Hamilton, evolutionary logic predicts that an animal with poor prospects of reproducing on his or her own should be predisposed to assist kin with better prospects so that at least some of their shared genes will be perpetuated. Among wolves, for example, both male and female helpers in the pack are likely to be genetically related to the alpha litter and to have good reasons for not trying to reproduce on their own: in a number of cooperatively breeding species (wild dogs, wolves, hyenas, dingoes, dwarf mongooses, marmosets), the helpers do try, but the dominant female is likely to bite their babies to death. The threat of coercion makes postponing ovulation the better part of valor, the least-bad option for females who must wait to breed until their circumstances improve, either through the death of a higher-ranking female or by finding a mate with an unoccupied territory.

One primate strategy is to line up extra fathers. Among common marmosets and several species of tamarins, females mate with several males, all of which help rear her young. As primatologist Charles T. Snowdon points out, in three of the four genera of Callitrichidae (*Callithrix, Saguinus,* and *Leontopithecus*), the more adult males the group has available to help, the more young survive. Among many of these species, females ovulate just after giving birth, perhaps encouraging males to stick around until after babies are born. (In cotton-top tamarins, males also undergo hormonal changes that prepare them to care for infants at the time of birth.) Among cooperative breeders of certain other species, such as wolves and jackals, pups born in the same litter can be sired by different fathers.

Human mothers, by contrast, don't ovulate again right after birth, nor do they produce offspring with more than one genetic father at a time. Ever inventive, though, humans solve the problem of enlisting help from several adult males by other means. In some cultures, mothers rely on a peculiar belief that anthropologists call partible paternity—the notion that a fetus is built up by contributions of semen from all the men with whom women have had sex in the ten months or so prior to giving birth. Among the Canela, a matrilineal tribe in Brazil studied for many years by William Crocker of the Smithsonian Institution, publicly sanctioned intercourse between women and men other than their husbands—sometimes many men—takes place during villagewide ceremonies. What might lead to marital disaster elsewhere works among the Canela because the men believe in partible paternity. Across a broad swath of South America—from Paraguay up into Brazil, westward to Peru, and northward to Venezuela—mothers rely on this convenient folk wisdom to line up multiple honorary fathers to help them provision both themselves and their children. Over hundreds of generations, this belief has helped children thrive in a part of the world where food sources are unpredictable and where husbands are as likely as not to return from the hunt empty-handed.

The Bari people of Venezuela are among those who believe in shared paternity, and according to anthropologist Stephen Beckerman, Bari children with more than one father do especially well. In Beckerman's study of 822 children, 80 percent of those who had both a "primary" father (the man married to their mother) and a "secondary" father survived to age fifteen, compared with 64 percent survival for those with a primary father alone. Not surprisingly, as soon as a Bari woman suspects she is pregnant, she accepts sexual advances from the more successful fishermen or hunters in her group. Belief that fatherhood can be shared draws more men into the web of possible paternity, which effectively translates into more food and more protection.

But for human mothers, extra mates aren't the only source of effective help. Older children, too, play a significant role in family survival. University of Nebraska anthropologists Patricia Draper and Raymond Hames have just shown that among !Kung hunters and gatherers living in the Kalahari Desert, there is a significant correlation between how many children a parent successfully raises and how many older siblings were on hand to help during that person's own childhood.

One primate strategy is to line up extra "fathers." In some species of marmosets, females mate with several males, all of which help her raise her young.

Older matrilineal kin may be the most valuable helpers of all. University of Utah anthropologists Kristen Hawkes and James O'Connell and their UCLA colleague Nicholas Blurton Jones, who have demonstrated the important food-gathering role of older women among Hazda hunter-gatherers in Tanzania, delight in explaining that since human life spans may extend for a few decades after menopause, older women become available to care for—and to provide vital food for—children born to younger kin. Hawkes, O'Connell, and Blurton Jones further believe that dating from the earliest days of Homo erectus, the survival of weaned children during food shortages may have depended on tubers dug up by older kin.

At various times in human history, people have also relied on a range of customs, as well as on coercion, to line up allomaternal assistance—for example, by using slaves or hiring poor women as wet nurses. But all the helpers in the world are of no use if they're not motivated to protect, carry, or provision babies. For both humans and nonhumans, this motivation arises in three main ways: through the manipulation of information about kinship; through appealing signals coming from the babies themselves; and, at the heart of it all, from the endocrinological and neural processes that induce individuals to respond to infants' signals. Indeed, all primates and many other mammals eventually respond to infants in a nurturing way if exposed long enough to their signals. Trouble is, "long enough" can mean very different things in males and females, with their very different response thresholds.

For decades, animal behaviorists have been aware of the phenomenon known as priming. A mouse or rat encountering a strange pup is likely to respond by either ignoring the pup or eating it. But presented with pup after pup, rodents of either sex eventually become sensitized to the baby and start caring for it. Even a male may gather pups into a nest and lick or huddle over them. Although nurturing is not a routine part of a male's repertoire, when sufficiently primed he behaves as a mother would. Hormonal change is an obvious candidate for explaining this transformation. Consider the case of the cooperatively breeding Florida scrub-jays studied by Stephan Schoech, of the University of Memphis. Prolactin, a protein hormone that initiates the secretion of milk in female mammals, is also present in male mammals and in birds of both sexes. Schoech showed that levels of prolactin go up in a male and female jay as they build their nest and incubate eggs and that these levels reach a peak when they feed their young. Moreover, prolactin levels rise in the jays' nonbreeding helpers and are also at their highest when they assist in feeding nestlings.

As it happens, male, as well as immature and nonbreeding female, primates can respond to infants' signals, although quite different levels of exposure and stimulation are required to get them going. Twenty years ago, when elevated prolactin levels were first reported in common marmoset males (by Alan Dixson, for *Callithrix jacchus*), many scientists refused to believe it. Later, when the finding was confirmed, scientists assumed this effect would be found only in fathers. But based on work by Scott Nunes, Jeffrey Fite, Jeffrey French, Charles Snowdon, Lucille Roberts, and many others—work that deals with a variety of species of marmosets and tamarins—we now know that all sorts of hormonal changes are associated with increased nurturing in males. For example, in the tufted-eared marmosets studied by French and colleagues, testosterone

levels in males went down as they engaged in caretaking after the birth of an infant. Testosterone levels tended to be lowest in those with the most paternal experience.

Genetic relatedness alone, in fact, is a surprisingly unreliable predictor of love. What matters are cues from infants and how we process these cues emotionally.

The biggest surprise, however, has been that something similar goes on in males of our own species. Anne Storey and colleagues in Canada have reported that prolactin levels in men who were living with pregnant women went up toward the end of the pregnancy. But the most significant finding was a 30 percent drop in testosterone in men right after the birth. (Some endocrinologically literate wags have proposed that this drop in testosterone levels is due to sleep deprivation, but this would probably not explain the parallel testosterone drop in marmoset males housed with parturient females.) Hormonal changes during pregnancy and lactation are, of course, indisputably more pronounced in mothers than in the men consorting with them, and no one is suggesting that male consorts are equivalent to mothers. But both sexes are surprisingly susceptible to infant signals—explaining why fathers, adoptive parents, wet nurses, and day-care workers can become deeply involved with the infants they care for.

Genetic relatedness alone, in fact, is a surprisingly unreliable predictor of love. What matters are cues from infants and how these cues are processed emotionally. The capacity for becoming emotionally hooked—or primed—also explains how a fully engaged father who is in frequent contact with his infant can become more committed to the infant's well-being than a detached mother will.

But we can't forget the real protagonist of this story: the baby. From birth, newborns are powerfully motivated to stay close, to root—even to creep—in quest of nipples, which they instinctively suck on. These are the first innate behaviors that any of us engage in. But maintaining contact is harder for little humans to do than it is for other primates. One problem is that human mothers are not very hairy, so a human mother not only has to position the baby on her breast but also has to keep him there. She must be motivated to pick up her baby even *before* her milk comes in, bringing with it a host of hormonal transformations.

Within minutes of birth, human babies can cry and vocalize just as other primates do, but human newborns can also read facial expressions and make a few of their own. Even with blurry vision, they engage in eye-to-eye contact with the people around them. Newborn babies, when alert, can see about eighteen inches away. When people put their faces within range, babies may reward this attention by looking back or even imitating facial expressions. Orang and chimp babies, too, are strongly attached to and interested in their mothers' faces. But unlike humans, other ape mothers and infants do not get absorbed in gazing deeply into each other's eyes.

To the extent that psychiatrists and pediatricians have thought about this difference between us and the other apes, they tend to attribute it to human mental agility and our ability to use language. Interactions between mother and baby, including vocal play and babbling, have been interpreted as protoconversations: revving up the baby to learn to talk. Yet even babies who lack face-to-face stimulation—babies born blind, say—learn to talk. Furthermore, humans are not the only primates to engage in the continuous rhythmic streams of vocalization known as babbling. Interestingly, marmoset and tamarin babies also babble. It may be that the infants of cooperative breeders are specially equipped to communicate with caretakers. This is not to say that babbling is not an important part of learning to talk, only to question which came first—babbling so as to develop into a talker, or a predisposition to evolve into a talker because among cooperative breeders, babies that babble are better tended and more likely to survive.

If humans evolved as cooperative breeders, the degree of a human mother's commitment to her infant should be linked to how much social support she herself can expect. Mothers in cooperatively breeding primate species can afford to bear and rear such costly offspring as they do only if they have help on hand. Maternal abandonment and abuse are very rarely observed among primates in the wild. In fact, the only primate species in which mothers are anywhere near as likely to abandon infants at birth as mothers in our own species are the other cooperative breeders. A study of cotton-top tamarins at the New England Regional Primate Research Center showed a 12 percent chance of abandonment if mothers had older siblings on hand to help them rear twins, but a 57 percent chance when no help was available. Overburdened mothers abandoned infants within seventy-two hours of birth.

This new way of thinking about our species' history, with its implications for children, has made me concerned about the future. So far, most Western researchers studying infant development have presumed that living in a nuclear family with a fixed division of labor (mom nurturing, dad providing) is the normal human adaptation. Most contemporary research on children's psychosocial development is derived from John Bowlby's theories of attachment and has focused on such variables as how available and responsive the mother is, whether the father is present or absent, and whether the child is in the mother's care or in day care. Sure enough, studies done with this model in mind always show that children with less responsive mothers are at greater risk.

In cooperative breeders, the degree of a mother's commitment to her infant should correlate with how much social support she herself can expect.

It is the baby, first and foremost, who senses how available and how committed its mother is. But I know of no studies that take into account the possibility that humans evolved as cooperative breeders and that a mother's responsiveness also happens to be a good indicator of her social supports. In terms of developmental outcomes, the most relevant factor might not be how securely or insecurely attached to the mother the baby is—the variable that developmental psychologists are trained to measure—but rather how secure the baby is in relation to all the people caring for him or her. Measuring attachment this way might help explain why even children whose relations with their mother suggest they are at extreme risk manage to do fine because of the interventions of a committed father, an older sibling, or a there-when-you-need-her grandmother.

The most comprehensive study ever done on how nonmaternal care affects kids is compatible with both the hypothesis that humans evolved as cooperative breeders and the conventional hypothesis that human babies are adapted to be reared exclusively by mothers. Undertaken by the National Institute of Child Health and Human Development (NICHD) in 1991, the seven-year study included 1,364 children and their families (from diverse ethnic and economic backgrounds) and was conducted in ten different U.S. locations. This extraordinarily ambitious study was launched because statistics showed that 62 percent of U.S. mothers with children under age six were working outside the home and that the majority of them (willingly or unwillingly) were back at work within three to five months of giving birth. Because this was an entirely new social phenomenon, no one really knew what the NICHD's research would reveal.

The study's main finding was that both maternal and hired caretakers' sensitivity to infant needs was a better predictor of a child's subsequent development and behavior (such traits as social "compliance," respect for others, and self-control were measured) than was actual time spent apart from the mother. In other words, the critical variable was not the continuous presence of the mother herself but rather how secure infants felt when cared for by someone else. People who had been convinced that babies need full-time care from mothers to develop normally were stunned by these results, while advocates of day care felt vindicated. But do these and other, similar findings mean that day care is not something we need to worry about anymore?

Not at all. We should keep worrying. The NICHD study showed only that day care was better than mother care if the mother was neglectful or abusive. But excluding such worst-case scenarios, the study showed no detectable ill effects from day care only when infants had a secure relationship with parents to begin with (which I take to mean that babies felt wanted) and only when the day care was of high quality. And in this study's context, "high quality" meant that the facility had a high ratio of caretakers to babies, that it had the same caretakers all the time, and that the caretakers were sensitive to infants' needs—in other words, that the day care staff acted like committed kin.

Bluntly put, this kind of day care is almost impossible to find. Where it exists at all, it's expensive. Waiting lists are long, even for cheap or inadequate care. The average rate of staff turnover in day care centers is 30 percent per year, primarily because these workers are paid barely the minimum wage (usually less, in fact, than parking-lot attendants). Furthermore, day care tends to be age-graded, so even at centers where staff members stay put, kids move annually to new teachers. This kind of day care is unlikely to foster trusting relationships.

What conclusion can we draw from all this? Instead of arguing over "mother care" versus "other care," we need to make day care better. And this is where I think today's evolution-minded researchers have something to say. Impressed by just how variable child-rearing conditions can be in human societies, several anthropologists and psychologists (including Michael Lamb, Patricia Draper, Henry Harpending, and James Chisholm) have suggested that babies are up to more than just maintaining the relationship with their mothers. These researchers propose that babies actually monitor mothers to gain information about the world they have been born into. Babies ask, in effect, Is this world filled with people who are going to provide for me and help me survive? Can I count on them to care about me? If the answer to those questions is yes, they begin to sense that developing a conscience and a capacity for compassion would be a great idea. If the answer is no, they may then be asking, Can I not afford to count on others? Would I be better off just grabbing what I need, however I can? In this case, empathy, or thinking about others' needs, would be more of a hindrance than a help.

For a developing baby and child, the most practical way to behave might vary drastically, depending on whether the mother has kin who help, whether the father is around, whether foster parents are well-meaning or exploitative. These factors, however unconsciously perceived by the child, affect important developmental decisions. Being extremely self-centered or selfish, being oblivious to others or lacking in conscience—traits that psychologists and child-development theorists may view as pathological—are probably quite adaptive traits for an individual who is short on support from other group members.

If I am right that humans evolved as cooperative breeders, Pleistocene babies whose mothers lacked social support and were less than fully committed to infant care would have been unlikely to survive. But once people started to settle down—10,000 or 20,000 or perhaps 30,000 years ago—the picture changed. Ironically, survival chances for neglected children increased. As people lingered longer in one place, eliminated predators, built walled houses, stored food—not to mention inventing things such as rubber nipples and pasteurized milk—infant survival became decoupled from continuous contact with a caregiver.

Since the end of the Pleistocene, whether in preindustrial or industrialized environments, some children have been surviving levels of social neglect that previously would have meant certain death. Some children get very little attention, even in the most benign of contemporary homes. In the industrialized world, children routinely survive caretaking practices that an Efe or a !Kung mother would find appallingly negligent. In traditional societies, no decent mother leaves her baby alone at any time, and traditional mothers are shocked to learn that Western mothers leave infants unattended in a crib all night.

In effect, babies ask: Is this world filled with people who are going to provide for me and help me survive? Can I count on them to care about me?

Without passing judgment, one may point out that only in the recent history of humankind could infants deprived of supportive human contact survive to reproduce themselves. Certainly there are a lot of humanitarian reasons to worry about this situation: one wants each baby, each child, to be lovingly cared for. From my evolutionary perspective, though, even more is at stake.

Even if we manage to survive what most people are worrying about—global warming, emergent diseases, rogue viruses, meteorites crashing into earth—will we still be human thousands of years down the line? By that I mean human in the way we currently define ourselves. The reason our species has managed to survive and proliferate to the extent that 6 billion people currently occupy the planet has to do with how readily we can learn to cooperate when we want to. And our capacity for empathy is one of the things that made us good at doing that.

At a rudimentary level, of course, all sorts of creatures are good at reading intentions and movements and anticipating what other animals are going to do. Predators from gopher snakes to lions have to be able to anticipate where their quarry will dart. Chimps and gorillas can figure out what another individual is likely to know or not know. But compared with that of humans, this capacity to entertain the psychological perspective of other individuals is crude.

During early childhood, through relationships with mothers and other caretakers, individuals learn to look at the world from someone else's perspective.

The capacity for empathy is uniquely well developed in our species, so much so that many people (including me) believe that along with language and symbolic thought, it is what makes us human. We are capable of compassion, of understanding other people's "fears and motives, their longings and griefs and vanities," as novelist Edmund White puts it. We spend time and energy worrying about people we have never even met, about babies left in dumpsters, about the existence of more than 12 million AIDS orphans in Africa.

Psychologists know that there is a heritable component to emotional capacity and that this affects the development of compassion among individuals. By fourteen months of age, identical twins (who share all genes) are more alike in how they react to an experimenter who pretends to painfully pinch her finger on a clipboard than are fraternal twins (who share only half their genes). But empathy also has a learned component, which has more to do with analytical skills. During the first years of life, within the context of early relationships with mothers and other committed caretakers, each individual learns to look at the world from someone else's perspective.

And this is why I get so worried. Just because humans have evolved to be smart enough to chronicle our species' histories, to speculate about its origins, and to figure out that we have about 30,000 genes in our genome is no reason to assume that evolution has come to a standstill. As gene frequencies change, natural selection acts on the outcome, the expression of those genes. No one doubts, for instance, that fish benefit from being able to see. Yet species reared in total darkness—as are the small, cave-dwelling characin of Mexico—fail to develop their visual capacity. Through evolutionary time, traits that are unexpressed are eventually lost. If populations of these fish are isolated in caves long enough, youngsters descended from those original populations will no longer be able to develop eyesight at all, even if reared in sunlight.

If human compassion develops only under particular rearing conditions, and if an increasing proportion of the species survives to breeding age without developing compassion, it won't make any difference how useful this trait was among our ancestors. It will become like sight in cave-dwelling fish.

No doubt our descendants thousands of years from now (should our species survive) will still be bipedal, symbol-generating apes. Most likely they will be adept at using sophisticated technologies. But will they still be human in the way we, shaped by a long heritage of cooperative breeding, currently define ourselves?

Critical Thinking

1. Why does the author say that human mothers need help in rearing a child? What was the "old answer" to this problem? What does the new evidence indicate?

2. What are "allomothers" and how do the Efe and Aka Pygmies illustrate their importance?

3. What is "cooperative breeding" and what have been its advantages for our ancestors?

4. What does it take to become a "cooperative breeder"? How do wild dogs illustrate this?

5. What is the "evolutionary logic" behind cooperative breeding?

6. Discuss "partible paternity" and its benefits in the cultures cited.

7. What other kinds of help are available to human mothers?

8. What is "priming" and how does it seem to come about?

9. Is genetic relatedness a reliable predictor of love? Explain.

10. What do human babies do to motivate mothers to nurture them? In what respect are humans different from apes? How important is babbling?

11. What have most Western researchers presumed to be the "normal human adaptation"? In terms of developmental outcomes, what is the most relevant factor, according to the author? How does the NICHD study bear upon this issue? What does the author have to say about day care?

12. Why is the author worried with regard to the human capacity for empathy?

This article was adapted from *"Cooperation, Empathy, and the Needs of Human Infants,"* a Tanner Lecture delivered at the University of Utah. It is used with the permission of the Tanner Lectures on Human Values, a Corporation, University of Utah, Salt Lake City.

From *Natural History*, May 2001, pp. 50–62. adapted from *Cooperation, Empathy, and the Needs of Human Infants*, a Tanner Lecture.
Copyright © 2001 Tanner Lectures on Human Values, Inc., University of Utah, Salt Lake City.

UNIT 4
The Fossil Evidence

Unit Selections

Learning Outcomes

After reading this unit, you will be able to:

- Describe what the last common ancestor of hominids and chimpanzees looked like.

- Determine under what circumstances bipedalism evolved and list its advantages.

- Draw the early hominid family tree.

- Explain why the fossil *Sediba* shows "one can no longer assign isolated bones to a genus."

- Discuss the successful adaptation of the Neanderthals with respect to anatomy, technology, and sociality.

- Describe what happened to the Neanderthals.

Student Website

www.mhhe.com/cls

Internet References

Fossil Hominids FAQ
   www.talkorigins.org/faqs/homs
Institute of Human Origins
   http://iho.asu.edu/node/27
Long Foreground: Human Prehistory
   www.wsu.edu/gened/learn-modules/top_longfor/lfopen-index.html

The Human Family's Earliest Ancestors

Studies of hominid fossils, like 4.4-million-year-old "Ardi," are changing ideas about human origins.

ANN GIBBONS

Tim White is standing with a group of restless men atop a ridge in the Afar desert of Ethiopia. A few of them are pacing back and forth, straining to see if they can spot fragments of beige bone in the reddish-brown rubble below, as eager to start their search as children at an Easter egg hunt. At the bottom of the hill is a 25-foot-long cairn of black rocks erected in the style of an Afar grave, so large it looks like a monument to a fallen hero. And in a way it is. White and his colleagues assembled it to mark the place where they first found traces, in 1994, of "Ardi," a female who lived 4.4 million years ago. Her skeleton has been described as one of the most important discoveries of the past century, and she is changing basic ideas about how our earliest ancestors looked and moved.

More than 14 years later, White, a wiry 59-year-old paleoanthropologist from the University of California at Berkeley, is here again, on an annual pilgrimage to see if seasonal rains have exposed any new bits of Ardi's bones or teeth. He often fires up the fossil hunters who work with him by chanting, "Hominid, hominid, hominid! Go! Go! Go!" But he can't let them go yet. Only a week earlier, an Alisera tribesman had threatened to kill White and two of his Ethiopian colleagues if they returned to these fossil beds near the remote village of Aramis, home of a clan of Alisera nomads. The threat is probably just a bluff, but White doesn't mess with the Alisera, who are renowned for being territorial and settling disputes with AK-47s. As a precaution, the scientists travel with six Afar regional police officers armed with their own AK-47s.

Arranging this meeting with tribal leaders to negotiate access to the fossil beds has already cost the researchers two precious days out of their five-week field season. "The best-laid plans change every day," says White, who has also had to deal with poisonous snakes, scorpions, malarial mosquitoes, lions, hyenas, flash floods, dust tornadoes, warring tribesmen and contaminated food and water. "Nothing in the field comes easy."

As we wait for the Alisera to arrive, White explains that the team returns to this hostile spot year after year because it's the only place in the world to yield fossils that span such a long stretch of human evolution, some six million years. In addition to Ardi, a possible direct ancestor, it is possible here to find hominid fossils from as recently as 160,000 years ago—an early

Homo sapiens like us—all the way back to *Ardipithecus kadabba,* one of the earliest known hominids, who lived almost si million years ago. At last count, the Middle Awash project, whic takes its name from this patch of the Afar desert and include 70 scientists from 18 nations, has found 300 specimens from seven different hominid species that lived here one after the other.

Ardi, short for *Ardipithecus ramidus,* is now the region's best-known fossil, having made news worldwide this past fall when White and others published a series of papers detailing her skeleton and ancient environment. She is not the oldest member of the extended human family, but she is by far the most complete of the early hominids; most of her skull and teeth as well as extremely rare bones of her pelvis, hands, arms, legs and feet have so far been found.

With sunlight beginning to bleach out the gray-and-beige terrain, we see a cloud of dust on the horizon. Soon two new Toyota Land Cruisers pull up on the promontory, and a half-dozen Alisera men jump out wearing Kufi caps and cotton sarongs, a few cinched up with belts that also hold long, curved daggers. Most of these clan "elders" appear to be younger than 40—few Alisera men seem to survive to old age.

After customary greetings and handshaking, White gets down on his hands and knees with a few fossil hunters to show the tribesmen how the researchers crawl on the ground, shoulder to shoulder, to look for fossils. With Ethiopian paleoanthropologist and project co-leader Berhane Asfaw translating to Amharic and another person translating from Amharic to Afariña, White explains that these stones and bones reveal the ancient history of humankind. The Alisera smile wanly, apparently amused that anyone would want to grovel on the ground for a living. They grant permission to search for fossils—for now. But they add one caveat. Someday, they say, the researchers must teach them how to get history from the ground.

The quest for fossils of human ancestors began in earnest after Charles Darwin proposed in 1871, in his book *The Descent of Man and Selection in Relation to Sex,* that humans probably arose in Africa. He didn't base his claim on hard evidence; the only hominid fossils then known were Neanderthals, who had lived in Europe less than 100,000 years ago. Darwin suggested that our "early progenitors" lived on the African continent because

A primary focal point of this book, as well as of the whole of physical anthropology, is the search for, and the interpretation of, fossil evidence for hominid (meaning human or humanlike) evolution. Paleoanthropologists are those who carry out this task by conducting painstaking excavations and detailed analyses that serve as a basis for understanding our past. Every fragment found is cherished like a ray of light that may help to illuminate the path taken by our ancestors in the process of becoming "us." At least, that is what we would like to believe. In reality, each discovery leads to further mystery, and for every fossil-hunting paleoanthropologist who thinks his or her find supports a particular theory, there are many others anxious to express their disagreement. How wonderful it would be, we sometimes think, in moments of frustration over inconclusive data, if the fossils would just speak for themselves, and every primordial piece of humanity were to carry with it a self-evident explanation for its place in the evolutionary story. Paleoanthropology would then be more of a quantitative problem of amassing enough material to reconstruct our ancestral development than a qualitative problem of interpreting what it all means. It would certainly be a simpler process, but would it be as interesting?

Most scientists tolerate, welcome, or even (dare it be said?) thrive on controversy, recognizing that diversity of opinion refreshes the mind, rouses students, and captures the imagination of the general public. After all, where would paleoanthropology be without the gadflies, the near-mythic heroes, and, lest we forget, the research funds they generate? Consider, for example, the issue of the differing roles played by males and females in the transition to humanity and all that it implies with regard to bipedalism, tool-making, and the origin of the family. Did bipedalism really evolve in the grasslands? (see "The Human Family's Earliest Ancestors"). Did bipedalism develop as a means of pursuing prey? Should the primary theme of human evolution be summed up as "man the hunter" and "woman the gatherer"? Indeed, for early hominid evolution, how about "man the hunted"?

Not all the research and theoretical speculations taking place in the field of paleoanthropology are so controversial. Most scientists, in fact, go about their work quietly and methodically, generating hypotheses that are much less explosive and yet have the cumulative effect of enriching our understanding of the details of human evolution. Our ability to glean from the fossil record is not completely without hope. In fact, informed speculation is what makes possible essays such as "Rethinking Neanderthals" by Joe Alper, and "Twilight of the Neandertals" by Kate Wong. Each is a fine example of careful, systematic, and thought-provoking work that is based upon an increased understanding of hominid fossil sites, as well as the more general environmental circumstances in which our predecessors lived.

As we mull over the controversies outlined in this unit, we should not take them as reflecting an inherent weakness of the

© Nick Koudis/Getty Images

field of paleoanthropology, but rather as symbolic of its strength: the ability and willingness to scrutinize, question, and reflect (endlessly) on every bit of evidence.

Contrary to the way that the proponents of creationism or "intelligent design theory" would have it, an admission of doubt is not an expression of ignorance but simply a frank recognition of the imperfect state of our knowledge. If we are to increase our understanding of ourselves, we must maintain an atmosphere of free inquiry without preconceived notions and unquestioning commitment to a particular point of view.

To paraphrase anthropologist Ashley Montagu, *while creationism embraces certainty without proof, science embraces proof without certainty.*

UNIT 4

The Fossil Evidence

Unit Selections

Learning Outcomes

After reading this unit, you will be able to:

- Describe what the last common ancestor of hominids and chimpanzees looked like.

- Determine under what circumstances bipedalism evolved and list its advantages.

- Draw the early hominid family tree.

- Explain why the fossil *Sediba* shows "one can no longer assign isolated bones to a genus."

- Discuss the successful adaptation of the Neanderthals with respect to anatomy, technology, and sociality.

- Describe what happened to the Neanderthals.

Student Website

www.mhhe.com/cls

Internet References

Fossil Hominids FAQ
www.talkorigins.org/faqs/homs
Institute of Human Origins
http://iho.asu.edu/node/27
Long Foreground: Human Prehistory
www.wsu.edu/gened/learn-modules/top_longfor/lfopen-index.html

to speculate about its origins, and to figure out that we have about 30,000 genes in our genome is no reason to assume that evolution has come to a standstill. As gene frequencies change, natural selection acts on the outcome, the expression of those genes. No one doubts, for instance, that fish benefit from being able to see. Yet species reared in total darkness—as are the small, cave-dwelling characin of Mexico—fail to develop their visual capacity. Through evolutionary time, traits that are unexpressed are eventually lost. If populations of these fish are isolated in caves long enough, youngsters descended from those original populations will no longer be able to develop eyesight at all, even if reared in sunlight.

If human compassion develops only under particular rearing conditions, and if an increasing proportion of the species survives to breeding age without developing compassion, it won't make any difference how useful this trait was among our ancestors. It will become like sight in cave-dwelling fish.

No doubt our descendants thousands of years from now (should our species survive) will still be bipedal, symbol-generating apes. Most likely they will be adept at using sophisticated technologies. But will they still be human in the way we, shaped by a long heritage of cooperative breeding, currently define ourselves?

Critical Thinking

1. Why does the author say that human mothers need help in rearing a child? What was the "old answer" to this problem? What does the new evidence indicate?

2. What are "allomothers" and how do the Efe and Aka Pygmies illustrate their importance?

3. What is "cooperative breeding" and what have been its advantages for our ancestors?

4. What does it take to become a "cooperative breeder"? How do wild dogs illustrate this?

5. What is the "evolutionary logic" behind cooperative breeding?

6. Discuss "partible paternity" and its benefits in the cultures cited.

7. What other kinds of help are available to human mothers?

8. What is "priming" and how does it seem to come about?

9. Is genetic relatedness a reliable predictor of love? Explain.

10. What do human babies do to motivate mothers to nurture them? In what respect are humans different from apes? How important is babbling?

11. What have most Western researchers presumed to be the "normal human adaptation"? In terms of developmental outcomes, what is the most relevant factor, according to the author? How does the NICHD study bear upon this issue? What does the author have to say about day care?

12. Why is the author worried with regard to the human capacity for empathy?

This article was adapted from *"Cooperation, Empathy, and the Needs of Human Infants,"* a Tanner Lecture delivered at the University of Utah. It is used with the permission of the Tanner Lectures on Human Values, a Corporation, University of Utah, Salt Lake City.

From *Natural History,* May 2001, pp. 50–62. adapted from *Cooperation, Empathy, and the Needs of Human Infants,* a Tanner Lecture.
Copyright © 2001 Tanner Lectures on Human Values, Inc., University of Utah, Salt Lake City.

its tropical climate was hospitable to apes, and because anatomical studies of modern primates had convinced him that humans were more "allied" with African apes (chimpanzees and gorillas) than Asian apes (orangutans and gibbons). Others disagreed, arguing that Asian apes were closer to modern humans.

As it happened, the first truly ancient remains of a hominid—a fossilized skullcap and teeth more than half a million years old—were found in Asia, on the island of Java, in 1891. "Java man," as the creature was called, was later classified as a member of *Homo erectus,* a species that arose 1.8 million years ago and may have been one of our direct ancestors.

So began a century of discovery notable for spectacular finds, in which the timeline of human prehistory began to take shape and the debate continued over whether Asia or Africa was the human birthplace.

In 1924, the Australian anatomist Raymond Dart, looking through a crate of fossils from a limestone quarry in South Africa, discovered a small skull. The first early hominid from Africa, the Taung child, as it was known, was a juvenile member of *Australopithecus africanus,* a species that lived one million to two million years ago, though at the time skeptical scientists said the chimpanzee-size braincase was too small for a hominid.

In 1959, archaeologist Louis Leakey and his wife Mary, working in Olduvai Gorge in Tanzania, discovered a bit of hominid jawbone that would later become known as *Paranthropus boisei.* The 1.75-million-year-old fossil was the first of many hominids the Leakeys, their son Richard and their associates would find in East Africa, strengthening the case that hominids indeed originated in Africa. Their work inspired American and European researchers to sweep through the Great Rift Valley, a geologic fault that runs through Kenya, Tanzania and Ethiopia and exposes rock layers that are millions of years old.

In 1974, paleoanthropologists Donald Johanson and Tom Gray, digging in Hadar, Ethiopia, found the partial skeleton of the earliest known hominid at the time—a female they called Lucy, after the Beatles' song "Lucy in the Sky with Diamonds," which was playing in camp as they celebrated. At 3.2 million years old, Lucy was remarkably primitive, with a brain and body about the size of a chimpanzee's. But her ankle, knee and pelvis showed that she walked upright like us.

This meant Lucy was a hominid—only humans and our close relatives in the human family habitually walk upright on the ground. A member of the species *Australopithecus afarensis,* which lived from 3.9 million to 2.9 million years ago, Lucy helped answer some key questions. She confirmed that upright walking evolved long before hominids began using stone tools—about 2.6 million years ago—and *before* their brains began to expand dramatically. But her upright posture and gait raised new questions. How long had it taken to evolve the anatomy to balance on two feet? What prompted some ancient ape to stand up and begin walking down the path toward humanness? And what kind of ape was it?

Lucy, of course, couldn't answer those questions. But what came before her? For 20 years after her discovery, it was as if the earliest chapter of the human story were missing.

One of the first teams to search for Lucy's ancestor was the Middle Awash project, which formed in 1981 when White and Asfaw joined Berkeley archaeologist J. Desmond Clark to search for fossils and stone tools in Ethiopia. They got off to a promising start—finding 3.9-million-year-old fragments of a skull and a slightly younger thighbone—but they were unable to return to the Middle Awash until 1990, because Ethiopian officials imposed a moratorium on searching for fossils while they rewrote their antiquities laws. Finally, in 1992, White's graduate student, Gen Suwa, saw a glint in the desert near Aramis. It was the root of a tooth, a molar, and its size and shape indicated that it belonged to a hominid. Suwa and other members of the Middle Awash project soon collected other fossils, including a child's lower jaw with a milk molar still attached. State-of-the-art dating methods indicated that they were 4.4 million years old.

The team proposed in the journal *Nature* in 1994 that the fossils—now known as *Ardipithecus ramidus*—represented the "long-sought potential root species for the Hominidae," meaning that the fossils belonged to a new species of hominid that could have given rise to all later hominids. The idea that it was a member of the human family was based primarily on its teeth—in particular, the absence of large, dagger-like canines sharpened by the lower teeth. Living and extinct apes have such teeth, while hominids don't. But the gold standard for being a hominid was upright walking. So was *A. ramidus* really a hominid or an extinct ape?

White joked at the time that he would be delighted with more fossils—in particular, a skull and thighbone. It was as if he had placed an order. Within two months, another graduate student of White's, Ethiopian paleoanthropologist Yohannes Haile-Selassie, spotted two pieces of a bone from the palm of a hand—their first sign of Ardi. The team members eventually found 125 pieces of Ardi's skeleton. She had been a muscular female who stood almost four feet tall but could have weighed as much as 110 pounds, with a body and brain roughly the same size as a chimpanzee's. As they got a good look at Ardi's body plan, they soon realized that they were looking at an entirely new type of hominid.

It was the find of a lifetime. But they were daunted by Ardi's condition. Her bones were so brittle that they crumbled when touched. White called them "road kill."

The researchers spent three field seasons digging out entire blocks of sedimentary rock surrounding the fossils, encasing the blocks in plaster and driving them to the National Museum of Ethiopia in Addis Ababa. In the museum lab, White painstakingly injected glue from syringes into each fragment and then used dental tools and brushes, often under a microscope, to remove the silty clay from the glue-hardened fossils. Meanwhile, Suwa, today a paleoanthropologist at the University of Tokyo, analyzed key fossils with modified CT scanners to see what was inside them and used computer imaging to digitally restore the crushed skull. Finally, he and anatomist C. Owen Lovejoy worked from the fossils and the computer images to make physical models of the skull and pelvis.

It's a measure of the particularity, complexity and thoroughness of the researchers' efforts to understand Ardi in depth that they took 15 years to publish their detailed findings, which appeared this past October in a series of 11 papers in the journal *Science.* In short, they wrote that Ardi and fossils from 35 other members of her species, all found in the Middle Awash, represented a new type of early hominid that wasn't much like a chimpanzee, gorilla or a human. "We have seen the ancestor and it's not a chimpanzee," says White.

This came as a surprise to researchers who had proposed that the earliest hominids would look and act a lot like chimpanzees. They are our closest living relatives, sharing 96 percent of our DNA, and they are capable of tool use and complex social behavior. But Ardi's discoverers proposed that chimpanzees have changed so dramatically as they have evolved over the past six million years or so, that today's chimpanzees make poor models for the last common ancestor we shared.

In his lab at Kent State University, Lovejoy recently demonstrated why Ardi is so unusual. He gently lined up four bones from Ardi's hand on his lab bench, and he showed how they fit together in a way that allowed Ardi's hand to bend far backward at the wrist. By comparison, a chimpanzee's wrist is stiff, which allows the animal to put its weight on its knuckles as it moves on the ground—knuckle walking. "If you wanted to evolve Ardi's hand, you couldn't do it from this," he said, waving a set of bones from a chimpanzee hand in the air. If Lovejoy is right, this means Ardi—and our upright-walking ancestors—never went through a knuckle-walking stage after they came down from the trees to live on the ground, as some experts have long believed.

As evidence that Ardi walked upright on the ground, Lovejoy pointed to a cast of her upper pelvic blades, which are shorter and broader than an ape's. They would have let her balance on one leg at a time while walking upright. "This is a monstrous change—this thing has been a biped for a very long time," Lovejoy said.

But Ardi didn't walk like us or, for that matter, like Lucy either. Ardi's lower pelvis, like a chimpanzee's, had powerful hip and thigh muscles that would have made it difficult to run as fast or as far as modern humans can without injuring her hamstrings. And she had an opposable big toe, so her foot was able to grasp branches, suggesting she still spent a lot of time in the trees—to escape predators, pick fruit or even sleep, presumably in nests made of branches and leaves. This unexpected combination of traits was a "shocker," says Lovejoy.

He and his colleagues have proposed that Ardi represents an early stage of human evolution when an ancient ape body plan was being remodeled to live in two worlds—in the trees and on the ground, where hominids increasingly foraged for plants, eggs and small critters.

The Ardi research also challenged the long-held views that hominids evolved in a grassy savanna, says Middle Awash project geologist Giday WoldeGabriel of Los Alamos National Laboratory. The Ardi researchers' thorough canvassing—"You crawl on your hands and knees, collecting every piece of bone, every piece of wood, every seed, every snail, every scrap," White says—indicates that Ardi lived in woodland with a closed canopy, so little light reached grass and plants on the forest floor. Analyzing thousands of specimens of fossilized plants and animals, as well as hundreds of samples of chemicals in sediments and tooth enamel, the researchers found evidence of such forest species as hackberry, fig and palm trees in her environment. Ardi lived alongside monkeys, kudu antelopes and peafowl—animals that prefer woodlands, not open grasslands.

Ardi is also providing insights into ancient hominid behavior. Moving from the trees to the ground meant that hominids became easier prey. Those that were better at cooperating could live in larger social groups and were less likely to become a big cat's next meal. At the same time, A. ramidus males were not much larger than females and they had evolved small, unsharpened canine teeth. That's similar to modern humans, who are largely cooperative, and in contrast to modern chimpanzees, whose males use their size to dominate females and brandish their dagger-like canines to intimidate other males.

As hominids began increasingly to work together, Lovejoy says, they also adopted other previously unseen behaviors—to regularly carry food in their hands, which allowed them to provision mates or their young more effectively. This behavior, in turn, may have allowed males to form tighter bonds with female mates and to invest in the upbringing of their offspring in a way not seen in African apes. All this reinforced the shift to life on the ground, upright walking and social cooperation, says Lovejoy.

Not everyone is convinced that Ardi walked upright, in part because the critical evidence comes from her pelvis, which was crushed. While most researchers agree that she is a hominid, based on features in her teeth and skull, they say she could be a type of hominid that was a distant cousin of our direct ancestor—a newfound offshoot on the human family tree. "I think it's solid" that Ardi is a hominid, if you define hominids by their skull and teeth, says Rick Potts, a paleoanthropologist at the Smithsonian's National Museum of Natural History. But, like many others who have not seen the fossils, he has yet to be convinced that the crushed but reconstructed pelvis proves upright walking, which could mean that Ardi might have been an extinct ape that was "experimenting" with some degree of upright walking. "The period between four million to seven million years is when we know the least," says Potts. "Understanding what is a great ape and what is a hominid is tough."

As researchers sort out where Ardi sits in the human family tree, they agree that she is advancing fundamental questions about human evolution: How can we identify the earliest members of the human family? How do we recognize the first stages of upright walking? What did our common ancestor with chimpanzees look like? "We didn't have much at all before," says Bill Kimbel, an Arizona State University paleoanthropologist. "*Ardipithecus* gives us a prism to look through to test alternatives."

After Ardi's discovery, researchers naturally began to wonder what came before her. They didn't have long to wait.

Starting in 1997, Haile-Selassie, now at the Cleveland Museum of Natural History, found fossils between 5.2 million and 5.8 million years old in the Middle Awash. A toe bone suggested its owner had walked upright. The bones looked so much like a primitive version of A. ramidus he proposed these fossils belonged to her direct ancestor—a new species he eventually named Ardipithecus kadabba.

In 2000, Martin Pickford of the College of France and Brigitte Senut of the National Museum of Natural History in Paris announced their team had found an even older hominid—13 fossils representing a species that lived six million years ago in the Tugen Hills of Kenya. Two of the fossils were thighbones, including one that provided the oldest direct evidence of upright walking in a hominid. They named this creature Orrorin tugenensis, drawing on a Tugen legend of the "original man" who settled the Tugen Hills. Informally, in honor of its year of discovery, they called it Millennium man.

Hot on the heels of that discovery came the most surprising one of all—a skull from Chad, about 1,500 miles west of the Great Rift Valley of eastern Africa where many of the most ancient hominids have been found. A Chadian student named Ahounta Djimdoumalbaye picked up a ball of rock on the floor of the Djurab Desert, where windstorms blow sand dunes like waves on a sea and expose fossils buried for millions of years. When Djimdoumalbaye turned over the stone, he stared into the vacant eye sockets of an ape-like face—the skull of a primate that lived six million to seven million years ago on the shores of an ancient lake. It had traits that suggested it was a hominid—a small lower face and canines and a skull that seemed to sit atop its spine, as in upright walkers. Paleontologist Michel Brunet, then of the University of Poitiers in France, introduced it as the oldest known hominid, *Sahelanthropus tchadensis*. (Its nickname is Toumaï, which means "hope of life" in the Goran language.) But proving that a skull walked upright is difficult, and questions linger about whether *Sahelanthropus* is a bona fide hominid or not.

Taken together, fossils discovered over the past 15 years have provided snapshots of several different creatures that were alive in Africa at the critical time when the earliest members of the human family were emerging. When these snapshots are added to the human family album, they double the time researchers can see back into our past—from Lucy at 3.2 million years to Toumaï at almost 7 million years.

One of the most sought-after fossils of that distant era was Lucy's direct ancestor. In 1994, 20 years after Lucy's skeleton was discovered, a team in Kenya led by Meave Leakey (the wife of Richard Leakey) found teeth and parts of a jaw as well as two pieces of shinbone that showed the creature walked upright. The fossils, named *Australopithecus anamensis*, were 4.1 million years old.

"This has been a fascinating 40 years to be in paleoanthropology," says Johanson, "one of the great times to be in this field." But, he adds, "there's still enormous confusion" about the murky time before 4 million years ago.

One thing that *is* clear is that these early fossils belong in a class by themselves. These species did not look or act like other known apes or like Lucy and other members of *Australopithecus*. They were large-bodied ground dwellers that stood up and walked on two legs. But if you watched them move, you would not mistake them for Lucy's species. They clung to life in the trees, but were poised to venture into more open country. In many ways, these early species resemble one another more than any fossils ever found before, as if there was a new developmental or evolutionary stage that our ancestors passed through before the transition was complete from ape to hominid. Indeed, when the skulls of Toumaï and Ardi are compared, the resemblance is "striking," says paleoanthropologist Christoph Zollikofer of the University of Zurich in Switzerland. The fossils are too far apart in time to be members of the same species, but their skulls are more like each other than they are like Lucy's species, perhaps signaling similar adaptations in diet or reproductive and social behavior.

The only way to find out how all these species are related to one another and to us is to find more bones. In particular, researchers need to find more overlapping parts of very early fossils so they can be compared directly—such as an upper end of a thighbone for both Ardi and Toumaï to compare with the upper thighbone of *O. tugenensis*.

At Aramis, as soon as the clan leaders gave the Middle Awash team their blessing, White began dispatching team members like an air traffic controller, directing them to fan out over the slope near Ardi's grave. The sun was high in the sky, though, making it hard to distinguish beige bone among the bleached out sediments. This time, the team found no new hominid fossils.

But one morning later that week, the team members drove up a dry riverbed to a site on the western margin of the Middle Awash. Only a few moments after hiking into the fossil beds, a Turkish postdoctoral researcher, Cesur Pehlevan, planted a yellow flag among the cobbles of the remote gully. "Tim!" he shouted. "Hominid?" White walked over and silently examined the molar, turning it over in his hand. White has the ability to look at a tooth or bone fragment and recognize almost immediately whether it belongs to a hominid. After a moment, he pronounced his verdict: "very good, Cesur. It's virtually unworn." The molar belonged to a young adult *A. kadabba*, the species whose fossils began to be found here in 1997. Now the researchers had one more piece to help fill in the portrait of this 5.8-million-year-old species.

"There's your discovery moment," said White. He reflected on the fossils they've bagged in this remote desert. "This year, we've got *A. kadabba, A. anamensis, A. garhi, H. erectus, H. sapiens*." That's five different kinds of hominids, most of which were unknown when White first started searching for fossils here in 1981. "The Middle Awash is a unique area," he said. "It is the only place on the planet Earth where you can look at the full scope of human evolution."

Critical Thinking

1. Why is the Middle Awash area of Ethiopiaa very important site for hominid fossil-hunting? Why is *Ardipithecus africanus,* in particular, so important?

2. Why did Charles Darwin contend that humans probably arose in Africa? How did "Java man" seem to contradict Darwin's view? How did *Australopithecus africanus* and *Paranthropus boisei* appear to support it?

3. Why was Lucy, a member of the species *Australopithecus afarensis,* so important and what key questions did she help answer?

4. What unexpected combination of traits of *Ardipithecus ramidus* made it a "shocker," according to Owen Lovejoy? What long-held view did the "Ardi" research challenge? What is the specific evidence for this challenge?

5. How is Ardi providing insights into ancient hominid behavior, according to Lovejoy?

6. Why is it that not everyone is convinced that Ardi walked upright?

7. What is even earlier evidence that there were hominids walking upright?

8. What *is* clear about these fossils that are earlier than Lucy? What do they have in common?

ANN GIBBONS is a correspondent for *Science* and the author of The First Human: The Race to Discover Our Earliest Ancestors.

First of Our Kind

**Sensational fossils from South Africa spark debate
over how we came to be human.**

KATE WONG

Sometime between three million and two million years ago, perhaps on a primeval savanna in Africa, our ancestors became recognizably human. For more than a million years their australopithecine predecessors—Lucy and her kind, who walked upright like us yet still possessed the stubby legs, tree-climbing hands and small brains of their ape forebears—had thrived in and around the continent's forests and woodlands. But their world was changing. Shifting climate favored the spread of open grasslands, and the early australopithecines gave rise to new lineages. One of these offshoots evolved long legs, tool making hands and an enormous brain. This was our genus, *Homo*, the primate that would rule the planet.

For decades paleoanthropologists have combed remote corners of Africa on hand and knee for fossils of *Homo's* earliest representatives, seeking to understand the details of how our genus rose to prominence. Their efforts have brought only modest gains—a jawbone here, a handful of teeth there. Most of the recovered fossils instead belong to either ancestral australopithecines or later members of *Homo*—creatures too advanced to illuminate the order in which our distinctive traits arose or the selective pressures that fostered their emergence. Specimens older than two million years with multiple skeletal elements preserved that could reveal how the *Homo* body plan came together eluded discovery. Scientists' best guess is that the transition occurred in East Africa, where the oldest fossils attributed to *Homo* have turned up, and that *Homo's* hallmark characteristics allowed it to incorporate more meat into its diet—a rich source of calories in an environment where fruits and nuts had become scarce. But with so little evidence to go on, the origin of our genus has remained as mysterious as ever.

Lee Berger thinks he has found a big piece of the puzzle. A paleoanthropologist at the University of the Witwatersrand in Johannesburg, South Africa, he recently discovered a trove of fossils that he and his team believe could revolutionize researchers' understanding of *Homo's* roots. In the white-walled confines of room 210 at the university's Institute for Human Evolution, he watches as Bernard Wood of George Washington University paces in front of the four plastic cases that have been removed from their fireproof safe and placed on a table clothed in royal blue velvet. The foam-lined cases are open, revealing the nearly two-million-year-old fossils inside. One holds pelvis and leg bones. Another contains ribs and vertebrae. A third displays arm bones and a clavicle. And a fourth houses a skull. On a counter opposite the table, more cases hold a second partial skeleton, including a nearly complete hand.

Wood, a highly influential figure in the field, pauses in front of the skull and leans in for a closer look. He strokes his beard as he considers the dainty teeth, the grapefruit-size brain-case. Straightening back up, he shakes his head. "I'm not often at a loss for words," he says slowly, almost as if to himself, "but wow. Just wow."

Berger grins. He has seen this reaction before. Since he unveiled the finds in 2010, scientists from all over the world have been flocking to his lab to gawk at the breathtaking fossils. Based on the unique anatomical package the skeletons present, Berger and his team assigned the remains to a new species, *Australopithecus sediba*. They furthermore propose that the combination of primitive Australopithecus traits and advanced *Homo* traits evident in the bones qualifies the species for a privileged place on the family tree: as the ancestor of *Homo*. The stakes are high. If Berger is right, paleoanthropologists will have to completely rethink where, when and how *Homo* got its start—and what it means to be human in the first place.

The Road Not Taken

In the middle of the rock-strewn dirt road that winds through the John Nash Nature Reserve, Berger brings the Jeep to a halt and points to a smaller road that branches right. For 17 years he had made the 40-kilometer trip northwest from Johannesburg to the 9,000-hectare parcel of privately owned wilderness and driven past this turnoff, continuing along the main road, past the resident giraffes and warthogs and wildebeests, to a cave he was excavating just a few kilometers away called Gladysvale. In 1948 American paleontologists Frank Peabody and Charles Camp came to this area to look for fossils of hominins (modern humans and their extinct relatives) on the advice of famed

South African paleontologist Robert Broom, who had found such fossils in the caves of Sterkfontein and Swartkrans, eight kilometers away. Peabody suspected that Broom had intentionally sent them on a wild goose chase, so unimpressed was he with the sites here. Little did Berger or the expeditioners before him know that had they only followed this smaller path—one of several miners' tracks used in the early 1900s to cart the limestone that built Johannesburg from quarries out to the main road—they would have made the discovery of a lifetime.

Berger, now 46 years old, never imagined he would find something like A. sediba. Although he thought *Homo* might have had roots in South Africa instead of East Africa, he knew the odds of making a big find were slim. Hominin fossils are extremely rare, so "you don't have any expectations," he reflects. What is more, he was focused on the so-called Cradle of Humankind, an already intensively explored region whose caves had long been yielding australopithecines generally considered to be more distantly related to *Homo* than the East African australopithecines seemed to be. And so Berger continued to toil at Gladysvale day after day, year after year. Because he found little in the way of hominins among the millions of animal fossils there—just scraps of a species called A. africanus—he busied himself with another goal: dating the site. A critical problem with interpreting the South African hominin fossils was that scientists had not yet figured out how to reliably determine how old they were. In East Africa, hominin fossils come from sediments sandwiched between layers of volcanic ash that blanketed the landscape during long-ago eruptions. Geologists can ascertain how old an ash layer is by analyzing its chemical "fingerprint." A fossil that originates from a layer of sediment that sits in between two volcanic ashes is thus intermediate in age between those two ashes. The cave sites in the Cradle of Humankind lack volcanic ashes. Through his 17 years of trial and error at Gladysvale, however, Berger and his colleagues hit on techniques that circumvented the problem of not having ash to work with.

Those techniques would soon come in very handy. On August 1, 2008, while surveying the reserve for potential new fossil sites in the area that he had identified using Google Earth, Berger turned right on the miners' track he had passed by for 17 years and followed it to a three- by four-meter hole in the ground blasted by the miners. Eyeballing the site, he found a handful of animal fossils—enough to warrant a trip back for a closer look. He returned on August 15 with his then nine-year-old son, Matthew, and dog, Tau. Matthew took off into the bush after Tau, and within minutes he shouted to his father that he had found a fossil. Berger doubted it was anything important—probably just an antelope bone—but in a show of fatherly support, he made his way over to inspect the find. There, protruding from a dark hunk of rock nestled in the tall grass by the corpse of a lightning-struck tree, was the tip of a collarbone.

As soon as Berger laid eyes on it, he knew it belonged to a hominin. In the months that followed he found more of the clavicle's owner, along with another partial skeleton, 20 meters away in the miners' pit. To date, Berger and his team have recovered more than 220 bones of A. sediba from the site—more than all the known early *Homo* bones combined. He christened the site Malapa, meaning "homestead" in the local Sesotho language. Using the approaches honed at Gladysvale, the geologists on Berger's team would later date the remains with remarkable precision to 1.977 million years ago, give or take 2,000 years.

A Patchwork Predecessor

That the Malapa Fossils include so many body parts is important because it means they can offer unique insights into the order in which key *Homo* traits appeared. And what they show very clearly is that quintessentially human features did not necessarily evolve as a package deal, as was thought. Take the pelvis and the brain, for example. Conventional wisdom holds that the broad, flat pelvis of australopithecines evolved into the bowl-shaped pelvis seen in the bigger-brained *Homo* to allow delivery of babies with larger heads. Yet A. sediba has a *Homo*-like pelvis with a broad birth canal in conjunction with a teeny brain—just 420 cubic centimeters, a third of the size of our own brain. This combination shows brain expansion was not driving the metamorphosis of the pelvis in A. sediba's lineage.

Not only do the A. sediba fossils mingle old and new versions of general features, such as brain size and pelvis shape, but the pattern repeats at deeper levels, like an evolutionary fractal. Analysis of the interior of the young male's braincase shows that the brain, while small, possessed an expanded frontal region, indicating an advanced reorganization of gray matter; the adult female's upper limb pairs a long arm—a primitive holdover from a tree-dwelling ancestor—with short, straight fingers adapted to making and using tools (although the muscle markings on the bones attest to powerful, apelike grasping capabilities). In some instances, the juxtaposition of old and new is so improbable that had the bones not been found joined together, researchers would have interpreted them as belonging to entirely different creatures. The foot, for instance, combines a heel bone like an ancient ape's with an anklebone like *Homo's*, according to Malapa team member Bernard Zipfel of the University of the Witwatersrand. It is as if evolution was playing Mr. Potato Head, as Berger puts it.

The extreme mosaicism evident in A. sediba, Berger says, should be a lesson to paleoanthropologists. Had he found any number of its bones in isolation, he would have classified them differently. Based on the pelvis, he could have called it H. erectus. The arm alone suggests an ape. The anklebone is a match for a modern human's. And like the blind men studying the individual parts of the elephant, he would have been wrong. "Sediba shows that one can no longer assign isolated bones to a genus," Berger asserts. That means, in his view, finds such as a 2.3-million-year-old upper jaw from Hadar, Ethiopia, that has been held up as the earliest trace of *Homo* cannot safely be assumed to have belonged to the *Homo* line.

Taking that jaw out of the running would make A. sediba older than any of the well-dated *Homo* fossils but still younger than A. afarensis, putting it in pole position for the immediate ancestor of the genus, Berger's team contends. Furthermore, considering A. sediba's advanced features, the researchers propose that it could be specifically ancestral to H. erectus (a portion of which is considered by some to be a different species called H. ergaster). Thus, instead of the traditional view in which A. afarensis begat H. habilis, which begat H. erectus, he submits that A. africanus is the likely ancestor of A. sediba, which then spawned H. erectus.

If so, that arrangement would relegate H. habilis to a dead-end side branch of the human family tree. It might even kick A. afarensis—long considered the ancestor of all later hominins, including A. africanus and *Homo*—to the evolutionary curb, too. Berger points out that A. sediba's heel is more primitive than that of A. afarensis, indicating that A. sediba either underwent an evolutionary reversal toward a more primitive heel or that it descended from a different lineage than the one that includes A. afarensis and A. africanus—one that has yet to be discovered.

"In the South, we have a saying: 'You dance with the girl you brought,'" quips Berger, who grew up on a farm in Sylvania, Ga. "And that is what paleoanthropologists have been doing" in trying to piece together the origin of *Homo* from the fossils that have turned up in East Africa. "Now we have to recognize there is more potential out there," he states. Maybe the East Side story of human origins is wrong. The traditional view of South Africa's oldest hominin fossils is that they represent a separate evolutionary experiment that ultimately fizzled out. A. sediba could turn the tables and reveal, in South Africa, another lineage, the one that ultimately gave rise to humankind as we know it (indeed, sediba is the Sesotho word for "fountain" or "wellspring").

William Kimbel of Arizona State University, who led the team that found the 2.3-million-year-old jawbone in Ethiopia, is having none of it. The idea that one needs a skeleton to classify a specimen is a "nonsensical argument," he retorts. The key is to find pieces of anatomy that contain diagnostic traits, he says, and the Hadar jaw has features clearly linking it to *Homo*, such as the parabolic shape formed by its tooth rows. Kimbel, who has seen the Malapa fossils but not studied them in depth, finds their *Homo*-like traits intriguing, although he is not sure what to make of them. He scoffs at the suggestion that they are directly ancestral to H. erectus, however. "I don't see how a taxon with a few characteristics that look like *Homo* in South Africa can be the ancestor [of *Homo*] when there's something in East Africa that is clearly *Homo* 300,000 years earlier," he declares, referring to the jaw.

Kimbel is not alone in rejecting the argument for A. sediba as the rootstock of *Homo*. "There are too many things that do not fit, particularly the dates and geography," comments Meave Leakey of the Turkana Basin Institute in Kenya, whose own research has focused on fossils from East Africa. "It is much more likely that the South African hominins are a separate radiation that took place in the south of the continent."

Rene Bobe of George Washington University says that if the A. sediba remains were older—say, around 2.5 million years old—they might make for a plausible *Homo* ancestor. But at 1.977 million years old, they are just too primitive in their overall form to be ancestral to fossils from Kenya's Lake Turkana region that are just a tad younger yet have many more indisputable Homo traits. Berger counters that A. sediba almost certainly existed as a species before the Malapa individuals. Bobe and others maintain that such information is not currently known. "Paleoanthropologists tend to think of the fossils they find as being in a key position within the [hominin] phylogenetic tree, and in many cases that's unlikely to be the situation," Bobe observes. From a statistical standpoint, "if you have [hominin] populations distributed across Africa, evolving in complex ways, why would the one you find be the ancestor?"

Berger has found a sympathetic ear in Wood, who says Berger is "absolutely right" that A. sediba demonstrates that isolated bones do not predict what the rest of the animal looks like. A. sediba shows that the combinations of traits evident from previous fossil discoveries do not exhaust the possibilities, Wood remarks. But he does not endorse the suggestion that A. sediba is the ancestor of Homo. "There are not many characters linking it to Homo," he notes, and A. sediba may have evolved those traits independently from the Homo lineage. "I just think sediba has got too much to do in order to evolve into [erectus]," Wood says.

Resolution of the issue of where A. sediba belongs in our family tree is hampered by the lack of a clear definition of the genus Homo. Coming up with one, however, is a taller order than it might seem. With so few specimens from the transition period, and most of them being scraps, identifying those features that first distinguished Homo from its australopithecine forebears—those traits that made us truly human—has proved challenging. The skeletons from Malapa expose just how vexing the situation is: they are so much more complete than any early Homo specimen that it is very difficult to compare them with anything. "Sediba may force us to come up with a definition," Berger says.

All in the Details

Whatever the position of the Malapa fossils in the family tree, they are poised to provide researchers with the most detailed portrait yet of an early hominin species, in part because they make up multiple individuals. In addition to the juvenile male and the adult female, the two most complete specimens, Berger's team has collected bones representing another four individuals, including a baby. Populations are incredibly rare in the human fossil record, and the individuals at Malapa have the added benefit of peerless preservation. Hominin bones that virtually never survive the ravages of deep time have turned up here: a paper-thin shoulder blade, the delicate sliver that is the first rib, pea-size finger bones, vertebrae with spiny projections intact. And a number of bones that were previously known only from fragments are complete. Before the discovery of Malapa, paleoanthropologists did not have a single complete arm from an early hominin, meaning that the limb lengths that are used to reconstruct such essential behaviors as locomotion are estimates. Even Lucy—the most complete hominin of such antiquity back when she was found in 1974—is missing significant chunks of her arm and leg bones. In the adult female from Malapa, in contrast, virtually the entire upper limb is preserved—from shoulder blade to hand. Only the very last digits of some of her fingers and some wristbones are missing, and Berger expects to find those—and the rest of the bones of both skeletons when he excavates the site (thus far the team has only collected bones visible from the surface, rather than systematically digging for buried material). From this evidence, researchers will be able to reconstruct how A. sediba matured, how it moved around the landscape and how members of the population varied from one another, among other things.

It is not only the bones that promise to tell new tales. Malapa has also yielded some other materials that could literally flesh out researchers' understanding of A. sediba. Paleontologists have long thought that during the fossilization process, all of an organism's organic components—such as skin, hair, organs, and so forth—are lost to decomposition, leaving behind only mineralized bone. But when Berger saw a CT scan of the skull of the young male, he noticed a place on the crown where there appeared to be an air space between the surface of the fossil and the contour of the actual bone. Examining the spot more closely, he observed a distinctive pattern on the surface that looked like the structural components of skin. He is now conducting extensive tests to determine whether the odd-looking patch on the male's crown and another on the female's chin—and similar patches on antelope bones from the site—are in fact skin.

Preserved skin, if confirmed as such, could reveal A. sediba's coloring and the density and patterning of its hair. Such evidence could also show the distribution of sweat glands—information that would provide insights into how well the species was able to regulate its body temperature, which in turn would have affected how active it was. Sweat glands could additionally offer clues to brain evolution: an effective means of keeping cool was a prerequisite for the emergence of large brain size—a trademark characteristic of Homo—because brains are temperature-sensitive. And if organic material is present, Berger might even be able to obtain DNA from the remains. Currently the oldest hominin DNA to have been sequenced is 100,000-year-old DNA from a Neandertal. But because the preservation conditions at Malapa were apparently exceptional, Berger has some hope of getting genetic information from the much older A. sediba specimens. In that event, scientists might be able to determine whether the adult female and young male really were mother and son, as has been suggested, and how, if at all, the other hominins at the site fit in. Moreover, such a discovery would prompt researchers at other early hominin sites to test for DNA, which, if successful, could settle debates over how the various hominin species were related.

Preservation of organic remains would be a first in hominin paleontology, and the Malapa team knows it will need extraordinary evidence to persuade the research community of such a claim. Thus far, however, the test results support the hypothesis, and Berger thinks the odds are very good that future analyses will bear it out. After all, similar claims have been made for organic material from dinosaur bones, and those are tens of millions of years older than the Malapa fossils. Organic preservation in hominin assemblages might even be fairly common, he suggests—it is just that no one ever thought to look for it.

Another thing no one thought to look for in a hominin this old? Tartar. The surfaces of the young male's molar teeth bear dark brown stains. Fossil preparators typically clean off the

teeth when readying hominin remains for study. But it occurred to Berger that the stains might actually be the same gunk we modern humans fend off with toothbrushes and pilgrimages to the dentist. Ancient tartar would provide valuable insights into the evolution of the hominin diet.

Previous studies of what early humans ate have looked at carbon isotope ratios in teeth, which can indicate whether an animal dined on so-called C3 plants, such as trees and shrubs, or C4 plants, such as certain grasses and sedges—or, in the case of carnivorous species, preyed on animals that ate those plant foods—or some combination thereof over its lifetime. Such evidence is indirect and nonspecific. Tartar, in contrast, is the remnants of the food itself. The team is currently studying tiny silica crystals called phytoliths that are embedded in the tartar. Phytoliths come from plants, and some plants make species-specific forms of the crystals. Studies of these phytoliths can thus reveal exactly which kinds of plants an animal ate just before it died. By analyzing the isotope ratios, phytoliths and wear marks on A. sediba's teeth that can signal whether an animal was chewing harder or softer foods in the weeks before it perished, the team should be able to glean a wealth of subsistence data. And because the researchers have bones from A. sediba individuals across a range of developmental stages, they might even be able to figure out what babies ate versus adult fare, for instance.

In a review paper published in Science last October, Peter S. Ungar of the University of Arkansas and Matt Sponheimer of the University of Colorado at Boulder observed that recent analyses have hinted at unexpected diversity and complexity in the diets of our predecessors. Whereas Ardipithecus ramidus, one of the earliest putative hominins, dined primarily on C3 foods, as savanna chimpanzees do, other early African hominins appear to have eaten a mix of C3 and C4 foods. One species, Paranthropus robustus, even ate a mostly C4 diet, as Thure Cerling of the University of Utah and his colleagues reported last June in the Proceedings of the National Academy of Sciences USA. Scientists will no doubt be eager to see where on the dietary spectrum A. sediba falls and how that picture fits with emerging clues about the paleoenvironment at Malapa, which appears to have included an abundance of grasses and trees. Perhaps the dietary evidence will shine a light on how A. sediba was using that dexterous hand, with its apparent adaptations to tool use—and, by the same token, whether it used its long, ape-like arms to forage in the trees.

End of Days

The final days of the Malapa hominins appear to have been grim ones. Possible drought conditions may have made water hard to come by. Berger suspects that the hominins, desperate for a drink, may have tried to climb down into the then 30- to 50-meter-deep underground cavern at Malapa to access a shallow pool of freshwater and, in so doing, tumbled to their deaths. Perhaps the boy fell in first, and the adult female—maybe his mother—tried to rescue him only to fall in herself. A menagerie of other beasts, from antelopes to zebras, met the same fate, becoming entombed alongside the hominins for posterity.

Intriguingly, geologic evidence from the site indicates that the fossil assemblage at Malapa formed right around the same time that the earth was undergoing a geomagnetic reversal—a mysterious event in which the planet's polarity flips and magnetic north becomes magnetic south. The timing raises the question of whether the reversal somehow played a role in the demise of these creatures.

Scientists know very little about why reversals occur and whether they precipitate environmental change. Some geologists have suggested that these events could conceivably wreak ecological havoc—by compromising the magnetic field that shields organisms from deadly radiation, for example, or by confusing the internal navigation systems of migratory birds and other animals that use the earth's magnetic field to orient themselves. As one of the only places in the world that has a terrestrial record of a reversal and a collection of fossils from the same time, Malapa could offer rare insights into what happens when the planet's poles trade places.

Other evidence might throw additional light on their deaths. The fossilized bones of a pregnant antelope and her fetus from Malapa could help scientists pinpoint the time of year that the hominins died to within a couple weeks: antelopes give birth within a very narrow interval in the spring, and analysis of the fetus should allow researchers to figure out how far along the antelope was before she died. Meanwhile traces of maggots and carrion beetles that set on the hominins after death could reveal how long the bodies were exposed before the cave's flowing sediments buried them.

In a sense, the work on A. sediba has only just begun. "You're walking all over hominin fossils," Berger tells visitors to Malapa on an austral spring morning in late November. They are standing on the rocky ground between the tree where Matthew found the clavicle and the mining pit where Berger found its owner. Climbing down into the pit, he points onlookers to bits of fossils peeking out of the rock and awaiting collection. The awestruck guests crane to glimpse an infant's arm bone, the lower jaw of a false saber-toothed cat, the area that appears to contain the rest of the young male's skeleton. Just by gathering remains exposed by the miners and the occasional rainstorm, the team has amassed one of the largest fossil hominin samples on record. Once the researchers begin excavating the roughly 500-square-meter site, Berger knows they will find more bones—many more. Extensive planning is under way to erect a structure to protect the site from the elements and serve as a state-of-the-art field laboratory for when they begin the formal excavation later this year, which will probe beyond the miners' leavings into the undisturbed parts of the deposit. Meanwhile, in the Malapa block lab at the University of the Witwatersrand, chunks of rock blasted from the miners' pit fill floor-to-ceiling shelves. Researchers will peer into the rocks with a CT scanner to look for hominin bones, including the adult female's missing skull.

So vast are Malapa's riches that Berger could probably spend the rest of his career working on them. Yet already he is thinking about where he wants to go next. A. sediba "has taught me that we really need a better record—and it's out there," he warrants. The mapping project that led Berger to Malapa identified more than three dozen new fossil sites in the Cradle alone that could potentially harbor hominin remains. He is lining up researchers to dig the most promising of those spots. Berger himself has his sights set farther afield. The Congo and Angola, among other places, have cave formations similar to the ones in the Cradle and have never been searched for hominin fossils, he observes. Perhaps there, in paleoanthropological terra incognita, he will find another unexpected emissary from the dawn of humankind that will rewrite the story of our origins once again.

Critical Thinking

1. How does the author summarize the relationship between changes in climate and in our ancestors' anatomy two million years ago?

2. In what respects is Australopithecus sediba a "patchwork predecessor"?

3. What is the "lesson to paleoanthropologists" regarding the extreme mosaicism?

4. How does Berger's interpretation of the fossil evidence differ from the traditional view? How do the paleoanthropologists working in East Africa counter Berger's claims?

5. In what ways are the Malapa fossils poised to provide researchers with the most detailed portrait yet of an early hominin species?

6. How does Berger describe what might have been the final days of the Malapa hominins? What might be the significance of the "geomagnetic upheaval"? How might other evidence throw additional light on their deaths?

7. In what sense has the work on A. sediba just begun?

Rethinking Neanderthals

Research suggests the so-called brutes fashioned tools, buried their dead, maybe cared for the sick and even conversed. But why, if they were so smart, did they disappear?

JOE ALPER

Bruno Maureille unlocks the gate in a chain-link fence, and we walk into the fossil bed past a pile of limestone rubble, the detritus of an earlier dig. We're 280 miles southwest of Paris, in rolling farm country dotted with long-haired cattle and etched by meandering streams. Maureille, an anthropologist at the University of Bordeaux, oversees the excavation of this storied site called Los Pradelles, where for three decades researchers have been uncovering, fleck by fleck, the remains of humanity's most notorious relatives, the Neanderthals.

We clamber 15 feet down a steep embankment into a swimming pool-size pit. Two hollows in the surrounding limestone indicate where shelters once stood. I'm just marveling at the idea that Neanderthals lived here about 50,000 years ago when Maureille, inspecting a long ledge that a student has been painstakingly chipping away, interrupts my reverie and calls me over. He points to a whitish object resembling a snapped pencil that's embedded in the ledge. "Butchered reindeer bone," he says. "And here's a tool, probably used to cut meat from one of these bones." The tool, or lithic, is shaped like a hand-size D.

All around the pit, I now see, are other lithics and fossilized bones. The place, Maureille says, was probably a butchery where Neanderthals in small numbers processed the results of what appear to have been very successful hunts. That finding alone is significant, because for a long time paleoanthropologists have viewed Neanderthals as too dull and too clumsy to use efficient tools, never mind organize a hunt and divvy, up the game. Fact is, this site, along with others across Europe and in Asia, is helping overturn the familiar conception of Neanderthals as dumb brutes. Recent studies suggest they were imaginative enough to carve artful objects and perhaps clever enough to invent a language.

Neanderthals, traditionally designated *Homo sapiens neanderthalensis,* were not only "human" but also, it turns out, more "modern" than scientists previously allowed. "In the minds of the European anthropologists who first studied them, Neanderthals were the embodiment of primitive humans, subhumans

if you will," says Fred H. Smith, a physical anthropologist at Loyola University in Chicago who has been studying Neanderthal DNA. "They were believed to be scavengers who made primitive tools and were incapable of language or symbolic thought." Now, he says, researchers believe that Neanderthals "were highly intelligent, able to adapt to a wide variety of ecological zones, and capable of developing highly functional tools to help them do so. They were quite accomplished."

Contrary to the view that Neanderthals were evolutionary failures—they died out about 28,000 years ago—they actually had quite a run. "If you take success to mean the ability to survive in hostile, changing environments, then Neanderthals were a great success," says archaeologist John Shea of the State University of New York at Stony Brook. "They lived 250,000 years or more in the harshest climates experienced by primates, not just humans." In contrast, we modern humans have only been around for 100,000 years or so and moved into colder, temperate regions only in the past 40,000 years.

Though the fossil evidence is not definitive, Neanderthals appear to have descended from an earlier human species, *Homo erectus,* between 500,000 to 300,000 years ago. Neanderthals shared many features with their ancestors—a prominent brow, weak chin, sloping skull and large nose—but were as big-brained as the anatomically modern humans that later colonized Europe, *Homo sapiens.* At the same time, Neanderthals were stocky, a build that would have conserved heat efficiently. From musculature marks on Neanderthal fossils and the heft of arm and leg bones, researchers conclude they were also incredibly strong. Yet their hands were remarkably like those of modern humans; a study published this past March in *Nature* shows that Neanderthals, contrary to previous thinking, could touch index finger and thumb, which would have given them considerable dexterity.

Neanderthal fossils suggest that they must have endured a lot of pain. "When you look at adult Neanderthal fossils, particularly the bones of the arms and skull, you see [evidence of] fractures," says Erik Trinkaus, an anthropologist at Washington University in St. Louis. "I've yet to see an adult Neanderthal skeleton that doesn't have at least one fracture, and in adults in their 30s, it's common to see multiple healed fractures." (That they suffered so many broken bones suggests they hunted large animals up close, probably stabbing prey with heavy spears—a risky tactic.) In addition, fossil evidence indicates that Neanderthals suffered from a wide range of ailments, including pneumonia and malnourishment. Still, they persevered, in some cases living to the ripe old age of 45 or so.

Perhaps surprisingly, Neanderthals must also have been caring: to survive disabling injury or illness requires the help of fellow clan members, paleoanthropologists say. A telling example came from an Iraqi cave known as Shanidar, 250 miles north of Baghdad, near the border with Turkey and Iran. There, archaeologist Ralph Solecki discovered nine nearly complete Neanderthal skeletons in the late 1950s. One belonged to a 40- to 45-year-old male with several major fractures. A blow to the left side of his head had crushed an eye socket and almost certainly blinded him. The bones of his right shoulder and upper arm appeared shriveled, most likely the result of a trauma that led to the amputation of his right forearm. His right foot and lower right leg had also been broken while he was alive. Abnormal wear in his right knee, ankle and foot shows that he suffered from injury-induced arthritis that would have made walking painful, if not impossible. Researchers don't know how he was injured but believe that he could not have survived long without a hand from his fellow man.

"This was really the first demonstration that Neanderthals behaved in what we think of as a fundamentally human way," says Trinkaus, who in the 1970s helped reconstruct and catalog the Shanidar fossil collection in Baghdad. (One of the skeletons is held by the Smithsonian Institution's National Museum of Natural History.) "The result was that those of us studying Neanderthals started thinking about these people in terms of their behavior and not just their anatomy."

Neanderthals inhabited a vast area roughly from present-day England east to Uzbekistan and south nearly to the Red Sea. Their time spanned periods in which glaciers advanced and retreated again and again, but the Neanderthals adjusted. When the glaciers moved in and edible plants became scarcer, they relied more heavily on large, hoofed animals for food, hunting the reindeer and wild horses that grazed the steppes and tundra.

Paleoanthropologists have no idea how many Neanderthals existed (crude estimates are in the many thousands), but archaeologists have found more fossils from Neanderthals than from any extinct human species. The first Neanderthal fossil was uncovered in Belgium in 1830, though nobody accurately identified it for more than a century. In 1848, the Forbes Quarry in Gibraltar yielded one of the most complete Neanderthal skulls ever found, but it, too, went unidentified, for 15 years. The name Neanderthal arose after quarrymen in Germany's Neander Valley found a cranium and several long bones in 1856; they gave the specimens to a local naturalist, Johann Karl Fuhlrott, who soon recognized them as the legacy of a previously unknown

type of human. Over the years, France, the Iberian Peninsula, southern Italy and the Levant have yielded abundances of Neanderthal remains, and those finds are being supplemented by newly opened excavations in Ukraine and Georgia. "It seems that everywhere we look, we're finding Neanderthal remains," says Loyola's Smith. "It's an exciting time to be studying Neanderthals."

Clues to some Neanderthal ways of life come from chemical analyses of fossilized bones, which confirm that Neanderthals were meat eaters. Microscopic studies hint at cannibalism; fossilized deer and Neanderthal bones found at the same site bear identical scrape marks, as though the same tool removed the muscle from both animals.

There are hints of cannibalism: deer and Neanderthal bones at the same site bear identical scrape marks.

The arrangement of fossilized Neanderthal skeletons in the ground demonstrates to many archaeologists that Neanderthals buried their dead. "They might not have done so with elaborate ritual, since there has never been solid evidence that they included symbolic objects in graves, but it is clear that they did not just dump their dead with the rest of the trash to be picked over by hyenas and other scavengers," says archaeologist Francesco d'Errico of the University of Bordeaux.

Paleoanthropologists generally agree that Neanderthals lived in groups of 10 to 15, counting children. That assessment is based on a few lines of evidence, including the limited remains at burial sites and the modest size of rock shelters. Also, Neanderthals were top predators, and some top predators, such as lions and wolves, live in small groups.

Steven Kuhn, an archaeologist at the University of Arizona, says experts "can infer quite a bit about who Neanderthal was by studying tools in conjunction with the other artifacts they left behind." For instance, recovered stone tools are typically fashioned from nearby sources of flint or quartz, indicating to some researchers that a Neanderthal group did not necessarily range far.

The typical Neanderthal tool kit contained a variety of implements, including large spear points and knives that would have been hafted, or set in wooden handles. Other tools were suitable for cutting meat, cracking open bones (to get at fat-rich marrow) or scraping hides (useful for clothing, blankets or shelter). Yet other stone tools were used for woodworking; among the very few wooden artifacts associated with Neanderthal sites are objects that resemble spears, plates and pegs.

I get a feel for Neanderthal handiwork in Maureille's office, where plastic milk crates are stacked three high in front of his desk. They're stuffed with plastic bags full of olive and tan flints from Les Pradelles. With his encouragement, I take a palm-size, D-shaped flint out of a bag. Its surface is scarred as though by chipping, and the flat side has a thin edge. I readily imagine I could scrape a hide with it or whittle a stick. The piece, Maureille says, is about 60,000 years old. "As you can see from the number of lithics we've found," he adds, referring to the crates piling up in his office, "Neanderthals were prolific and accomplished toolmakers."

Among the new approaches to Neanderthal study is what might be called paleo-mimicry, in which researchers themselves fashion tools to test their ideas. "What we do is make our own tools out of flint, use them as a Neanderthal might have, and then look at the fine detail of the cutting edges with a high-powered microscope," explains Michael Bisson, chairman of anthropology at McGill University in Montreal. "A tool used to work wood will have one kind of wear pattern that differs from that seen when a tool is used to cut meat from a bone, and we can see those different patterns on the implements recovered from Neanderthal sites." Similarly, tools used to scrape hide show few microscopic scars, their edges having been smoothed by repeated rubbing against skin, just as stropping a straight razor will hone its edge. As Kuhn, who has also tried to duplicate Neanderthal handicraft, says: "There is no evidence of really fine, precise work, but they were skilled in what they did."

Based on the consistent form and quality of the tools found at sites across Europe and western Asia, it appears likely that Neanderthal was able to pass along his toolmaking techniques to others. "Each Neanderthal or Neanderthal group did not have to reinvent the wheel when it came to their technologies," says Bisson.

The kinds of tools that Neanderthals began making about 200,000 years ago are known as Mousterian, after the site in France where thousands of artifacts were first found. Neanderthals struck off pieces from a rock "core" to make an implement, but the "flaking" process was not random; they evidently examined a core much as a diamond cutter analyzes a rough gemstone today, trying to strike just the spot that would yield "flakes," for knives or spear points, requiring little sharpening or shaping.

Around 40,000 years ago, Neanderthals innovated again. In what passes for the blink of an eye in paleoanthropology, some Neanderthals were suddenly making long, thin stone blades and hafting more tools. Excavations in southwest France and northern Spain have uncovered Neanderthal tools betraying a more refined technique involving, Kuhn speculates, the use of soft hammers made of antler or bone.

What happened? According to the conventional wisdom, there was a culture clash. In the early 20th century, when researchers first discovered those "improved" lithics—called Châtelperronian and Uluzzian, depending on where they were found—they saw the relics as evidence that modern humans, Homo sapiens or Cro-Magnon, had arrived in Neanderthal territory. That's because the tools resembled those unequivocally associated with anatomically modern humans, who began colonizing western Europe 38,000 years ago. And early efforts to assign a date to those Neanderthal lithics yielded time frames consistent with the arrival of modern humans.

But more recent discoveries and studies, including tests that showed the lithics to be older than previously believed, have prompted d'Errico and others to argue that Neanderthals advanced on their own. "They could respond to some change in their environment that required them to improve their technology," he says. "They could behave like modern humans."

Meanwhile, these "late" Neanderthals also discovered ornamentation, says d'Errico and his archaeologist colleague João Zilhão of the University of Lisbon. Their evidence includes items made of bone, ivory and animal teeth marked with grooves and perforations. The researchers and others have also found dozens of pieces of sharpened manganese dioxide—black crayons, essentially—that Neanderthals probably used to color animal skins or even their own. In his office at the University of Bordeaux, d'Errico hands me a chunk of manganese dioxide. It feels silky, like soapstone. "Toward the end of their time on earth," he says, "Neanderthals were using technology as advanced as that of contemporary anatomically modern humans and were using symbolism in much the same way."

Generally, anthropologists and archaeologists today proffer two scenarios for how Neanderthals became increasingly resourceful in the days before they vanished. On the one hand, it may be that Neanderthals picked up a few new technologies from invading humans in an effort to copy their cousins. On the other, Neanderthals learned to innovate in parallel with anatomically modern human beings, our ancestors.

Most researchers agree that Neanderthals were skilled hunters and craftsmen who made tools, used fire, buried their dead (at least on occasion), cared for their sick and injured and even had a few symbolic notions. Likewise, most researchers believe that Neanderthals probably had some facility, for language, at least as we usually think of it. It's not far-fetched to think that language skills developed when Neanderthal groups mingled and exchanged mates; such interactions may have been necessary for survival, some researchers speculate, because Neanderthal groups were too small to sustain the species. "You need to have a breeding population of at least 250 adults, so some kind of exchange had to take place," says archaeologist Ofer Bar-Yosef of Harvard University. "We see this type of behavior in all hunter-gatherer cultures, which is essentially what Neanderthals had."

But if Neanderthals were so smart, why did they go extinct? "That's a question we'll never really have an answer to," says Clive Finlayson, who runs the Gibraltar Museum, "though it doesn't stop any of us from putting forth some pretty elaborate scenarios." Many researchers are loath even to speculate on the cause of Neanderthals' demise, but Finlayson suggests that a combination of climate change and the cumulative effect of repeated population busts eventually did them in. "I think it's the culmination of 100,000 years of climate hitting Neanderthals hard, their population diving during the cold years, rebounding some during warm years, then diving further when it got cold again," Finlayson says.

As Neanderthals retreated into present-day southern Spain and parts of Croatia toward the end of their time, modern human beings were right on their heels. Some researchers, like Smith, believe that Neanderthals and Cro-Magnon humans probably mated, if only in limited numbers. The question of whether Neanderthals and modern humans bred might be resolved within a decade by scientists studying DNA samples from Neanderthal and Cro-Magnon fossils.

As Neanderthals retreated, modern humans were right on their heels. The two may have mated—or tried to.

But others argue that any encounter was likely to be hostile. "Brotherly love is not the way I'd describe any interaction between different groups of humans," Shea says. In fact, he speculates that modern humans were superior warriors and wiped out the Neanderthals. "Modern humans are very competitive and really good at using projectile weapons to kill from a distance," he says, adding they also probably worked together better in large groups, providing a battlefield edge.

In the end, Neanderthals, though handy, big-brained, brawny and persistent, went the way of every human species but one. "There have been a great many experiments at being human preceding us and none of them made it, so we should not think poorly of Neanderthal just because they went extinct," says Rick Potts, head of the Smithsonian's Human Origins Program. "Given that Neanderthal possessed the very traits that we think guarantee our success should make us pause about our place here on earth."

Critical Thinking

1. Discuss the general ways in which Neanderthals should be considered successful—and not failures.

2. What features did they share with their ancestors, *Homo erectus*? With anatomically modern humans?

3. Why were they stocky in build? What indications are there that they were incredibly strong? In what way were their hands like those of modern humans?

4. What indications are there that they must have endured a lot of pain?

5. Why can we conclude that they were very caring?

6. How did the Neanderthals adjust when the glaciers moved in?

7. Why is there a "hint" of cannibalism? That they buried their dead?

8. Why do we think that they lived in groups of about 10 to 15? That each group did not range far?

9. What kinds of tools did the Neanderthals have?

10. What is "paleo-mimcry" and how has it helped us to understand Neanderthal tool-making?

11. How do we know that they were able to pass along tool-making techniques?

12. In what sense was the Mousterian flaking process not random?

13. In what ways did the Neanderthals innovate again around 40,000 years ago?

14. What two scenarios are preferred to explain Neanderthals' increasing resourcefulness? What do most researchers agree upon about Neanderthals?

15. Why is it not far-fetched to think that they had language?

16. Discuss the differing points of view as to what may have happened to the Neanderthals.

17. Why should we not think poorly of them just because they went extinct? What should make us pause about our place on earth?

Joe Alper, a freelance writer in Louisville, Colorado, is a frequent contributor to *Science* magazine. This is his first article for *Smithsonian*.

Twilight of the Neandertals

Paleoanthropologists know more about Neandertals than any other extinct human. But their demise remains a mystery, one that gets curiouser and curiouser.

KATE WONG

Some 28,000 years ago in what is now the British territory of Gibraltar, a group of Neandertals eked out a living along the rocky Mediterranean coast. They were quite possibly the last of their kind. Elsewhere in Europe and western Asia, Neandertals had disappeared thousands of years earlier, after having ruled for more than 200,000 years. The Iberian Peninsula, with its comparatively mild climate and rich array of animals and plants, seems to have been the final stronghold. Soon, however, the Gibraltar population, too, would die out, leaving behind only a smattering of their stone tools and the charred remnants of their campfires.

Ever since the discovery of the first Neandertal fossil in 1856, scientists have debated the place of these bygone humans on the family tree and what became of them. For decades two competing theories have dominated the discourse. One holds that Neandertals were an archaic variant of our own species, *Homo sapiens,* that evolved into or was assimilated by the anatomically modern European population. The other posits that the Neandertals were a separate species, *H. neanderthalensis,* that modern humans swiftly extirpated on entering the archaic hominid's territory.

Over the past decade, however, two key findings have shifted the fulcrum of the debate away from the question of whether

Hypothesis 1
Did Climate Change Doom the Neandertals?

Starting perhaps around 55,000 years ago, climate in Eurasia began to swing wildly from frigid to mild and back again in the span of decades. During the cold snaps, ice sheets advanced and treeless tundra replaced wooded environments across much of the Neandertals' range. Shifts in the available prey animals accompanied these changes. Wide spacing between past climate fluctuations allowed diminished Neandertal populations sufficient time to bounce back and adapt to the new conditions.

This time, however, the rapidity of the changes may have made recovery impossible. By 30,000 years ago only a few pockets of Neandertals survived, hanging on in the Iberian Peninsula, with its comparatively mild climate and rich resources. These groups were too small and fragmented to sustain themselves, however, and eventually they disappeared.

Key Concepts

- Neandertals, our closest relatives, ruled Europe and western Asia for more than 200,000 years. But sometime after 28,000 years ago, they vanished.
- Scientists have long debated what led to their disappearance. The latest extinction theories focus on climate change and subtle differences in behavior and biology that might have given modern humans an advantage over the Neandertals.

—The Editors

Neandertals and moderns made love or war. One is that analyses of Neandertal DNA have yet to yield the signs of interbreeding with modern humans that many researchers expected to see if the two groups mingled significantly. The other is that improvements in dating methods show that rather than disappearing immediately after the moderns invaded Europe, starting a little more than 40,000 years ago, the Neandertals survived for nearly 15,000 years after moderns moved in—hardly the rapid replacement adherents to the blitzkrieg theory envisioned.

These revelations have prompted a number of researchers to look more carefully at other factors that might have led to Neandertal extinction. What they are finding suggests that the answer involves a complicated interplay of stresses.

A World in Flux

One of the most informative new lines of evidence bearing on why the Neandertals died out is paleoclimate data. Scholars have known for some time that Neandertals experienced both glacial conditions and milder interglacial conditions during their long reign. In recent years, however, analyses of isotopes trapped in primeval ice, ocean sediments and pollen retrieved from such locales as Greenland, Venezuela and Italy have enabled investigators to reconstruct a far finer-grained picture of the climate shifts that occurred during a period known as oxygen isotope stage 3 (OIS-3). Spanning the time between roughly 65,000 and 25,000 years ago, OIS-3 began with moderate conditions and culminated with the ice sheets blanketing northern Europe.

Considering that Neandertals were the only hominids in Europe at the beginning of OIS-3 and moderns were the only ones there by the end of it, experts have wondered whether the plummeting temperatures might have caused the Neandertals to perish, perhaps because they could not find enough food or keep sufficiently warm. Yet arguing for that scenario has proved tricky for one essential reason: Neandertals had faced glacial conditions before and persevered.

In fact, numerous aspects of Neandertal biology and behavior indicate that they were well suited to the cold. Their barrel chests and stocky limbs would have conserved body heat, although they would have additionally needed clothing fashioned from animal pelts to stave off the chill. And their brawny build seems to have been adapted to their ambush-style hunting of large, relatively solitary mammals—such as woolly rhinoceroses—that roamed northern and central Europe during the cold snaps. (Other distinctive Neandertal features, such as the form of the prominent brow, may have been adaptively neutral traits that became established through genetic drift, rather than selection.)

But the isotope data reveal that far from progressing steadily from mild to frigid, the climate became increasingly unstable heading into the last glacial maximum, swinging severely and abruptly. With that flux came profound ecological change: forests gave way to treeless grassland; reindeer replaced certain kinds of rhinoceroses. So rapid were these oscillations that over the course of an individual's lifetime, all the plants and animals that a person had grown up with could vanish and be replaced with unfamiliar flora and fauna. And then, just as quickly, the environment could change back again.

It is this seesawing of environmental conditions—not necessarily the cold, per se—that gradually pushed Neandertal populations to the point of no return, according to scenarios posited by such experts as evolutionary ecologist Clive Finlayson of the Gibraltar Museum, who directs the excavations at several cave sites in Gibraltar. These shifts would have demanded that Neandertals adopt a new way of life in very short order. For example, the replacement of wooded areas with open grassland would have left ambush hunters without any trees to hide behind, he says. To survive, the Neandertals would have had to alter the way they hunted.

Some Neandertals did adapt to their changing world, as evidenced by shifts in their tool types and prey. But many probably died out during these fluctuations, leaving behind ever more fragmented populations. Under normal circumstances, these archaic humans might have been able to bounce back, as they had previously, when the fluctuations were fewer and farther between. This time, however, the rapidity of the environmental change left insufficient time for recovery. Eventually, Finlayson argues, the repeated climatic insults left the Neandertal populations so diminished that they could no longer sustain themselves.

The results of a genetic study published this past April in *PLoS One* by Virginie Fabre and her colleagues at the University of the Mediterranean in Marseille support the notion that Neandertal populations were fragmented, Finlayson says. That analysis of Neandertal mitochondrial DNA found that the Neandertals could be divided into three subgroups—one in western Europe, another in southern Europe and a third in western Asia—and that population size ebbed and flowed.

Invasive Species

For other researchers, however, the fact that the Neandertals entirely disappeared only after moderns entered Europe clearly indicates that the invaders had a hand in the extinction, even if the newcomers did not kill the earlier settlers outright. Probably, say those who hold this view, the Neandertals ended up competing with the incoming moderns for food and gradually lost ground. Exactly what ultimately gave moderns their winning edge remains a matter of considerable disagreement, though.

One possibility is that modern humans were less picky about what they ate. Analyses of Neandertal bone chemistry conducted

---

Resurrecting the Neandertal

Later this year researchers led by Svante Pääbo of the Max Planck Institute for Evolutionary Anthropology in Leipzig, Germany, are expected to publish a rough draft of the Neandertal genome. The work has prompted speculation that scientists might one day be able to bring back this extinct human. Such a feat, if it were technically possible, would raise all sorts of ethical quandaries: What rights would a Neandertal have? Would this individual live in a lab, or a zoo, or a household?

Moral concerns aside, what could researchers actually learn from a resurrected Neandertal? The answer is: less than you might think. A Neandertal born and raised in a modern setting would not have built-in Ice Age wisdom to impart to us, such as how to make a Mousterian stone tool or bring down a woolly rhinoceros. Indeed, he would not be able to tell scholars anything about the culture of his people. It is possible, however, that studying Neandertal biology and cognition could reveal as yet unknown differences between these archaic hominids and modern ones that might have given moderns a survival advantage.

Hypothesis 2
Were the Neandertals Outsmarted by Modern Humans?

A long-standing theory of Neandertal extinction holds that modern humans outcompeted Neandertals with their superior smarts. But mounting evidence indicates that Neandertals engaged in many of the same sophisticated behaviors once attributed to moderns alone (*table*). The findings reveal that at least some Neandertals were capable of symbolic thought—and therefore probably language—and that they had the tools and the know-how to pursue a wide range of foods. Still, these practices seem to have been more entrenched in modern human culture than in that of Neandertals, which may have given moderns the upper hand.

Table   Evidence of Modern Behavior among Neandertals

Trait	Common	Occasional	Absent	Uncertain
Art				√
Pigment use	√			
Jewelry		√		
Symbolic burial of dead				√
Long-distance exchange				√
Microliths		√		
Barbed points			√	
Bone tools		√		
Blades		√		
Needles			√	
Exploitation of marine resources		√		
Bird hunting		√		
Division of labor			√	

by Hervé Bocherens of the University of Tubingen in Germany suggest that at least some of these hominids specialized in large mammals, such as woolly rhinoceroses, which were relatively rare. Early modern humans, on the other hand, ate all manner of animals and plants. Thus, when moderns moved into Neandertal territory and started taking some of these large animals for themselves, so the argument goes, the Neandertals would have been in trouble. Moderns, meanwhile, could supplement the big kills with smaller animals and plant foods.

"Neandertals had a Neandertal way of doing things, and it was great as long as they weren't competing with moderns," observes archaeologist Curtis W. Marean of Arizona State University. In contrast, Marean says, the moderns, who evolved under tropical conditions in Africa, were able to enter entirely different environments and very quickly come up with creative ways to deal with the novel circumstances they encountered. "The key difference is that Neandertals were just not as advanced cognitively as modern humans," he asserts.

Marean is not alone in thinking that Neandertals were one-trick ponies. A long-standing view holds that moderns outsmarted the Neandertals with not only their superior tool technology and survival tactics but also their gift of gab, which might have helped them form stronger social networks. The Neandertal dullards, in this view, did not stand a chance against the newcomers.

But a growing body of evidence indicates that Neandertals were savvier than they have been given credit for. In fact, they apparently engaged in many of the behaviors once believed to be strictly the purview of modern humans. As paleoanthropologist Christopher B. Stringer of London's Natural History Museum puts it, "the boundary between Neandertals and moderns has gotten fuzzier."

Sites in Gibraltar have yielded some of the most recent findings blurring the line between the two human groups. In September 2008 Stringer and his colleagues reported on evidence that Neandertals at Gorham's Cave and next-door Vanguard Cave hunted dolphins and seals as well as gathered shellfish. And as yet unpublished work shows that they were eating birds and rabbits, too. The discoveries in Gilbraltar, along with finds from a handful of other sites, upend the received wisdom that moderns alone exploited marine resources and small game.

More evidence blurring the line between Neandertal and modern human behavior has come from the site of Hohle Fels in southwestern Germany. There paleoanthropologist Bruce Hardy of Kenyon College was able to compare artifacts made by Neandertals who inhabited the cave between 36,000 and 40,000 years ago with artifacts from modern humans who resided there between 33,000 and 36,000 years ago under similar climate and environmental conditions. In a presentation given this past April to the Paleoanthropology Society in Chicago, Hardy reported that his analysis of the wear patterns on the tools and the residues from substances with which the tools came into contact revealed that although the modern humans created a larger variety of tools than did the Neandertals, the groups engaged in mostly the same activities at Hohle Fels.

These activities include such sophisticated practices as using tree resin to bind stone points to wooden handles, employing stone points as thrusting or projectile weapons, and crafting implements from bone and wood. As to why the Hohle Fels Neandertals made fewer types of tools than did the moderns who lived there afterward, Hardy surmises that they were able to get the job done without them. "You don't need a grapefruit spoon to eat a grapefruit," he says.

The claim that Neandertals lacked language, too, seems unlikely in light of recent discoveries. Researchers now know that at least some of them decorated their bodies with jewelry and probably pigment. Such physical manifestations of symbolic behavior are often used as a proxy for language when reconstructing behavior from the archaeological record. And in 2007 researchers led by Johannes Krause of the Max Planck Institute for Evolutionary Anthropology in Leipzig, Germany, reported that analyses of Neandertal DNA have shown that these hominids had the same version of the speech-enabling gene *FOXP2* that modern humans carry.

Tiebreakers

With the gap between Neandertal and modern human behavior narrowing, many researchers are now looking to subtle differences in culture and biology to explain why the Neandertals lost out. "Worsening and highly unstable climatic conditions would have made competition among human groups all the more fierce," reflects paleoanthropologist Katerina Harvati, also at Max Planck. "In this context, even small advantages would become extremely important and might spell the difference between survival and death."

Stringer, for his part, theorizes that the moderns' somewhat wider range of cultural adaptations provided a slightly superior buffer against hard times. For example, needles left behind by modern humans hint that they had tailored clothing and tents, all the better for keeping the cold at bay. Neandertals, meanwhile, left behind no such signs of sewing and are believed by some to have had more crudely assembled apparel and shelters as a result.

Neandertals and moderns may have also differed in the way they divvied up the chores among group members. In a paper published in *Current Anthropology* in 2006, archaeologists Steven L. Kuhn and Mary C. Stiner, both at the University of Arizona, hypothesized that the varied diet of early modern Europeans would have favored a division of labor in which men hunted the larger game and women collected and prepared nuts, seeds and berries. In contrast, the Neandertal focus on large game probably meant that their women and children joined in the hunt, possibly helping to drive animals toward the waiting men. By creating both a more reliable food supply and a safer environment for rearing children, division of labor could have enabled modern human populations to expand at the expense of the Neandertals.

However the Neandertals obtained their food, they needed lots of it. "Neandertals were the SUVs of the hominid world," says paleoanthropologist Leslie Aiello of the Wenner-Gren Foundation in New York City. A number of studies aimed at estimating Neandertal metabolic rates have concluded that these archaic hominids required significantly more calories to survive than the rival moderns did.

Hominid energetics expert Karen Steudel-Numbers of the University of Wisconsin–Madison has determined, for example, that the energetic cost of locomotion was 32 percent higher in Neandertals than in anatomically modern humans, thanks to the archaic hominids' burly build and short shinbones, which would have shortened their stride. In terms of daily energy needs, the Neandertals would have required somewhere between 100 and 350 calories more than moderns living in the same climates, according to a model developed by Andrew W. Froehle of the University of California, San Diego, and Steven E. Churchill of Duke University. Modern humans, then, might have outcompeted Neandertals simply by virtue of being more fuel-efficient: using less energy for baseline functions meant that moderns could devote more energy to reproducing and ensuring the survival of their young.

One more distinction between Neandertals and moderns deserves mention, one that could have enhanced modern survival in important ways. Research led by Rachel Caspari of Central Michigan University has shown that around 30,000 years ago, the number of modern humans who lived to be old enough to be grandparents began to skyrocket. Exactly what spurred this increase in longevity is uncertain, but the change had two key consequences. First, people had more reproductive years, thus increasing their fertility potential. Second, they had more time over which to acquire specialized knowledge and pass it on to the next generation—where to find drinking water in times of drought, for instance. "Long-term survivorship gives the potential for bigger social networks and greater knowledge stores," Stringer comments. Among the shorter-lived Neandertals, in contrast, knowledge was more likely to disappear, he surmises.

More clues to why the Neandertals faded away may come from analysis of the Neandertal genome, the full sequence of which is due out this year. But answers are likely to be slow to surface, because scientists know so little about the functional significance of most regions of the modern genome, never mind the Neandertal one. "We're a long way from being able to read what the [Neandertal] genome is telling us," Stringer says. Still, future analyses could conceivably pinpoint cognitive or metabolic differences between the two groups, for example, and provide a more definitive answer to the question of whether Neandertals and moderns interbred.

The Stone Age whodunit is far from solved. But researchers are converging on one conclusion: regardless of whether climate or competition with moderns, or some combination thereof, was the prime mover in the decline of the Neandertals, the precise factors governing the extinction of individual populations of these archaic hominids almost certainly varied from group to group. Some may have perished from disease, others from inbreeding. "Each valley may tell its own story," Finlayson remarks.

As for the last known Neandertals, the ones who lived in Gibraltar's seaside caves some 28,000 years ago, Finlayson is certain that they did not spend their days competing with moderns, because moderns seem not to have settled there until thousands of years after the Neandertals were gone. The rest of their story, however, remains to be discovered.

More to Explore

Older Age Becomes Common Late in Human Evolution. Rachel Caspari and Sang-Hee Lee in *Proceedings of the National Academy of Sciences USA,* Vol. 101, No. 30, pages 10895–10900; July 27, 2004.

Rapid Ecological Turnover and Its Impact on Neanderthal and Other Human Populations. Clive Finlayson and José S. Carrión in *Trends in Ecology and Evolution,* vol. 22, no. 4, pages 213–222; 2007.

Heading North: An Africanist Perspective on the Replacement of Neanderthals by Modern Humans. Curtis W. Marean in *Rethinking the Human Revolution.* Edited by Paul Mellars et al. McDonald Institute for Archaeological Research, Cambridge, 2007.

Neanderthal Exploitation of Marine Mammals in Gibraltar. C. B. Stringer et al. in *Proceedings of the National Academy of Sciences USA,* vol. 105, no. 38, pages 14319–14324; September 23, 2008.

Critical Thinking

1. What have been the two competing theories regarding the relationship between Neanderthals and ourselves? What two key findings have shifted the fulcrum of the debate?

2. Why would the "see sawing" of environmental conditions contribute to Neanderthal extinction in spite of their biological adaptations to the cold?

3. What evidence is there that Neanderthal populations were fragmented?

4. What have been the claims that modern humans had something to do with Neanderthals' extinction? What is the counter-evidence?

5. What may have been the "tiebreakers" that caused the Neanderthals to lose out, and why?

UNIT 5
Late Hominid Evolution

Unit Selections

Learning Outcomes

After reading this Unit, you will be able to:

- Discuss when, where, and how modern humans evolved.

- Discuss whether the modern humans that came out of Africa replaced archaic *Homo sapiens* or mated with them.

- Explain how the human family tree looks more like a thickly branched bush.

- Discuss the phrase, "Upper Paleolithic Revolution" in terms of what it proposed and what evidence now challenges the notion.

- Explain why humans have such an extended period of childhood.

- Discuss the importance of longevity with respect to the human lifespan.

- Why is a big, sophisticated brain an advantage in life?

- Discuss the limits to human intelligence and how they can be overcome.

- Discuss the top ten myths about the human brain in terms of the scientific evidence.

- Explain why humans are the most hairless of the primates.

Student Website

www.mhhe.com/cls

Internet References

Human Prehistory
http://users.hol.gr/~dilos/prehis.htm

Max Planck Institute for Evolutionary Anthropology
www.eva.mpg.de/english/index.htm

The most important aspect of human evolution is also the most difficult to decipher from the fossil evidence: our development as sentient, social beings, capable of communicating by means of language.

We detect hints of incipient humanity in the form of crudely chipped tools, the telltale signs of a home base, or the artistic achievements of ornaments and cave art. Yet none of these indicators of a distinctly hominid way of life can provide us with the nuances of the everyday lives of these creatures, their social relations, or their supernatural beliefs, if any. Most of what remains is the rubble of bones and stones from which we interpret what we can of their lifestyle, thought processes, and ability to communicate.

It is understandable, then, that some questions regarding our most recent ancestors have yet to be fully answered. Did we derive entirely from people who represented a second wave of migration out of Africa and who replaced the archaic members of our species, i.e., the remnants of a much earlier migration, according to the "replacement hypothesis"? Or did our modern *Homo sapiens* ancestors mate with archaic sapiens, as proposed in the "multiregional theory"? Recent evidence seems to say the answer is not as clear-cut as either side of the controversy would have it, that there was certainly some replacement and that there was also some degree of admixture (see "A New View of the Birth of *Homo sapiens*"). Did modern *Homo sapiens* truly usher in an "Upper Paleolithic Revolution," involving art, mortuary rituals, personal adornments, and more complex food-getting technologies and strategies? Or did such innovations come about on a piecemeal basis, scattered in time and place depending upon the needs of the people, including the archaic members of our species? Evidence cited in "Refuting a Myth About Human Origins" suggests the latter.

Beyond the anatomical and technological adaptations, questions have arisen as to how our hominid forebears organized themselves socially and whether modern-day human behavior is inherited as a legacy of our evolutionary past or is a learned product of contemporary circumstances. Attempts to address these questions have given rise to the technique referred to as the "ethnographic analogy." This is a method whereby anthropologists use "ethnographies," or field studies, of modern-day hunters and gatherers whose lives we take to be the best

© Digital Vision

approximations we have to what life might have been like for our ancestors (see "The Birth of Childhood" and "The Evolution of Grandparents"). Granted, these contemporary foragers have been living under conditions of environmental and social change just as industrial peoples have. Nevertheless, it seems that, at least in some aspects of their lives, they have not changed as much as we have. So, if we are to make any enlightened assessments of prehistoric behavior patterns, we are better off looking at them than at ourselves.

As if to show that controversial interpretations of the evidence are not limited to the earlier hominid period, in this unit we also see how long-held beliefs about recent human evolution are being shattered. Hominid migrations are being revised by new evidence coming from fossils, archaeology, and even DNA (see "Meet the New Human Family"). Mythologies about the brain abound, in spite of scientific evidence to the contrary ("Top Ten Myths About the Brain"). And, finally, alas, there really are limits to intelligence ("The Limits of Intelligence"), which seem to be constrained by the laws of physics.

For some scientists, the revelations of this unit fit in quite comfortably with previously held positions; for others it seems that reputations, as well as theories, are at stake.

A New View of the Birth of *Homo sapiens*

New genomic data are settling an old argument about how our species evolved.

Ann Gibbons

For 27 years, Chris Stringer and Milford Wolpoff have been at odds about where and how our species was born. Stringer, a paleoanthropologist at the Natural History Museum in London, held that modern humans came out of Africa, spread around the world, and replaced, rather than mated with, the archaic humans they met. But Wolpoff, of the University of Michigan, Ann Arbor, argued that a single, worldwide species of human, including archaic forms outside of Africa, met, mingled and had offspring, and so produced *Homo sapiens*. The battle has been long and bitter: When reviewing a manuscript in the 1980s, Wolpoff scribbled "Stringer's desperate argument" under a chart; in a 1996 book, Stringer wrote that "attention to inconvenient details has never been part of the Wolpoff style." At one tense meeting, the pair presented opposing views in rival sessions on the same day—and Wolpoff didn't invite Stringer to the meeting's press conference. "It was difficult for a long time," recalls Stringer.

Then, in the past year, geneticists announced the nearly complete nuclear genomes of two different archaic humans: Neandertals, and their enigmatic eastern cousins from southern Siberia. These data provide a much higher resolution view of our past, much as a new telescope allows astronomers to see farther back in time in the universe. When compared with the genomes of living people, the ancient genomes allow anthropologists to thoroughly test the competing models of human origins for the first time.

The DNA data suggest not one but at least two instances of interbreeding between archaic and modern humans, raising the question of whether *H. sapiens* at that point was a distinct species (see box, The Species Problem). And so they appear to refute the complete replacement aspect of the Out of Africa model. "[Modern humans] are certainly coming out of Africa, but we're finding evidence of low levels of admixture wherever you look," says evolutionary geneticist Michael Hammer of the University of Arizona in Tucson. Stringer admits: "The story has undoubtedly got a whole lot more complicated."

But the genomic data don't prove the classic multiregionalism model correct either. They suggest only a small amount of interbreeding, presumably at the margins where invading moderns met archaic groups that were the worldwide descendants of *H. erectus,* the human ancestor that left Africa 1.8 million years ago. "I have lately taken to talking about the best model as replacement with hybridization, . . . [or] 'leaky replacement,'" says paleogeneticist Svante Pääbo of the Max Planck Institute for Evolutionary Anthropology in Leipzig, lead author of the two nuclear genome studies.

The new picture most resembles so-called assimilation models, which got relatively little attention over the years. "This means so much," says Fred Smith of Illinois State University in Normal, who proposed such a model. "I just thought 'Hallelujah! No matter what anybody else says, I was as close to correct as anybody.'"

Evolving Models

Stringer and others first proposed Africa as the birthplace of modern humans back in the mid-1980s. The same year, researchers published a landmark study that traced the maternally inherited mitochondrial DNA (mtDNA) of all living people to a female ancestor that lived in Africa about 200,000 years ago, dubbed mitochondrial Eve. She caught the attention of the popular press, landing on the cover of *Newsweek* and *Time*.

Additional studies of living people—from Y chromosomes to snippets of nuclear DNA to the entire mtDNA genome—consistently found that Africans were the most diverse genetically. This suggests that modern humans arose in Africa, where they had more time to accumulate mutations than on other continents (*Science,* 17 November 2006, p. 1068). Meanwhile, ancient DNA technology also took off. Pääbo's group sequenced first a few bits of Neandertal mitochondrial DNA in 1997, then the entire mitochondrial genomes of several Neandertals—and found them to be distinct from those of living people. So ancient DNA, too, argued against the idea of mixing between Neandertals and moderns. Over the years the replacement model became the leading theory, with only a stubborn few, including Wolpoff, holding to multiregionalism.

The Species Problem

Our ancestors had sex with at least two kinds of archaic humans at two different times and places—and those liaisons produced surviving children, according to the latest ancient DNA research (see main text). But were the participants in these prehistoric encounters members of separate species? Doesn't a species, by definition, breed only with others of that species?

These are the questions paleogeneticist Svante Pääbo dodged twice last year. His team published two papers proposing that both Neandertals and mysterious humans from Denisova Cave in Siberia interbred with ancient modern humans. But the researchers avoided the thorny question of species designation and simply referred to Neandertals, Denisovans, and modern humans as "populations." "I think discussion of what is a species and what is a subspecies is a sterile academic endeavor," says Pääbo, who works at the Max Planck Institute for Evolutionary Anthropology in Leipzig, Germany.

The question of how to define a species has divided researchers for centuries. Darwin's words in *On the Origin of Species* still hold: "No one definition has satisfied all naturalists." However, many scientists use the biological species concept proposed by Ernst Mayr: "groups of actually or potentially interbreeding natural populations, which are reproductively isolated from other such groups."

The draft versions of the Neandertal and Denisovan nuclear genomes show low levels of interbreeding between each of them and modern humans. Apply Mayr's definition strictly, and all three must be considered *Homo sapiens*. "They mated with each other. We'll call them the same species," says molecular anthropologist John Hawks of the University of Wisconsin, Madison.

But that's a minority view among paleoanthropologists. Many consider Neandertals a species separate from modern humans because the anatomical and developmental differences are "an order of magnitude higher than anything we can observe between extant human populations," says Jean-Jacques Hublin, a co-author of Pääbo's at Max Planck. In the real world, he says, Mayr's concept doesn't hold up: "There are about 330 closely related species of mammals that interbreed, and at least a third of them can produce fertile hybrids."

There's also no agreed upon yardstick for how much morphologic or genetic difference separates species. That's why Pääbo's team avoided the species question a second time with respect to the Denisovans. These hominins are known only from a scrap of bone, a single tooth, and their DNA. They are genetically closest to Neandertals. The genetic distance between Denisovans and Neandertals, in fact, is only 9% larger than that between a living Frenchman and a living San Bushman in Africa, both of whom belong to *H. sapiens*. But so far Neandertals seem to have low genetic diversity, based on the DNA of six Neandertals from Russia to Spain. To Pääbo's team, that makes the difference from the Denisovans significant.

Also, the Denisovan tooth doesn't look much like that of a Neandertal. So the team considers them a distinct population but declined to name a new species. "Why take a stand on it when it will only lead to discussions and no one will have the final word?" asks Pääbo.

—A.G.

Yet there were a few dissenting notes. A few studies of individual genes found evidence of migration from Asia into Africa, rather than vice versa. Population geneticists warned that complete replacement was unlikely, given the distribution of alleles in living humans. And a few paleoanthropologists proposed middle-of-the-road models. Smith, a former student of Wolpoff's, suggested that most of our ancestors arose in Africa but interbred with local populations as they spread out around the globe, with archaic people contributing to about 10% of living people's genomes. At the University of Hamburg in Germany, Gunter Brauer similarly proposed replacement with hybridization, but with a trivial amount of interbreeding. But neither model got much traction; they were either ignored or lumped in with multiregionalism. "Assimilation got kicked so much," recalls Smith.

Over time, the two more extreme models moved toward the middle, with most multiregionalists recognizing that the chief ancestors of modern humans arose in Africa. "The broad line of evolution is pretty clear: Our ancestors came out of Africa," says biological anthropologist John Relethford of the State University of New York College at Oneonta. "But what happens next is kind of complex."

Genes from the Past

Then in May 2010 came the Neandertals' complete nuclear genome, sequenced from the bones of three female Neandertals who lived in Croatia more than 38,000 years ago. Pääbo's international team found that a small amount—1% to 4%—of the nuclear DNA of Europeans and Asians, but not of Africans, can be traced to Neandertals. The most likely model to explain this, Pääbo says, was that early modern humans arose in Africa but interbred with Neandertals in the Middle East or Arabia before spreading into Asia and Europe, about 50,000 to 80,000 years ago (*Science,* 7 May 2010, pp. 680, 710).

Seven months later, on 23 December, the team published in *Nature* the complete nuclear genome of a girl's pinky finger from Denisova Cave in the Altai Mountains of southern Siberia. To their surprise, the genome was neither a Neandertal's nor a modern human's, yet the girl was alive at the same time, dating to at least 30,000 years ago and probably older than 50,000 years. Her DNA was most like a Neandertal's, but her people were a distinct group that had long been separated from Neandertals.

By comparing parts of the Denisovan genome directly with the same segments of DNA in 53 populations of living people, the team found that the Denisovans shared 4% to 6% of their DNA with Melanesians from Papua New Guinea and the Bougainville Islands. Those segments were not found in Neandertals or other living humans.

The most likely scenario for how all this happened is that after Neandertal and Denisovan populations split about 200,000 years ago, modern humans interbred with Neandertals as they left Africa in the past 100,000 years. Thus Neandertals left their mark in the genomes of living Asians and Europeans, says co-author Montgomery Slatkin, a population geneticist at the University of California, Berkeley. Later, a subset of this group of moderns—who carried some Neandertal DNA—headed east toward Melanesia and interbred with the Denisovans in Asia on the way. As a result, Melanesians inherited DNA from both Neandertals and Denisovans, with as much as 8% of their DNA coming from archaic people, says co-author David Reich, a population geneticist at Harvard Medical School in Boston.

This means *H. sapiens* mixed it up with at least two different archaic peoples, in at least two distinct times and places. To some, that's starting to sound a lot like multiregionalism. "It's hard to explain how good I feel about this," says Wolpoff, who says that seeing complete replacement falsified twice in 1 year was beyond his wildest expectations. "It was a good year."

And yet the interbreeding with archaic humans seems limited—from 1% to 8% of some living people's genomes. Stringer and many others don't consider it full-scale multiregional continuity. "I think interbreeding was at a low level," says Slatkin, who says that if there had been a great deal of admixture, the genetic data would have revealed it already. Low levels of interbreeding suggest that either archaic people mated with moderns only rarely—or their hybrid offspring had low fitness and so produced few viable offspring, says population geneticist Laurent Excoffier of the University of Bern in Switzerland.

In any case, Reich notes that at least 90% of our genomes are inherited from African ancestors who replaced the archaic people on other continents but hybridized with them around the margins. And that scenario most closely backs the assimilation models proposed by Smith and Brauer.

Of course, it's possible that future data will overturn today's "leaky replacement" model. Slatkin says he cannot rule out an alternative explanation for the data: The "archaic" DNA thought to have come from mating with Neandertals could instead stem from a very ancient ancestor that we shared with Neandertals. Most modern humans retained those archaic sequences, but Africans lost them. But Slatkin says this "doesn't seem very plausible," because it requires modern human populations with the archaic DNA and those without it to have been partially isolated from each other in Africa for hundreds of thousands of years. And it seems even less probable that Melanesians and Denisovans are the only groups that retained a second set of archaic DNA motifs from a common ancestor shared by all modern humans, Neandertals and Denisovans. If those explanations do prove true, replacement would not be falsified.

In the wake of the big genome studies, other researchers such as Hammer are scrutinizing DNA from more living humans to further test the model. Researchers are also trying to pinpoint when admixture happened, which has significant consequences. At just what point did we evolve from archaic humans to become "modern" humans? "There are still archaic [genetic] features floating around until amazingly recently, until 40,000 years ago," says Hammer. He wonders whether the process of becoming modern took longer and was more complex than once thought. "There's no line you can draw and say everything after this is modern. That's the elephant in the room."

Meanwhile, paleoanthropologists are searching for fossils in Asia that might belong to the enigmatic Denisovan population—and might yield more ancient DNA. Paleoanthropologist Russell Ciochon of the University of Iowa in Iowa City and Wolpoff say there are several known, ambiguous fossils in Asia that might be candidates for early Denisovans. "I believe things were going on in Asia that we just don't know about," says Ciochon. "Before this paper on the Denisovans, we didn't have any insight into this. Now, with this nuclear genome, I find myself talking about 'the Denisovans.' It's already had an impact."

As for Stringer and Wolpoff, both now in their 60s, their battle has mellowed. Their views, while still distinct, have converged somewhat, and they shared a beer at a Neandertal meeting last year. "The reason we get on well now," says Stringer, "is we both think we've been proved right."

Critical Thinking

1. Discuss the evidence for the "replacement model" and the "multiregional model" for the origins of modern humans.

2. What evidence is there for a "leaky replacement model"?

3. What is the "species problem" and how does it relate to an understanding of modern human origins?

Meet the New Human Family

Once we shared the planet with other human species, competing with them and interbreeding with them. Today we stand alone, but our rivals' genes live on inside us—even as their remarkable stories are only now coming to light.

JILL NEIMARK

A single, unforgettable image comes to mind when we ponder human origins: a crouching ape slowly standing and morphing into a tall, erect human male poised to conquer every bit of habitable land on this planet. We walk this earth—we, this unparalleled experiment in evolution—reflexively assuming we are the crown of creation. Certainly we are rare and strange: As biological anthropologist Owen Lovejoy of Kent State University says, "The chances that a creature like us will ever happen again are so small that I can't even measure them."

But that ascent-of-man picture is looking as dated as the flat earth. A series of scientific and technological breakthroughs have altered much of our fundamental understanding of human evolution. In the new view, the path to *Homo sapiens* was amazingly dilatory and indirect. Along the way, our planet witnessed many variations on the human form, multiple migrations out of Africa, interspecies trysts, and extinctions that ultimately wiped out all hominid species except one. "Human evolution used to seem simple and linear," says paleoanthropologist William Jungers of the State University of New York at Stony Brook. "Now, you look at almost any time slice and you see diversity. We may be special and we may be lucky, but we're far from the only human experiment."

Unexpected fossil finds keep showing us an ever-expanding variety of human and prehuman species. Probably the most stunning of these recent discoveries is *Ardipithecus ramidus,* an ancestor who displayed a fantastical mosaic of ape and human traits. *A. ramidus* apparently climbed trees but also walked upright some 4.4 million years ago—more than half a million years before the long-accepted origin of bipedalism.

Our ideas about later human evolution, meanwhile, have been shattered by the remains of a tiny, novel human species with a small but intricately folded brain. Called *Homo floresiensis* and nicknamed the "hobbit" people, this species found in Indonesia rewrites the scientific story of how humans migrated out of Africa and came to populate the whole world. The hobbits overlapped in time and space with *Homo sapiens,* showing that even in relatively recent history more than one human species shared our planet—a situation evocative of the colorful world of J. R. R. Tolkien's Middle-earth, but undeniably real.

There were times when more than one human species shared our planet. But why, after so many human experiments, are we the only ones left standing?

The emerging field of paleogenetics has brought perhaps the most surprising news of all. Using DNA sequencing, scientists have learned that anatomically modern humans interbred with *Homo neanderthalensis,* or the Neanderthals, probably around 60,000 years ago in the Middle East, before they fanned out to populate Europe and Asia. We not only shared the planet with our cousins but shared our DNA as well. Today 1 to 4 percent of the genome for populations living outside of Africa is Neanderthal. A similar form of genetic analysis has also just revealed an entirely new human group, previously unknown: the Denisovans, cousins to Neanderthals. All we have of them so far is a fragment of a 50,000-year-old pinkie finger and most of a molar, found in a cave in Denisova, Siberia. But those fragments were enough to determine that humans living in New Guinea today carry nearly 5 percent Denisovan DNA.

As anthropologists use all the latest tools—genomics, computer analysis, and increasingly sophisticated imaging—to extract deep secrets from the latest fossil finds, they are replacing the "ascent of man" with a captivating new picture of the human family. It edges us decisively closer to understanding not only where we came from but also what made us so much more successful than other, superficially similar primates. "Our relatives, the gorillas and chimpanzees, are still living in the forest in a little piece of West Africa," Lovejoy says, "and orangutans have survived on two islands in Southeast Asia, but we have evolved rapidly and are everywhere."

Why, after so many human experiments, are we the only ones left standing?

Ardi, the Human Mosaic

One tantalizing answer comes from an international team of dozens of scientists, including Lovejoy and paleoanthropologist Tim White of the University of California, Berkeley. (The two are the Batman and Robin of the paleoanthropological world, envied and resented for their daring deeds.) Their most notable find is the remarkably complete remains of a 4.4-million-year-old young adult female *Ardipithecus ramidus,* a creature nicknamed Ardi, which they announced in the journal *Science* in 2009. Along with more than 100 other fossils representing nearly 40 other *Ardipithecus* individuals, Ardi was discovered in the scorched landscape of Ethiopia's Afar Rift, a place where torrential rains regularly wash up traces of ancient stone and bone from different eras. "The rift is our time machine," says White, who has been working in the area since 1981. "Its as if Mother Nature is revealing our roots with every rainstorm. We now have hominid remains dating as far back as 5.7 million years and as recently as 80,000 years. We see the deep past here through narrow temporal and spatial windows—walk a mile in any direction and you are either hundreds of thousands of years earlier or later because you are walking on eroding sediments from different slices of time."

By painstakingly reassembling partially crumbled or smashed specimens, analyzing tooth enamel to determine diet and habitat, and peering inside skeletal bone using powerful high-resolution micro-CT scans (like medical CT scans but with much higher radiation than could ever be used on a patient), the researchers have uncovered what White calls "a complex locomotor hybrid, a creature the likes of which had never been seen." Translation: Ardi climbed trees with her apelike hands and powerfully built, grasping big toe yet also walked on the ground in her woodland habitat.

Was Ardi a true biped? White and his collaborators looked to the remains of her upper leg and pelvis for clues. After years analyzing digital re-creations of the damaged bones, the group concluded what they had long suspected: The lower part of Ardi's hip was powerfully primitive, adapted for climbing. In contrast, the upper part of the hip, the ilium, was surprisingly broad—a humanlike adaptation for walking on the ground. As far as Lovejoy is concerned, Ardi is the perfectly logical precursor to Lucy, a small-bodied human ancestor that lived more than a million years after Ardi. For years, *Australopithecus afarensis,* the species to which Lucy belonged, was regarded as the first truly bipedal hominid. No longer. "Ardi's adaptations did all the hard evolutionary work for Lucy," says Lovejoy, an expert on Lucy's anatomy. "The mosaic Ardi pelvis fits with its equally mosaic foot and reveals, for the first time, how hominids became bipedal."

For the team at Middle Awash, the part of the rift where Ardi was found, *A. ramidus* teeth offered another surprise: The males of the species lack the long, fanglike canines that are a hallmark of aggression in apes. Their canines are short and blunt, a signature human trait, one carried over much later by Lucy as well. Lovejoy was startled to see that such a crucial marker of aggression disappeared so early in human evolution. He now suspects this happened because *A. ramidus* males no longer needed to bare sharp fangs to scare off competing males and ensure female sexual favors. Instead, the males traveled long distances to seek out food for their chosen females, then walked back on their hind legs, carrying provisions in their hands. Bringing females extra food elicited sexual loyalty, and the steady food supply led to reproductive success and expansion on a new scale.

If Ardi's skeleton was an unexpected mosaic, her habitat was even more curious. The Middle Awash scientists analyzed more than 150,000 vertebrate fossils from the site, from rats to foxes to saber-toothed cats, along with hundreds of geologic samples, to arrive at a detailed understanding of Ardi's habitat. "It was like a whole series of snapshots across an ancient landscape," White says.

For decades anthropologists have argued the "savanna hypothesis": that bipedalism evolved on the savannas of Africa as spreading grasslands forced our ancestors to walk increasing distances across open territory. As White and his team analyzed their evidence, they realized that Ardi must have lived in the woods. In that case, bipedalism must have emerged for different reasons. "Since her species was already bipedal and already had reduced canines, those characteristics were not the result of adaptation to savanna," White says.

But Ardi's most important legacy could be the light she sheds on our last common ancestor, that mysterious creature that ultimately gave rise to both today's humans and our closest living relatives, the chimpanzees. "There's a big gap in our knowledge about our past," White says, "and it lies down there somewhere about 7 million years ago in the form of a last common ancestor. It may never be found. But Ardi tells us what that creature looked like, and it's something we never expected."

The long-favored view is that the last common ancestor must have been similar to a chimp, with more evolutionary change occurring subsequently on the human branch of the family. But Ardi's anatomy suggests that our last common ancestor was like neither a human nor a chimpanzee. The shape of Ardi's hands makes the point. Their anatomy contains bony structures that would have allowed her to walk comfortably on her palms, more like monkeys than like living apes. "The Ardi wrist is wholly unlike a modern ape wrist," Lovejoy says. "Apes can't bend their wrist backward, and it's the bending of the wrist backward that allowed Ardi to walk on the palms." In contrast, modern apes like gorillas, chimpanzees, and bonobos walk on their knuckles, an adaptation that was always assumed to be ancient.

Not everyone likes these surprises. "People are tightly invested in the chimp as a model for our ancestors," White says. "The idea that the chimpanzee is basically a living missing link is deeply embedded in paleoanthropology. Ardi is not particularly chimpanzee-like, and we've gotten a lot of extreme pushback on that."

University of Toronto paleoanthropologist David Begun is one of the skeptics. "Ardi lived at least 2½ or 3 million years after the split of chimps and humans," Begun says. "The idea that this fossil tells us what the last common ancestor looks like is unfounded. Ardi is a spectacular discovery, but it may actually be an early side branch of hominids that is not even

The Human Family Bush

In the new view, the human family tree looks more like a thickly branched bush. *Ardipithecus ramidus,* or "Ardi," one of the earliest human relatives, appears near the base. Likely human relatives predating Ardi—*Sahelanthropus tchadensis, Orrorin tugensis,* and *Ardipithecus kadabba*—are known only from fragmentary remains; all probably walked upright. About 4 million years ago, Ardi may have given rise to the chimp-size australopithecines including *A. anamensis.* Like Ardi, the australopithecines were adapted to life both in trees and on the ground. One of their descendants, the *Paranthropus* genus, had massive chewing muscles that enabled them to eat tough foods, including nuts. Two million years ago, the most recent of these rugged relatives (*P. robustus* and *P. boisei*) lived contemporaneously with the first members of the *Homo* genus—our own. Although today we are the only human species, as recently as 30,000 years ago we shared the planet with at least three others. *H. floresiensis, H. neanderthalensis* (Neanderthals), and the recently discovered Denisovans; evidence suggests we interbred with at least the latter two.

"Some people have a hard time wrapping their minds around the anatomical mosaic that Ardi represents and its implications for human origins," he says. "You're able, as you take those sand grains away from the fossil, to see a creature that nobody has seen for the last four and a half million years."

Flo, the Hobbit Person

"Big" has been the sine qua non of our success as humans. Relative to our ancestors and most of our primate cousins, we have large bodies, long limbs, and oversize brains. It seemed that only in our bigness could we stride out of Africa and across the planet. But maybe bigness was unnecessary. That is the message from a strange Indonesian fossil belonging to a previously unknown species of the human family: *Homo floresiensis,* the hobbit people. If *Ardipithecus* has utterly upset our notions about early human origins, the hobbits have altered our thinking about late human evolution by showing us, among other things, that small might be just as adept.

Relative to our ancestors, we have big bodies, long limbs, and large brains. It seemed that only in our bigness could we stride out of Africa, but maybe bigness was unnecessary.

directly related to Lucy or humans. Its naïve to think every fossil you find is directly on the line leading to humans. And if we evolved from a monkeylike quadruped," as Lovejoy's analysis of Ardi's hands suggests, "then all our extensive anatomy related to suspension and hanging would have evolved in parallel to the great apes. That's possible but unlikely."

Others question whether Ardi was truly a biped. William Jungers, the Stony Brook paleoanthropologist, and a group of colleagues spent several days in White's lab last year. After examining the casts and digital images, Jungers decided that "Ardi was at best a facultative biped," a creature that is capable of walking but somewhat inefficiently. That description also fits modern chimps, gibbons, and even capuchin monkeys. Jungers also questions the idea that male food-gathering turned *A. ramidus* into upright walkers. "Owen's provisioning theory is untestable," he says. "Striding bipedalism is obviously a dandy adaptation, but there is no shortage of colorful and plausible speculations as to why it occurred, from thermoregulation to sexual displays, from looking over tall grasses to wading through the water."

Even the savanna hypothesis is not dead yet. Geochemist Thure Cerling of the University of Utah and seven other geologists and anthropologists recently questioned the ecological reconstruction from White's team. Cerling reexamined the soil and tooth enamel data provided by White and concluded instead that Ardi lived in a bush-savanna, with less than a quarter of the area providing canopy cover. "I believe their data indicate a significant savanna influence," Cerling says. White heatedly disagrees. The point is that Ardi's particular habitat was woodland, he says, even if savanna was nearby.

Ardi has been hit with one potshot after another since she was unveiled to the world. Tim White's answer to all the objections?

The ancestors of hobbits probably left the rift area of Africa (Ardi's home) for Southeast Asia on foot about 2 million years ago, ultimately crossing treacherous ocean waters to land on the narrow, 230-mile-long Indonesian island of Flores. More amazing, hobbits seem to have survived into modern times alongside modern humans; they fashioned stone tools, hunted cooperatively, and even cooked with fire—all with a brain just one-third the size of that of a typical *Homo sapiens* adult.

The key hobbit skeleton is an adult female named LB1 for the place where it was found: a vast, open, sun-drenched limestone cave called Liang Bua, on Flores. In the tradition of giving notable hominid fossils familiar names, LB1 was nicknamed Flo. In addition to Flo, archaeologist Michael Morwood of the University of Wollongong in Australia found partial remains of as many as 14 other individuals in the same cave, all of them presented to the world in the journal *Nature* in 2004.

After the publication of Morwood s article, the hobbit immediately became a scientific and media sensation. Flo is "one of the most complete fossils found anywhere until you get to true burials, like in Neanderthals and early modern humans," says Jungers, who has been closely involved in *Homo floresiensis* research.

Flo and her species lived on Flores from about 90,000 years ago until about 14,000 years ago, when they were wiped out—perhaps by a volcanic eruption, or perhaps by competition with modern humans. If they did interact with humans, the hobbits may have inspired the local legends of a small, hairy, humanlike creature that some Flores natives call the Ebu Gogo (which loosely translates to the "grandparent who eats anything"), anthropologist Gregory Forth of the University of Alberta speculates.

Flo's body shape was truly unexpected: she was just 3.3 feet tall and weighed about 60 pounds. She walked upright on large, flat feet unsuited to running and had a prominent brow, primitive teeth, no chin, short legs, and mysteriously long arms.

But it was her small head and brain that prompted the most fascination, fury, and often derision. Critics swiftly objected, saying that the specimen was not what it seemed. Some suggested Flo was a diseased modern human, related to pygmies but suffering from a condition like microcephaly, which causes the brain and head to be pathologically small. Others proposed she was simply a late form of *Homo erectus,* a tall, strong human ancestor that spread into Southeast Asia at least 1.5 million years ago but, in this instance, "dwarfed," as sometimes happens to species isolated on an island. Or maybe hobbits had descended from *Australopithecus afarensis*—Lucy's kin—since that species was a highly adaptable biped that spread over great masses of African land.

Morwood and other experts have dismissed each of these explanations in turn. "If our interpretation is right, we're dealing with hominids that came out of Africa more than 1.8 million years ago, before the emergence of *erectus*," Morwood says.

"The face and teeth are all wrong for australopiths," adds Jungers. "As for dwarfing, if *Homo erectus* were its ancestor, it would have had to do more than dwarf; it would have had to re-evolve a more primitive body design from head to toe."

Such arguments quickly established who Flo is not. Establishing exactly who she *is* has taken a lot longer, but slowly a consensus has emerged. Using CAT scans, digital imaging, statistical analysis, and computer reconstructions of the brain, anthropologists have determined that the little hobbit is most likely a normal, nondiseased human, albeit one with a very unusual form.

If so, *homo floresiensis* crushes our cherished notions about the key human trait of bigness, both in body and in brain. Jungers is not surprised. "Ask yourself why something would have to be large and evolve long hind limbs to get out of Africa in the first place," he says. "That idea is crazy. We now think Flo's ancestor was possibly an isolated remnant of an early human species that left Africa almost 2 million years ago. We know for certain that Flo's ancestors were on Flores at least a million years ago, because we've found stone tools on the island that are that old." Morwood has begun hunting for stone tools on the nearby and much larger Indonesian island of Sulawesi, where he hopes to find fossils ancestral to the Flores group.

One pressing question hanging over the discovery: How did Flo's ancestors cross the deep, seemingly impassable waters from mainland Southeast Asia to their island home? Jungers speculates that a giant tsunami like the one that hit the region in 2004 swept them out to sea. Survivors clinging to trees could have been washed ashore on Sulawesi, only to migrate to nearby Flores after that. This early hominid species was small, and on Flores it might have become even smaller in response to the limited resources.

In their extreme focus on early human evolution in Africa, scientists may have missed major clues about our ancestry still buried in other parts of the world. That is another message from Flo. Asia in particular could be full of surprises, Jungers believes. "Perhaps hominids spread throughout the Southeast Asian archipelagos earlier and more extensively than we've realized. What about early man in the Indian subcontinent? In remote areas of China? There's so much yet to be discovered," he says.

How did Flo's ancestors cross the waters? Jungers speculates that a giant tsunami swept them out to sea. Some clung to trees and were washed ashore.

Still, the biggest shock is the fact that Flo's puny brain—no bigger than a chimpanzee's—was so capable. "The hobbit discovery challenges the idea that intelligence is directly proportional to brain size," Morwood says.

"We're talking about a creature that was fairly well advanced," adds archaeologist Carol Lentfer of the University of Queensland in Australia. "It was able to use stone tools to make other tools." Relics unearthed in Flores indicate that the hobbits used large stones as hammers to knap and chip away at stone flakes, shaping them into cutting tools. The fabrication methods did not change significantly over time, however. Flakes were created with an average of about nine blows per tool from as far back as 100,000 years ago right up to the time of the hobbits' extinction.

Those simplest of stone tools had far-ranging consequences. "With a chip of stone you had a hammer; you could crush things more effectively than with an elephant's molar," says anthropologist Rick Potts, director of the Smithsonian's Human Origins Program. "With a sharp flake you could cut more effectively than with a carnivore's canine. A whole world opened up for humanity with the use of simple stone tools." Evidence of butchery and fire on animal bones found near hobbit remains suggests that these early humans enjoyed a good barbecue, usually of baby elephants, huge rats, and deadly Komodo dragons that they hunted and killed.

So how did Flo and her kin manage such big achievements using their little heads? Through resculpting the brain itself, it seems. The first evidence of this trend came as long ago as 1925, when South African anthropologist Raymond Dart published controversial findings in *Nature* on the first known australopithecus, called the Taung child. Dart argued that a brain structure called the lunate sulcus had been thrust back into a human position and that parts of the brain linked with higher cognitive functions had expanded. In his interpretation, Lucy's relatives had already started reorganizing their little brains a long time ago.

Biological anthropologist Dean Falk did not expect to see anything like that when she got to work on models of hobbit skulls at Florida State University in Tallahassee. To create a virtual version of the hobbit brain, Falk's colleague, engineer Kirk Smith, of the Mallinckrodt Institute of Radiology in St. Louis, used three-dimensional CAT scans that Morwood's team had taken of its fossilized skull and braincase. Smith's replica could be sliced, diced, twirled, and viewed in picturesque detail by Falk and her team. The scans show that the hobbit brain was uniquely folded and unusually complex. "It was beautiful, and the temporal lobes were really wide, which is an advanced feature," says Falk, who has since moved her lab to the School for Advanced Research in Santa Fe, New Mexico. "At the very front were two enormous convolutions in an area associated with executive functions like planning ahead, again a complex feature."

In the size-matters world of anthropology, these studies were a revelation. Flo's brain was "globally reorganized in comparison with the brains of apes," Jungers says. "That means that brain architecture and function are not always tightly constrained by size."

Neanderthal, the Rival and Mate

"There's a mantra in paleoanthropology," Jungers says, "and it goes like this: We need more fossils." Even with profound and important surprises like Ardi and Flo, scientists argue endlessly over their meaning. Because there are still so few complete fossils and so many gaps in the overall fossil record, interpretations abound. But now that increasingly powerful genomic technology can definitively identify a species from a fragment of bone or uncover Neanderthal genes embedded in the DNA of modern humans, there is less room for debate.

When paleontologists study fossils through bone shape alone, they can only broadly infer the relationship between two hominids, no matter how many fossils they collect. By going inside those bones and siphoning DNA—the genetic essence of long-dead ancestors—scientists can now use sequencing technology to make exact measurements of the similarities between groups. Using these techniques, says biologist Svante Pääbo of the Max Planck Institute for Evolutionary Anthropology in Leipzig, Germany, "you can determine, quantitatively, how much extinct human forms have contributed to the human form today."

Hominid paleogenomics has advanced quickly since biologists started analyzing the Neanderthal genome in 1997. Today, DNA can be sequenced from bone bits that a few years ago were regarded as far too eroded and contaminated to yield relevant results. Although some bones are still out of reach (Ardi is far too old, and Flo's bones too poorly preserved), others are yielding phenomenal insights. The latest gene-sequencing technologies developed by biotech companies 454 Life Sciences and Illumina can analyze several million DNA fragments at a time.

Using the same techniques being applied in medicine and forensics, Pääbo's team is filling in the fossil record in formerly inconceivable ways. Last year they announced that modern humans outside Africa carry 1 to 4 percent Neanderthal genes. To reach this conclusion, Pääbo and his team spent years sequencing the complete genome of three Neanderthal bones from the Vin-dija Cave in Croatia and compared the results with the genomes of five modern humans from southern Africa, West Africa, Papua New Guinea, China, and Western Europe. They found that the Neanderthal genome shows more similarity with non-African modern humans throughout Europe and Asia than with African modern humans, suggesting that the gene flow between us and Neanderthals most likely occurred outside Africa as humans were en route to Europe, Asia, and New Guinea.

This pattern of gene flow means humans and Neanderthals must have mated at some point. The notion of such interspecies trysts had long been only a theory. "We thought if we did interbreed, it might have been when modern humans came to Europe, about 30,000 to 40,000 years ago," Pääbo says. But when placed under genetic scrutiny, the bones tell a different tale.

The likeliest place for human-Neanderthal romance was the Middle East, where bones of both humans and Neanderthals have been found. "Modern humans appeared in the Middle East before 100,000 years ago, and Neanderthals were there at least 60,000 years ago—providing a likely 30,000-year window of opportunity for interbreeding before Neanderthals disappeared," Pääbo says.

The more we learn about Neanderthals, the more we stand to learn about ourselves. By comparing our DNA with that of our big-boned relatives, Pääbo has already found spots in the modern human genome that appeared after we diverged from our Neanderthal cousins and evolved apart. These may be the very genes that enhanced our survival. Examples include modern human gene variants for cognitive development. Unique genes for skin morphology and physiology could be other examples. "We will ultimately catalog everything that has changed in our genome in the last 300,000 years since we shared a common ancestor with the Neanderthals," Pääbo says.

And there is more to the story. In what could be the biggest triumph of paleogenomics, Pääbo and his colleagues have just extracted another evolutionary secret from especially sparse fossil remains. In 2010 the team discovered a new kind of human, cousins to Neanderthals called Denisovans, by sequencing DNA from a 50,000-year-old pinkie finger found in a high-altitude Siberian cave in Denisova. Based on the genetic evidence, the Denisovans lived in Asia from about 400,000 to 50,000 years ago and also interbred with the ancestors of modern-day humans—in this case, ones living in Asia. "We were examining mitochondrial DNA [found within the energy factories of cells and transmitted only by the mother] from that pinkie finger to find out if it was from a Neanderthal," Pääbo says. "Instead it turned out to be something completely different." Subsequent sequencing of the nuclear genome followed, revealing that the pinkie came from a previously unknown hominid group, similar to Neanderthals, that migrated east toward Asia while Neanderthals migrated west. Modern humans in New Guinea still carry genomes with nearly 5 percent Denisovan DNA.

Sequencing technology has advanced so far that, these days, fresh evolutionary insights do not necessarily require any fossils at all: Within our DNA, we modern humans provide a genomic window onto what came before. At the University of New Mexico in Albuquerque, genetic anthropologists Jeffrey Long, Keith Hunley, and Sarah Joyce used computers to analyze genetic data from 2,000 people in 100 modern human populations in Africa, Europe, Asia, Oceania, and the Americas. In much the same way that forensic scientists compare DNA samples to catch criminals, the New Mexico researchers compared 619 "micro-satellite" positions on genomes, creating a digital evolutionary tree of the groups. There seemed to be two periods of interbreeding between modern and ancient humans (such as Neanderthals, perhaps Denisovans, and other large-brained hominid cousins).

Those two periods of interbreeding occurred after humans left Africa—first about 60,000 years ago in the eastern Mediterranean, and more recently about 45,000 years ago in eastern Asia. Offspring from the first interbreeding went on to migrate to Europe, Asia, and North America. The second mating in eastern Asia further altered the genetic makeup of people in New Guinea and possibly Australia. The findings mean our species did not branch off from all the others as sharply and irrevocably as we like to think, Long says. "This is giving us a window on human evolution where we see that there were these periods of flux and ebbs and flows in our gene pool."

The Future of Our Past

With each discovery come new questions about our identity. "Over the next 10 years, projects like the Neanderthal genome will lead to a contentious debate about what it means to be human," Rick Potts says. "To my mind, if you had to crystallize the human essence in one word, it would be *adaptability*. That goes all the way back to Lucy." William Jungers calls members of Lucy's genus, the australopiths, the "ultimate morphological generalists." They accommodated huge amounts of climate change, were able to survive where there were lots of trees and very few trees, and expanded across Africa for millions of years in the face of overwhelming challenges. We are the bearers of Lucy's legacy, able to live in igloos or space shuttles and interconnect instantaneously through technology that confounds our own imagination.

Ardi's kin launched that adaptability with their complex, versatile anatomy. Flo's relatives, swept unceremoniously onto an isolated island, adjusted and thrived. Even the Neanderthals, themselves doomed, managed to share space with *Homo sapiens* long enough to spread their genes. They still live in us. Yet out of all these species, only our species became a global success. As much as we resemble our relatives, there clearly is something special about us.

"Imagine a long-lived alien observing Earth through geologic time," White says. "It would be pretty darn monotonous for a million years. We showed up anatomically about 150,000 years ago, and we are a very bizarre primate compared with all the others. Our feet don't grasp. We walk only on two legs. Our braincase is massive. Our face and front teeth are almost infantile. Human breasts don't cycle with lactation. They remain 'enlarged' throughout adulthood. We are different in every possible way."

And then, over just the past two centuries or so, came a far more epochal change. The number of *Homo sapiens* on the planet skyrocketed. Our technology altered every aspect of the global ecosystem. Was all of this potential locked away in our brains and in our genes? Is it tethered to the same traits that allowed us to survive competing with and mating with our cousins, the Neanderthals and Denisovans? What will a few more generations bring?

"In art, in exploration, in technology, modern humans seem to have it over these other forms," Pääbo says. "The million-dollar question seeks the genetic reason for some of that." But he is cautious as well. "We are more numerous and spread over more parts of the globe, but we haven't lived on this planet very long." At the very least, we can expect our talent to render more astounding discoveries about our past—once as invisible and mute as a long-buried fossil in some deep cleft of rock but now exhumed and decoded by that unique brain that sets our species apart.

Critical Thinking

1. In what respects is the simple and linear view of the "ascent of man" dated and wrong?

2. In what ways does *Ardipithecus ramidus* display a mosaic of ape and human traits? Be familiar with the contrasting points of view drawn from the evidence. What is the significance of the relatively blunt and small canines, according to Owen Lovejoy?

3. How do Morwood and others answer those who think it is a dwarf-like descendant of *Homo erectus* or an australopithecine? How does *Homo floresiensis* challenge established views on human brain and body size and migration?

4. How has paleogenomics changed our views on whether or not Neanderthal genes survive in living populations?

5. In what sense is the human essence adaptability?

From *Discover*, May 2011, pp. 48, 50–51, 53–55, 76. Copyright © 2011 by Discover Syndication. Reprinted by permission via PARS International.

Refuting a Myth About Human Origins

Homo sapiens emerged once, not as modern-looking people first and as modern-behaving people later.

JOHN J. SHEA

For decades, archeologists have believed that modern behaviors emerged among *Homo sapiens* tens of thousands of years after our species first evolved. Archaeologists disagreed over whether this process was gradual or swift, but they assumed that *Homo sapiens* once lived who were very different from us. These people were not "behaviorally modern," meaning they did not routinely use art, symbols and rituals; they did not systematically collect small animals, fish, shellfish and other difficult-to-procure foods; they did not use complex technologies: Traps, nets, projectile weapons and watercraft were unknown to them.

Premodern humans—often described as "archaic *Homo sapiens*"—were thought to have lived in small, vulnerable groups of closely related individuals. They were believed to have been equipped only with simple tools and were likely heavily dependent on hunting large game. Individuals in such groups would have been much less insulated from environmental stresses than are modern humans. In Thomas Hobbes's words, their lives were "solitary, nasty, brutish and short." If you need a mental image here, close your eyes and conjure a picture of a stereotypical caveman. But archaeological evidence now shows that some of the behaviors associated with modern humans, most importantly our capacity for wide behavioral variability, actually did occur among people who lived very long ago, particularly in Africa. And a conviction is growing among some archaeologists that there was no sweeping transformation to "behavioral modernity" in our species' recent past.

As Misia Landau argued nearly a quarter of a century ago in the essay "Human Evolution as Narrative" (*American Scientist*, May–June 1984), prescientific traditions of narrative explanation long encouraged scientists to envision key changes in human evolution as holistic transformations. The idea of an archaic-to-modern human transition in *Homo sapiens* arises, in part, from this narrative tradition. All this makes for a satisfying story, but it is not a realistic framework for understanding the actual, complex and contingent course of human evolution. Most evolutionary changes are relatively minor things whose consequences play out incrementally over thousands of generations.

In order to better understand human prehistory, I recommend another approach, one that focuses on behavioral variability.

This trait, easily observed among recent humans, is becoming more apparent in the archaeological record for early *Homo sapiens*. Prehistoric people lived in different ways in different places at different times. We must seek out and explain those differences, for, in evolution, only differences matter. Thinking about prehistoric human behavioral variability in terms of various adaptive strategies offers an attractive way to explain these differences. But first, we need to discard an incorrect and outdated idea about human evolution, the belief that prehistoric *Homo sapiens* can be divided into "archaic" and "modern" humans.

An Idea Is Born

Archaeology's concept of archaic versus modern humans developed as prehistoric archaeological research spread from Europe to other regions. The study of prehistoric people began in Europe during the 19th century in scientific societies, museums and universities. By the 1920s, discoveries made at a number of European archaeological sites had prompted a consensus about the Paleolithic Period, which is now dated from 12,000 to nearly 2.6 million years ago. Archaeologists divided this period into Lower (oldest), Middle, and Upper (youngest) Paleolithic phases. Distinctive stone-tool assemblages—or "industries"—characterized each phase. Archaeologists identified these industries by the presence of diagnostic artifact types, such as Acheulian hand axes (Lower Paleolithic), Mousterian scrapers made of Levallois flakes (Middle Paleolithic), and Aurignacian prismatic blades and carved antler points (Upper Paleolithic). The fact that tools from more recent industries were lighter, smaller and more heavily modified suggested there was a trend toward greater technological and cultural sophistication in the Paleolithic sequence. European Upper Paleolithic industries were associated exclusively with *Homo sapiens* fossils and Lower and Middle Paleolithic industries were associated with earlier hominins (*Homo heidelbergensis* and *Homo neanderthalensis*). This supported the idea that there were important evolutionary differences between modern *Homo sapiens* and earlier archaic hominins.

Early Upper Paleolithic contexts in Europe preserve evidence for prismatic blade production, carved bone tools, projectile weaponry, complex hearths, personal adornments, art, long-distance trade, mortuary rituals, architecture, food storage and specialized big-game hunting, as well as systematic exploitation of smaller prey and aquatic resources. Furthermore, the variability of these behaviors within the Upper Paleolithic is much greater than that seen in earlier periods. In much the same way that anthropologists have documented cultural variability among recent humans, archaeologists can easily tell whether a particular carved bone point or bone bead is from a site in Spain, France or Germany. Not surprisingly, most prehistorians accept that the archaeology of the Upper Paleolithic is, in effect, "the archaeology of us."

Lower and Middle Paleolithic stone tools and other artifacts found in Europe and elsewhere vary within a narrow range of simple forms. Properly equipped and motivated modern-day flintknappers (people who make stone tools) can turn out replicas of any of these tools in minutes, if not seconds. Many of the differences among Lower and Middle Paleolithic artifacts simply reflect variation in rock types and the extent to which tools were resharpened. Geographic and chronological differences among Middle and Lower Paleolithic tools mostly involve differences in relative frequencies of these simple tool types. Nearly the same range of Lower and Middle Paleolithic stone tool types are found throughout much of Europe, Africa and Asia.

The differences between the Lower/Middle and Upper Paleolithic records in Europe are so pronounced that from the 1970s onward prehistorians have described the transition between them as "The Upper Paleolithic Revolution." This regional phenomenon went global in the late 1980s after a conference at Cambridge University entitled "The Human Revolution." This revolution was portrayed as a watershed event that set recent modern humans apart from their archaic predecessors and from other hominins, such as *Homo neanderthalensis*. The causes of this assumed transformation were hotly debated. Scientists such as Richard Klein attributed the changes to the FOXP2 polymorphism, the so-called language gene. But the polymorphism was eventually discovered in Neanderthal DNA too. Many researchers—such as Christopher Henshilwood of the University of Witwatersrand, Curtis Marean of Arizona State University, Paul Mellars of the University of Cambridge, April Nowell of the University of Victoria and Phil Chase of the University of Pennsylvania—continue to see symbolic behavior as a crucial component of behavioral modernity. Yet as João Zilhão of the University of Bristol and Francesco d'Errico of the University of Bordeaux have argued, finds of mineral pigments, perforated beads, burials and artifact-style variation associated with Neanderthals challenge the hypothesis that symbol use, or anything else for that matter, was responsible for a quality of behavioral modernity unique to *Homo sapiens*.

The Missing Revolution

In fact, fossil evidence threatening the Upper Paleolithic revolution hypothesis emerged many decades ago. At about the same time the Paleolithic framework was developed during the 1920s and 1930s, European-trained archaeologists began searching for human fossils and artifacts in the Near East, Africa and Asia.

Expatriate and colonial archaeologists such as Dorothy Garrod and Louis Leakey expected that the European archaeological record worked as a global model for human evolution and used the European Paleolithic framework to organize their observations abroad. Very quickly, however, they discovered a mismatch between their expectations and reality when *Homo sapiens* remains outside Europe were found with Lower or Middle Paleolithic artifacts. Archaeologists started assuming then that the remains dated to periods just before the Upper Paleolithic revolution. But in fact, those discoveries, as well as more recent finds, challenge the notion that the revolution ever occurred.

In Europe, the oldest *Homo sapiens* fossils date to only 35,000 years ago. But studies of genetic variation among living humans suggest that our species emerged in Africa as long as 200,000 years ago. Scientists have recovered *Homo sapiens* fossils in contexts dating to 165,000 to 195,000 years ago in Ethiopia's Lower Omo Valley and Middle Awash Valley. Evidence is clear that early humans dispersed out of Africa to southern Asia before 40,000 years ago. Similar modern-looking human fossils found in the Skhul and Qafzeh caves in Israel date to 80,000 to 120,000 years ago. *Homo sapiens* fossils dating to 100,000 years ago have been recovered from Zhiren Cave in China. In Australia, evidence for a human presence dates to at least 42,000 years ago. Nothing like a human revolution precedes *Homo sapiens'* first appearances in any of these regions. And all these *Homo sapiens* fossils were found with either Lower or Middle Paleolithic stone tool industries.

There are differences between the skeletons of these early *Homo sapiens* and Upper Paleolithic Europeans. The best-documented differences involve variation in skull shape. Yet, as Daniel Lieberman of Harvard University writes in the recently published *The Evolution of the Human Head,* we are just beginning to understand the genetic and behavioral basis for variation in human skulls. It makes no sense whatsoever to draw major evolutionary distinctions among humans based on skull shape unless we understand the underlying sources of cranial variation. There is no simple morphological dividing line among these fossil skulls. Most fossils combine "primitive" (ancestral) characteristics as well as "derived" (recently evolved) ones. Even if physical anthropologists divided prehistoric humans into archaic and modern groups, it would be foolish for archaeologists to invoke this difference as an explanation for anything unless we knew how specific skeletal differences related to specific aspects of behavior preserved in the archaeological record.

Early *Homo sapiens* fossils in Africa and Asia are associated with "precocious," or unexpectedly early evidence for modern behaviors such as those seen in the European Upper Paleolithic. They include intensive fish and shellfish exploitation, the production of complex projectile weapons, the use of symbols in the form of mineral pigments and perforated shells, and even rare burials with grave goods in them. But as Erella Hovers and Anna Belfer-Cohen of The Hebrew University of Jerusalem argued in a chapter of *Transitions Before the Transition,* "Now You See It, Now You Don't—Modern Human Behavior in the Middle Paleolithic," much of this evidence is recursive. It is not a consistent feature of the archaeological record. Evidence for one or more of these modern behaviors appears at a few sites or for a few thousand years in one region or another, and then it vanishes. If behavioral modernity were both a derived condition and a landmark development in the course of human history, one would hardly expect it to disappear for prolonged periods in our species' evolutionary history.

For me, the most surprising aspect about the debate regarding when *Homo sapiens* became human is that archaeologists have not tested the core hypothesis that there were significant behavioral differences between the earliest and more recent members of our species. Because modernity is a typological category, it is not easy to test this hypothesis. One is either behaviorally modern or not. And, not all groups classified as behaviorally modern have left clear and unambiguous evidence for that modernity at all times and in all contexts. For example, expedient and opportunistic flintknapping of river pebbles and cobbles by living humans often creates stone tools indistinguishable from the pebble tools knapped by *Homo habilis* or *Homo erectus*. This similarity reflects the nature of the tool-making strategies, techniques and raw materials, not the evolutionary equivalence of the toolmakers. Thus, the archaeological record abounds in possibilities of false-negative findings about prehistoric human behavioral modernity.

This issue caught my interest in 2002 while I was excavating 195,000-year-old archaeological sites associated with early *Homo sapiens* fossils in the Lower Omo River Valley Kibish Formation in Ethiopia. I am an archaeologist, but I am also a flintknapper. Nothing about the stone tools from Omo Kibish struck me as archaic or primitive. (When I teach flintknapping at my university, I have ample opportunity to see what happens when people with rudimentary skills try to knap stone and how those skills vary with experience and motivation.) The Omo Kibish tools showed that their makers had great versatility in effectively knapping a wide range of rock types. This set me to thinking: Have we been asking the wrong questions about early humans' behavior?

A Better Way

Documenting and analyzing behavioral variability is a more theoretically sound approach to studying differences among prehistoric people than searching for the transition to behavioral modernity. Nearly everything humans do, we do in more than one identifiably different way. As Richard Potts of the Smithsonian Institution argued in *Humanity's Descent* in 1996, our species' capacity for wide behavioral variability appears to be uniquely derived. No other animal has as wide a behavioral repertoire as *Homo sapiens* does. And variability can be investigated empirically, quantitatively, and with fewer problems than occur in ranking prehistoric people in terms of their modernity.

One way to gauge early *Homo sapiens'* behavioral variability is to compare their lithic technologies. Lithics, or stone tools, are nearly indestructible and are found everywhere hominins lived in Pleistocene times. Stone tools do not tell us everything we might wish to know about prehistoric human behavior, but they are no less subject to the selective pressures that create variation in other types of archaeological evidence.

Lithic artifacts made by recent humans are more complex and variable than those associated with early hominins. Early Paleolithic stone tools are more complex and variable than those made by nonhuman primates. Thus, there is reason to expect that analysis of these tools will produce a valid signal about early *Homo sapiens'* capacity for behavioral variability. Eastern Africa is an especially good place in which to compare early and later *Homo sapiens'* stone technology because that region preserves our species' longest continuous archaeological record. Restricting this comparison to eastern Africa minimizes the complicating effects of geographic constraints on stone-tool technology.

One of the most popular ways of describing variation among stone-tool industries is a framework that the British archaeologist Grahame Clark proposed in *World Prehistory: A New Synthesis* (1969). This framework describes lithic technological variability in terms of five modes of core technology. (In flintknapping, "cores" are the rocks from which flakes are struck, with the flakes later developed into various kinds of tools.) Variation in core technology is thought to reflect differences in ecological adaptations. Clark's framework is a crude instrument, but it can be made into a reasonably sensitive register of technological variability if we simply note which of these modes are represented in each of a series of lithic assemblages. When it is applied to sites in eastern Africa dating 284,000 to 6,000 years ago, a more complex view of prehistoric life there emerges. One does not see a steady accumulation of novel core technologies since our species first appeared or anything like a "revolution." Instead one sees a persistent pattern of wide technological variability.

What does this variability mean? Archaeologists' understanding of lithic technology continues to grow, from experiments, from studies of recent stone-tool-using groups and from contextual clues in the archaeological record. Our understanding is far from perfect, but we do know enough to make some plausible interpretations. Pebble-core reduction (mode 1 in Clark's framework), in which toolmakers strike flakes opportunistically from rounded pebbles or cobbles, is the simplest way to obtain a cutting edge from stone. Stone tools are still made this way in rural parts of eastern Africa. Its ubiquity in the archaeological assemblages probably reflects a stable strategy of coping expediently with unpredictable needs for cutting edges.

Large bifacial core tools (mode 2) are thought to have been dual-purpose tools. Their heft and long ratting edges make them effective in heavy-duty tasks, such as woodworking or the butchering of large animal carcasses. Thinner flakes knapped from bifacial core tools can be used for lighter-duty cutting or retouched into more functionally specialized forms. In recent archaeological contexts, large bifacial cutting tools are often correlated with people who moved their residences frequently, whereas expedient pebble cores are correlated with more lengthy occupations. High topographic relief and wide seasonal variation in rainfall make residential stability a difficult thing for even recent eastern African pastoralist groups to achieve. The persistence of this technology may reflect relatively high residential mobility among prehistoric eastern Africans.

The behavioral correlates of Levallois prepared-core technology (mode 3) are less clear, if only because the term encompasses so many different core-knapping strategies. Some archaeologists see Levallois prepared cores as reflecting knappers' efforts to obtain desired tool shapes, or to produce relatively broad and thin flakes that efficiently recover cutting edge. These hypotheses are not mutually exclusive, and in the long run, each of them probably explains some part of why people made such cores in eastern Africa for a very long time.

Prismatic-blade core technology (mode 4) involves detaching long rectangular flakes one after another from a cone-shaped core. The most widely repeated hypothesis about the appeal of prismatic-blade production is that it produces greater amounts of ratting edge per unit mass of stone than other strategies. However, recent experiments by Metin Eren at Southern Methodist University and his colleagues have shown that this hypothesis is wrong. A far more likely appeal of this strategy is that the blades' morphological consistency makes them easier to attach to a handle. Attaching a stone tool to a handle vastly increases leverage and mechanical efficiency, but it also restricts the range of tool movement and limits the portion of the tool that can be resharpened. The comings and goings of blade core technology in eastern Africa probably reflect a complex interplay of these strategic considerations.

Differing amounts of geometric microlithic technology (mode 5) are preserved in the most ancient and most recent assemblages in the east African sample. Geometric microliths are small tools made by segmenting blades or flakes and shaping them into triangles, rectangles, crescents and other geometric forms by blunting one or more of their edges. Too small to have been useful while hand-held, geometric microliths were almost certainly used as hafted tools. They are easy to attach to handles, making them suitable for use as projectile armatures, woodworking tools and aids to preparing plant foods. Archaeologists view microlithic stone-tool technology as a strategy for optimizing versatility and minimizing risk. Microlithic technologies first appear and proliferate among African and Eurasian human populations from about 50,000 years ago to around 10,000 years ago. This was a period of hypervariable climate, and it makes a certain amount of sense that humans at that time devised versatile and efficiently transportable stone tools. If, for example, climate change required people to frequently shift from hunting game to reaping grasses and back again, using microlith-barbed arrows and microlith-edged sickles would allow them to do this efficiently, without any major change to their technological strategies. Because microlithic took are small, they preserve high ratios of cutting edge to mass. This means that if climate shifts required more seasonal migrations, individuals transporting microliths would be carrying the most cutting edge per unit mass of stone. Variability in the use of microlithic technology in eastern Africa probably reflects strategic responses to environmental unpredictability along with efforts to cope with increased subsistence risk by optimizing versatility in stone-tool technology.

How do the differences between earlier and later eastern African core technologies compare to variation among recent stone-tool-using humans? The range of variability in recent human stone-tool technology is greater than that in the eastern African sample. All five of Clark's modes are to be found among the lithic technology of recent humans. Yet some technologies are not represented in the African sample. For example, more than 30,000 years ago in Australia, and later elsewhere, people began grinding and polishing the edges of stone tools. Such grinding and polishing reduces friction during work, making cutting tools more efficient to use and resharpen. In the New World, ancestral Native American flintknappers deployed a wide range of bifacial-core technologies fundamentally different from those seen in eastern Africa. They used these tools in contexts ranging from hunter-gatherer campsites on the Great Plains to Mesoamerican city-states like Teotihuacan. Differences in recent stone-tool technology reflect variability in adaptive strategies. No anthropologists in their right minds would attribute this variability to evolutionary differences among recent humans. If this kind of explanation makes so little sense in the present, what possible value can it have for explaining past behavioral variability among *Homo sapiens*?

The lithic evidence reviewed here challenges the hypothesis that there were significant behavioral differences between the earliest and more recent members of our species in eastern Africa. Obviously, there is more to human behavioral variability than what is reflected in stone tools. Using Clark's technological modes to capture that variability, as described here, is just a first step. But it is a step forward. This emphasis on variability will gain strength if and when it is supported by more detailed analyses of the stone tools and by other archaeological evidence.

Abandoning a Myth

One could view these findings as just another case of precocious modern behavior by early *Homo sapiens* in Africa, but I think they have a larger lesson to teach us. After all, something is only precocious if it is unexpected. The hypothesis that there were skeletally modern-looking humans whose behavioral capacities differed significantly from our own is not supported by uniformitarian principles (explanations of the past based on studies of the present), by evolutionary theory or by archaeological evidence. There are no known populations of *Homo sapiens* with biologically constrained capacities for behavioral variability. Generations of anthropologists have sought in vain for such primitive people in every corner of the world and have consistently failed to find them. The parsimonious interpretation of this failure is that such humans do not exist.

Nor is there any reason to believe that behaviorally archaic *Homo sapiens* ever did exist. If there ever were significant numbers of *Homo sapiens* individuals with cognitive limitations on their capacity for behavioral variability, natural selection by intraspecific competition and predation would have quickly and ruthlessly winnowed them out. In the unforgiving Pleistocene environments in which our species evolved, reproductive isolation was the penalty for stupidity, and lions and wolves were its cure. In other words: No villages, no village idiots. If any such cognitive "winner take all" wipeout event ever happened, it was probably among earlier hominins (*Homo ergaster/erectus* or

Homo heidelbergensis) or during the evolutionary differentiation of our species from these hominin ancestors.

Dividing *Homo sapiens* into modern and archaic or pre-modern categories and invoking the evolution of behavioral modernity to explain the difference has never been a good idea. Like the now-discredited scientific concept of race, it reflects hierarchical and typological thinking about human variability that has no place in a truly scientific anthropology. Indeed, the concept of behavioral modernity can be said to be worse than wrong, because it is an obstacle to understanding. Time, energy and research funds that could have been spent investigating the sources of variability in particular behavioral strategies and testing hypotheses about them have been wasted arguing about behavioral modernity.

Anthropology has already faced this error. Writing in the early 20th century, the American ethnologist Franz Boas railed against evolutionary anthropologists who ranked living human societies along an evolutionary scale from primitive to advanced. His arguments found an enthusiastic reception among his colleagues, and they remain basic principles of anthropology to this day. A similar change is needed in the archaeology of human origins. We need to stop looking at artifacts as expressions of evolutionary states and start looking at them as byproducts of behavioral strategies.

The differences we discover among those strategies will lead us to new and very different kinds of questions than those we have asked thus far. For instance, do similar environmental circumstances elicit different ranges of behavioral variability? Are there differences in the stability of particular behavioral strategies? Are certain strategies uniquely associated with particular hominin species, and if so, why? By focusing on behavioral variability, archaeologists will move toward a more scientific approach to human-origins research. The concept of behavioral modernity, in contrast, gets us nowhere.

Even today, a caveman remains the popular image of what a prehistoric person looked like. This individual usually is shown with enlarged eyebrows, a projecting face, long hair and a beard. The stereotypical caveman is inarticulate and dim-witted, and possesses a limited capacity for innovation. In 2006, GEICO commercials put an ironic twist on this image. Their cavemen were more intelligent, articulate, creative and culturally sophisticated than many "modern" people. In a striking case of life imitating art, recent archaeological discoveries are overturning long-standing misconceptions about early human behavior.

Bibliography

Bar-Yosef, O. 2002. The Upper Paleolithic revolution. *Annual Review of Anthropology* 31:363–393.

Clark, G. 1969. *World Prehistory: A New Synthesis.* Cambridge: Cambridge University Press.

Klein, R. G. 2009. *The Human Career,* third edition. Chicago: University of Chicago Press.

Landau, M. L. 1984. Human evolution as narrative. *American Scientist* 72:262–268.

McBrearty, S., and A. S. Brooks. 2000. The revolution that wasn't: A new interpretation of the origin of modern human behavior. *Journal of Human Evolution* 39:453–563.

Mellars, P., and C. Stringer. 1989. *The Human Revolution: Behavioural and Biological Perspectives on the Origins of Modern Humans.* Edinburgh: Edinburgh University Press.

Nowell, A. 2010. Defining behavioral modernity in the context of Neandertal and anatomically modern human populations. *Annual Review of Anthropology* 39:437–452.

Potts, R. 1998. Variability selection and hominid evolution. *Evolutionary Anthropology* 7(3):81–96.

Shea, J. J. 2008. The Middle Stone Age archaeology of the Lower Omo Valley Kibish Formation: Excavations, lithic assemblages, and inferred patterns of early *Homo sapiens* behavior. *Journal of Human Evolution* 55(3):448–485.

Shea, J. J. 2011. *Homo sapiens* is as *Homo sapiens* was: Behavioral variability versus "behavioral modernity" in Paleolithic archaeology. *Current Anthropology* 52(l):l–35.

Critical Thinking

1. What is meant by "behaviorally modern" in the context of this article and how were "pre-modern" people presumed to live by most archeologists?

2. How did archeologists perceive the technological stages of the Paleolithic period and their associations with fossil hominin remains?

3. What is meant by the "Upper Paleolithic Revolution" and how is it explained? What kinds of finds associated with Neanderthals challenge this view?

4. In what sense and where has there been a "mismatch" between the fossil record and archeologists' expectations?

5. What is the problem with associating cranial variation among early humans with actual behavior?

6. What are some of the specific kinds of modern behavior found among early modern humans in Africa and Asia? What is the significance of the fact that these behaviors are "not a consistent feature of the archeological record"?

7. Why is it difficult to test the core hypothesis about the presumed relationship between modern technology and modern-looking *Homo sapiens*?

8. What alternative approach does the author propose? Why is eastern Africa an especially good place to compare early and later *Homo sapiens'* technology?

9. Be familiar with Graham Clarke's five modes of core technology and the benefits of each.

10. Why is it that the range of variability in recent human stone tools is greater than that found in just the east African sample? How does this help to invalidate the assumption that stone tool variation in the fossil record reflects stages of human evolution?

11. Why does the author say, "We need to stop looking at artifacts as expressions of evolutionary states and start looking at them as byproducts of behavioral strategies"?

JOHN J. SHEA is a professor of anthropology at Stony Brook University and a research associate with the Turkana Basin Institute in Kenya. He earned his PhD at Harvard University in 1991 and has conducted research in Israel, Jordan, Ethiopia, Eritrea, Kenya, and Tanzania. Two of his key scientific articles are "The origins of lithic projectile point technology: Evidence from Africa, the Levant, and Europe"

(*Journal of Archaeological Science,* 2006) and "Stone age visiting cards revisited: A strategic perspective on the lithic technology of early hominin dispersal" (*Vertebrate Paleobiology and Paleoanthropology,* 2010). His forthcoming book will be titled *Paleolithic and Neolithic Stone Tools of the Near East: A Guide.* Shea is a professional flintknapper whose work appears in numerous documentaries and in exhibits at the Smithsonian Institution and the American Museum of Natural History. Address: Anthropology Department, Stony Brook University, Stony Brook, NY 11794-4364. E-mail: john.shea@sunysb.edu.

The Birth of Childhood

Unlike other apes, humans depend on their parents for a long period after weaning. But when—and why—did our long childhood evolve?

ANN GIBBONS

Mel was just 3.5 years old when his mother died of pneumonia in 1987 in Tanzania. He had still been nursing and had no siblings, so his prospects were grim. He begged weakly for meat, and although adults gave him scraps, only a 12-year-old named Spindle shared his food regularly, protected him, and let him sleep with him at night. When Spindle took off for a month, another adolescent, Pax, came to Mel's rescue, giving him fruit and a place to sleep until Spindle returned. Mel survived to age 10.

Fortunately for Mel, he was an orphan chimpanzee living in the Gombe Stream National Park rather than a small child living in the slums of a big city. With only sporadic care from older children, a 3-year-old human orphan would not have survived.

Mel's story illustrates the uniqueness of one facet of human life: Unlike our close cousins the chimpanzees, we have a prolonged period of development after weaning, when children depend on their parents to feed them, until at least age 6 or 7. Street children from Kathmandu to Rio de Janeiro do not survive on their own unless they are at least 6. "There's no society where children can feed themselves after weaning," says anthropologist Kristen Hawkes of the University of Utah in Salt Lake City. By contrast, "chimpanzees don't have childhoods. They are independent soon after weaning," says anthropologist Barry Bogin of Loughborough University in Leicestershire, U.K.

Humans are also the only animals that stretch out the teenage years, having a final growth spurt and delaying reproduction until about 6 years after puberty. On average, women's first babies arrive at age 19, with a worldwide peak of first babies at age 22.5. This lengthy period of development—comprised of infancy, juvenile years, and adolescence—is a hallmark of the human condition; researchers have known since the 1930s that we take twice as long as chimpanzees to reach adulthood. Even though we are only a bit bigger than chimpanzees, we mature and reproduce a decade later and live 2 to 3 decades longer, says Bogin.

Given that we are unique among mammals, researchers have been probing how this pattern of growth evolved. They have long scrutinized the few, fragile skulls and skeletons of ancient children and have now developed an arsenal of tools to better gauge how childhood has changed over the past 3 million years. Researchers are scanning skulls and teeth of every known juvenile with electron microscopes, micro-computed tomography scans, or powerful synchrotron x-rays and applying state-of-the-art methods to create three-dimensional virtual reconstructions of the skulls of infants and the pelvises of mothers. They're analyzing life histories in traditional cultures to help understand the advantages of the human condition. In addition, some new fossils are appearing. . . . Researchers report the first nearly complete pelvis of a female *Homo erectus,* which offers clues to the prenatal growth of this key human species.

All of this is creating some surprises. One direct human ancestor, whose skeleton looks much like our own, turns out to have grown up much faster than we do. The life histories of our closest evolutionary cousins, the Neandertals, remain controversial, but some researchers suspect that they may have had the longest childhoods of all. The new lines of evidence are helping researchers close in on the time when childhood began to lengthen. "Evidence suggests that much of what makes our life history unique took shape during the evolution of the genus *Homo* and not before," says anthropologist Holly Smith of the University of Michigan, Ann Arbor.

Live Fast, Die Young

Back in 1925, Australian anatomist Raymond Dart announced the discovery of that rarest of rare specimens, the skull of an early hominin child. Dart estimated that the australopithecine he called the Taung baby had been about 6 years old when it died about 2 million years ago, because its first permanent molar had erupted. As modern parents know, the first of the baby teeth fall out and the first permanent molars appear at about age 6. Dart assumed that early hominins—the group made up of humans and our ancestors but not other apes—matured on much the same schedule as we do, an assumption held for 60 years. Growing up slowly was seen as a defining character of the human lineage.

Childhood Stages

	Age at Weaning (Years)	Age at Eruption of First Molar (Years)	Female Age at First Breeding (Years) (Estimated by 3rd Molar Eruption in Fossils)	Average Maximum Life Span (Years)
Chimpanzees, *Pan troglodytes*	4.0	4.0	11.5	45
Lucy, *Australopithecus afarensis*	4.0?	4.0?	11.5	45
Homo erectus	?	4.5	14.5 (est.)	60? (est.)
Modern humans, *Homo sapiens*	2.5	6.0	19.3	70

Milestones. Key events show that modern humans live slower and die later than our ancestors did.

Then in 1984, anatomists Christopher Dean and Timothy Bromage tested a new method to calculate the chronological ages of fossil children in a lab at University College London (UCL). Just as botanists add up tree rings to calculate the age of a tree, they counted microscopic lines on the surface of teeth that are laid down weekly as humans grow. The pair counted the lines on teeth of australopithecine children about as mature as the Taung child and were confounded: These hominin children were only about 3.5 years old rather than 6. They seemed to be closer to the chimpanzee pattern, in which the first permanent molar erupts at about age 3.5. "We concluded that [the australopithecines] were more like living great apes in their pace of development than modern humans," says Dean.

Their report in *Nature* in 1985 shook the field and focused researchers on the key questions of when and why our ancestors adopted the risky strategy of delaying reproduction. Many other slow-growing, large-bodied animals, such as rhinos, elephants, and chimpanzees, are now threatened with extinction, in part because they delay reproduction so long that their offspring risk dying before they replace themselves. Humans are the latest to begin reproducing, yet we seem immune from those risks, given that there are 6.6 billion of us on the planet. "When did we escape those constraints? When did we extend our childhood?" asks biological anthropologist Steven Leigh of the University of Illinois, Urbana-Champaign.

The Taung baby and the other australopithecine children, including the relatively recent discovery of a stunning fossil of a 3-year-old *Australopithecus afarensis* girl from Dikika, Ethiopia, show that it happened after the australopithecines. So researchers have zeroed in on early *Homo*, which appeared in Africa about 2 million years ago.

Unfortunately, there are only a few jaw bits of early *Homo* infants and young children to nail down their ages. Most of what we know comes from a single skeleton, a *H. erectus* boy who died about 1.6 million years ago near Lake Turkana, Kenya. *H. erectus* was among the first human ancestors to share many key elements of the modern human body plan, with a brain considerably larger than that of earlier hominins. And unlike the petite australopithecines, this Turkana youth was big: He weighed 50 kilograms, stood 163 centimeters tall, and looked like he was 13 years old, based on modern human standards. Yet two independent tooth studies suggested ages from 8 or 9 to 10.5 years old.

Now a fresh look at the skeleton concludes that, despite the boy's size, he was closer to 8 years old when he died. Dean and Smith make this case in a paper in press in an edited volume, *The First Humans: Origin of the Genus* Homo. The skeleton and tooth microstructure of the boy and new data on other members of his species suggest that he attained more of his adult height and mass earlier than modern human children do. Today, "you won't find an 8-year-old boy with body weight, height, and skeletal age that are so much older," says Dean.

He and Smith concluded that the boy did not experience a "long, slow period of growth" after he was weaned but grew up earlier, more like a chimpanzee. They estimate the species' age at first reproduction at about 14.5, based on the eruption of its third molar, which in both humans and chimpanzees erupts at about the age they first reproduce. This 8-year-old Turkana Boy was probably more independent than a 13-year-old modern human, the researchers say, suggesting that *H. erectus* families were quite different from ours and did not stay together as long.

The new, remarkably complete female pelvis, however, suggests that life history changes had begun in *H. erectus*. Researchers led by Sileshi Semaw of the Stone Age Institute at Indiana University, Bloomington, found the pelvis in the badlands of Gona, Ethiopia. They present a chain of inference that leads from pelvis, to brain size, to life history strategy.

They assume that the nearly complete pelvis belongs to *H. erectus*, because other *H. erectus* fossils were found nearby and because it resembles fragmentary pelvises for the species. Lead author Scott Simpson of Case Western Reserve University in Cleveland, Ohio, paints a vivid picture of a short female with wide hips and an "obstetrically capacious" pelvic opening that could have birthed babies with brain sizes of up to 315 milliliters. That's 30% to 50% of the adult brain size for this species and larger than previously predicted based on a reconstruction of the Turkana Boy's incomplete pelvis. However, the new estimate does match with newborn brain size predicted by the size of adult brains in *H. erectus*, says Jeremy DeSilva of Worcester State College in Massachusetts, who made such calculations online in September in the *Journal of Human Evolution*.

The wide pelvis suggests *H. erectus* got a head start on its brain development, putting on extra gray matter in utero rather than later in childhood. That's similar to living people, whose brains grow rapidly before birth, says Simpson. But if *H. erectus*'s fetal growth approached that of modern humans, it built proportionately more of its brain before birth, because its brain never became as massive as our own.

Thus, *H. erectus* grew its brain before birth like a modern human, while during childhood it grew up faster like an ape. With a brain developing early, *H. erectus* toddlers may have spent less time as helpless children than modern humans do, says paleoanthropologist Alan Walker of Pennsylvania State University in State College. This suggests *H. erectus* children were neither chimplike nor humanlike but perhaps somewhere in between: "Early *H. erectus* possessed a life history unlike any species living today," write Dean and Smith. "If you look at its morphology, it fits in our genus, *Homo*," says Smith. "But in terms of life history, they fit with australopithecines."

Live Slow, Die Old?

If *H. erectus* was just beginning to slow down its life history, when did humans take the last steps, to our current late-maturing life plan? Three juvenile fossil members of *H. antecessor,* who died 800,000 years ago in Atapuerca, Spain, offer tantalizing clues. An initial study in 1999, based on rough estimates of tooth eruption, found that this species matured like a modern human, says José María Bermúdez de Castro of the Museo Nacional de Ciencias Naturales in Madrid. Detailed studies of tooth microstructure are eagerly awaited to confirm this.

In the meantime, another recent study has shown that childhood was fully extended by the time the first members of our species, *H. sapiens,* appeared in northern Africa about 200,000 years ago. In 2007, researchers examined the daily, internal tooth lines of a *H. sapiens* child who lived 160,000 years ago in Jebel Irhoud, Morocco. They used x-rays from a powerful particle accelerator in Grenoble, France (*Science,* 7 December 2007, p. 1546), to study the teeth without destroying them and found that the 8-year-old Jebel Irhoud child had grown as slowly as a modern 8-year-old, according to Harvard University paleoanthropologist Tanya Smith, who coled the study.

That analysis narrowed the window of time when humans evolved the last extension of our childhood to between 800,000 years ago and 200,000 years ago. To constrain it still further, Tanya Smith and her colleagues recently trained their x-ray vision on our closest relatives: the extinct Neandertals, who shared their last ancestor with us about 500,000 years ago. First, the researchers sliced a molar of a Belgian Neandertal that was at the same stage of dental development as the 8-year-old Jebel Irhoud child and counted its internal growth lines. They found that it had reached the same dental milestones more rapidly and proposed that Neandertals grew up faster than we do. That suggests that a fully extended childhood evolved only in our species, in the past 200,000 years.

But Tanya Smith's results conflict with earlier studies by Dean and colleagues who also sliced Neandertal teeth and found that they had formed slowly, like those of modern humans. The case is not closed: Smith and paleontologist Paul Tafforeau of the European Synchrotron Radiation Facility in Grenoble, France, spent weeks last year imaging juvenile Neandertals and early members of *H. sapiens,* and they expect to publish within a year.

Meanwhile, new data with implications for Neandertal growth rates are coming in from other sources. The brain sizes of a Neandertal newborn and two infants show that they were at the upper end of the size range for modern humans, suggesting that their brains grew faster than ours after birth, according to virtual reconstructions by Christoph Zollikofer and anthropologist Marcia Ponce de León of the University of Zurich (*Science,* 12 September, p. 1429).

Those rapidly growing brains don't necessarily imply a rapid life history, warn Zollikofer and Ponce de León. They argue that because Neandertals' brains were more massive, they did not complete brain growth earlier than modern humans even though they grew at a faster rate. "They have to get those bigger brains somehow," says Holly Smith. For now, Neandertals' life history remains controversial.

Why Wait?

If childhood began to change in *H. erectus* and continued to get longer in our own species and possibly Neandertals, then the next question is why. What advantage did our ancestors gain from delaying reproduction so long? Many researchers agree that childhood allows us to learn from others, in order to improve our survival skills and prepare us to be better parents. Historically, researchers have also argued that humans need a long childhood to allow enough time for our larger brain to mature.

But in fact, a big brain doesn't directly cause the extension of childhood, because the brain is built relatively early. "Everyone speaks about slow human development, but the human brain develops very fast," says Zollikofer. It doubles in size in the first year of life and achieves 95% of its adult size by the age of 5 (although white matter grows at least to age 18). "We get our brains done; then, we sit around for much longer than other species before we reproduce," says Leigh. "It's almost like humans are building the outside, getting the scaffolding of the house up early, and then filling in after that."

However, there's a less direct connection between brains and life history: Big brains are so metabolically expensive that primates must postpone the age of reproduction in order to build them, according to a paper last year in the *Journal of Human Evolution* (*Science,* 15 June 2007, p. 1560). "The high metabolic costs of rapid brain growth require delayed maturation so that mothers can bear the metabolic burdens associated with high brain growth," says Leigh. "Fast brain growth tells us that maturation is late."

That's why Ponce de León and Zollikofer think that the Neandertals' rapid brain growth implies late, rather than early, maturation: Neandertal mothers must have been large and strong—and by implication, relatively old—to support infants with such big, fast-growing brains. Indeed, say the Zurich pair, Neandertals may have had even longer childhoods than we do now. Childhood, like brain size, may have reached its zenith in Neandertals and early *H. sapiens*. As our brains got smaller over the past 50,000 years, we might have begun reproducing slightly earlier than Neandertals.

To explore such questions, recent interdisciplinary studies are teasing out the reproductive advantages of waiting to become parents. Many analyses cite an influential life history model by evolutionary biologist Eric Charnov of the University of New Mexico, Albuquerque. The model shows that it pays to have babies early if parents face a high risk of death. Conversely, mammals that face a lower risk of dying benefit if they wait to reproduce, because older mothers can grow bigger, stronger bodies that grow bigger babies, who are more likely to survive. "The driving force of a prolonged life history schedule is almost certainly a reduction in mortality rates that allows growth and life span to extend and allows for reproduction to extend further into adulthood in a more spread-out manner," says Dean.

Researchers such as Loughborough's Bogin have applied Charnov's model to modern humans, proposing that delaying reproduction creates higher quality human mothers. Indeed, humans start having babies 8 years later than chimpanzees, and both species stop by about age 45 to 50. But once human mothers begin, they more than make up for their delayed start, pushing out babies on average 3.4 years apart in traditional forager societies without birth control, compared with 5.9 years for wild chimpanzees, says Bogin. This rapid-fire reproduction produces more babies for human hunter-gatherers, who have peak fertility rates of 0.31 babies per given year compared with 0.22 for chimpanzees. And human mothers who start even later than age 19 have more surviving babies. For example, in the 1950s, the Anabaptist Hutterites of North America, who eschewed birth control, had their first babies on average at age 22 and then bore children every 2 years. They produced an amazing nine children per mother, says Bogin, who has studied the group.

Such fecundity, however, requires a village or at least an extended family with fathers and grandmothers around to help provision and care for the young. That's something that other primates cannot provide consistently, if at all, says Hawkes (*Science*, 25 April 1997, p. 535). She proposed that grandmothers' provisioning allows mothers to wean early and have babies more closely together, a vivid example of the way humans use social connections to overcome biological constraints—and allow mothers to have more babies than they could raise on their own. "Late maturation works well for humans because culture lets us escape the constraints other primates have," says Leigh.

The key is to find out when our ancestors were weaned, says Holly Smith. Younger weaning implies that mothers had enough social support to feed weaned children and space babies more closely. "Weaning tells us when *Homo* species start stacking their young," says Smith. Indeed, Dean and Louise Humphrey of the Natural History Museum in London are testing a method that detects the chemical signature of weaning in human teeth. Humans may be slow starters, but our social safety net has allowed us to stack our babies closely together—and so win the reproductive sweepstakes, leaving chimpanzees, and the extinct Neandertals, far behind.

Critical Thinking

1. How does the case of Mel illustrate the contrast between chimpanzee and human childhood?

2. How do humans contrast with chimpanzees in terms of maturation and reproduction?

3. How were Dean and Bromage able to recalculate the age of the Taung child? What key questions did this cause researchers to focus upon?

4. What can be said about the Turkana boy and why? What is the estimate of this species' first reproduction? How would *H. erectus* families been different from ours?

5. What does the wide *H. erectus* pelvis suggest about its brain development and its life history?

6. What is the evidence as to when our ancestors took the last steps to our current late-maturing life plan?

7. Why does similar evidence for Neanderthals continue to be ambiguous?

8. What are the possible advantages to a long childhood? Why is the idea of allowing for brain growth not a likely explanation?

9. What is the advantage to postponing the age of reproduction?

10. Under what circumstance does it pay to have babies early? What is the benefit of having babies later? How do humans compare favorably with chimpanzees in this regard? Why does such fecundity require a village?

11. What would the time of weaning tell us about our ancestors?

The Evolution of Grandparents

Senior citizens may have been the secret of our species' success.

RACHEL CASPARI

During the summer of 1963, when I was six years old, my family traveled from our home in Philadelphia to Los Angeles to visit my maternal relatives. I already knew my grandmother well: she helped my mother care for my twin brothers, who were only 18 months my junior, and me. When she was not with us, my grandmother lived with her mother, whom I met that summer for the first time. I come from a long-lived family. My grandmother was born in 1895, and her mother in the 1860s; both lived almost 100 years. We stayed with the two matriarchs for several weeks. Through their stories, I learned about my roots and where I belonged in a social network spanning four generations. Their reminiscences personally connected me to life at the end of the Civil War and the Reconstruction era and to the challenges my ancestors faced and the ways they persevered.

My story is not unique. Elders play critical roles in human societies around the globe, conveying wisdom and providing social and economic support for the families of their children and larger kin groups. In our modern era, people routinely live long enough to become grandparents. But this was not always the case. When did grandparents become prevalent, and how did their ubiquity affect human evolution?

Research my colleagues and I have been conducting indicates that grandparent-aged individuals became common relatively recently in human prehistory and that this change came at about the same time as cultural shifts toward distinctly modern behaviors—including a dependence on sophisticated symbol-based communication of the kind that underpins art and language. These findings suggest that living to an older age had profound effects on the population sizes, social interactions and genetics of early modern human groups and may explain why they were more successful than archaic humans, such as the Neandertals.

Live Fast, Die Young

The first step in figuring out when grandparents became a fixture in society is assessing the typical age breakdown of past populations—what percent were children, adults of childbearing age and parents of those younger adults? Reconstructing the demography of ancient populations is tricky business, however. For one thing, whole populations are never preserved in the fossil record. Rather paleontologists tend to recover fragments of individuals. For another, early humans did not necessarily mature at the same rate as modern humans. In fact, maturation rates differ even among contemporary human populations. But a handful of sites have yielded high enough numbers of human fossils in the same layers of sediment that scientists can confidently assess the age at death of the remains—which is key to understanding the makeup of a prehistoric group.

A rock-shelter located in the town of Krapina in Croatia, about 40 kilometers northwest of the city of Zagreb, is one such site. More than a century ago Croatian paleontologist Dragutin Gorjanović-Kramberger excavated and described the fragmentary remains of perhaps as many as 70 Neandertal individuals there, most of which came from a layer dated to about 130,000 years ago. The large number of fossils found close to one another, the apparently rapid accumulation of the sediments at the site and the fact that some of the remains share distinctive, genetically determined features all indicate that the Krapina bones approximate the remains of a single population of Neandertals. As often happens in the fossil record, the best-preserved remains at Krapina are teeth because the high mineral content of teeth protects them from degradation. Fortunately, teeth are also one of the best skeletal elements for determining age at death, which is achieved by analyzing surface wear and age-related changes in their internal structure.

In 1979, before I began my research into the evolution of grandparents, Milford H. Wolpoff of the University of Michigan at Ann Arbor published a paper, based on dental remains, that assessed how old the Krapina Neandertals were when they died. Molar teeth erupt sequentially. Using one of the fastest eruption schedules observed in modern-day humans as a guide, Wolpoff estimated that the first, second and third molars of Neandertals erupted at ages that rounded to six, 12 and 15, respectively. Wear from chewing accumulates at a steady pace over an individual's lifetime, so when the second molar emerges, the first already has six years of wear on it, and when the third emerges, the second has three years of wear on it.

Working backward, one can infer, for instance, that a first molar with 15 years of wear on it belonged to a 21-year-old Neandertal, a second molar with 15 years of wear on it belonged to a 27-year-old and a third molar with 15 years of wear on it belonged to a 30-year-old. (These estimates have an uncertainty of plus or minus one year.) This wear-based seriation method for determining age at death, adapted from a technique developed by dental researcher A.E.W. Miles in 1963, works best on samples with large numbers of juveniles, which Krapina has in abundance. The method loses accuracy when applied to the teeth of elderly individuals, whose tooth crowns can be too worn to evaluate reliably and in some cases may even be totally eroded.

Wolpoff's work indicated that the Krapina Neandertals died young. In 2005, a few years after I began researching the evolution of longevity, I decided to take another look at this sample using a novel approach. I wanted to make sure that we were not missing older individuals as a result of the inherent limitations of wear-based seriation. Working with Jakov Radovčić of the Croatian Natural History Museum in Zagreb, Steven A. Goldstein, Jeffrey A. Meganck and Dana L. Begun, all at Michigan, and undergraduate students from Central Michigan University, I developed a new nondestructive method—using high-resolution three-dimensional microcomputed tomography (μCT)—to reassess how old the Krapina individuals were when they died. Specifically, we looked at the degree of development of a type of tissue within the tooth called secondary dentin; the volume of secondary dentin increases with age and provides a way to assess how old an individual was at death when the tooth crown is too worn to be a good indicator.

Our initial findings, supplemented with scans provided by the Max Planck Institute for Evolutionary Anthropology in Leipzig, corroborated Wolpoff's results and validated the wear-based seriation method: the Krapina Neandertals had remarkably high mortality rates; no one survived past age 30. (This is not to say that Neandertals across the board never lived beyond 30. A few individuals from sites other than Krapina were around 40 when they died.)

By today's standards, the Krapina death pattern is unimaginable. After all, for most people age 30 is the prime of life. And hunter-gatherers lived beyond 30 in the recent past. Yet the Krapina Neandertals are not unique among early humans. The few other human fossil localities with large numbers of individuals preserved, such as the approximately 600,000-year-old Sima de los Huesos site in Atapuerca, Spain, show similar patterns. The Sima de los Huesos people had very high levels of juvenile and young adult mortality, with no one surviving past 35 and very few living even that long. It is possible that catastrophic events or the particular conditions under which the remains became fossilized somehow selected against the preservation of older individuals at these sites. But the broad surveys of the human fossil record—including the material from these unusually rich sites and other sites containing fewer individuals—that my colleagues and I have conducted indicate that dying young was the rule, not the exception. To paraphrase words attributed to British philosopher Thomas Hobbes, prehistoric life really was nasty, brutish and short.

Rise of the Grandparents

This new μCT approach has the potential to provide a high-resolution picture of the ages of older individuals in other fossil human populations. But a few years ago, before we hit on this technique, Sang-Hee Lee of the University of California, Riverside, and I were ready to start looking for evidence of changes in longevity over the course of human evolution. We turned to the best approach available at the time: wear-based seriation.

We faced a daunting challenge, though. Most human fossils do not come from sites, such as Krapina, that preserve so many individuals that the remains can be considered reflective of their larger populations. And the smaller the number of contemporaneous individuals found at a site, the more difficult it is to reliably estimate how old members were when they died because of the statistical uncertainties associated with small samples.

But we realized that we could get at the question of when grandparents started becoming common in another way. Instead of asking how long individuals lived, we asked how many of them lived to be old. That is, rather than focusing on absolute ages, we calculated relative ages and asked what proportion of adults survived to the age at which one could first become a grandparent. Our objective was to evaluate changes over evolutionary time in the ratio of older to younger adults—the so-called OY ratio. Among primates, including humans up until very recently, the third molar erupts at about the same time that an individual becomes an adult and reaches reproductive age. Based on data from Neandertals and contemporary hunter-gatherer populations, we inferred that fossil humans got their third molars and had their first child at around age 15. And we considered double that age to mark the beginning of grandparenthood—just as some women today can potentially give birth at age 15 and those women can become grandmothers when their own children reach age 15 and reproduce.

For our purposes, then, any archaic individual judged to be 30 years old or more qualified as an older adult—one old enough to have become a grandparent. But the beauty of the OY ratio approach is that regardless of whether maturation occurred at 10, 15 or 20 years, the number of older and younger individuals in a sample would be unaffected because the start of older adulthood would change accordingly. And because we were only looking to place the fossils in these two broad categories, we could include large numbers of smaller fossil samples in our analysis without worrying about uncertainties in absolute ages.

We calculated the OY ratios for four large aggregates of fossil samples totaling 768 individuals spanning a period of three million years. One aggregate comprised later australopithecines—those primitive relatives of "Lucy," who lived in East Africa and South Africa from three million to 1.5 million years ago. Another aggregate consisted of early members of our genus, *Homo*, from around the globe who lived between two million and 500,000 years ago. The third group was the European Neandertals from 130,000 to 30,000 years ago. And the last consisted of modern Europeans from the early Upper Paleolithic period, who lived between about 30,000 and 20,000 years ago and left behind sophisticated cultural remains.

Although we expected to find increases in longevity over time, we were unprepared for how striking our results would turn out to be. We observed a small trend of increased longevity over time among all samples, but the difference between earlier humans and the modern humans of the Upper Paleolithic was a dramatic fivefold increase in the OY ratio. Thus, for every 10 young adult Neandertals who died between the ages of 15 and 30, there were only four older adults who survived past age 30; in contrast, for every 10 young adults in the European Upper Paleolithic death distribution, there were 20 potential grandparents. Wondering whether the higher numbers of burials at Upper Paleolithic sites might account for the high number of older adults in that sample, we re-analyzed our Upper Paleolithic sample, using only those remains that had not been buried. But we got similar results. The conclusion was inescapable: adult survivorship soared very late in human evolution.

Biology or Culture?

Now that Lee and I had established that the number of potential grandparents surged at some point in the evolution of anatomically modern humans, we had another question on our hands: What was it that brought about this change? There were two possibilities. Either longevity was one of the constellations of genetically controlled traits that biologically distinguished anatomically modern humans from their predecessors, or it did not come along with the emergence of modern anatomy and was instead the result of a later shift in behavior. Anatomically modern humans did not burst onto the evolutionary scene making the art and advanced weaponry that define Upper Paleolithic culture. They originated long before those Upper Paleolithic Europeans, more than 100,000 years ago, and for most of that time they and their anatomically archaic contemporaries the Neandertals used the same, simpler Middle Paleolithic technology. (Members of both groups appear to have dabbled in making art and sophisticated weapons before the Upper Paleolithic, but these traditions were ephemeral compared with the ubiquitous and enduring ones that characterize that later period.) Although our study indicated that a large increase in grandparents was unique to anatomically modern humans, it alone could not distinguish between the biological explanation and the cultural one, because the modern humans we looked at were both anatomically and behaviorally modern. Could we trace longevity back to earlier anatomically modern humans who were not yet behaviorally modern?

To address this question, Lee and I analyzed Middle Paleolithic humans from sites in western Asia dating to between about 110,000 and 40,000 years ago. Our sample included both Neandertals and modern humans, all associated with the same comparatively simple artifacts. This approach allowed us to compare the OY ratios of two biologically distinct groups (many scholars consider them to be separate species) who lived in the same region and had the same cultural complexity. We found that the Neandertals and modern humans from western Asia had statistically identical OY ratios, ruling out the possibility that a biological shift accounted for the increase in adult survivorship seen in Upper Paleolithic Europeans. Both

western Asian groups had roughly even proportions of older and younger adults, putting their OY ratios between those of the Neandertals and early modern humans from Europe.

Compared with European Neandertals, a much larger proportion of western Asian Neandertals (and modern humans) lived to be grandparents. This is not unexpected—the more temperate environment of western Asia would have been far easier to survive in than the harsh ecological conditions of Ice Age Europe. Yet if the more temperate environment of western Asia accounts for the elevated adult survivorship seen in the Middle Paleolithic populations there, the longevity of Upper Paleolithic Europeans is even more impressive. Despite living in much harsher conditions, the Upper Paleolithic Europeans had an OY ratio more than double that of the Middle Paleolithic modern humans.

Senior Moments

We do not know exactly what those Upper Paleolithic Europeans started doing culturally that allowed so many more of them to live to older age. But there can be no doubt that this increased adult survivorship itself had far-reaching effects. As Kristen Hawkes of the University of Utah, Hillard Kaplan of the University of New Mexico and others have shown in their studies of several modern-day hunter-gatherer groups, grandparents routinely contribute economic and social resources to their descendants, increasing both the number of offspring their children can have and the survivorship of their grandchildren. Grandparents also reinforce complex social connections—like my grandmother did in telling stories of ancestors that linked me to other relatives in my generation. Such information is the foundation on which human social organization is built.

Elders transmit other kinds of cultural knowledge, too—from environmental (what kinds of plants are poisonous or where to find water during times of drought, for example) to technological (how to weave a basket or knap a stone knife, perhaps). Studies led by Pontus Strimling of Stockholm University have shown that repetition is a critical factor in the transmission of the rules and traditions of one's culture. Multigenerational families have more members to hammer home important lessons. Thus, longevity presumably fostered the intergenerational accumulation and transfer of information that encouraged the formation of intricate kinship systems and other social networks that allow us to help and be helped when the going gets tough.

Increases in longevity would also have translated into increases in population size by adding an age group that was not there in the past and that was still fertile. And large populations are major drivers of new behaviors. In 2009 Adam Powell of University College London and his colleagues published a paper in *Science* showing that population density figures importantly in the maintenance of cultural complexity. They and many other researchers argue that larger populations promoted the development of extensive trade networks, complex systems of cooperation, and material expressions of individual and group identity (jewelry, body paint, and so on). Viewed in that light, the hallmark features of the Upper Paleolithic—the explosive increase in the use of symbols, for instance, or the incorporation of exotic materials in tool manufacture—look as though they might well have been consequences of swelling population size.

Growing population size would have affected our forebears another way, too: by accelerating the pace of evolution. As John Hawks of the University of Wisconsin-Madison has emphasized, more people mean more mutations and opportunities for advantageous mutations to sweep through populations as their members reproduce. This trend may have had an even more striking effect on recent humans than on Upper Paleolithic ones, compounding the dramatic population growth that accompanied the domestication of plants 10,000 years ago. In their 2009 book *The 10,000 Year Explosion,* Gregory Cochran and Henry Harpending, both at the University of Utah, describe multiple gene variants—from those influencing skin color to those that determine tolerance of cow milk—that arose and spread swiftly over the past 10,000 years, thanks to the ever larger numbers of breeding individuals.

The relation between adult survivorship and the emergence of sophisticated new cultural traditions, starting with those of the Upper Paleolithic, was almost certainly a positive feedback process. Initially a by-product of some sort of cultural change, longevity became a prerequisite for the unique and complex behaviors that signal modernity. These innovations in turn promoted the importance and survivorship of older adults, which led to the population expansions that had such profound cultural and genetic effects on our predecessors. Older and wiser, indeed.

Critical Thinking

1. What are the critical roles played by elders around the world?

2. When did grandparent-aged individuals become common in human prehistory? What do these findings suggest?

3. Why is reconstructing the demography of ancient populations a tricky business? Why were sites such as Krapina useful in this regard?

4. How was Wolpoff able to estimate the ages of death at Krapina?

5. Describe the high mortality rates among the Neandertals at Krapina. How does this compare to today's standards? What indications are there that dying young was the rule?

6. Why did the author use the OY (older to younger adults) ratio?

7. What four aggregates of fossil samples were used?

8. What were the results?

9. What were the two possible explanations for increased longevity? Why was it important to know if longevity could be traced back to the early anatomically modern humans?

10. What was found in comparing Middle Paleolithic Neandertals with modern humans in western Asia? What was the significance of this find? How did western Asian Neandertals compare to the European Neandertals?

11. Why was the longevity of the Upper Paleolithic Europeans impressive?

12. Discuss the far-reaching effects that increased adult survivorship must have had on humanity.

A Bigger, Better Brain

Observations of chimpanzees and dolphins strengthen the notion that humanlike intelligence may not be uniquely human.

MADDALENA BEARZI AND CRAIG STANFORD

When the orange sun rises in the east of Gombe National Park in Tanzania, it takes time to cross the mountain ridge above and warm the forest below. There, a party of chimpanzees is waking up. One by one they roll over, look up at the morning sky and slowly revive themselves. Each sits sleepily on the branch supporting his or her nest, peeing quietly onto the ground many meters below. Every tree has an ape or two, and one towering Chrysophyllum tree holds several nests. In minutes, the silent band descends to sit like boulders on the hillside.

Then, as if on cue, one of the older males gets up and begins walking from the sleeping area, heading north. Several males follow, but two walk instead to the west toward a lake. A mother and her infant embark southward, alone. A couple of young males stay put; later they will travel to the east, up into the rugged hills. What started out at dawn as a nesting party of 26 chimpanzees fragments into at least five separate parties of one to eight chimpanzees each, all venturing into a day of multiple decisions and complicated social encounters.

At the opposite side of the world, dawn begins to light up the coast of the Yucatan Peninsula in Mexico. Like clockwork, a group of dolphins passes the fisherman's rickety wharf at this time. Gordo, a chubby male bottlenose with a clear, deep notch halfway down his dorsal fin, is the first to appear in the morning mist. He makes his way slowly westward along the shoreline; the rest of the gang, a football field behind, follows. As the sun brightens, one dark grey body after another passes the pier. They are 14: a female with her calf and 12 others. Twenty or so meters past the wharf, they cluster together next to a colorful string of moored pangas. Some dive, others mill about at the surface.

A few at a time, the dolphins explore the sandy bottom with no sign of hurry while another group of dolphins leisurely joins them from the opposite direction. They are now 23 with a couple of calves next to their mothers, all tightly grouped in a murky patch of water that likely hides a fishy meal. Suddenly, the circle unwinds in two lively threads: Five animals move steadily back toward the wharf in a monklike procession; the others disappear quickly to the west. The sun is already high on the horizon. What seemed for a moment to be a singular and cohesive group has reshuffled and divided, ready for the complex tasks and interactions that will make up their day.

Chimpanzees and dolphins look completely different. One resembles people, more or less. The other has the body of a cruise missile. One has hands that can skillfully manipulate a tool, delicately groom a partner or converse in sign language. The other has no hands at all. Chimpanzees swing through the trees of African forests. Dolphins dive deep in oceans. These mammals, about as closely related as mice and elephants, haven't had a common ancestor for nearly 100 million years. It takes dissection to see how their organs and limbs share common features.

One of us (Maddalena) is a marine mammalogist who has studied bottlenose and other dolphin species for nearly 20 years in Santa Monica Bay, near Los Angeles, and other parts of the world. The other (Craig) is a primatologist who has observed chimpanzees and gorillas in Africa for more than 15 years. As unlikely as it might seem, we find more parallel behavioral traits in these species than we do in more closely related animals. What's even more compelling is that many of these distinctive traits are also found in humans—an observation that may have implications for the origin of human intelligence.

Humanlike intelligence may not be a quality that could only have emerged from our own recent evolutionary lineage. Instead convergent evolution could have played a role. Evidence for this argument is not yet irrefutable but it is increasing. And it all starts with one unusual quality shared by humans, chimpanzees and dolphins: the large size of their brains. The various dolphin species, the four great apes and Homo sapiens possess brains that are the cognitive crowning glory of Earth's millions of species.

A Rare Intelligence

Of all the species on our planet, only a handful has possessed a high degree of intellect: apes and humans (including many extinct forms of both), dolphins, whales, and some others, such as elephants. The brains of an ape and a dolphin differ in their external morphology and neuroanatomical organization, in particular their cortical cytoarchitecture, which in dolphins has less cellular differentiation. Despite these differences, primate (including human) and dolphin brains share important similarities. For one, the brains of dolphins and apes increased in size and complexity over their evolutionary history. Both possess a high encephalization quotient (EQ) due to their unusually large brain-to-body-size ratios. EQ is the ratio of an animal's actual brain size to its expected brain size based on measurements of other animals its size. In both dolphins and apes, the neocortex is also more elaborately developed compared to that of other animals. Also distinctive is the neocortical gyrification, or folding of the cerebral cortex—which in dolphins surpasses that of any primate—and the presence of spindleshaped neurons, called Von Economo neurons, which have been linked in people to social fluency and the ability to sense what others think. Only recently were those neurons found in bottlenose dolphins.

But why is a big, sophisticated brain an advantage in life? Dinosaurs had puny brains but flourished for hundreds of millions of years. Intelligence is an adaptation, but not necessarily the only or even the most effective one. What works best for a given organism depends on its environmental context. Some creatures have changed precious little over many millions of years. Other lineages, such as primates and cetaceans, have undergone dramatic changes and a mushrooming of brain size in just a few million years. Natural selection has acted to favor intelligence when it conferred survival and reproductive benefits and when it complemented traits that were genetically hard-wired.

Brain power has allowed dolphins and apes to possess communication and social skills so complex that we are only now beginning to understand how they work. Unlike most animals, apes and dolphins live in fluid societies and engage in relationships that require accurate memories of who is a friend and who owes whom a favor. The social alliances they become a part of can change as their needs change. Great apes possess an intellect often referred to as Machiavellian. They remember favors owed and debts incurred and they operate in a "service economy" of behavior exchange. Male chimpanzees form paramilitary patrol parties and hunting parties. They also shift alliances in accordance with their self-interest. They may work with one group to manipulate a female for sexual access and with another to overthrow an alpha male. We used to think that some of these alliances were based entirely on kinship. Anthony Goldberg and Richard Wrangham showed some years ago, however, that such coalitions are not necessarily based on genetic relatedness.

Some dolphins also form coalitions of males in order to sexually coerce females. As was very recently observed by David Lusseau of the University of Aberdeen in Scotland, these groupings can also cooperate to overthrow other male coalitions. The alliances allow for highly complex behavioral "agreements" between males of the same school who cooperate in pairs and triplets to sequester females likely to be in estrus. In other

contexts, dolphins can also practice deceit and deception, practices that require a theory of mind—the ability to perceive mental states in oneself and in others. Stan Kuczaj of the University of Southern Mississippi and his colleagues observed intentional deception in Kelly, a female dolphin kept in captivity. Kelly had been trained—along with her tank-mates—to retrieve objects from the pool in exchange for fish. After all the other dolphins had finished with their retrieval chores and gone their own way, Kelly appeared at the surface with some objects of unknown origin in the hope of gaining more fish. After searching the pool, Kelly's trainer discovered a secret cache of "toys" that the dolphin had astutely concealed under a drain cover. Day after day, she had collected objects inadvertently dropped into the pool by tourists, to be used for barter with her trainers for fish. On closer observation, it also became clear that Kelly was extremely careful not to add or remove objects from her cache when other dolphins were present.

Great apes also seem to be skilled at deceiving one another. In Tanzania, one of us (Craig) once watched a low-ranking male chimpanzee named Beethoven use deception to mate with a female despite the presence of the alpha male called Wilkie. As a party of chimpanzees sat in a forest clearing, Beethoven made a charging display through the middle of the group, his hair standing on end and his arched posture indicating bravado. As a low-ranking male, this was taken by the alpha Wilkie as an act of insubordination. As Beethoven charged past Wilkie and into dense thickets, Wilkie pursued and launched into his own display, dragging branches, drumming tree trunks with his feet and generally trying to be maximally impressive. With Wilkie absorbed in his display of dominance, Beethoven furtively made his way back to the clearing and mated with an eagerly awaiting female.

Intelligence Opens the Toolbox

Our understanding of how chimpanzees and dolphins apply their intelligence to tool use is expanding as well. Jane Goodall and others showed decades ago that chimpanzees use sticks to harvest insects. A 2007 report by primatologist Jill Pruetz taught us more: She and her colleagues, working in Senegal, observed a chimpanzee use a stick it had peeled to a tapered end as a weapon to hunt another mammal, something once only seen in humans. The chimpanzee jabbed the stick into tree cavities until it found a bushbaby, a squirrel-sized primate, which the stick extracted. Although not exactly a spear, the stick was evidence that the chimpanzee had foreseen a problem in immobilizing and extracting its intended prey and had devised a solution.

Dolphins do not have hands to use tools, but wild Indian Ocean bottlenose dolphin females are the first "tool-using cetacean" ever documented. Marine biologist Rachel Smolker and colleagues in the early 1980s observed these animals carrying a large cone-shaped sponge on the tip of their elongated beaks, or rostra, like a mask. These "nose mittens" were used for protection against stinging organisms or sand abrasion, or to extract prey from the sea floor. In a 2005 publication, Michael Kriitzen of the University of Zurich and his colleagues, using mitochondrial DNA analyses, concluded that "sponging" was socially transmitted vertically within a single matrilineal group, from mother sponge-carriers to their female offspring.

Knowing how to use a tool is not the fundamental adaptation that a large brain provides. Instead, a large brain conveys the ability to learn and to imitate another's behavior to appropriate its benefits. Tools allow chimpanzees to harvest protein, fat and carbohydrates that would be otherwise unavailable. The added nutrition can help a gestating or lactating female through an otherwise lean time of year, and enhance her reproductive output over the course of her long life. The ability to respond to rapidly changing dynamics in the social group, such as when males form coalitions to control females, is not limited to higher primates and dolphins, but it certainly typifies many species among them. In each case, these skills require years of learning. But the payoff is a potential reproductive windfall.

For many years the study of chimpanzee technological culture consisted mostly of anecdotes, which are fascinating but not always convincing. But when chimpanzee researchers obtained enough long-term data that they were able to analyze cultural traditions from a range of field sites, they found unequivocal evidence for a systematic pattern of these traditions. Using tool use and other cultural data from the seven longest-running field studies in Africa, Andrew Whiten of the University of St. Andrews and his colleagues in 1999 found at least 39 behaviors that could be attributable to the influence of learned traditions. This number may seem rather limited compared with the myriad examples of such behavior in our species, where almost everything is learned at some level. But compared with other nonhuman animals, it is a long list. The logical conclusion here is that animals that live by their wits, as it were, tend to be like chimpanzees and us—big-brained and with a long period of growth and maturation during which key life skills can be acquired by watching one's elders and peers.

We can ask how and why certain cultural traditions, whether technological or social behavior, arise and spread. Biological evolution occurs primarily via natural selection and is preserved through the transfer of genetic material from one generation to the next. It is also an inefficient process, because of the time required for genes to pass to the next generation, and because each reproductive act requires (in all higher animals) the reshuffling of genes from mother and father. Cultural "evolution" does not require the massive shuffling of the genetic deck that can slow the rate of change to a glacial pace. If a cultural trait confers on its user higher odds of survival and enhanced reproduction, then it has a good chance of being passed on. Even though the tool-use innovation, for example, has no genetic basis, the tradition of its use, once established, should spread, to the reproductive benefit of the inventor. Thus an entirely nongenetic feature could have a long-term effect on the species. Only a few groups of animals on this planet exhibit cultural traits. Higher primates certainly are cultural animals. Cetaceans also exhibit elements of culture. A good example of social learning in dolphins is the vertical cultural transmission of foraging and feeding specializations and vocal dialects.

John Ford, for instance, reported what he calls "interpod call mimicry" in the wild, showing that killer whales are capable of vocal learning.

Language Building Blocks

Scientists disagree about whether dolphins have language capabilities but evidence persists that they may, depending on how one defines it. In one of the best-known cases, Louis Herman and his colleagues at the Kewalo Basin Marine Mammal Lab in Honolulu in the 1980s devised two artificial languages to teach to bottlenose dolphins at their facility. Neither language approximated human conversation, but both were based on a set of grammatical rules. One was computer-generated and included high-pitched words. The other was a sign language conveyed by trainers' arm and hand signals.

In an underwater classroom, two animals, Ake and Phoenix, were taught a series of sentences, including some commands describing how to take a Frisbee through a particular hoop or to swim under another dolphin. The dolphins also displayed the ability to recognize meaningless phrases. When a trainer occasionally said something that didn't make sense in the created languages, for instance, Ake ignored the command.

Evidence that apes can acquire and use language, including sign language, has grown over decades. Perhaps the most persuasive evidence of language capability in nonhuman apes comes from primatologist Sue Savage-Rumbaugh, who for 30 years was affiliated with Georgia State University's Language Research Center. Kanzi, a male bonobo she worked with, learned to communicate by touching symbols on a lexicon board and understand some spoken English. Savage-Rumbaugh estimated he could produce 300 words himself and could understand more than 1,000 when spoken.

Work by Savage-Rumbaugh and many other researchers has conclusively settled at least two arguments over ape language. First, she demonstrated that apes understand and employ the concept of reference, using words as symbols to represent things in their environment. Second, they can spontaneously use and combine these words to make requests, give information and comment on the world around them. If there is a difference between what Kanzi comprehends and what a human toddler understands, scientists have not yet discovered it.

Evidence also exists that dolphins and chimpanzees can recognize themselves as individuals. Chimpanzees, gorillas, bonobos and orangutans not only recognize themselves in mirrors but also are able to understand that paint blotches they observe in mirrors during experiments were placed on their bodies. The same holds true for bottlenose dolphins. These experiments do not prove that the animals are self-aware in human terms. But they do provide evidence that these animals exhibit cognition, as does their behavior in the wild.

Large brains likely also help these animals succeed in foraging. Both chimpanzees and dolphins feed on widely scattered, temporarily available food. Many species of dolphins chase schools of fish; chimpanzees chase the fleeting appearances of ripe fruits in tree crowns. These two dietary specialties keep them moving all day long, in search of the next school, the next patch. Predicting where and when to search is one challenge. Chimpanzees have the spatial memory of forest rangers. They monitor particular fruit trees in the weeks leading up to the ripening of a crop and return to the right spot day after day until the bounty is gone. Dolphins have a taller order; they have to know where to locate rapidly moving fish schools without such obvious landmarks as trees, streams and mountains. For this they have sonar, a wonderfully evolved system that humans only relatively recently were able to replicate for their own uses. But in addition to their purely sensory adaptations, dolphins put their intelligence (and memory) to good use to find fish.

Chimpanzees mostly eat fruit but, like dolphins, they do hunt. And their hunting is social. They will attack groups of monkeys they encounter during their rambles in search of fruit in African forests. The chase, capture and kill are heart stopping, often gruesome, and always illustrative of the chimpanzees' social nature. To a lion, the zebra it is chasing may be only a meal, but to a chimpanzee the chance to kill and share prey is not only nutritional, but socially significant as well. The monkeys and pigs and antelopes the chimpanzees capture sometimes become pawns in the social dynamics of the group. Researchers in a range of studies across Africa have shown that males use meat to negotiate new alliances, rub salt in the wounds of old rivals and secure status that a chimpanzee without prey cannot. Adult and adolescent males do most of the hunting, making about 90 percent of the kills recorded at Gombe. Females also hunt but more often receive a share of meat from the male who either captured the meat or stole it from the captor. Although lone chimpanzees, both male and female, sometimes hunt by themselves, most hunts are social.

For many dolphin species, hunting is also a social affair. Dolphins are efficient predators who use both agility and braininess to achieve success. Killer whales, the largest dolphins, display one of the most cooperative hunting practices. Feeding at the top of the food chain, transient killer whales prey on small marine mammals such as seals lying on beaches or slabs of ice, and scientists have observed coordinated and intentional stranding by killer whales in the waters of Patagonia. On occasion, the killing of a pinniped represents a learning lesson for the calf, which will use the same technique throughout its life. In groups, they also attack whales much larger than themselves without any sign of fear or hesitation and with a high degree of predatory success.

Being such accomplished ocean hunters makes dolphins a valuable asset for other ocean dwellers in search of a meal. In the coastal waters of Los Angeles, one of us (Maddalena) frequently observes sea lions in proximity to dolphins during feeding and foraging activities. Two predatory species travel and feed together, with no evident hostility or competition. Sea lions capitalize on the superior food-finding ability of echolocating common dolphins to find their own prey. The diverse hunting strategies employed by dolphin and ape societies are an excellent gauge of their social complexity, and another example of how brain complexity, social complexity and ecological complexity are all linked.

Familiar Yet Threatened

These growing insights into the intelligence of great apes and dolphins are emerging as these animals become increasingly threatened worldwide. As we reach farther and farther into tropical forests in search of timber, farmland and spaces for human dwellings, we disrupt the apes' terrestrial habitat. The ongoing hunting of these animals is also taking a toll. And as we continue to use the oceans as our dumping ground, we threaten dolphins' habitat. The incidental catching of nontarget species in commercial fishing activity, known as bycatch, is just one of the major problems facing these animals today. Many conservationists believe that a century from now, great apes will survive only in a few carefully protected sanctuaries or in captivity. Dolphin populations are much less visible than those of great apes but the threats to them are also insidious. Today, several dolphin species are either critically endangered, endangered, threatened or of unknown status.

As scientists who have spent many years studying dolphins and apes in the wild, we believe that our research must incorporate respect and a sense of stewardship for the animals we study. We have both reached the same conclusion: Without conservation and protection of these species and the ecosystems in which they live, they will not survive to see the next century. Sadly, this projection comes just as we are beginning to better understand their complex abilities and social interactions.

Bibliography

Bearzi, M., and C. B. Stanford. 2008. *Beautiful Minds: The Parallel Lives of Great Apes and Dolphins.* Cambridge: Harvard University Press.

Butti, C, C. C. Sherwood, A. Y. Hakeem, J. M. Allman, and P. R. Hof. 2009. Total number and volume of Von Economo neurons in the cerebral cortex of cetaceans. *The Journal of Comparative Neurology, Research in Systems Neuroscience* 515:243–259.

Goldberg, T. L., and R. W. Wrangham. 1997. Genetic correlates of social behaviour in wild chimpanzees: Evidence from mitochondrial DNA. *Animal Behaviour* 54:559–570.

Kriitzen, M., J. Mann, M. R. Heithaus, R. C. Connor, L. Bejder, and W. B. Sherwin. 2005. Cultural transmission of tool use in bottlenose dolphins. Proceedings of the National Academy of Sciences of the U.S.A. 105:8939–8943.

Lusseau, D. 2007. Why are male social relationships complex in the Doubtful Sound bottlenose dolphin population? *PLoS ONE* 2(4):e348.

Marino, L. 2002. Convergence of complex cognitive abilities in cetaceans and primates. *Brain, Behavior and Evolution* 59:21–32.

Marino, L. 1996. What can dolphins tell us about primate evolution? *Evolutionary Anthropology* 5:73–110.

Marino, L. et al. 2007. Cetaceans have complex brains for complex cognition. *PLoS Biology* 139:966–972.

Pruetz, J. D., and P. Bertolani. 2007. Savanna chimpanzees, *Pan troglodytes verus,* hunt with tools. *Current Biology* 17:1–6.

Reiss, D., B. McCowan, and L. Marino. 1997. Communicative and other cognitive characteristics of bottlenose dolphins. *Trends in Cognitive Sciences* 1:123–156.

Reiss, D., and L. Marino. 2001. Mirror self-recognition in the bottlenose dolphin: A case of cognitive convergence. Proceedings of the National Academy of Sciences 98:5937–5942.

Smolker, R., A. Richards, R. Connor, J. Mann, and P. Berggren. 1997. Sponge carrying by dolphins (*Delphindea, Tursiops sp.*) A foraging specialization involving tool use? *Ethology* 103:454–465.

Stanford, C. 2007. *Apes of the Impenetrable Forest*. Upper Saddle River, NJ: Prentice Hall (Primate Field Studies Series).

Whiten, A., J. Goodall, W. C. McGrew, T. Nishida, V. Reynolds, Y. Sugiyama, C. E. G. Tutin, R. W. Wrangham, and C. Boesch. 1999. Cultures in chimpanzees. *Nature* 399:682–685.

Critical Thinking

1. What are some of the important similarities shared by primate and dolphin brains?

2. Why is a big, sophisticated brain an advantage in the social life of both dolphins and chimpanzees?

3. How do chimpanzees and dolphins each apply their intelligence to tool use?

4. What are the other, more fundamental advantages of having a large brain?

5. What have long-term studies revealed about tool use and how it is acquired?

6. Why is "cultural evolution" rather than natural selection a more effective way of transferring technological or social behavior?

7. How do the authors assess the language ability and cognition among chimpanzees and dolphins?

8. How have large brains helped both chimpanzees and dolphins in foraging for food?

MADDALENA BEARZI is president and cofounder of the Ocean Conservation Society and a nature and travel journalist. She received her PhD in biology at the University of California, Los Angeles, and has studied dolphins and whales in California and other parts of the world for more than 20 years. **CRAIG STANFORD** is a professor of anthropology and biological sciences at the University of Southern California and codirector of its Jane Goodall Research Center. He received his PhD in anthropology from the University of California, Berkeley, and has conducted field research on great apes in Africa for more than 15 years.

The Limits of Intelligence

The laws of physics may well prevent the human brain from evolving into an ever more powerful thinking machine.

DOUGLAS FOX

Santiago Ramó y Cajal, the Spanish Nobel-winning Biologist who mapped the neural anatomy of insects in the decades before World War I, likened the minute circuitry of their vision-processing neurons to an exquisite pocket watch. He likened that of mammals, by comparison, to a hollow-chested grandfather clock. Indeed, it is humbling to think that a honeybee, with its milligram-size brain, can perform tasks such as navigating mazes and landscapes on a par with mammals. A honeybee may be limited by having comparatively few neurons, but it surely seems to squeeze everything it can out of them.

At the other extreme, an elephant, with its five-million-fold larger brain, suffers the inefficiencies of a sprawling Mesopotamian empire. Signals take more than 100 times longer to travel between opposite sides of its brain—and also from its brain to its foot, forcing the beast to rely less on reflexes, to move more slowly, and to squander precious brain resources on planning each step.

We humans may not occupy the dimensional extremes of elephants or honeybees, but what few people realize is that the laws of physics place tough constraints on our mental faculties as well. Anthropologists have speculated about anatomic roadblocks to brain expansion—for instance, whether a larger brain could fit through the birth canal of a bipedal human. If we assume, though, that evolution can solve the birth canal problem, then we are led to the cusp of some even more profound questions.

One might think, for example, that evolutionary processes could increase the number of neurons in our brain or boost the rate at which those neurons exchange information and that such changes would make us smarter. But several recent trends of investigation, if taken together and followed to their logical conclusion, seem to suggest that such tweaks would soon run into physical limits. Ultimately those limits trace back to the very nature of neurons and the statistically noisy chemical exchanges by which they communicate. "Information, noise and energy are inextricably linked," says Simon Laughlin, a theoretical neuroscientist at the University of Cambridge. "That connection exists at the thermodynamic level."

Do the laws of thermodynamics, then, impose a limit on neuron-based intelligence, one that applies universally, whether in birds, primates, porpoises or praying mantises? This question apparently has never been asked in such broad terms, but the scientists interviewed for this article generally agree that it is a question worth contemplating. "It's a very interesting point," says Vijay Balasubramanian, a physicist who studies neural coding of information at the University of Pennsylvania. "I've never even seen this point discussed in science fiction."

Intelligence is of course a loaded word: it is hard to measure and even to define. Still, it seems fair to say that by most metrics, humans are the most intelligent animals on earth. But as our brain has evolved, has it approached a hard limit to its ability to process information? Could there be some physical limit to the evolution of neuron-based intelligence—and not just for humans but for all of life as we know it?

That Hungry Tapeworm in Your Head

The most intuitively obvious way in which brains could get more powerful is by growing larger. And indeed, the possible connection between brain size and intelligence has fascinated scientists for more than 100 years. Biologists spent much of the late 19th century and the early 20th century exploring universal themes of life—mathematical laws related to body mass, and to brain mass in particular, that run across the animal kingdom. One advantage of size is that a larger brain can contain more neurons, which should enable it to grow in complexity as well. But it was clear even then that brain size alone did not determine intelligence: a cow carries a brain well over 100 times larger than a mouse's, but the cow isn't any smarter. Instead brains seem to expand with body size to carry out more trivial functions: bigger bodies might, for example, impose a larger workload of neural housekeeping chores unrelated to intelligence, such as monitoring more tactile nerves, processing signals from larger retinas and controlling more muscle fibers.

Eugene Dubois, the Dutch anatomist who discovered the skull of *Homo* erectus in Java in 1892, wanted a way to estimate the intelligence of animals based on the size of their fossil skulls, so he worked to define a precise mathematical relation between the brain size and body size of animals—under the assumption that animals with disproportionately large brains would also be smarter. Dubois and others amassed an ever growing database of brain and body weights; one classic treatise reported the body, organ and gland weights of 3,690 animals, from wood roaches to yellow-billed egrets to two-toed and three-toed sloths.

Dubois's successors found that mammals' brains expand more slowly than their bodies—to about the ¾ power of body mass. So a muskrat, with a body 16 times larger than a mouse's, has a brain about eight times as big. From that insight came the tool that Dubois had sought: the encephalization quotient, which compares a species' brain mass with what is predicted based on body mass. In other words, it indicates by what factor a species deviates from the ¾ power law. Humans have a quotient of 7.5 (our brain is 7.5 times larger than the law predicts); bottlenose dolphins sit at 5.3; monkeys hover as high as 4.8; and oxen—no surprise there—slink around at 0.5. In short, intelligence may depend on the amount of neural reserve that is left over after the brain's menial chores, such as minding skin sensations, are accounted for. Or to boil it down even more: intelligence may depend on brain size in at least a superficial way.

As brains expanded in mammals and birds, they almost certainly benefited from economies of scale. For example, the greater number of neural pathways that any one signal between neurons can travel means that each signal implicitly carries more information, implying that the neurons in larger brains can get away with firing fewer times per second. Meanwhile, however, another, competing trend may have kicked in. "I think it is very likely that there is a law of diminishing returns" to increasing intelligence indefinitely by adding new brain cells, Balasubramanian says. Size carries burdens with it, the most obvious one being added energy consumption. In humans, the brain is already the hungriest part of our body: at 2 percent of our body weight, this greedy little tapeworm of an organ wolfs down 20 percent of the calories that we expend at rest. In newborns, it's an astounding 65 percent.

Staying in Touch

Much of the energetic burden of brain size comes from the organ's communication networks: in the human cortex, communications account for 80 percent of energy consumption. But it appears that as size increases, neuronal connectivity also becomes more challenging for subtler, structural reasons. In fact, even as biologists kept collecting data on brain mass in the early to mid-20th century, they delved into a more daunting enterprise: to define the "design principles" of brains and how these principles are maintained across brains of different sizes.

A typical neuron has an elongated tail called the axon. At its end, the axon branches out, with the tips of the branches forming synapses, or contact points, with other cells. Axons, like telegraph wires, may connect different parts of the brain or may bundle up into nerves that extend from the central nervous system to the various parts of the body.

In their pioneering efforts, biologists measured the diameter of axons under microscopes and counted the size and density of nerve cells and the number of synapses per cell. They surveyed hundreds, sometimes thousands, of cells per brain in dozens of species. Eager to refine their mathematical curves by extending them to ever larger beasts, they even found ways to extract intact brains from whale carcasses. The five-hour process, meticulously described in the 1880s by biologist Gustav Adolf Guldberg, involved the use of a two-man lumberjack saw, an ax, a chisel and plenty of strength to open the top of the skull like a can of beans.

These studies revealed that as brains expand in size from species to species, several subtle but probably unsustainable changes happen. First, the average size of nerve cells increases. This phenomenon allows the neurons to connect to more and more of their compatriots as the overall number of neurons in the brain increases. But larger cells pack into the cerebral cortex less densely, so the distance between cells increases, as does the length of axons required to connect them. And because longer axons mean longer times for signals to travel between cells, these projections need to become thicker to maintain speed (thicker axons carry signals faster).

Researchers have also found that as brains get bigger from species to species, they are divided into a larger and larger number of distinct areas. You can see those areas if you stain brain tissue and view it under a microscope: patches of the cortex turn different colors. These areas often correspond with specialized functions, say, speech comprehension or face recognition. And as brains get larger, the specialization unfolds in another dimension: equivalent areas in the left and right hemispheres take on separate functions—for example, spatial versus verbal reasoning.

For decades this dividing of the brain into more work cubicles was viewed as a hallmark of intelligence. But it may also reflect a more mundane truth, says Mark Changizi, a theoretical neurobiologist at 2AI Labs in Boise, Idaho: specialization compensates for the connectivity problem that arises as brains get bigger. As you go from a mouse brain to a cow brain with 100 times as many neurons, it is impossible for neurons to expand quickly enough to stay just as well connected. Brains solve this problem by segregating like-functioned neurons into highly interconnected modules, with far fewer long-distance connections between modules. The specialization between right and left hemispheres solves a similar problem: it reduces the amount of information that must flow between the hemispheres, which minimizes the number of long, interhemispheric axons that the brain needs to maintain. "All of these seemingly complex things about bigger brains are just the backbends that the brain has to do to satisfy the connectivity problem" as it gets larger, Changizi argues. "It doesn't tell us that the brain is smarter."

Jan Karbowski, a computational neuroscientist at the Polish Academy of Sciences in Warsaw, agrees. "Somehow brains have to optimize several parameters simultaneously, and there must be trade-offs," he says. "If you want to improve one thing, you screw up something else." What happens, for example, if you expand the corpus callosum (the bundle of axons connecting right and left hemispheres) quickly enough to maintain constant connectivity as brains expand? And what if you thicken those axons, so the transit delay for signals traveling between hemispheres does not increase as brains expand? The results would not be pretty. The corpus callosum would expand—and push the hemispheres apart—so quickly that any performance improvements would be neutralized.

These trade-offs have been laid into stark relief by experiments showing the relation between axon width and conduction speed. At the end of the day, Karbowski says, neurons do get larger as brain size increases, but not quite quickly enough to stay equally well connected. And axons do get thicker as brains expand, but not quickly enough to make up for the longer conduction delays.

Keeping axons from thickening too quickly saves not only space but energy as well, Balasubramanian says. Doubling the width of an axon doubles energy expenditure, while increasing the velocity of pulses by just 40 percent or so. Even with all of this corner cutting, the volume of white matter (the axons) still grows more quickly than the volume of gray matter (the main body of neurons containing the cell nucleus) as brains increase in size. To put it another way, as brains get bigger, more of their volume is devoted to wiring rather than to the parts of individual cells that do the actual computing, which again suggests that scaling size up is ultimately unsustainable.

The Primacy of Primates

It is easy, with this dire state of affairs, to see why a cow fails to squeeze any more smarts out of its grapefruit-size brain than a mouse does from its blueberry-size brain. But evolution has also achieved impressive workarounds at the level of the brain's building blocks. When Jon H. Kaas, a neuroscientist at Vanderbilt University, and his colleagues compared the morphology of brain cells across a spectrum of primates in 2007, they stumbled onto a game changer—one that has probably given humans an edge.

Kaas found that unlike in most other mammals, cortical neurons in primates enlarge very little as the brain increases in size. A few neurons do increase in size, and these rare ones may shoulder the burden of keeping things well connected. But the majority do not get larger. Thus, as primate brains expand from species to species, their neurons still pack together almost as densely. So from the marmoset to the owl monkey—a doubling in brain mass—the number of neurons roughly doubles, whereas in rodents with a similar doubling of mass the number of neurons increases by just 60 percent. That difference has huge consequences. Humans pack 100 billion neurons into 1.4 kilograms of brain, but a rodent that had followed its usual neuron-size scaling law to reach that number of neurons would now have to drag around a brain weighing 45 kilograms. And metabolically speaking, all that brain matter would eat the varmint out of house and home. "That may be one of the factors in why the large rodents don't seem to be [smarter] at all than the small rodents," Kaas says.

Having smaller, more densely packed neurons does seem to have a real impact on intelligence. In 2005 neurobiologists Gerhard Roth and Urusula Dicke, both at the University of Bremen in Germany, reviewed several traits that predict intelligence across species (as measured, roughly, by behavioral complexity) even more effectively than the encephalization quotient does. "The only tight correlation with intelligence," Roth says, "is in the number of neurons in the cortex, plus the speed of neuronal activity," which decreases with the distance between neurons and increases with the degree of myelination of axons. Myelin is fatty insulation that lets axons transmit signals more quickly.

If Roth is right, then primates' small neurons have a double effect: first, they allow a greater increase in cortical cell number as brains enlarge; and second, they allow faster communication, because the cells pack more closely. Elephants and whales are reasonably smart, but their larger neurons and bigger brains lead to inefficiencies. "The packing density of neurons is much lower," Roth says, "which means that the distance between neurons is larger and the velocity of nerve impulses is much lower."

In fact, neuroscientists have recently seen a similar pattern in variations within humans: people with the quickest lines of communication between their brain areas also seem to be the brightest. One study, led in 2009 by Martijn P. van den Heuvel of the University Medical Center Utrecht in the Netherlands, used functional magnetic resonance imaging to measure how directly different brain areas talk to one another—that is, whether they talk via a large or a small number of intermediary areas. Van den Heuvel found that shorter paths between brain areas correlated with higher IQ. Edward Bullmore, an imaging neuroscientist at the University of Cambridge, and his collaborators obtained similar results the same year using a different approach. They compared working memory (the ability to hold several numbers in one's memory at once) among 29 healthy people. They then used magnetoencephalographic recordings from their subjects' scalp to estimate how quickly communication flowed between brain areas. People with the most direct communication and the fastest neural chatter had the best working memory.

It is a momentous insight. We know that as brains get larger, they save space and energy by limiting the number of direct connections between regions. The large human brain has relatively few of these long-distance connections. But Bullmore and van den Heuvel showed that these rare, nonstop connections have a disproportionate influence on smarts: brains that scrimp on resources by cutting just a few of them do noticeably worse. "You pay a price for intelligence," Bullmore concludes, "and the price is that you can't simply minimize wiring."

Intelligence Design

If communication between neurons, and between brain areas, is really a major bottleneck that limits intelligence, then evolving neurons that are even smaller (and closer together, with faster communication) should yield smarter brains. Similarly, brains might become more efficient by evolving axons that can carry signals faster over longer distances without getting thicker. But something prevents animals from shrinking neurons and axons beyond a certain point. You might call it the mother of all limitations: the proteins that neurons use to generate electrical pulses, called ion channels, are inherently unreliable.

Ion channels are tiny valves that open and close through changes in their molecular folding. When they open, they allow ions of sodium, potassium or calcium to flow across cell membranes, producing the electrical signals by which neurons communicate. But being so minuscule, ion channels can get flipped open or closed by mere thermal vibrations. A simple biology experiment lays the defect bare. Isolate a single ion channel on the surface of a nerve cell using a microscopic glass tube, sort of like slipping a glass cup over a single ant on a sidewalk. When you adjust the voltage on the ion channel—a maneuver that causes it to open or close—the ion channel does not flip on and off reliably like your kitchen light does. Instead it flutters on and off randomly. Sometimes it does not open at all; other times it opens when it should not. By changing the voltage, all you do is change the likelihood that it opens.

It sounds like a horrible evolutionary design flaw—but in fact, it is a compromise. "If you make the spring on the channel too loose, then the noise keeps on switching it," Laughlin says—as happens in the biology experiment described earlier. "If you make the spring on the channel stronger, then you get less noise," he says, "but now it's more work to switch it," which forces neurons to spend more energy to control the ion channel. In other words, neurons save energy by using hair-trigger ion channels, but as a side effect the channels can flip open or close accidentally. The trade-off means that ion channels are reliable only if you use large numbers of them to "vote" on whether or not a neuron will generate an impulse. But voting becomes problematic as neurons get smaller. "When you reduce the size of neurons, you reduce the number of channels that are available to carry the signal," Laughlin says. "And that increases the noise."

In a pair of papers published in 2005 and 2007, Laughlin and his collaborators calculated whether the need to include enough ion channels limits how small axons can be made. The results were startling. "When axons got to be about 150 to 200 nanometers in diameter, they became impossibly noisy," Laughlin says. At that point, an axon contains so few ion channels that the accidental opening of a single channel can spur the axon to deliver a signal even though the neuron did not intend to fire. The brain's smallest axons probably already hiccup out about six of these accidental spikes per second. Shrink them just a little bit more, and they would blather out more than 100 per second. "Cortical gray matter neurons are working with axons that are pretty close to the physical limit," Laughlin concludes.

This fundamental compromise between information, energy and noise is not unique to biology. It applies to everything from optical-fiber communications to ham radios and computer chips. Transistors act as gatekeepers of electrical signals, just like ion channels do. For five decades engineers have shrunk transistors steadily, cramming more and more onto chips to produce ever faster computers. Transistors in the latest chips are 22 nanometers. At those sizes, it becomes very challenging to "dope" silicon uniformly (doping is the addition of small quantities of other elements to adjust a semiconductor's properties). By the time they reach about 10 nanometers, transistors will be so small that the random presence or absence of a single atom of boron will cause them to behave unpredictably.

Engineers might circumvent the limitations of current transistors by going back to the drawing board and redesigning chips to use entirely new technologies. But evolution cannot start from scratch: it has to work within the scheme and with the parts that have existed for half a billion years, explains Heinrich Reichert, a developmental neurobiologist at the University of Basel in Switzerland—like building a battleship with modified airplane parts.

Moreover, there is another reason to doubt that a major evolutionary leap could lead to smarter brains. Biology may have had a wide range of options when neurons first evolved, but 600 million years later a peculiar thing has happened. The brains of the honeybee, the octopus, the crow and intelligent mammals, Roth points out, look nothing alike at first glance. But if you look at the circuits that underlie tasks such as vision, smell, navigation and episodic memory of event sequences, "very astonishingly they all have absolutely the same basic arrangement." Such evolutionary convergence usually suggests that a certain anatomical or physiological solution has reached maturity so that there may be little room left for improvement.

Perhaps, then, life has arrived at an optimal neural blueprint. That blueprint is wired up through a step-by-step choreography in which cells in the growing embryo interact through signaling molecules and physical nudging, and it is evolutionarily entrenched.

Bees Do It

So have humans reached the physical limits of how complex our brain can be, given the building blocks that are available to us? Laughlin doubts that there is any hard limit on brain function the way there is one on the speed of light. "It's more likely you just have a law of diminishing returns," he says. "It becomes less and less worthwhile the more you invest in it." Our brain can pack in only so many neurons; our neurons can establish only so many connections among themselves; and those connections can carry only so many electrical impulses per second. Moreover, if our body and brain got much bigger, there would be costs in terms of energy consumption, dissipation of heat and the sheer time it takes for neural impulses to travel from one part of the brain to another.

The human mind, however, may have better ways of expanding without the need for further biological evolution. After all, honeybees and other social insects do it: acting in concert with their hive sisters, they form a collective entity that is smarter than the sum of its parts. Through social interaction we, too, have learned to pool our intelligence with others.

And then there is technology. For millennia written language has enabled us to store information outside our body, beyond the capacity of our brain to memorize. One could argue that the Internet is the ultimate consequence of this trend toward outward expansion of intelligence beyond our body. In a sense, it could be true, as some say, that the Internet makes you stupid: collective human intelligence—culture and computers—may have reduced the impetus for evolving greater individual smarts.

Critical Thinking

1. How do the honeybees and elephants exhibit the dimensional extremes of brain function?

2. How do the laws of physics place tough constraints on human mental faculties?

3. Why might it make sense that an increase in brain size would allow for an increase in intelligence? Why does brain size alone not determine intelligence?

4. In what respect does there seem to be a relationship between brain size and intelligence?

5. Why might there be a "law of diminishing returns" with respect to brain size and intelligence?

6. What happens as a result of increase in brain size with respect to the average size of nerve cells, their density, the length of axons and the time it takes for signals to travel between cells? Why must there be a division into distinct areas, including right and left hemispheres, as well?

7. In what sense are there "trade-offs"? In what sense is scaling size up "ultimately unsustainable"?

8. How have primates, including humans, gained an advantage with respect to the size and density of neurons? What effects do such differences have just among humans?

9. How do ion channels prevent neurons from becoming too small, which in turn place a limit on intelligence?

10. How is it that our neural blueprint may be evolutionarily entrenched in a way that chip technology is not?

11. How might the human mind have better ways of expanding without the need for further biological evolution?

Top Ten Myths About the Brain

When it comes to this complex, mysterious, fascinating organ, what do—and don't—we know?

Laura Helmuth

1. We use only 10 percent of our brains

This one sounds so compelling—a precise number, repeated in pop culture for a century, implying that we have huge reserves of untapped mental powers. But the supposedly unused 90 percent of the brain is not some vestigial appendix. Brains are expensive—it takes a lot of energy to build brains during fetal and childhood development and maintain them in adults. Evolutionarily, it would make no sense to carry around surplus brain tissue. Experiments using PET or fMRI scans show that much of the brain is engaged even during simple tasks, and injury to even a small bit of brain can have profound consequences for language, sensory perception, movement or emotion.

True, we have some brain reserves. Autopsy studies show that many people have physical signs of Alzheimer's disease (such as amyloid plaques among neurons) in their brains even though they were not impaired. Apparently we can lose some brain tissue and still function pretty well. And people score higher on IQ tests if they're highly motivated, suggesting that we don't always exercise our minds at 100 percent capacity.

2. "Flashbulb memories" are precise, detailed and persistent

We all have memories that feel as vivid and accurate as a snapshot, usually of some shocking, dramatic event—the assassination of President Kennedy, the explosion of the space shuttle Challenger, the attacks of September 11, 2001. People remember exactly where they were, what they were doing, who they were with, what they saw or heard. But several clever experiments have tested people's memory immediately after a tragedy and again several months or years later. The test subjects tend to be confident that their memories are accurate and say the flashbulb memories are more vivid than other memories. Vivid they may be, but the memories decay over time just as other memories do. People forget important details and add incorrect ones, with no awareness that they're recreating a muddled scene in their minds rather than calling up a perfect, photographic reproduction.

3. It's all downhill after 40 (or 50 or 60 or 70)

It's true, some cognitive skills do decline as you get older. Children are better at learning new languages than adults—and never play a game of concentration against a 10-year-old unless you're prepared to be humiliated. Young adults are faster than older adults to judge whether two objects are the same or different; they can more easily memorize a list of random words, and they are faster to count backward by sevens.

But plenty of mental skills improve with age. Vocabulary, for instance—older people know more words and understand subtle linguistic distinctions. Given a biographical sketch of a stranger, they're better judges of character. They score higher on tests of social wisdom, such as how to settle a conflict. And people get better and better over time at regulating their own emotions and finding meaning in their lives.

4. We have five senses

Sure, sight, smell, hearing, taste and touch are the big ones. But we have many other ways of sensing the world and our place in it. Proprioception is a sense of how our bodies are positioned. Nociception is a sense of pain. We also have a sense of balance—the inner ear is to this sense as the eye is to vision—as well as a sense of body temperature, acceleration and the passage of time.

Compared with other species, though, humans are missing out. Bats and dolphins use sonar to find prey; some birds and insects see ultraviolet light; snakes detect the heat of warm-blooded prey; rats, cats, seals and other whiskered creatures use their "vibrissae" to judge spatial relations or detect movements; sharks sense electrical fields in the water; birds, turtles and even bacteria orient to the earth's magnetic field lines.

By the way, have you seen the taste map of the tongue, the diagram showing that different regions are sensitive to salty, sweet, sour or bitter flavors? Also a myth.

5. Brains are like computers

We speak of the brain's processing speed, its storage capacity, its parallel circuits, inputs and outputs. The metaphor fails at pretty much every level: the brain doesn't have a set memory capacity that is waiting to be filled up; it doesn't perform computations in the way a computer does; and even basic visual perception isn't a passive receiving of inputs because we actively interpret, anticipate and pay attention to different elements of the visual world.

There's a long history of likening the brain to whatever technology is the most advanced, impressive and vaguely mysterious. Descartes compared the brain to a hydraulic machine. Freud likened emotions to pressure building up in a steam engine. The brain later resembled a telephone switchboard and then an electrical circuit before evolving into a computer; lately it's turning into a Web browser or the Internet. These metaphors linger in clichés: emotions put the brain "under pressure" and some behaviors are thought to be "hard-wired." Speaking of which . . .

6. The brain is hard-wired

This is one of the most enduring legacies of the old "brains are electrical circuits" metaphor. There's some truth to it, as with many metaphors: the brain is organized in a standard way, with certain bits specialized to take on certain tasks, and those bits are connected along predictable neural pathways (sort of like wires) and communicate in part by releasing ions (pulses of electricity).

But one of the biggest discoveries in neuroscience in the past few decades is that the brain is remarkably plastic. In blind people, parts of the brain that normally process sight are instead devoted to hearing. Someone practicing a new skill, like learning to play the violin, "rewires" parts of the brain that are responsible for fine motor control. People with brain injuries can recruit other parts of the brain to compensate for the lost tissue.

7. A conk on the head can cause amnesia

Next to babies switched at birth, this is a favorite trope of soap operas: Someone is in a tragic accident and wakes up in the hospital unable to recognize loved ones or remember his or her own name or history. (The only cure for this form of amnesia, of course, is another conk on the head.)

In the real world, there are two main forms of amnesia: anterograde (the inability to form new memories) and retrograde (the inability to recall past events). Science's most famous amnesia patient, H.M., was unable to remember anything that happened after a 1953 surgery that removed most of his hippocampus. He remembered earlier events, however, and was able to learn new skills and vocabulary, showing that encoding "episodic" memories of new experiences relies on different brain regions than other types of learning and memory do. Retrograde amnesia can be caused by Alzheimer's disease, traumatic brain injury (ask an NFL player), thiamine deficiency or other insults. But a brain injury doesn't selectively impair autobiographical memory—much less bring it back.

8. We know what will make us happy

In some cases we haven't a clue. We routinely overestimate how happy something will make us, whether it's a birthday, free pizza, a new car, a victory for our favorite sports team or political candidate, winning the lottery or raising children. Money does make people happier, but only to a point—poor people are less happy than the middle class, but the middle class are just as happy as the rich. We overestimate the pleasures of solitude and leisure and underestimate how much happiness we get from social relationships.

On the flip side, the things we dread don't make us as unhappy as expected. Monday mornings aren't as unpleasant as people predict. Seemingly unendurable tragedies—paralysis, the death of a loved one—cause grief and despair, but the unhappiness doesn't last as long as people think it will. People are remarkably resilient.

9. We see the world as it is

We are not passive recipients of external information that enters our brain through our sensory organs. Instead, we actively search for patterns (like a Dalmatian dog that suddenly appears in a field of black and white dots), turn ambiguous scenes into ones that fit our expectations (it's a vase; it's a face) and completely miss details we aren't expecting. In one famous psychology experiment, about half of all viewers told to count the number of times a group of people pass a basketball do not notice that a guy in a gorilla suit is hulking around among the ball-throwers.

We have a limited ability to pay attention (which is why talking on a cellphone while driving can be as dangerous as drunk driving), and plenty of biases about what we expect or want to see. Our perception of the world isn't just "bottom-up"—built of objective observations layered together in a logical way. It's "top-down," driven by expectations and interpretations.

10. Men are from Mars, women are from Venus

Some of the sloppiest, shoddiest, most biased, least reproducible, worst designed and most over interpreted research in the history of science purports to provide biological explanations for differences between men and women. Eminent neuroscientists once claimed that head size, spinal ganglia or brain stem structures were responsible for women's inability to think creatively, vote logically or practice medicine. Today the theories are a bit more sophisticated: men supposedly have more specialized brain hemispheres, women more elaborate emotion circuits. Though there are some differences (minor and uncorrelated with any particular ability) between male and female brains, the main problem with looking for correlations with behavior is that sex differences in cognition are massively exaggerated.

Women are thought to outperform men on tests of empathy. They do—unless test subjects are told that men are particularly good at the test, in which case men perform as well as or better than women. The same pattern holds in reverse for tests of spatial reasoning. Whenever stereotypes are brought to mind, even by something as simple as asking test subjects to check a box next to their gender, sex differences are exaggerated. Women college students told that a test is something women usually do poorly on, do poorly. Women college students told that a test is something college students usually do well on, do well. Across countries—and across time—the more prevalent the belief is that men are better than women in math, the greater the difference in girls' and boys' math scores. And that's not because girls in Iceland have more specialized brain hemispheres than do girls in Italy.

Certain sex differences are enormously important to us when we're looking for a mate, but when it comes to most of what our brains do most of the time—perceive the world, direct attention, learn new skills, encode memories, communicate (no, women don't speak more than men do), judge other people's emotions (no, men aren't inept at this)—men and women have almost entirely overlapping and fully Earth-bound abilities.

Critical Thinking

1. Why does it not make evolutionary sense that we use only 10 percent of our brains? What evidence is there that we do at least have some brain reserves?

2. Are "flashbulb memories" precise, detailed and persistent? Explain.

3. Do all cognitive skills decline after age 40? Explain.

4. Do we have more than five senses? Explain. In what respects are humans "missing out?" Is there a "taste map of the tongue?"

5. In what ways are brains *not* like computers? What kinds of metaphors have been used before and why?

6. In what respects is the brain "hardwired" and in what respects can it be "rewired"?

7. What two types of amnesia are there? Can a conk on the head cause memory loss? Can it bring back memories?

8. In what ways do we overestimate and underestimate how happy something is going to make us?

9. Do we really see the world as it is? Explain.

10. How does the author assess the many claimed biological differences between men and women?

From *Smithsonian*, May 20, 2011. Copyright © 2011 by Laura Helmuth. Reprinted by permission of the author.

The Naked Truth

Recent findings lay bare the origins of human hairlessness—and hint that naked skin was a key factor in the emergence of other human traits.

NINA G. JABLONSKI

Among primates, humans are unique in having nearly naked skin. Every other member of our extended family has a dense covering of fur—from the short, black pelage of the howler monkey to the flowing copper coat of the orangutan—as do most other mammals. Yes, we humans have hair on our heads and elsewhere, but compared with our relatives, even the hairiest person is basically bare.

How did we come to be so denuded? Scholars have pondered this question for centuries. Finding answers has been difficult, however: most of the hallmark transitions in human evolution—such as the emergence of upright walking—are recorded directly in the fossils of our predecessors, but none of the known remains preserves impressions of human skin. In recent years, though, researchers have realized that the fossil record does contain indirect hints about our transformation from hirsute to hairless. Thanks to these clues and insights gleaned over the past decade from genomics and physiology, I and others have pieced together a compelling account of why and when humans shed their fur. In addition to explaining a very peculiar quirk of our appearance, the scenario suggests that naked skin itself played a crucial role in the evolution of other characteristic human traits, including our large brain and dependence on language.

Key Concepts

- Humans are the only primate species that has mostly naked skin.
- Loss of fur was an adaptation to changing environmental conditions that forced our ancestors to travel longer distances for food and water.
- Analyses of fossils and genes hint at when this transformation occurred.
- The evolution of hairlessness helped to set the stage for the emergence of large brains and symbolic thought.

—The Editors

Hairy Situations

To understand why our ancestors lost their body hair, we must first consider why other species have coats in the first place. Hair is a type of body covering that is unique to mammals. Indeed, it is a defining characteristic of the class: all mammals possess at least some hair, and most of them have it in abundance. It provides insulation and protection against abrasion, moisture, damaging rays of sunlight, and potentially harmful parasites and microbes. It also works as camouflage to confuse predators, and its distinctive patterns allow members of the same species to recognize one another. Furthermore, mammals can use their fur in social displays to indicate aggression or agitation: when a dog "raises its hackles" by involuntarily elevating the hairs on its neck and back, it is sending a clear signal to challengers to stay away.

Yet even though fur serves these many important purposes, a number of mammal lineages have evolved hair that is so sparse

Benefits of Hairlessness
Furry Vs. Naked

Naked human skin is better at ridding the body of excess heat than is fur-covered skin. Mammals possess three types of glands for the purpose: apocrine, eccrine and sebaceous. In most mammals the outermost layer of the skin, known as the epidermis, contains an abundance of apocrine glands. These glands cluster around hair follicles and coat the fur in a lather of oily sweat. Evaporation of this sweat, which cools the animal by drawing heat away from the skin, occurs at the surface of the fur. But the more the animal perspires, the less effectively it eliminates heat because the fur becomes matted, hampering evaporation. In the human epidermis, in contrast, eccrine glands predominate. These glands reside close to the skin surface and discharge thin, watery sweat through tiny pores. In addition to evaporating directly from the skin surface, this eccrine sweat vaporizes more readily than apocrine sweat, thus permitting improved cooling.

and fine as to serve no function. Many of these creatures live underground or dwell exclusively in the water. In subterranean mammals, such as the naked mole rat, hairlessness evolved as a response to living in large underground colonies, where the benefits of hair are superfluous because the animals cannot see one another in the dark and because their social structure is such that they simply huddle together for warmth. In marine mammals that never venture ashore, such as whales, naked skin facilitates long-distance swimming and diving by reducing drag on the skin's surface. To compensate for the lack of external insulation, these animals have blubber under the skin. In contrast, semiaquatic mammals—otters, for example—have dense, waterproof fur that traps air to provide positive buoyancy, thus decreasing the effort needed to float. This fur also protects their skin on land.

The largest terrestrial mammals—namely, elephants, rhinoceroses and hippopotamuses—also evolved naked skin because they are at constant risk of overheating. The larger an animal is, the less surface area it has relative to overall body mass and the harder it is for the creature to rid its body of excess heat. (On the flip side, mice and other small animals, which have a high surface-to-volume ratio, often struggle to retain sufficient heat.) During the Pleistocene epoch, which spans the time between two million and 10,000 years ago, the mammoths and other relatives of modern elephants and rhinoceroses were "woolly" because they lived in cold environments, and external insulation helped them conserve body heat and lower their food intake. But all of today's megaherbivores live in sweltering conditions, where a fur coat would be deadly for beasts of such immense proportions.

Human hairlessness is not an evolutionary adaptation to living underground or in the water—the popular embrace of the so-called aquatic ape hypothesis notwithstanding [see box on next page]. Neither is it the result of large body size. But our bare skin is related to staying cool, as our superior sweating abilities suggest.

Sweating It Out

Keeping cool is a big problem for many mammals, not just the giant ones, especially when they live in hot places and generate abundant heat from prolonged walking or running. These animals must carefully regulate their core body temperature because their tissues and organs, specifically the brain, can become damaged by overheating.

Mammals employ a variety of tactics to avoid burning up: dogs pant, many cat species are most active during the cooler evening hours, and many antelopes can off-load heat from the blood in their arteries to blood in small veins that has been cooled by breathing through the nose. But for primates, including humans, sweating is the primary strategy. Sweating cools the body through the production of liquid on the skin's surface that then evaporates, drawing heat energy away from the skin in the process. This whole-body cooling mechanism operates according to the same principle as an evaporative cooler (also known as a swamp cooler), and it is highly effective in preventing the dangerous overheating of the brain, as well as of other body parts.

Not all sweat is the same, however. Mammalian skin contains three types of glands—sebaceous, apocrine and eccrine—that together produce sweat. In most species, sebaceous and apocrine glands are the dominant sweat glands and are located near the base of hair follicles. Their secretions combine to coat hairs with an oily, sometimes foamy, mixture (think of the lather a racehorse generates when it runs). This type of sweat helps to cool the animal. But its ability to dissipate heat is limited. G. Edgar Folk, Jr., of the University of Iowa and his colleagues showed nearly two decades ago that the effectiveness of cooling diminishes as an animal's coat becomes wet and matted with this thick, oily sweat. The loss of efficiency arises because evaporation occurs at the surface of the fur, not at the surface of the skin itself, thus impeding the transfer of heat. Under conditions of duress, heat transfer is inefficient, requiring that the animal drink large amounts of water, which may not be readily available. Fur-covered mammals forced to exercise energetically or for prolonged periods in the heat of day will collapse from heat exhaustion.

Humans, in addition to lacking fur, possess an extraordinary number of eccrine glands—between two million and five million—that can produce up to 12 liters of thin, watery sweat a day. Eccrine glands do not cluster near hair follicles; instead they reside relatively close to the surface of the skin and discharge sweat through tiny pores. This combination of naked skin and watery sweat that sits directly atop it rather than collecting in the fur allows humans to eliminate excess heat very efficiently. In fact, according to a 2007 paper in *Sports Medicine* by Daniel E. Lieberman of Harvard University and Dennis M. Bramble of the University of Utah, our cooling system is so superior that in a marathon on a hot day, a human could outcompete a horse.

Showing Some Skin

Because humans are the only primates that lack coats and have an abundance of eccrine glands, something must have happened since our hominid lineage diverged from the line leading to our closest living relative, the chimpanzee, that favored the emergence of naked, sweaty skin. Perhaps not surprisingly, the transformation seems to have begun with climate change.

By using fossils of animals and plants to reconstruct ancient ecological conditions, scientists have determined that starting around three million years ago the earth entered into a phase of global cooling that had a drying effect in East and Central Africa, where human ancestors lived. With this decline in regular rainfall, the wooded environments favored by early hominids gave way to open savanna grasslands, and the foods that our ancestors the australopithecines subsisted on—fruits, leaves, tubers and seeds—became scarcer, more patchily distributed and subject to seasonal availability, as did permanent sources or freshwater. In response to this dwindling of resources, our forebears would have had to abandon their relatively leisurely foraging habits for a much more consistently active way of life just to stay hydrated and obtain enough calories, traveling ever longer distances in search of water and edible plant foods.

Alternative Ideas
Why the Aquatic Ape Theory Doesn't Hold Water

Among the many theories that attempt to explain the evolution of naked skin in humans, the aquatic ape theory (AAT)—which posits that humans went through an aquatic phase in their evolution—has attracted the most popular attention and support. First enunciated by English zoologist Sir Alister Hardy in a popular scientific article in 1960, the AAT later found a champion in writer Elaine Morgan, who continues to promote the theory in her lectures and writings. The problem is, the theory is demonstrably wrong.

The AAT holds that around five million to seven million years ago tectonic upheavals in the Rift Valley of East Africa cut early human ancestors off from their preferred tropical forest environments. As a result, they had to adapt to a semiaquatic life in marshes, along coasts and in floodplains, where they lived for about a million years. Evidence of this aquatic phase, Morgan argues, comes from several anatomical features humans share with aquatic and semiaquatic mammals but not with savanna mammals. These traits include our bare skin, a reduced number of apocrine glands, and fat deposits directly under the skin.

The AAT is untenable for three major reasons. First, aquatic mammals themselves differ considerably in the degree to which they exhibit Morgan's aquatic traits. Thus, there is no simple connection between, say, the amount of hair an animal has and the environment in which it lives. Second, the fossil record shows that watery habitats were thick with hungry crocodiles and aggressive hippopotamuses. Our small, defenseless ancestors would not have stood a chance in an encounter with such creatures. Third, the AAT is overly complex. It holds that our forebears shifted from a terrestrial way of life to a semiaquatic one and then returned to living on terra firma full-time. As John H. Langdon of the University of Indianapolis has argued, a more straightforward interpretation of the fossil record is that humans always lived on land, where the driving force behind the evolution of naked skin was climate change that favored savanna grasslands over woodlands. And from a scientific perspective, the simplest explanation is usually the correct one.

—N.J.

It is around this time that hominids also began incorporating meat into their diet, is revealed by the appearance of stone tools and butchered animal bones in the archaeological record around 2.6 million years ago. Animal foods are considerably richer in calories than are plant foods, but they are rarer on the landscape. Carnivorous animals therefore, need to range farther and wider than their herbivorous counterparts to procure a sufficient amount of food. Prey animals are also moving targets, save for the occasional carcass, which means predators must expend that much more energy to obtain their meal. In the case of human hunters and scavengers, natural selection morphed the apelike proportions of the australopithecines, who still spent some time in the trees, into a long-legged body built for sustained striding and running. (This modern form also no doubt helped our ancestors avoid becoming dinner themselves when out in the open.)

But these elevated activity levels came at a price: a greatly increased risk of overheating. Beginning in the 1980s, Peter Wheeler of Liverpool John Moores University in England published a series of papers in which he simulated how hot ancestral humans would have become out on the savanna. Wheeler's work, together with research my colleagues and I published in 1994, shows that the increase in walking and running, during which muscle activity builds up heat internally, would have required that hominids both enhance their eccrine sweating ability and lose their body hair to avoid overheating.

When did this metamorphosis occur? Although the human fossil record does not preserve skin, researchers do have a rough idea of when our forebears began engaging in modern patterns of movement. Studies conducted independently by Lieberman and Christopher Ruff of Johns Hopkins University have shown that by about 1.6 million years ago an early member of our genus called *Homo ergaster* had evolved essentially modern body proportions, which would have permitted prolonged walking and running. Moreover, details of the joint surfaces of the ankle, knee and hip make clear that these hominids actually exerted themselves in this way. Thus, according to the fossil evidence, the transition to naked skin and an eccrine-based sweating system must have been well under way by 1.6 million years ago to offset the greater heat loads that accompanied our predecessors' newly strenuous way of life.

Another clue to when hominids evolved naked skin has come from investigations into the genetics of skin color. In an ingenious study published in 2004, Alan R. Rogers of the University

When Nakedness Evolved
Ancestors on the Move

Although the fossil record does not preserve any direct evidence of ancient human skin, scientists can estimate when nakedness evolved based on other fossil clues. Protohumans such as the australopithecines probably led relatively sedentary lives, as today's apes do, because they lived in or near wooded environments rich in plant foods and freshwater. But as woodlands shrank and grasslands expanded, later ancestors, such as *Homo ergaster*, had to travel ever farther in search of sustenance—including meat. This species, which arose by 1.6 million years ago, was probably the first to possess naked skin and eccrine sweat, which would have offset the body heat generated by such elevated activity levels.

Beating the Heat

Naked skin is not the only adaptation humans evolved to maintain a healthy body temperature in the sweltering tropics where our ancestors lived. They also developed longer limbs, increasing their surface-to-volume ratio, which in turn facilitated the loss of excess heat. That trend seems to be continuing even today. The best evidence of this sustained adaptation comes from populations in East Africa, such as the Dinka of southern Sudan. It is surely no coincidence that these people, who live in one of the hottest places on earth, also have extremely long limbs.

Why do modern humans exhibit such a wide range of limb proportions? As our forebears migrated out of tropical Africa into cooler parts of the world, the selection pressures changed, allowing for a variety of body shapes to evolve.

Of Lice and Men

In recent years researchers have looked to lice for clues to why humans lost their body hair. In 2003 Mark Pagel of the University of Reading in England and Walter Bodmer of John Radcliffe Hospital in Oxford proposed that humans shed their fur to rid their bodies of disease-spreading lice and other fur-dwelling parasites and to advertise the health of their skin. Other investigators have studied head and body lice for insight into how long after becoming bare-skinned our ancestors began to cover up with clothing.

Although body lice feed on blood, they live on clothing. Thus, the origin of body lice provides a minimum estimate for the dawn of hominid garb. By comparing gene sequences of organisms, investigators can learn roughly when the species arose. Such analyses in lice indicate that whereas head lice have plagued humans from the start, body lice evolved much later. The timing of their appearance hints that humans went naked for more than a million years before getting dressed.

of Utah and his colleagues examined sequences of the human *MC1R* gene, which is among the genes responsible for producing skin pigmentation. The team showed that a specific gene variant always found in Africans with dark pigmentation originated as many as 1.2 million years ago. Early human ancestors are believed to have had pinkish skin covered with black fur, much as chimpanzees do, so the evolution of permanently dark skin was presumably a requisite evolutionary follow-up to the loss of our sun-shielding body hair. Rogers's estimate thus provides a minimum age for the dawn of nakedness.

Skin Deep

Less certain than why and when we became naked is how hominids evolved bare flesh. The genetic evidence for the evolution of nakedness has been difficult to locate because many genes contribute to the appearance and function of our skin. Nevertheless, hints have emerged from large-scale comparisons of the sequences of DNA "code letters," or nucleotides, in the entire genomes of different organisms. Comparison of the human and chimp genomes reveals that one of the most significant differences between chimp DNA and our own lies in the genes that code for proteins that control properties of the skin. The human versions of some of those genes encode proteins that help to make our skin particularly waterproof and scuff-resistant—critical properties, given the absence of protective fur. This finding implies that the advent of those gene variants contributed to the origin of nakedness by mitigating its consequences.

The outstanding barrier capabilities of our skin arise from the structure and makeup of its outermost layer, the stratum corneum (SC) of the epidermis. The SC has what has been described as a bricks-and-mortar composition. In this arrangement, multiple layers of flattened dead cells called corneocytes, which contain the protein keratin and other substances, are the bricks; ultrathin layers of lipids surrounding each of the corneocytes make up the mortar.

Most of the genes that direct the development of the SC are ancient, and their sequences are highly conserved among vertebrates. That the genes undergirding the human SC are so distinctive signifies, therefore, that the advent of those genes was important to survival. These genes encode the production of a unique combination of proteins that occur only in the epidermis, including novel types of keratin and involucrin. A number of laboratories are currently attempting to unravel the precise mechanisms responsible for regulating the manufacture of these proteins.

Other researchers are looking at the evolution of keratins in body hair, with the aim of determining the mechanisms responsible for the sparseness and fineness of body hair on the surface of human skin. To that end, Roland Moll of Philipps University in Marburg, Germany, and his colleagues have shown that the keratins present in human body hair are extremely fragile, which is why these hairs break so easily compared with those of other animals. This finding, detailed in a paper Moll published in 2008, suggests that human hair keratins were not as important to survival as the hair keratins of other primates were over the course of evolution and thus became weak.

Another question geneticists are eager to answer is how human skin came to contain such an abundance of eccrine glands. Almost certainly this accumulation occurred through changes in the genes that determine the fate of epidermal stem cells, which are unspecialized, in the embryo. Early in development, groups of epidermal stem cells in specific locations interact with cells of the underlying dermis, and genetically driven chemical signals within these niches direct the differentiation of the stem cells into hair follicles, eccrine glands, apocrine glands, sebaceous glands or plain epidermis. Many research groups are now investigating how epidermal stem cell niches are established and maintained, and this work should clarify what directs the fate of embryonic epidermal cells and how more of these cells become eccrine sweat glands in humans.

Not Entirely Nude

However it was that we became naked apes, evolution did leave a few body parts covered. Any explanation of why humans lost their fur therefore must also account for why we retain it in some places. Hair in the armpits and groin probably serves both to propagate pheromones (chemicals that serve to elicit a behavioral response from other individuals) and to help keep these areas lubricated during locomotion. As for hair on the head, it was most likely retained to help shield against excess heat on the top of the head. That notion may sound paradoxical, but having dense hair on the head creates a barrier layer of air between the sweating scalp and the hot surface of the hair. Thus, on a hot, sunny day the hair absorbs the heat while the barrier layer of air remains cooler, allowing sweat on the scalp to evaporate into that layer of air. Tightly curled hair provides the optimum head covering in this regard, because it increases the thickness of the space between the surface of the hair and the scalp, allowing air to blow through. Much remains to be discovered about the evolution of human head hair, but it is possible that tightly curled hair was the original condition in modern humans and that other hair types evolved as humans dispersed out of tropical Africa.

With regard to our body hair, the question is why it is so variable. There are many populations whose members have hardly any body hair at all and some populations of hirsute folks. Those with the least body hair tend to live in the tropics, whereas those with the most tend to live outside the tropics. Yet the hair on these nontropical people provides no warmth to speak of. These differences in hairiness clearly stem to some extent from testosterone, because males in all populations have more body hair than females do. A number of theories aimed at explaining this imbalance attribute it to sexual selection. For example, one posits that females prefer males with fuller beards and thicker body hair because these traits occur in tandem with virility and strength. Another proposes that males have evolved a preference for females with more juvenile features. These are interesting hypotheses, but no one has actually tested them in a modern human population; thus, we do not know, for instance, whether hairy men are in fact more vigorous or fecund than their sleeker counterparts. In the absence of any empirical evidence, it is still anybody's guess why human body hair varies the way it does.

Naked Ambitions

Going furless was not merely a means to an end; it had profound consequences for subsequent phases of human evolution. The loss of most of our body hair and the gain of the ability to dissipate excess body heat through eccrine sweating helped to make possible the dramatic enlargement of our most temperature-sensitive organ, the brain. Whereas the australopithecines had a brain that was, on average, 400 cubic centimeters—roughly the size of a chimp's brain—*H. ergaster* had a brain twice that large. And within a million years the human brain swelled another 400 cubic centimeters, reaching its modern size. No doubt other factors influenced the expansion of our gray matter—the adoption of a sufficiently caloric diet to fuel this energetically demanding tissue, for example. But shedding our body hair was surely a critical step in becoming brainy.

Going furless was not merely a means to an end; it had profound consequences for subsequent phases of human evolution.

Our hairlessness also had social repercussions. Although we can technically raise and lower our hackles when the small muscles at the base of our hair follicles contract and relax, our body hairs are so thin and wispy that we do not put on much of a show compared with the displays of our cats and dogs or of our chimpanzee cousins. Neither do we have the built-in advertising—or camouflage—offered by zebra stripes, leopard spots, and the like. Indeed, one might even speculate that universal human traits such as social blushing and complex facial expressions evolved to compensate for our lost ability to communicate through our fur. Likewise, body paint, cosmetics, tattoos and other types of skin decoration are found in various combinations in all cultures, because they convey group membership, status and other vital social information formerly encoded by fur. We also employ body postures and gestures to broadcast our emotional states and intentions. And we use language to speak our mind in detail. Viewed this way, naked skin did not just cool us down—it made us human.

More to Explore

Skin Deep. Nina G. Jablonski and George Chaplin in *Scientific American,* vol. 287, no. 4, pages 74–81; October 2002.

Genetic Variation at the MC1R Locus and the Time since Loss of Human Body Hair. Alan R. Rogers, D. Iltis and S. Wooding in *Current Anthropology,* vol. 45, no. 1, pages 105–108; February 2004.

Initial Sequence of the Chimpanzee Genome and Comparison with the Human Genome. Chimpanzee Sequencing and Analysis Consortium in *Nature,* vol. 437, pages 69–87; September 1, 2005.

Skin: A Natural History. Nina G. Jablonski. University of California Press, 2006.

The Evolution of Marathon Running: Capabilities in Humans. Daniel E. Lieberman and Dennis M. Bramble in *Sports Medicine,* vol. 37, nos. 4–5, pages 288–290; 2007.

Critical Thinking

1. What benefits does body hair provide for various mammals?
2. Why have some mammal lineages evolved hair so sparse and fine as to serve no function?

3. What is human bare skin related to, according to the author?

4. Why is keeping cool important for some mammals?

5. In contrast to other mammals, what is the primary strategy for keeping cool among primates?

6. How is the human system of cooling more effective than that of other mammals?

7. How does the evolution of the human cooling system relate to changes in environment, food accessibility, and the availability of water? How did the switch to meat-eating result in a long-legged body built for sustained striding and running?

8. At what price did this elevated activity come? What was required, according to Peter Wheeler?

9. When was the transition to naked skin and an eccrine-based sweating system well under way, according to the fossil evidence?

10. Why did evolution leave a few body parts covered?

11. Why is tightly curled hair thought to be the original condition in modern humans?

12. How has going furless had profound effects upon making us human?

NINA G. JABLONSKI is head of the anthropology department at Pennsylvania State University. Her research focuses on the natural history of human skin, the origin of bipedalism, the evolution and biogeography of Old World monkeys, and the paleoecology of mammals that lived during the past two million years. She has conducted fieldwork in China, Kenya and Nepal. This is her second article for *Scientific American*. The first, co-authored with George Chaplin and published in October 2002, described the evolution of human skin color.

UNIT 6

Human Diversity

Unit Selections

Learning Outcomes

After reading this Unit, you will be able to:

- Explain why genes influence everything about us but determine very little.
- Discuss why some ethnic groups do better than others at certain sports.
- Explain why skin color varies among humans.
- Discuss whether the human species can be subdivided into racial categories and support your position.
- Explain how and why the concept of race developed.
- Discuss both the positive and negative aspects of racial classification.
- Determine to what extent height is a barometer of the health of a society and explain why.
- Explain why forensic anthropology is important to society.

Student Website

www.mhhe.com/cls

Internet References

Forensic Science Reference Page
   www.lab.fws.gov
Human Genome Project Information
   www.ornl.gov/TechResources/Human_Genome/home.html
OMIM Home Page-Online Mendelian Inheritance in Man
   www.ncbi.nlm.nih.gov
Zeno's Forensic Page
   www.forensic.to/forensic.html

The field of biological anthropology has come a long way since the days when one of its primary concerns was the classification of human beings according to racial type. Although human diversity is still a matter of major interest in terms of how and why we differ from one another, most anthropologists have concluded that human beings cannot be sorted into sharply distinct entities (see "How Real Is Race?: Using Anthropology to Make Sense of Human Diversity"). Without denying the fact of human variation throughout the world, the prevailing view today is that the differences between us exist along geographical gradients, as differences in degree, rather than in terms of separate and discrete entities as perceived in the past.

One of the old ways of looking at human "races" was that each such group was a subspecies of humans that, if left reproductively isolated long enough, would eventually evolve into separate species. While this concept of subspecies, or racial varieties within a species, would seem to apply to some living creatures (such as the dog and wolf or the horse and zebra) and might even be relevant to hominid diversification in the past, the current consensus is that it does not apply today, at least not within the human species.

A more recent attempt to salvage the idea of human races has been to perceive them not so much as reproductively isolated entities, but as many clusters of gene frequencies, separable only by the fact that the proportions of traits (such as skin color, hair form, etc.) differ in each artificially constructed group. Some scientists in the area of forensic physical anthropology appreciate the practical value of this approach (see "Dead Men Do Tell Tales"). In a similar manner, our ability to reconstruct human prehistory is dependent upon an understanding of human variation (as in "Skin Deep" by Nina G. Jablonski and George Chaplin, and "The Tall and the Short of It" by Barry Bogin).

Lest anyone think that anthropologists are "in denial" regarding the existence of human races and that some of the viewpoints expressed in this section are merely expressions of contemporary political correctness, it should be pointed out that serious, scholarly attempts to classify people in terms of precise, biological units have been going on now for 200 years, and, so far, nothing of scientific value has come of them.

Complicating the matter is the fact that there are actually two concepts of race: the strictly biological one, as described above, and the one of popular culture, which has been around since time immemorial. These two ways of thinking have resulted not only in fuzzy thinking about racial biology, but they have led to confusion as to which traits are truly biological in origin and which ones are environmentally and socially influenced

© IT Stock/PunchStock

(see "Can White Men Jump?: Ethnicity, Genes, Culture, and Success"). This confusion has infected the way we think about people and, therefore, the way we treat each other in the social arena.

What we should recognize, claim most anthropologists, is that, despite the superficial physical and biological differences between us, when it comes to intelligence, all human beings are basically the same. The degrees of variation within our species may be accounted for by the subtle, and changing, selective forces experienced as one moves from one geographical area to another. However, no matter what the environmental pressures have been, the same intellectual demands have been made upon all of us. This is not to say, of course, that we do not vary from each other as individuals. Rather, what is being said is that when we look at these artificially created groups of people called "races," we find a varying range of intellectual skills within each group. Indeed, even when we look at traits other than intelligence, we find much greater variation within each group than we find between groups.

It is time, therefore, to put the idea of human races to rest, at least as far as science is concerned. If such notions remain in the realm of social discourse, then so be it. That is where the problems associated with notions of race have to be solved anyway. At least, says Marks, in speaking for the anthropological community: "You may group humans into a small number of races if you want to, but you are denied biology as a support for it."

Can White Men Jump?

Ethnicity, Genes, Culture, and Success

Clusters of ethnic and geographical athletic success prompt suspicions of hidden genetic advantages. The real advantages are far more nuanced—and less hidden.

DAVID SHENK

At the 2008 Summer Olympics in Beijing, the world watched in astonishment as the tiny island of Jamaica captured six gold medals in track and field and eleven overall. Usain Bolt won (and set world records in) both the men's 100-meter and the men's 200-meter races. Jamaican women took the top three spots in the 100-meter and won the 200-meter as well. "They brought their A game. I don't know where we left ours," lamented American relay runner Lauryn Williams.

A poor, underdeveloped nation of 2.8 million people—one-hundredth the size of the United States—had somehow managed to produce the fastest humans alive.

How?

Within hours, geneticists and science journalists rushed in with reports of a "secret weapon": biologically, it turned out that almost all Jamaicans are flush with alpha-actinin-3, a protein that drives forceful, speedy muscle contractions. The powerful protein is produced by a special gene variant called *ACTN3,* at least one copy of which can be found in 98 percent of Jamaicans—far higher than in many other ethnic populations.

An impressive fact, but no one stopped to do the math. Eighty percent of Americans also have at least one copy of *ACTN3*—that amounts to 240 million people. Eighty-two percent of Europeans have it as well—that tacks on another 597 million potential sprinters. "There's simply no clear relationship between the frequency of this variant in a population and its capacity to produce sprinting superstars," concluded geneticist Daniel MacArthur.

What, then, is the Jamaicans' secret sauce?

This is the same question people asked about champion long-distance runners from Finland in the 1920s and about great Jewish basketball players from the ghettos of Philadelphia and New York in the 1930s. Today, we wonder how tiny South Korea turns out as many great female golfers as the United States—and how the Dominican Republic has become a factory for male baseball players.

The list goes on and on. It turns out that sports excellence commonly emerges in geographic clusters—so commonly, in fact, that a small academic discipline called "sports geography" has developed over the years to help understand it. What they've discovered is that there's never a single cause for a sports cluster. Rather, the success comes from many contributions of climate, media, demographics, nutrition, politics, training, spirituality, education, economics, and folklore. In short, athletic clusters are not genetic, but systemic.

Unsatisfied with this multifaceted explanation, some sports geographers have also transformed themselves into sports geneticists. In his book *Taboo: Why Black Athletes Dominate Sports and Why We're Afraid to Talk About It,* journalist Jon Entine insists that today's phenomenal black athletes— Jamaican sprinters, Kenyan marathoners, African American basketball players, etc.—are propelled by "high performance genes" inherited from their West and East African ancestors. Caucasians and Asians don't do as well, he says, because they don't share these advantages. "White athletes appear to have a physique between central West Africans and East Africans," Entine writes. "They have more endurance but less explosive running and jumping ability than West Africans; they tend to be quicker than East Africans but have less endurance."

In the finer print, Entine acknowledges that these are all grosser-than-gross generalizations. He understands that there are extraordinary Asian and Caucasian athletes in basketball, running, swimming, jumping, and cycling. (In fact, blacks do not even dominate the latter three of these sports as of 2008.) In his own book, Entine quotes geneticist Claude Bouchard: "They key point is that these biological characteristics *are not unique* to either West or East African blacks. These characteristics are seen in all populations, including whites." (Italics mine.) (Entine also acknowledges that we haven't in fact found the actual genes he's alluding to. "These genes will likely be identified early in the [twenty-first century]," he predicts.)

Actual proof for his argument is startlingly thin. But Entine's message of superior genes seems irresistible to a world steeped in gene-giftedness—and where other influences and dynamics are nearly invisible.

Take the running Kenyans. Relatively new to international competition, Kenyans have in recent years become overwhelmingly dominant in middle- and long-distance races. "It's pointless for me to run on the pro circuit," complained American 10,000-meter champion Mike Mykytok to *The New York Times* in 1998. "With all the Kenyans, I could set a personal best time, still only place 12th and win $200."

Ninety percent of the top-performing Kenyans come from the Kalenjin tribe in the Great Rift Valley region of western Kenya, where they have a centuries-old tradition of long-distance running. Where did this tradition come from? Kenyan-born journalist John Manners suggests it came from cattle raiding. Further, he proposes how a few basic economic incentives became a powerful evolutionary force. "The better a young man was at raiding [cattle]—in large part a function of his speed and endurance—the more cattle he accumulated," Manners says. "And since cattle were what a prospective husband needed to pay for a bride, the more a young man had, the more wives he could buy, and the more children he was likely to father. It is not hard to imagine that such a reproductive advantage might cause a significant shift in a group's genetic makeup over the course of a few centuries."

Whatever the precise origin, it is true that the Kalenjin have long had a fierce dedication to running. But it wasn't until the 1968 Olympics that they became internationally renowned for their prowess, thanks to the extraordinary runner Kipchoge Keino.

The son of a farmer and ambitious long-distance runner, Keino caught the running bug early in life. He wasn't the most precocious or "natural" athlete among his peers, but running was simply woven into the fabric of his life: along with his schoolmates, Keino ran many miles per day as a part of his routine. "I used to run from the farm to school and back," he recalled. "We didn't have a water tap in the house, so you run to the river, take your shower, run home, change, [run] to school . . . Everything is running." Slowly, Keino emerged as a serious competitor. He built himself a running track on the farm where his family worked and by his late teens was showing signs of international-level performance. After some success in the early 1960s, he competed admirably in the 1964 Olympics and became the leader of the Kenyan running team for the 1968 games in Mexico City. It was Kenya's fourth Olympics.

In Mexico City, things did not begin well for Keino. After nearly collapsing in pain during his first race, the 10,000 meters, he was diagnosed with gallstones and ordered by doctors not to continue. At the last minute, though, he stubbornly decided to race the 1,500 meters and hopped in a cab to Mexico City's Aztec Stadium. Caught in terrible traffic, Keino did the only thing he could do, the thing he'd been training his whole life for: he jumped out of the cab and ran the last mile to the event, arriving on the track only moments before the start of the race, winded and very sick. Still, when the gun sounded,

Keino was off, and his performance that day shattered the world record and left his rival, American Jim Ryun, in the dust.

The dramatic victory made Keino one of the most celebrated men in all Africa and helped catalyze a new interest in world-class competition. Athletic halls and other venues all over Kenya were named after him. World-class coaches like Fred Hardy and Colm O'Connell were recruited to nurture other Kenyan aspirants. In the decades that followed, the long-standing but profit-less Kalenjin running tradition became a well-oiled economic-athletic engine. Sports geographers point to many crucial ingredients in Kenya's competitive surge but no single overriding factor. High-altitude training and mild year-round climate are critical, but equally important is a deeply ingrained culture of asceticism—the postponement of gratification—and an overriding preference for individual over team sports. (Soccer, the overwhelming Kenyan favorite, is all but ignored among the Kalenjin; running is all.) In testing, psychologists discovered a particularly strong cultural "achievement orientation," defined as the inclination to seek new challenges, attain competence, and strive to outdo others. And then there was the built-in necessity as virtue: as Keino mentioned, Kalenjin kids tend to run long distances as a practical matter, an average of eight to twelve kilometers per day from age seven.

Joke among elite athletes: How can the rest of the world defuse Kenyan running superiority? Answer: Buy them school buses.

With the prospect of international prize money, running in Kenya has also become a rare economic opportunity to catapult oneself into Western-level education and wealth. Five thousand dollars in prize money is a very nice perk for an American; for a Kenyan, it is instant life-changing wealth. Over time, a strong culture of success has also bred even more success. The high-performance benchmark has stoked higher and higher levels of achievement—a positive feedback loop analogous to technological innovation in Silicon Valley, combat skills among Navy SEALs, and talents in other highly successful microcultures. In any competitive arena, the single best way to inspire better performance is to be surrounded by the fiercest possible competitors and a culture of extreme excellence. Success begets success.

There is also an apparent sacrificial quality particular to Kenyan training, wherein coaches can afford to push their athletes to extreme limits in a way that coaches in other parts of the world cannot. *Sports Illustrated*'s Alexander Wolff writes that with a million Kenyan schoolboys running so enthusiastically, "coaches in Kenya can train their athletes to the outer limits of endurance—up to 150 miles a week—without worrying that their pool of talent will be meaningfully depleted. Even if four out of every five runners break down, the fifth will convert that training into performance."

And what of genetics? Are Kenyans the possessors of rare endurance genes, as some insist? No one can yet know for sure, but the new understanding of GxE[1] and some emergent truths in genetic testing strongly suggest otherwise, in two important ways:

1. Despite Appearances to the Contrary, Racial and Ethnic Groups Are *Not* Genetically Discrete

Skin color is a great deceiver; actual genetic differences between ethnic and geographic groups are very, very limited. All human beings are descended from the same African ancestors, and it is well established among geneticists that there is roughly ten times more genetic variation within large populations than there is between populations. "While ancestry is a useful way to classify species (because species are isolated gene pools, most of the time)," explains University of Queensland philosopher of biology John Wilkins, "it is rarely a good way to classify populations within species . . . [and definitely not] in humans. We move about too much."

By no stretch of the imagination, then, does any ethnicity or region have an exclusive lock on a particular body type or secret high-performance gene. Body shapes, muscle fiber types, etc., are actually quite varied and scattered, and true athletic potential is widespread and plentiful.

2. Genes Don't Directly Cause Traits; They Only Influence the System

Consistent with other lessons of GxE, the surprising finding of the $3 billion Human Genome Project is that only in rare instances do specific gene variants directly cause specific traits or diseases. Far more commonly, they merely increase or decrease the likelihood of those traits/diseases. In the words of King's College developmental psychopathologist Michael Rutter, genes are "probabilistic rather than deterministic."

As the search for athletic genes continues, therefore, the overwhelming evidence suggests that researchers will instead locate genes prone to certain types of interactions: gene variant A in combination with gene variant B, provoked into expression by X amount of training + Y altitude + Z will to win + a hundred other life variables (coaching, injury rate, etc.), will produce some specific result R. What this means, of course, is that we need to dispense rhetorically with the thick firewall between biology (nature) and training (nurture). The reality of GxE assures that each person's genes interact with his climate, altitude, culture, meals, language, customs, and spirituality—everything—to produce unique life trajectories. Genes play a critical role, but as dynamic instruments, not a fixed blueprint. A seven- or fourteen- or twenty-eight-year-old outfitted with a certain height, shape, muscle-fiber proportion, and so on is not that way merely because of genetic instruction.

As for John Manners's depiction of cattle-raiding Kenyans becoming genetically selected to be better and better runners over the generations, it's an entertaining theory that fits well with the popular gene-centric view of natural selection. But developmental biologists would point out that you could take exactly the same story line and flip the conclusion on its head: the fastest man earns the most wives and has the most kids—but rather than passing on quickness genes, he passes on crucial external ingredients, such as the knowledge and means to attain maximal nutrition, inspiring stories, the most propitious attitude and habits, access to the best trainers, the most leisure time to pursue training, and so on. This nongenetic aspect of inheritance is often overlooked by genetic determinists: culture, knowledge, attitudes, and environments are also passed on in many different ways.

The case for the hidden performance gene is even further diminished in the matter of Jamaican sprinters, who turn out to be a quite heterogeneous genetic group—nothing like the genetic "island" that some might imagine. On average, Jamaican genetic heritage is about the same as African American heritage, with roughly the same mix of West African, European, and native American ancestry. That's on average; individually, the percentage of West African origin varies widely, from 46.8 to 97.0 percent. Jamaicans are therefore *less* genetically African and *more* European and native American than their neighboring Barbadians and Virgin Islanders. "Jamaica . . . may represent a 'crossroads' within the Caribbean," conclude the authors of one DNA study. Jamaica was used as a "transit point by colonists between Central and South America and Europe [which] may have served to make Jamaica more cosmopolitan and thus provided more opportunities for [genetic] admixture to occur. *The large variance in both the global and individual admixture estimates in Jamaica attests to the cosmopolitan nature of the island.*"

In other words, Jamaica would be one of the very last places in the region expected to excel, according to a gene-gift paradigm.

Meanwhile, specific cultural explanations abound for the island's sprinting success—and for its recent competitive surge. In Jamaica, track events are beloved. The annual high school Boys' and Girls' Athletic Championships is as important to Jamaicans as the Super Bowl is to Americans. "Think Notre Dame football," write *Sports Illustrated*'s Tim Layden and David Epstein. "Names like Donald Quarrie and Merlene Ottey are holy on the island. In the United States, track and field is a marginal, niche sport that pops its head out of the sand every four years and occasionally produces a superstar. In Jamaica . . . it's a major sport. When *Sports Illustrated* [recently] visited the island . . . dozens of small children showed up for a Saturday morning youth track practice. That was impressive. That they were all wearing spikes was stunning."

With that level of intensity baked right into the culture, it's no surprise that Jamaicans have for many decades produced a wealth of aggressive, ambitious young sprinters. Their problem, though, was that for a long time they didn't have adequate college-level training resources for these promising teenagers. Routinely, the very best athletes would leave the country for Britain (Linford Christie) or Canada (Ben Johnson) and often never return.

Then, in the 1970s, former champion sprinter Dennis Johnson did come back to Jamaica to create a college athletic program based on what he'd experienced in the United States.

That program, now at the University of Technology in Kingston, became the new core of Jamaican elite training. After a critical number of ramp-up years, the medals started to pour in. It was the final piece in the systemic machinery driven by national pride and an ingrained sprinting culture.

Psychology was obviously a critical part of the mix. "We genuinely believe that we'll conquer," says Jamaican coach Fitz Coleman. "It's a mindset. We're small and we're poor, but we believe in ourselves." On its own, it might seem laughable that self-confidence can turn a tiny island into a breeding ground for champion sprinters. But taken in context of the developmental dynamic, psychology and motivation become vital. Science has demonstrated unequivocally that a person's mindset has the power to dramatically affect both short-term capabilities and the long-term dynamic of achievement. In Jamaica, sprinting is a part of the national identity. Kids who sprint well are admired and praised; their heroes are sprinters; sprinting well provides economic benefits and ego gratification and is even considered a form of public service.

All things considered, it seems obvious that the mind is the most athletic part of any Jamaican athlete's body.

The notion that the mind is of such paramount importance to athletic success is something that we all have to accept and embrace if we're going to advance the culture of success in human society. Within mere weeks of British runner Roger Bannister becoming the first human being to crack the four-minute mile, several other runners also broke through. Bannister himself later remarked that while biology sets ultimate limits to performance, it is the mind that plainly determines how close individuals come to those absolute limits.

And we keep coming closer and closer to them. "The past century has witnessed a progressive, indeed remorseless improvement in human athletic performance," writes South African sports scientist Timothy David Noakes. The record speed for the mile, for example, was cut from 4:36 in 1865 to 3:43 in 1999. The one-hour cycling distance record increased from 26 kilometers in 1876 to 49 kilometers in 2005. The 200-meter freestyle swimming record decreased from 2:31 in 1908 to 1:43 in 2007. Technology and aerodynamics are a part of the story, but the rest of it has to do with training intensity, training methods, and sheer competitiveness and desire. It used to be that 67 kilometers per week was considered an aggressive level of training. Today's serious Kenyan runners, Noakes points out, will cover 230 kilometers per week (at 6,000 feet in altitude).

These are not superhumans with rare super-genes. They are participants in a culture of the extreme, willing to devote more, to ache more, and to risk more in order to do better. Most of us will understandably want nothing to do with that culture of the extreme. But that is our choice.

Note

1. Genetics times Environment, meaning that an individual's observable characteristics are the result of the dynamic interaction between one's genes and the environment in which one develops.

Critical Thinking

1. What is "sports geography"? What has been discovered about "sports clusters"?

2. What have been the claims of "sports geneticists" such as Jon Entine? How does the author counter this point of view?

3. What are the motives for running among the Kalenjin tribe of Kenya?

4. How was running woven into the fabric of Kipchoge Keino's life?

5. What have been the "crucial ingredients in Kenya's competitive surge"?

6. What has been the "feedback loop" in this "culture of success"?

7. What is the "sacrificial quality particular to Kenyan training"?

8. In what two important ways does our understanding of GxE (meaning that genes interact with the environment rather than simply genes plus environment accounting for traits) strongly suggest that genes alone are not responsible for Kenyan running endurance?

9. How does the author respond to the claim that the cattle-raiding Kenyans are becoming genetically selected for better running?

10. Explain how and why there is not likely to be a "hidden performance gene" for running among Jamaicans as opposed to other ethnic groups?

11. Why would Jamaica be one of the very last places in the region expected to excel, according to a gene-gift paradigm?

12. What specific cultural explanations abound for the island's sprinting success? What was once the "problem" in this respect? How was this problem solved?

13. Why is psychology "a critical part of the mix"? How does breaking the four-minute mile illustrate this point? What is meant by the "culture of the extreme"?

Skin Deep

Throughout the world, human skin color has evolved to be dark enough to prevent sunlight from destroying the nutrient folate but light enough to foster the production of vitamin D.

NINA G. JABLONSKI AND GEORGE CHAPLIN

Among primates, only humans have a mostly naked skin that comes in different colors. Geographers and anthropologists have long recognized that the distribution of skin colors among indigenous populations is not random: darker peoples tend to be found nearer the equator, lighter ones closer to the poles. For years, the prevailing theory has been that darker skins evolved to protect against skin cancer. But a series of discoveries has led us to construct a new framework for understanding the evolutionary basis of variations in human skin color. Recent epidemiological and physiological evidence suggests to us that the worldwide pattern of human skin color is the product of natural selection acting to regulate the effects of the sun's ultraviolet (UV) radiation on key nutrients crucial to reproductive success.

From Hirsute to Hairless

The evolution of skin pigmentation is linked with that of hairlessness, and to comprehend both these stories, we need to page back in human history. Human beings have been evolving as an independent lineage of apes since at least seven million years ago, when our immediate ancestors diverged from those of our closest relatives, chimpanzees. Because chimpanzees have changed less over time than humans have, they can provide an idea of what human anatomy and physiology must have been like. Chimpanzees' skin is light in color and is covered by hair over most of their bodies. Young animals have pink faces, hands, and feet and become freckled or dark in these areas only as they are exposed to sun with age. The earliest humans almost certainly had a light skin covered with hair. Presumably hair loss occurred first, then skin color changed. But that leads to the question, When did we lose our hair?

The skeletons of ancient humans—such as the well-known skeleton of Lucy, which dates to about 3.2 million years ago—give us a good idea of the build and the way of life of our ancestors. The daily activities of Lucy and other hominids that lived before about three million years ago appear to have been similar to those of primates living on the open savannas of Africa today.

They probably spent much of their day foraging for food over three to four miles before retiring to the safety of trees to sleep.

By 1.6 million years ago, however, we see evidence that this pattern had begun to change dramatically. The famous skeleton of Turkana Boy—which belonged to the species *Homo ergaster*—is that of a long-legged, striding biped that probably walked long distances. These more active early humans faced the problem of staying cool and protecting their brains from overheating. Peter Wheeler of John Moores University in Liverpool, England, has shown that this was accomplished through an increase in the number of sweat glands on the surface of the body and a reduction in the covering of body hair. Once rid of most of their hair, early members of the genus *Homo* then encountered the challenge of protecting their skin from the damaging effects of sunlight, especially UV rays.

Built-In Sunscreen

In chimpanzees, the skin on the hairless parts of the body contains cells called melanocytes that are capable of synthesizing the dark-brown pigment melanin in response to exposure to UV radiation. When humans became mostly hairless, the ability of the skin to produce melanin assumed new importance. Melanin is nature's sunscreen: it is a large organic molecule that Overview/Skin Color Evolution serves the dual purpose of physically and chemically filtering the harmful effects of UV radiation; it absorbs UV rays, causing them to lose energy, and it neutralizes harmful chemicals called free radicals that form in the skin after damage by UV radiation.

Anthropologists and biologists have generally reasoned that high concentrations of melanin arose in the skin of peoples in tropical areas because it protected them against skin cancer. James E. Cleaver of the University of California at San Francisco, for instance, has shown that people with the disease xeroderma pigmentosum, in which melanocytes are destroyed by exposure to the sun, suffer from significantly higher than normal rates of squamous and basal cell carcinomas, which are usually easily treated. Malignant melanomas are more frequently fatal, but

Overview/Skin Color Evolution

- After losing their hair as an adaptation for keeping cool, early hominids gained pigmented skins. Scientists initially thought that such pigmentation arose to protect against skin-cancer-causing ultra-violet [UV] radiation.
- Skin cancers tend to arise after reproductive age, however. An alternative theory suggests that dark skin might have evolved primarily to protect against the breakdown of folate, a nutrient essential for fertility and for fetal development.
- Skin that is too dark blocks the sunlight necessary for catalyzing the production of vitamin D, which is crucial for maternal and fetal bones. Accordingly, humans have evolved to be light enough to make sufficient vitamin B yet dark enough to protect their stores of folate.
- As a result of recent human migrations, many people now live in areas that receive more [or less] UV radiation than is appropriate for their skin color.

they are rare (representing 4 percent of skin cancer diagnoses) and tend to strike only light-skinned people. But all skin cancers typically arise later in life, in most cases after the first reproductive years, so they could not have exerted enough evolutionary pressure for skin protection alone to account for darker skin colors. Accordingly, we began to ask what role melanin might play in human evolution.

The Folate Connection

In 1991 one of US (Jablonski) ran across what turned out to be a critical paper published in 1978 by Richard F. Branda and John W. Eaton, now at the University of Vermont and the University of Louisville, respectively. These investigators showed that light-skinned people who had been exposed to simulated strong sunlight had abnormally low levels of the essential B vitamin folate in their blood. The scientists also observed that subjecting human blood serum to the same conditions resulted in a 50-percent loss of folate content within one hour.

The significance of these findings to reproduction—and hence evolution—became clear when we learned of research being conducted on a major class of birth defects by our colleagues at the University of Western Australia. There Fiona J. Stanley and Carol Bower had established by the late 1980s that folate deficiency in pregnant women is related to an increased risk of neural tube defects such as spina bifida, in which the arches of the spinal vertebrae fail to close around the spinal cord. Many research groups throughout the world have since confirmed this correlation, and efforts to supplement foods with folate and to educate women about the importance of the nutrient have become widespread.

We discovered soon afterward that folate is important not only in preventing neural tube defects but also in a host of other

processes. Because folate is essential for the synthesis of DNA in dividing cells, anything that involves rapid cell proliferation, such as spermatogenesis (the production of sperm cells), requires folate. Male rats and mice with chemically induced folate deficiency have impaired spermatogenesis and are infertile. Although no comparable studies of humans have been conducted, Wai Yee Wong and his colleagues at the University Medical Center of Nijmegen in the Netherlands have recently reported that folic acid treatment can boost the sperm counts of men with fertility problems.

Such observations led us to hypothesize that dark skin evolved to protect the body's folate stores from destruction. Our idea was supported by a report published in 1996 by Argentine pediatrician Pablo Lapunzina, who found that three young and otherwise healthy women whom he had attended gave birth to infants with neural tube defects after using sun beds to tan themselves in the early weeks of pregnancy. Our evidence about the breakdown of folate by UV radiation thus supplements what is already known about the harmful (skin-cancer-causing) effects of UV radiation on DNA.

Human Skin on the Move

The earliest members of *Homo sapiens,* or modern humans, evolved in Africa between 120,000 and 100,000 years ago and had darkly pigmented skin adapted to the conditions of UV radiation and heat that existed near the equator. As modern humans began to venture out of the tropics, however, they encountered environments in which they received significantly less UV radiation during the year. Under these conditions their high concentrations of natural sunscreen probably proved detrimental. Dark skin contains so much melanin that very little UV radiation, and specifically very little of the shorter-wavelength UVB radiation, can penetrate the skin. Although most of the effects of UVB are harmful, the rays perform one indispensable function: initiating the formation of vitamin D in the skin. Dark-skinned people living in the tropics generally receive sufficient UV radiation during the year for UVB to penetrate the skin and allow them to make vitamin D. Outside the tropics this is not the case. The solution, across evolutionary time, has been for migrants to northern latitudes to lose skin pigmentation.

The connection between the evolution of lightly pigmented skin and vitamin D synthesis was elaborated by W. Farnsworth Loomis of Brandeis University in 1967. He established the importance of vitamin D to reproductive success because of its role in enabling calcium absorption by the intestines, which in turn makes possible the normal development of the skeleton and the maintenance of a healthy immune system. Research led by Michael Holick of the Boston University School of Medicine has, over the past 20 years, further cemented the significance of vitamin D in development and immunity. His team also showed that not all sunlight contains enough UVB to stimulate vitamin D production. In Boston, for instance, which is located at about 42 degrees north latitude, human skin cells begin to produce vitamin D only after mid-March. In the wintertime there isn't enough UVB to do the job. We realized that this was another piece of evidence essential to the skin color story.

During the course of our research in the early 1990s, we searched in vain to find sources of data on actual UV radiation levels at the earth's surface. We were rewarded in 1996, when we contacted Elizabeth Weatherhead of the Cooperative Institute for Research in Environmental Sciences at the University of Colorado at Boulder. She shared with us a database of measurements of UV radiation at the earth's surface taken by NASA's Total Ozone Mapping Spectrophotometer satellite between 1978 and 1993. We were then able to model the distribution of UV radiation on the earth and relate the satellite data to the amount of UVB necessary to produce vitamin D.

We found that the earth's surface could be divided into three vitamin D zones: one comprising the tropics, one the subtropics and temperate regions, and the last the circumpolar regions north and south of about 45 degrees latitude. In the first, the dosage of UVB throughout the year is high enough that humans have ample opportunity to synthesize vitamin D all year. In the second, at least one month during the year has insufficient UVB radiation, and in the third area not enough UVB arrives on average during the entire year to prompt vitamin D synthesis. This distribution could explain why indigenous peoples in the tropics generally have dark skin, whereas people in the subtropics and temperate regions are lighter-skinned but have the ability to tan, and those who live in regions near the poles tend to be very light skinned and burn easily.

One of the most interesting aspects of this investigation was the examination of groups that did not precisely fit the predicted skin-color pattern. An example is the Inuit people of Alaska and northern Canada. The Inuit exhibit skin color that is somewhat darker than would be predicted given the UV levels at their latitude. This is probably caused by two factors. The first is that they are relatively recent inhabitants of these climes, having migrated to North America only roughly 5,000 years ago. The second is that the traditional diet of the Inuit is extremely high in foods containing vitamin D, especially fish and marine mammals. This vitamin D-rich diet offsets the problem that they would otherwise have with vitamin D synthesis in their skin at northern latitudes and permits them to remain more darkly pigmented.

Our analysis of the potential to synthesize vitamin D allowed us to understand another trait related to human skin color: women in all populations are generally lighter-skinned than men. (Our data show that women tend to be between 3 and 4 percent lighter than men.) Scientists have often speculated on the reasons, and most have argued that the phenomenon stems from sexual selection—the preference of men for women of lighter color. We contend that although this is probably part of the story, it is not the original reason for the sexual difference. Females have significantly greater needs for calcium throughout their reproductive lives, especially during pregnancy and lactation, and must be able to make the most of the calcium contained in food. We propose, therefore, that women tend to be lighter-skinned than men to allow slightly more UVB rays to penetrate their skin and thereby increase their ability to produce vitamin D. In areas of the world that receive a large amount of UV radiation, women are indeed at the knife's edge of natural selection, needing to maximize the photoprotective function of their skin on the one hand and the ability to synthesize vitamin D on the other.

Where Culture and Biology Meet

As modern humans moved throughout the Old World about 100,000 years ago, their skin adapted to the environmental conditions that prevailed in different regions. The skin color of the indigenous people of Africa has had the longest time to adapt because anatomically modern humans first evolved there. The skin-color changes that modern humans underwent as they moved from one continent to another—first Asia, then Austro-Melanesia, then Europe and, finally, the Americas—can be reconstructed to some extent. It is important to remember, however, that those humans had clothing and shelter to help protect them from the elements. In some places, they also had the ability to harvest foods that were extraordinarily rich in vitamin D, as in the case of the Inuit. These two factors had profound effects on the tempo and degree of skin-color evolution in human populations.

Africa is an environmentally heterogeneous continent. A number of the earliest movements of contemporary humans outside equatorial Africa were into southern Africa. The descendants of some of these early colonizers, the Khoisan (previously known as Hottentots), are still found in southern Africa and have significantly lighter skin than indigenous equatorial Africans do—a clear adaptation to the lower levels of UV radiation that prevail at the southern extremity of the continent.

Interestingly, however, human skin color in southern Africa is not uniform. Populations of Bantu-language speakers who live in southern Africa today are far darker than the Khoisan. We know from the history of this region that Bantu speakers migrated into this region recently—probably within the past 1,000 years—from parts of West Africa near the equator. The skin-color difference between the Khoisan and Bantu speakers such as the Zulu indicates that the length of time that a group has inhabited a particular region is important in understanding why they have the color they do.

Cultural behaviors have probably also strongly influenced the evolution of skin color in recent human history. This effect can be seen in the indigenous peoples who live on the eastern and western banks of the Red Sea. The tribes on the western side, which speak so-called Nilo-Hamitic languages, are thought to have inhabited this region for as long as 6,000 years. These individuals are distinguished by very darkly pigmented skin and long, thin bodies with long limbs, which are excellent biological adaptations for dissipating heat and intense UV radiation. In contrast, modern agricultural and pastoral groups on the eastern bank of the Red Sea, on the Arabian Peninsula, have lived there for only about 2,000 years. These earliest Arab people, of European origin, have adapted to very similar environmental conditions by almost exclusively cultural means—wearing heavy protective clothing and devising portable shade in the form of tents. (Without such clothing, one would have expected their skin to have begun to darken.) Generally speaking, the more recently a group has migrated into an area, the more extensive its cultural, as opposed to biological, adaptations to the area will be.

Perils of Recent Migrations

Despite great improvements in overall human health in the past century, some diseases have appeared or reemerged in populations that had previously been little affected by them. One of these is skin cancer, especially basal and squamous cell carcinomas, among light-skinned peoples. Another is rickets, brought about by severe vitamin D deficiency, in dark-skinned peoples. Why are we seeing these conditions?

As people move from an area with one pattern of UV radiation to another region, biological and cultural adaptations have not been able to keep pace. The light-skinned people of northern European origin who bask in the sun of Florida or northern Australia increasingly pay the price in the form of premature aging of the skin and skin cancers, not to mention the unknown cost in human life of folate depletion. Conversely, a number of dark-skinned people of southern Asian and African origin now living in the northern U.K., northern Europe or the northeastern U.S. suffer from a lack of UV radiation and vitamin D, an insidious problem that manifests itself in high rates of rickets and other diseases related to vitamin D deficiency.

The ability of skin color to adapt over long periods to the various environments to which humans have moved reflects the importance of skin color to our survival. But its unstable nature also makes it one of the least useful characteristics in determining the evolutionary relations between human groups. Early Western scientists used skin color improperly to delineate human races, but the beauty of science is that it can and does correct itself. Our current knowledge of the evolution of human skin indicates that variations in skin color, like most of our physical attributes, can be explained by adaptation to the environment through natural selection. We look ahead to the day when the vestiges of old scientific mistakes will be erased and replaced by a better understanding of human origins and diversity. Our variation in skin color should be celebrated as one of the most visible manifestations of our evolution as a species.

More to Explore

The Evolution of Human Skin Coloration. Nina G. Jablonski and George Chaplin in *Journal of Human Evolution,* vol. 39, no. 1, pages 57–106; July 1, 2000. An abstract of the article is available online at www.idealibrary.com/links/doi/10.1006/jhev.2000.0403.

Why Skin Comes in Colors. Blake Edgar in *California Wild,* vol. 53, no. 1, pages 6–7; Winter 2000. The article is also available at www.calacademy.org/calwild/winter2000/html/horizons.html.

The Biology of Skin Color: Black and White. Gina Kirchweger in *Discover,* vol. 22, no. 2, pages 32–33; February 2001. The article is also available at www.discover.com/feb_01/featbiology.html.

Critical Thinking

1. Why did our ancestors lose most of their body hair? What was the resulting challenge?

2. What is the function of melanin?

3. What is the relationship between light skin, exposure to the sun, and skin cancer? Why is this insufficient to explain darker skin colors?

4. Discuss the evidence that relates skin color to folate deficiency.

5. How do the authors describe the earliest member of *Homo sapiens,* or modern humans in this context? Why would skin color become lighter as people moved out of the tropics? How is vitamin D production important to health?

6. Discuss the three vitamin D zones on the earth's surface and how they help to explain skin color variations.

7. Why don't the Inuit precisely fit the predicted skin color pattern?

8. Why do women tend to be lighter skinned than men?

9. What two factors have had profound effects on the tempo and degree of skin color evolution in human populations? Give some examples.

10. Discuss the "perils of recent migrations" and the examples cited.

11. Why is skin color unreliable as a means to delineate human races?

12. Why should we celebrate our variation in skin color?

Nina G. Jablonski and **George Chaplin** work at the California Academy of Sciences in San Francisco, where Jablonski is Irvine Chair and curator of anthropology and Chaplin is a research associate in the department of anthropology. Jablonski's research centers on the evolutionary adaptations of monkeys, apes and humans. She is particularly interested in how primates have responded to changes over time in the global environment. Chaplin is a private geographic information systems consultant who specializes in describing and analyzing geographic trends in biodiversity. In 2001 he was awarded the Student of the Year prize by the Association of Geographic Information in London for his master's thesis on the environmental correlates of skin color.

How Real Is Race?

Using Anthropology to Make Sense of Human Diversity

Race is not a scientifically valid biological category, and yet it remains important as a socially constructed category. Once educators grasp this concept, they can use the suggestions and resources the authors offer here to help their students make sense of race.

Carol Mukhopadhyay and Rosemary C. Henze

Surely we've all heard people say there is only one race—the human race. We've also heard and seen overwhelming evidence that would seem to contradict this view. After all, the U.S. Census divides us into groups based on race, and there are certainly observable physical differences among people—skin color, nose and eye shape, body type, hair color and texture, and so on. In the world of education, the message of racial differences as biological "facts" is reinforced when we are told that we should understand specific learning styles and behavior patterns of black, Asian, Native American, white, and Latino children and when books such as *The Bell Curve* make pseudoscientific claims about race and learning.[1]

How can educators make sense of these conflicting messages about race? And why should they bother? Whether we think of all human beings as one race, or as four or five distinct races, or as hundreds of races, does anything really change? If we accept that the concept of race is fundamentally flawed, does that mean that young African Americans are less likely to be followed by security guards in department stores? Are people going to stop thinking of Asians as the "model" minority? Will racism become a thing of the past?

Many educators understandably would like to have clear information to help them teach students about human biological variability. While multicultural education materials are now widely available, they rarely address basic questions about why we look different from one another and what these biological differences do (and do not) mean. Multicultural education emphasizes respecting differences and finding ways to include all students, especially those who have been historically marginalized. Multicultural education has helped us to understand racism and has provided a rich body of literature on antiracist teaching strategies, and this has been all to the good. But it has not helped us understand the two concepts of race: the biological one and the social one.

In this article, we explain what anthropologists mean when they say that "races don't exist" (in other words, when they reject the concept of race as a scientifically valid biological category) and why they argue instead that "race" is a socially constructed category. We'll also discuss why this is such an important understanding and what it means for educators and students who face the social reality of race and racism every day. And finally, we'll offer some suggestions and resources for teachers who want to include teaching about race in their classes.

Why Race Isn't Biologically Real

For the past several decades, biological anthropologists have been arguing that races don't really exist, or, more precisely, that the concept of race has no validity as a biological category. What exactly does this mean?

First, anthropologists are unraveling a deeply embedded ideology, a long-standing European and American racial world view.[2] Historically, the idea of race emerged in Europe in the 17th and 18th centuries, coinciding with the growth of colonialism and the transatlantic slave trade. Attempts were made to classify humans into "natural," geographically distinct "races," hierarchically ordered by their closeness to God's original forms. Europeans were, not surprisingly, at the top, with the most perfect form represented by a female skull from the Caucasus Mountains, near the purported location of Noah's ark and the origin of humans. Hence the origins of the racial term "Caucasian" or "Caucasoid" for those of European ancestry.[3]

In the late 19th century, anthropologists sought to reconstruct human prehistory and trace the evolution of human cultural institutions. Physical and cultural evolution were seen as moving in tandem; "advances" in human mental capacity were thought to be responsible for human cultural inventions, such as marriage, family, law, and agriculture. If cultural "evolution" was propelled by biological evolution, according to this logic, the more "advanced" cultures must be more biologically and intellectually evolved. Physical indicators of evolutionary rank, such as skull size, were sought in order to classify and rank human groups along an evolutionary path from more "primitive" to more "advanced" races.

Nineteenth-century European scientists disagreed on when the "races" began. Theologians had long argued that there was "one human origin," Adam and Eve, and that certain races subsequently "degenerated" (predictably, the non-Europeans). Some evolutionary scientists, however, began to argue for multiple origins, with distinct races evolving in different places and times. By the beginning of the 20th century, European and American science viewed races as natural, long-standing divisions of the human species, evolving at different rates biologically and hence culturally. By such logic was racial inequality naturalized and legitimized.

When contemporary scientists, including anthropologists, assert that races are not scientifically valid, they are rejecting at least three fundamental premises of this old racial ideology: 1) the archaic subspecies concept, 2) the divisibility of contemporary humans into scientifically valid biological groupings, and 3) the link between racial traits and social, cultural, and political status.

1. *There were no distinct, archaic human subspecies.* The first premise anthropologists reject is that humans were originally divided, by nature or God, into a small set of biologically distinct, fixed species, subspecies, or races. Anthropologists now know conclusively, from fossil and DNA evidence, that contemporary humans are one variable species, with our roots in Africa, which moved out of Africa into a wide range of environments around the world, producing hundreds, perhaps thousands, of culturally and genetically distinct populations. Local populations, through natural selection as well as random genetic mutation, acquired some distinctive genetic traits, such as shovel-shaped incisor teeth, hairy ears, or red hair. Adaptation to human cultural inventions—such as agriculture, which creates concentrations of water that allow malaria-carrying mosquitoes to breed—also produced higher frequencies of sickle-cell genes (related to malaria resistance) in human populations in some parts of Africa, India, Arabia, and the Mediterranean.[4] At the same time, continuous migration and intermating between local populations prevented us from branching off into distinct subspecies or species and instead created a richer and more variable gene pool, producing new combinations and permutations of the human genome.

Human prehistory and history, then, are a continuing story of fusion and fission, of a myriad of populations, emerging and shifting over time and space, sometimes isolated temporarily, then fusing and producing new formations. There have been thousands and thousands of groups throughout human history, marrying in and, more often, out; they have disappeared and reemerged in new forms over time.

In short, there are no "basic" or "ancient" races; there are no stable, "natural," permanent, or even long-standing groupings called races. There have never have been any "pure" races. All human populations are historically specific mixtures of the human gene pool. This is human evolution, and we see these same processes at work in the 19th and 20th centuries and today. "Races" are ephemeral—here today, gone tomorrow.

2. *Contemporary humans are not divisible into biological races.* When anthropologists say races aren't biologically real, they also reject the idea that *modern* humans can be divided into scientifically valid, biologically distinct groupings or races. For races to be real as biological categories, the classification must be based on objective, consistent, and reliable biological criteria. The classification system must also have predictive value that will make it useful in research.

Scientists have demonstrated that both the concept of race and racial criteria are subjective, arbitrary, and inconsistently applied.[5] U.S. racial categories, such as the ones used in the Census, aren't valid in part because the biological attributes used to define races and create racial classifications rely on only a few visible, superficial, genetic traits—such as skin color and hair texture—and ignore the remaining preponderance of human variation. Alternative, equally visible racial classifications could be constructed using such criteria as hair color, eye color, height, weight, ear shape, or hairiness. However, there are less visible genetic traits that have far greater biological significance. For example, there are at least 13 genetic factors related to hemoglobin, the protein that helps carry oxygen to tissues, and there is also significant variation in the ABO, RH, and other blood systems. We could create racial classifications based on genetic factors that affect susceptibility to diabetes or to certain kinds of breast cancer or to the ability to digest milk. In sum, given the variety of possible biologically based traits for classifying human beings, the criteria used in U.S. racial categorizations are highly arbitrary and subjective. Our discussion here focuses on the U.S. concept of race. While racial concepts are no doubt similar in Canada and Europe, this is not true in other parts of the Americas.[6]

The number of potential biologically based racial groupings is enormous. Not only are there millions of genetic traits, but most genetic traits—even culturally salient but superficial traits such as skin color, hair texture, eye shape, and eye color—do not cluster together. Darker skin can cluster with straight hair as well as with very curly hair or with hairy or nonhairy bodies; paler skin can cluster with straight or curly hair or with black or blond hair or with lighter to darker eyes. Each trait could produce a different racial classification. For example, if one used height as a criterion rather than skin pigmentation, then the Northern Afghan population would be in the same racial category as the Swedes and the Tutsi of Rwanda. There are huge numbers of genetically influenced traits, visible and nonvisible, which could be used to classify humans into biologically distinct groups. There is no "natural" classification—no co-occurring clusters of racial traits. There are just alternatives, with different implications and uses.

Racial classifications are also unscientific because they are unreliable and unstable over time. Individuals cannot reliably be "raced," partly because the criteria are so subjective and unscientific. Robert Hahn, a medical anthropologist, found that 37% of babies described as Native American on their birth certificates ended up in a different racial category on their death certificates.[7] Racial identifications by forensic anthropologists, long touted as accurate, have been shown to be disturbingly unreliable, even in relatively ethnically homogeneous areas, such as Missouri and Ohio.[8] Forensic evidence from such urban areas as San Jose, California, or New York City is even more problematic.

Racial categories used by the U.S. Census Bureau have changed over time. In 1900, races included "mulatto, quadroon, or octoroon" in addition to "black." Southern Europeans and Jews were deemed to be separate races before World War II. Asian Indians ("Hindus") were initially categorized as "Caucasoid"—except for voting rights. The number and definitions of races in the most recent U.S. Census reflect the instability—and hence unreliability—of the concept of race. And U.S. racial classifications simply don't work in much of the rest of the world. Brazil is a classic, often-studied example, but they also don't work in South Asia, an area that includes over one-fifth of the world's population.

Historical and contemporary European and American racial categories are huge, biologically diverse macro-categories. Members of the same racial group tend to be similar in a few genetic ways that are often biologically irrelevant. Moreover, the genetic variability found within each racial grouping is far greater than the genetic similarity. Africa, by itself, is home to distinct populations whose average height ranges from less than five feet (the Mbuti) to over six feet (the Tutsi). Estimates suggest that contemporary racial variation accounts for less than 7% of all human genetic variation.[9] U.S. races, then, are not biologically distinct or biologically meaningful, scientifically based groupings of the human species.

3. *Race as biology has no scientific value.* An additional critique of the concept of race is that racial categories, as defined biologically, are not very useful in understanding other phenomena, whether biological or cultural.

There is no substantial evidence that race, as a biological category, and "racial" characteristics, such as skin color, hair texture, and eye shape, are causally linked to behavior, to capacities, to individual and group accomplishments, to cultural institutions, or to propensities to engage in any specific activities. In the area of academic achievement, the focus on race as biology can lead researchers to ignore underlying nonbiological causal factors. One classic study found that controlling for socioeconomic and other environmental variables eliminated purported "racial" differences in I.Q. scores and academic achievement between African American, Mexican American, and European American students.[10]

Health professionals have also critiqued the concept of race. Alan Goodman and others have shown that race does not help physicians with diagnosis, prevention, or treatment of medical diseases.[11] Racial categories and a false ideology of race as "biology" encourage both doctors and their patients to view medical conditions as necessarily genetic, ignoring possible environmental sources. Hypertension, infant birthweights, osteoporosis, ovarian cysts—all traditionally viewed as "racial"

(i.e., genetically based)—now seem to reflect environmental rather than racially linked genetic factors. The Centers for Disease Control concluded in 1993 that most associations between race and disease have no genetic or biological basis and that the concept of "race" is therefore not useful in public health.

As a result of recent evolution and constant interbreeding between groups of humans, two individuals from different "races" are just as likely to be more similar to one another genetically than two individuals from the same "race." This being so, race-as-biology has no predictive value.

If Not Race, Then What?

Classifications are usually created for some purpose. Alan Goodman and other biological anthropologists suggest that investigators focus on using traits relevant to the problem at hand. For example, if a particular blood factor puts an individual at risk for a disease, then classify individuals on that basis for that purpose.

Some suggest using the term "population" or "breeding population" to refer to the multitude of small, often geographically localized, groups that have developed high frequencies of one or more somewhat distinctive biological traits (e.g., shovel-shaped incisors) in response to biological, historical, and cultural factors. But others point out that there could be thousands of such groups, depending on the classifying criteria used, and that the groups would be merging and recombining over time and space. Moreover, the variability "captured" would reflect only a fraction of the variability in the human species.

Most anthropologists now use the concept of "clines" to help understand how genetic traits are distributed.[12] New data indicate that biological traits, such as blood type or skin color, are distributed in geographic gradations or "clines"; that is, the frequency of a trait varies continuously over a geographic area. For example, the genes for type B blood increase in frequency in an east-to-west direction (reflecting, in part, the travels of Genghis Khan and his army). In contrast, skin pigmentation grades from north to south, with increasing pigmentation as one gets closer to the equator. The frequency of the gene for sickle cell decreases from West Africa moving northeast.

Virtually all traits have distinct geographic distributions. Genes controlling skin color, body size and shape (head, limbs, lips, fingers, nose, ears), hairiness, and blood type are each distributed in different patterns over geographic space. Once again, for biological races to exist, these traits would have to co-vary, but they don't. Instead, biological traits produce a nearly infinite number of potential races. This is why anthropologists conclude that there are no scientifically distinguishable biological races—only thousands of clines!

So What Is Race Then?

We hope we have made the point that the concept of separate, biologically distinct human races is not scientifically defensible. Unfortunately, racial ideology, by focusing on a few physical attributes, traps us into a discourse about race as biology rather than race as a cultural construction. The concept of race is a cultural invention, a culturally and historically specific way of thinking about, categorizing, and treating human beings.[13] It is about social divisions within society, about social categories and identities, about power and privilege. It has been and remains a particular type of ideology for legitimizing social inequality between groups with different ancestries, national origins, and histories. Indeed, the concept of race is also a major system of social identity, affecting one's own self-perception and how one is perceived and treated by others.

But race does have a biological component, one that can trick us into thinking that races are scientifically valid, biological subdivisions of the human species. As noted earlier, geographically localized populations—as a result of adaptation, migration, and chance—tend to have some characteristic physical traits. While these may be traits that characterize an entire population, such as hairy ears, it is more accurate to talk about the relative frequency of a particular trait, such as blood type O, in one population as compared to another, or the relative amount of pigmentation of individuals in a population, relative to other populations. Some traits, such as skin color, reflect climatic conditions; others, such as eye color and shape, probably reflect random, historical processes and migration patterns. The U.S. was peopled by populations from geographically distinct regions of the world—voluntary immigrants, forced African slaves, and indigenous American groups. Therefore, dominant northwestern European ethnic groups, such as the English and Germans, were able to exploit certain visually salient biological traits, especially skin color, as markers of race.

The effectiveness of these physical traits as markers of one's race depended, of course, on their being preserved in future generations. So dominant cultural groups created elaborate social and physical barriers to mating, reproduction, and marriage that crossed racial lines. The most explicit were the so-called anti-miscegenation laws, which outlawed sex between members of different races, whether married or not. These laws were not declared unconstitutional by the U.S. Supreme Court until the 1967 case of *Loving v. Virginia*.[14] Another vehicle was the cultural definition of kinship, whereby children of interracial (often forced) matings acquired the racial status of their lower-ranking parent; this was the so-called one-drop rule or hypodescent. Especially during the time of slavery, the lower-ranking parent was generally the mother, and thus the long-standing European cultural tradition of affiliating socially "legitimate" children with the father's kinship group was effectively reversed.

In contrast, there have been fewer social or legal barriers in the U.S. to mating and marriage between Italians, British, Germans, Swedes, and others of European ancestry. Consequently, the physical and cultural characteristics of European regional populations are less evident in the U.S. With intermarriage, distinct European identities were submerged in the culturally relevant macroracial category of "white"—more accurately, European American.

Thus even the biological dimension of contemporary racial groupings is the result of sociocultural processes. That is, humans as cultural beings first gave social significance to some physical differences between groups and then tried to perpetuate these "racial markers" by preventing social and physical intercourse between members of the groups. Although the dominant racial ideology was about maintaining racial "purity," the issue was not about biology; it was about maintaining social, political, and economic privilege.[15]

Why Is This Understanding Important for Educators?

We hope we've convinced you that race isn't biologically "real" and that race in the U.S. and elsewhere is a historical, social, and cultural creation. But so what? What is the significance of this way of viewing race for teachers, students, and society?

1. *The potential for change.* First, it is important to understand that, while races are biological fictions, they are social realities. Race may not be "real" in a biological sense, but it surely is "real" socially, politically, economically, and psychologically. Race and racism profoundly structure who we are, how we are treated, how we treat others, and our access to resources and rights.

Perhaps the most important message educators can take from the foregoing discussion is that race, racial classifications, racial stratification, and other forms of racism, including racial ideology, rather than being part of our biology, are part of our culture. Like other cultural forms, both the concept of race and our racial classifications are part of a system we have created. This means that we have the ability to change the system, to transform it, and even to totally eradicate it. Educators, in their role as transmitters of official culture, are particularly well poised to be active change agents in such a transformation.

But how, you may well ask, can teachers or anybody else make people stop classifying by race? And are there any good reasons to do so? These familiar categories—black, white, Asian, Native American, and so on—seem so embedded in U.S. society. They seem so "natural." Of course, that's how culture works. It seems "natural" to think of chicken, but not rats, as food. But, as we have shown above, the labels and underlying constructs that we use to talk about human diversity are unstable, depending on particular social, political, and historical contexts. Individuals in positions of authority, of course, have the ability to change them institutionally. But ordinary people also have the ability to change how they classify and label people in their everyday lives.

Several questions arise at this point. Do we as educators consciously want to change our way of conceptualizing and discussing human biological variation? What makes the "race as biology" assumption so dangerous? Are we going to continue to classify people by race, even while recognizing that it is a social construct? What vested interests do people have in holding onto—or rejecting—racial categories? How can we become more sophisticated in our understanding of how systems of classification work while also becoming more critical of our own ways of classifying people? Are there alternative ways of thinking about, classifying, and labeling human beings that might be more empowering for students, teachers, and community members? By eliminating or changing labels, will we change the power structures that perpetuate privilege and entitlement? Moving beyond race as biology forces us to confront these and other issues.

2. *The dangers of using racial classifications.* Categories and classifications are not intrinsically good or bad. People have always grouped others in ways that were important within a given society. However, the myth of race as biology is dangerous because it conflates physical attributes, such as skin color, with unrelated qualities, such as intelligence. Racial labels delude people into thinking that race predicts such other outcomes and behaviors as achievement in sports, music, or school; rates of employment; pregnancies outside marriage; or drug use. Race was historically equated with intelligence and, on that basis, was used to justify slavery and educational discrimination; it later provided the rationale that supported the genocide of Jews, blacks, Gypsies, and other "inferior" races under Hitler. So using racial categories brings along this history, like unwanted baggage.

Macroracial categories are dangerous in that the categories oversimplify and mask complex human differences. Saying that someone is Asian tells us virtually nothing concrete, but it brings with it a host of stereotypes, such as "model minority," "quiet," "good at math," "inscrutable," and so on. Yet the Asian label includes a wide range of groups, such as Koreans, Filipinos, and Vietnamese, with distinct histories and languages. The same is true for "white," a term that homogenizes the multiple nationalities, languages, and cultures that constitute Europe. The label "African American" ignores the enormous linguistic, physical, and cultural diversity of the peoples of Africa. The term "black" conflates people of African descent who were brought to the U.S. as slaves with recent immigrants from Africa and the Caribbean. These macroracial labels oversimplify and reduce human diversity to four or five giant groups. Apart from being bad science, these categories don't predict anything helpful—yet they have acquired a life of their own.

Macroracial categories, such as those used in the U.S. Census and other institutional data-collection efforts, force people to use labels that may not represent their own self-identity or classifying system. They must either select an existing category or select "other"—by definition, a kind of nonidentity. The impossibility, until recently, of selecting more than one ethnic/racial category implicitly stigmatizes multiracial individuals. And the term "mixed" wrongly implies that there are such things as "pure" races, an ideology with no basis in science. The recent expansion of the number of U.S. Census categories still cannot accommodate the diversity of the U.S. population, which includes people whose ancestry ranges from Egypt, Brazil, Sri Lanka, Ghana, and the Dominican Republic to Iceland and Korea.

3. *How macroracial categories have served people in positive ways.* Having noted some negative aspects, it is equally important to discuss how macroracial categories also serve society. Recall that labels are not intrinsically "good" or "bad." It depends on what people do with them. During the 1960s, the U.S. civil rights movement helped bring about consciousness and pride in being African American. This consciousness— known by terms such as ethnic pride and black power—united people who had been the victims of racism and oppression. From that consciousness sprang such educational interventions as black and Chicano history classes, ethnic studies departments, Afrocentric schools, and other efforts to empower young people. The movement to engender pride in and knowledge of one's ancestry has had a powerful impact. Many individuals are deeply attached to these racial labels as part of a positive identity. As one community activist put it, "Why should I give up being a race? I like being a race."

Racial classification can also have positive impact by allowing educators to monitor how equitably our institutions are serving the public. Racial categories are used by schools to disaggregate data on student outcomes, including achievement, attendance, discipline, course placements, college attendance rates, and other areas of school and student performance. These data are then used to examine whether certain groups of students are disproportionately represented in any outcome areas. For example, a school might discover that the percentage of Latino students who receive some type of disciplinary intervention is higher than that for other school populations. The school can then consider what it can do to change this outcome. Teachers might ask, Is there something about the way Latino students are treated in the school that leads to higher disciplinary referral rates? What other factors might be involved?

The racial classifications that educators use to monitor student outcome data reflect our society's social construction of race. As such, the categories represent groups that have been historically disenfranchised, oppressed, or marginalized. Without data disaggregated by race, gender, and other categories, it would be difficult to identify problems stemming from race-based institutional and societal factors that privilege certain groups, such as the widespread U.S. practice of tracking by so-called ability. Without data broken out according to racial, gender, and ethnic categories, schools would not be able to assess the positive impact intervention programs have had on different groups of students.

4. *Shifting the conversation from biology to culture.* One function of the myth of race as biology has been to distract us from the underlying causes of social inequality in the United States. Dismantling the myth of race as biology means that we must now shift our focus to analyzing the social, economic, political, and historical conditions that breed and serve to perpetuate social inequality. For educators, this means helping students to recognize and understand socioeconomic stratification, who benefits and who is harmed by racial discrimination, and how we as individuals and institutional agents can act to dismantle ideologies, institutions, and practices that harm young people.

There is another, more profound implication of the impermanence of race. Culture, acting collectively, and humans, acting individually, can make races disappear. That is, we can mate and marry across populations, thus destroying the racial "markers" that have been used to facilitate categorization and differential treatment of people of different ancestry and social rank. An understanding of human biological variation reveals the positive, indeed essential, role that intermating and intermarriage have played in human evolution and human adaptation. Rather than "mongrelizing" a "pure species," mating between different populations enriches the genetic pool. It is society, rather than nature—and socially and economically stratified societies, for the most part—that restricts social and sexual intercourse and severely penalizes those who mate across racial and other socially created lines.

Suggestions and Resources for Educators

Anthropological knowledge about race informs us about what race is and is not, but it cannot guide educational decision making. The underlying goal of social justice can help educators in making policy decisions, such as whether to use racial and ethnic categories to monitor educational outcomes. As long as we continue to see racially based disparities in young peoples' school achievement, then we must monitor and investigate the social conditions that produce these disparities. We must be careful, however, to avoid "biologizing" the classification; that is, we must avoid assuming genetic explanations for racial differences in behaviors and educational outcomes or even diseases.

As we pursue a more socially just world, educators should also continue to support young people's quest for knowledge about the history and struggles of their own people, as well as those of other groups, so that students in the future will not be able to point to their textbooks and say, "My people are not included in the curriculum." In the process, we can encourage both curiosity about and respect for human diversity, and we can emphasize the importance that historical and social context plays in creating social inequality. We can also encourage comparative studies of racial and other forms of social stratification, further challenging the notion that there is a biological explanation for oppression and inequality. In short, students will understand that there is no biological explanation for a group's historical position as either oppressed—or oppressor. We can encourage these studies to point out variations and fine distinctions within human racial groupings.

In addition to viewing the treatment of race and racial categories through a social-justice lens, we would apply another criterion that we call "depth of knowledge." We believe that it is important to challenge and inspire young people by exposing them to the best of our current knowledge in the sciences, social sciences, and other disciplines. Until now, most students in our education system have not been exposed to systematic, scientifically based teaching about race and human biological variation. One reason is that many social studies teachers may think they lack sufficient background in genetics and human biology. At the same time, many biology teachers may feel uncomfortable teaching about race as a social construct. The null move for teachers seems to be to say that we should all be "color blind." However, this does not help educate students about human diversity, both biological and social. In rare cases when students have the opportunity to engage in studies of race, ethnicity, culture, and ways to end racism, they are both interested and intellectually challenged.[16] One high school teacher who teaches students about race said he wants to dispel the notion

that teaching about diversity is "touchy feely." "We don't just want to touch diversity; we want to approach it academically. . . . We feel we have a definite discipline."[17]

Rather than shield students and ourselves from current scientific knowledge about race, including its contradictions and controversies, we submit that educators should be providing opportunities for students to learn what anthropologists, geneticists, and other scientists, including social scientists, have to say about human biological variation and the issue of race. Particularly in middle schools, high schools, and beyond, students should be involved in inquiry projects and social action projects, in critical examination of the labels we currently use, and in analysis of the reasons for and against using them in particular contexts. Rather than tell students that they should or should not use racial labels (except for slurs), educators should be creating projects in which students explore together the range of possible ways of classifying people and the implications and political significance of alternative approaches in different contexts.

We would like to conclude by offering readers some ideas for student inquiry and by suggesting some resources that can serve to get teachers in all subject areas started on the quest to learn about human biological variation and ways to teach about it.

1. *Ideas for student inquiry.* Here are some examples of how teachers might engage students in critically examining the social, historical, and cultural construction of racial categories.

- Have students create and employ alternative "racial" classification schemes using as many observable and nonobservable physical differences as they can think of (e.g., foot size, height, ear shape, eyebrow shape, waist/shoulder ratio, hairiness). What do the groups look like? What does this tell us about macroracial classifications based on skin pigmentation and other surface features?

- Show students U.S. Census forms from 1870, 1950, and 2000, and ask them to place themselves in the most appropriate category.[18] Or show a photograph of a person of multiple ethnic ancestry and ask students to place this person in one of the categories from these three censuses. Ask them why they think the census form has changed over time and what that says about the meaning of "race."

- Ask immigrant students to investigate the racial/ethnic categories used in their country of origin and to reflect on how well they mesh with the U.S. categories. For example, have students from Mexico taken on an identity as Latino or Hispanic? And what does it mean for them to become part of a larger "macro" race in the U.S.?[19]

- Ask students how they feel when someone asks them to "represent their race." For example, how do students who identify themselves as African Americans feel when someone asks, "How do African Americans feel about this issue?" or "What's the African American perspective on this?"

- Discuss "reverse discrimination." When did this term come into use and why? Who is being discriminated against when discrimination is reversed?

- Discuss "political correctness." Where did this term come from? Who uses it and for what purposes? And why did it emerge?

2. *Resources for teachers.* The following examples will give readers a place to start in compiling resources available for teaching about race.

- Two major anthropological associations have produced highly readable position statements on the topic of race and human biological variation. First, the American Anthropological Association website features both the AAA position and a summary of testimony given in conjunction with the debates on the 2000 census categories. Second, the official statement of the American Association of Physical Anthropologists has appeared in that organization's journal.[20]

- The American Anthropological Association is making a special effort to disseminate understandings about race and human variation to the broader public. *AnthroNotes,* designed for precollege teachers, is a superb resource that offers concrete approaches to teaching about race, human diversity, and human evolution. It is available at no charge from the Anthropology Outreach Office (anthroutreach@nmnh.si.edu). Several past issues of *AnthroNotes* treat race and ethnicity.[21] Anthropologists have produced materials for precollege teachers and teacher educators that deal with cultural diversity; some include strategies for teaching about culture and human diversity.[22] Others provide useful overviews of relevant topics.[23]

- The AAA is currently engaged in a public education initiative called Understanding Race and Human Variation, which will involve a traveling museum exhibit and a website. The Ford Foundation has contributed one million dollars to this project.

- In 1999, the AAA created a special commission called the Anthropology Education Commission (AEC) to "help achieve significant progress towards the integration of anthropological concepts, methods, and issues into pre-K through community college and adult education as a means of increasing public understanding of anthropology." The two teaching modules by Leonard Lieberman and by Lieberman and Patricia Rice, which we cited above, are available at no charge on the AEC website (www.aaanet.org/committees/commissions/aec). The AEC webpage contains extensive resources that teachers can use to teach anthropological concepts and methods, including some that address race.

Anthropologists recognize an obligation to disseminate their knowledge of human biological variation and the social construction of race to the wider public. We hope that this article and the resources we have provided will contribute to this effort.

Notes

1. Richard Herrnstein and Charles Murray, *The Bell Curve: Intelligence and Class Structure in American Life* (New York: Free Press, 1994).

2. Audrey Smedley, *Race in North America: Origin and Evolution of a Worldview* (Boulder, Colo.: Westview Press, 1998).

3. Jonathan Marks, *Human Biodiversity: Genes, Race, and History* (New York: Aldine de Gruyter, 1995).

4. Leonard Lieberman and Patricia Rice, "Races or Clines?," p. 7, available on the Anthropology Education Commission page of the American Anthropological Association website, www.aaanet.org/committees/commissions/aec—click on Teaching About Race.

5. George J. Armelagos and Alan H. Goodman, "Race, Racism, and Anthropology," in Alan H. Goodman and Thomas L. Leatherman, eds., *Building a New Biocultural Synthesis: Political-Economic Perspectives on Human Biology* (Ann Arbor: University of Michigan Press, 1998).

6. Jeffrey M. Fish, "Mixed Blood," in James Spradley and William McCurdy, eds., *Conformity and Conflict,* 11th ed. (New York: Allyn & Bacon, 2002), pp. 270–80.

7. Alan Goodman, "Bred in the Bone?," *Sciences,* vol. 37, no. 2, 1997, p. 24.

8. Ibid., p. 22.

9. Leonard Lieberman, "'Race' 1997 and 2001: A Race Odyssey," available on the Anthropology Education Commission page of the American Anthropological Association website, www.aaanet.org/committees/commissions/aec—click on Teaching About Race.

10. Jane Mercer, "Ethnic Differences in IQ Scores: What Do They Mean? (A Response to Lloyd Dunn)," *Hispanic Journal of Behavioral Sciences,* vol. 10, 1988, pp. 199–218.

11. Goodman, op. cit.

12. Lieberman and Rice, op. cit.

13. Carol Mukhopadhyay and Yolanda Moses, "Reestablishing 'Race' in Anthropological Discourse," *American Anthropologist,* vol. 99, 1997, pp. 517–33.

14. Janet Hyde and John DeLamater, *Understanding Human Sexuality,* 6th ed. (New York: McGraw-Hill, 1997).

15. Smedley, op. cit.

16. Karen Donaldson, *Through Students' Eyes: Combating Racism in United States Schools* (Westport, Conn.: Praeger, 1996); and Rosemary C. Henze, "Curricular Approaches to Developing Positive Interethnic Relations," *Journal of Negro Education,* vol. 68, 2001, pp. 529–49.

17. Henze, p. 539.

18. American Anthropological Association. (2002). Front End Evaluation of *Understanding Race and Human Variability.* Arlington, VA: American Anthropological Association.

19. Clara Rodriguez, *Changing Race: Latinos, the Census, and the History of Ethnicity in the United States* (New York: New York University Press, 2000); and Gilberto Arriaza, "The School Yard as a Stage: Missing Culture Clues in Symbolic Fighting," *Multicultural Education Journal,* Spring 2003, in press.

20. American Anthropological Association, "AAA Statement on Race," www.aaanet.org/stmts/racepp.htm; and American Association of Physical Anthropologists, "AAPA Statement on Biological Aspects of Race," *American Journal of Physical Anthropology,* vol. 101, 1996, pp. 569–70.

21. Alison S. Brooks et al., "Race and Ethnicity in America," in Ruth O. Selig and Marilyn R. London, eds., *Anthropology Explored: The Best of Smithsonian AnthroNotes* (Washington, D.C.: Smithsonian Institution Press), pp. 315–26; E. L. Cerrini-Long, "Ethnicity in the U.S.A.: An Anthropological Model," *AnthroNotes,* vol. 15, no. 3, 1993; William L. Merrill, "Identity Transformation in Colonial Northern Mexico," *AnthroNotes,* vol. 19, no. 2, 1997, pp. 1–8; and Boyce Rensberger, "Forget the Old Labels: Here's a New Way to Look at Race," *AnthroNotes,* vol. 18, no. 1, 1996, pp. 1–7.

22. Hilda Hernandez and Carol C. Mukhopadhyay, *Integrating Multicultural Perspectives in Teacher Education: A Curriculum Resource Guide* (Chico: California State University, 1985); and Conrad P. Kottak, R. Furlow White, and Patricia Rice, eds. *The Teaching of Anthropology: Problems, Issues, and Decisions* (Mountain View, Calif.: Mayfield Publishing, 1996).

23. Faye Harrison, "The Persistent Power of 'Race' in the Cultural and Political Economy of Racism," *Annual Review of Anthropology,* vol. 24, 1995, pp. 47–74; and Ida Susser and Thomas Patterson, eds., *Cultural Diversity in the United States: A Critical Reader* (Malden, Mass.: Blackwell, 2001).

Critical Thinking

1. What physical characteristics do the authors list as being the basis for racial divisions?

2. What is the historical origin of the concept of race?

3. On what three bases do contemporary scientists criticize the traditional race concept? Explain each.

4. What are some of the "less visible genetic traits that have far greater biological significance"? How would racial classifications based on these look?

5. How have racial classifications used by the U.S. Census Bureau changed over time?

6. What does it mean to say that the genetic variation within each racial grouping is greater than the genetic similarity?

7. What evidence exists that race or racial characteristics are causally linked to behavior? What about the relationship between race and health? What were some of the traditional "racial" health problems? How are they now viewed?

8. What terms have anthropologists sought to replace "race" with? What is the meaning of each of these terms? Which term do the authors seem to prefer?

9. Why was the United States, in particular, a place where racial ideas found fertile ground? What are anti-miscegenation laws? What is "hypodescent" or the "one-drop rule"?

10. What do you think about the prospects for change? What has your experience of race been in your own educational background?

11. What are some of the dangers of racial classifications listed by the authors? What are some of the problems they mention with the terms "Asian," "African American," and "black"?

12. What are some of the positive ways "macroracial categories have served people"?

13. What is the point (as they advise) of "shifting the conversation from biology to culture"?

14. What do you think of the suggestions they make ("ideas for student inquiry") for teaching about the notion of race?

CAROL MUKHOPADHYAY is a professor in the Department of Anthropology, San Josè State University, San Josè, Calif., where **ROSEMARY C. HENZE** is an associate professor in the Department of Linguistics and Language Development. They wish to thank Gilberto Arriaza, Paul Erickson, Alan Goodman, and Yolanda Moses for their comments on this article.

The Tall and the Short of It

BARRY BOGIN

Baffled by your future prospects? As a biological anthropologist, I have just one word of advice for you: plasticity. *Plasticity* refers to the ability of many organisms, including humans, to alter themselves—their behavior or even their biology—in response to changes in the environment. We tend to think that our bodies get locked into their final form by our genes, but in fact we alter our bodies as the conditions surrounding us shift, particularly as we grow during childhood. Plasticity is as much a product of evolution's fine-tuning as any particular gene, and it makes just as much evolutionary good sense. Rather than being able to adapt to a single environment, we can, thanks to plasticity, change our bodies to cope with a wide range of environments. Combined with the genes we inherit from our parents, plasticity accounts for what we are and what we can become.

Anthropologists began to think about human plasticity around the turn of the century, but the concept was first clearly defined in 1969 by Gabriel Lasker, a biological anthropologist at Wayne State University in Detroit. At that time scientists tended to consider only those adaptations that were built into the genetic makeup of a person and passed on automatically to the next generation. A classic example of this is the ability of adults in some human societies to drink milk. As children, we all produce an enzyme called lactase, which we need to break down the sugar lactose in our mother's milk. In many of us, however, the lactase gene slows down dramatically as we approach adolescence—probably as the result of another gene that regulates its activity. When that regulating gene turns down the production of lactase, we can no longer digest milk.

Lactose intolerance—which causes intestinal gas and diarrhea—affects between 70 and 90 percent of African Americans, Native Americans, Asians, and people who come from around the Mediterranean. But others, such as people of central and western European descent and the Fulani of West Africa, typically have no problem drinking milk as adults. That's because they are descended from societies with long histories of raising goats and cattle. Among these people there was a clear benefit to being able to drink milk, so natural selection gradually changed the regulation of their lactase gene, keeping it functioning throughout life.

That kind of adaptation takes many centuries to become established, but Lasker pointed out that there are two other kinds of adaptation in humans that need far less time to kick in. If people have to face a cold winter with little or no heat, for example, their metabolic rates rise over the course of a few weeks and they produce more body heat. When summer returns, the rates sink again.

Lasker's other mode of adaptation concerned the irreversible, lifelong modification of people as they develop—that is, their plasticity. Because we humans take so many years to grow to adulthood, and because we live in so many different environments, from forests to cities and from deserts to the Arctic, we are among the world's most variable species in our physical form and behavior. Indeed, we are one of the most plastic of all species.

In an age when DNA is king, it's worth considering why Americans are no longer the world's tallest people, and some Guatemalans no longer pygmies.

One of the most obvious manifestations of human malleability is our great range of height, and it is a subject I've made a special study of for the last 25 years. Consider these statistics: in 1850 Americans were the tallest people in the world, with American men averaging 5'6". Almost 150 years later, American men now average 5'8", but we have fallen in the standings and are now only the third tallest people in the world. In first place are the Dutch. Back in 1850 they averaged only 5'4"—the shortest men in Europe—but today they are a towering 5'10". (In these two groups, and just about everywhere else, women average about five inches less than men at all times.)

So what happened? Did all the short Dutch sail over to the United States? Did the Dutch back in Europe get an infusion of "tall genes"? Neither. In both America and the Netherlands life got better, but more so for the Dutch, and height increased as a result. We know this is true thanks in part to studies on how height is determined. It's the product of plasticity in our childhood and in our mothers' childhood as well. If a girl is undernourished and suffers poor health, the growth of her body, including her reproductive system, is usually reduced. With a shortage of raw materials, she can't build more cells to construct a bigger body; at the same time, she has to invest what materials she can get into repairing already existing cells and tissues from the damage caused by disease. Her shorter stature as an adult is the result of a compromise her body makes while growing up.

Such a woman can pass on her short stature to her child, but genes have nothing to do with it for either of them. If she becomes pregnant, her small reproductive system probably won't be able to supply a normal level of nutrients and oxygen to her fetus. This harsh environment reprograms the fetus to grow more slowly than it would if the woman was healthier, so she is more likely to give birth to a smaller baby. Low-birth-weight babies (weighing less than 5.5 pounds) tend to continue their prenatal program of slow growth through childhood. By the time they are teenagers, they are usually significantly shorter than people of normal birth weight. Some particularly striking evidence of this reprogramming comes from studies on monozygotic twins, which develop from a single fertilized egg cell and are therefore identical genetically. But in certain cases, monozygotic twins end up being nourished by unequal portions of the placenta. The twin with the smaller fraction of the placenta is often born with low birth weight, while the other one is normal. Follow-up studies show that this difference between the twins can last throughout their lives.

As such research suggests, we can use the average height of any group of people as a barometer of the health of their society. After the turn of the century both the United States and the Netherlands began to protect the health of their citizens by purifying drinking water, installing sewer systems, regulating the safety of food, and, most important, providing better health care and diets to children. The children responded to their changed environment by growing taller. But the differences in Dutch and American societies determined their differing heights today. The Dutch decided to provide public health benefits to all the public, including the poor. In the United States, meanwhile, improved health is enjoyed most by those who can afford it. The poor often lack adequate housing, sanitation, and health care. The difference in our two societies can be seen at birth: in 1990 only 4 percent of Dutch babies were born at low birth weight, compared with 7 percent in the United States. For white Americans the rate was 5.7 percent, and for black Americans the rate was a whopping 13.3 percent. The disparity between rich and poor in the United States carries through to adulthood: poor Americans are shorter than the better-off by about one inch. Thus, despite great affluence in the United States, our average height has fallen to third place.

People are often surprised when I tell them the Dutch are the tallest people in the world. Aren't they shrimps compared with the famously tall Tutsi (or "Watusi," as you probably first encountered them) of Central Africa? Actually, the supposed great height of the Tutsi is one of the most durable myths from the age of European exploration. Careful investigation reveals that today's Tutsi men average 5'7" and that they have maintained that average for more than 100 years. That means that back in the 1800s, when puny European men first met the Tutsi, the Europeans suffered strained necks from looking up all the time. The two-to-three-inch difference in average height back then could easily have turned into fantastic stories of African giants by European adventurers and writers.

The Tutsi could be as tall or taller than the Dutch if equally good health care and diets were available in Rwanda and Burundi, where the Tutsi live. But poverty rules the lives of most African people, punctuated by warfare, which makes the conditions for growth during childhood even worse. And indeed, it turns out that the Tutsi and other Africans who migrate to Western Europe or North America at young ages end up taller than Africans remaining in Africa.

At the other end of the height spectrum, Pygmies tell a similar story. The shortest people in the world today are the Mbuti, the Efe, and other Pygmy peoples of Central Africa. Their average stature is almost 4'9" for adult men and 4'6" for women. Part of the reason Pygmies are short is indeed genetic: some evidently lack the genes for producing the growth-promoting hormones that course through other people's bodies, while others are genetically incapable of using these hormones to trigger the cascade of reactions that lead to growth. But another important reason for their small size is environmental. Pygmies living as hunter-gatherers in the forests of Central African countries appear to be undernourished, which further limits their growth. Pygmies who live on farms and ranches outside the forest are better fed than their hunter-gatherer relatives and are taller as well. Both genes and nutrition thus account for the size of Pygmies.

Peoples in other parts of the world have also been labeled pygmies, such as some groups in Southeast Asia and the Maya of Guatemala. Well-meaning explorers and scientists have often claimed that they are genetically short, but here we encounter another myth of height. A group of extremely short people in New Guinea, for example, turned out to eat a diet deficient in iodine and other essential nutrients. When they were supplied with cheap mineral and vitamin supplements, their supposedly genetic short stature vanished in their children, who grew to a more normal height.

Another way for these so-called pygmies to stop being pygmies is to immigrate to the United States. In my own research, I study the growth of two groups of Mayan children. One group lives in their homeland of Guatemala, and the other is a group of refugees living in the United States. The Maya in Guatemala live in the village of San Pedro, which has no safe source of drinking water. Most of the water is contaminated with fertilizers and pesticides used on nearby agricultural fields. Until recently, when a deep well was dug, the townspeople depended on an unreliable supply of water from rain-swollen streams. Most homes still lack running water and have only pit toilets. The parents of the Mayan children work mostly at clothing factories and are paid only a few dollars a day.

One way for the so-called pygmies of Guatemala to stop being pygmies is to immigrate to the United States.

I began working with the schoolchildren in this village in 1979, and my research shows that most of them eat only 80 percent of the food they need. Other research shows that almost 30 percent of the girls and 20 percent of the boys are deficient in iodine, that most of the children suffer from intestinal parasites, and that many have persistent ear and eye infections. As a consequence, their health is poor and their height reflects it: they average about three inches shorter than better-fed Guatemalan children.

The Mayan refugees I work with in the United States live in Los Angeles and in the rural agricultural community of Indiantown in central Florida. Although the adults work mostly in minimum-wage jobs, the children in these communities are generally better off than their counterparts in Guatemala. Most Maya arrived in the 1980s as refugees escaping a civil war as well as a political system that threatened them and their children. In the United States they found security and started new lives, and before long their children began growing faster and bigger. My data show that the average increase in height among the first generation of these immigrants was 2.2 inches, which means that these so-called pygmies have undergone one of the largest single-generation increases in height ever recorded. When people such as my own grandparents migrated from the poverty of rural life in Eastern Europe to the cities of the United States just after World War I, the increase in height of the next generation was only about one inch.

One reason for the rapid increase in stature is that in the United States the Maya have access to treated drinking water and to a reliable supply of food. Especially critical are school breakfast and lunch programs for children from low-income families, as well as public assistance programs such as the federal Woman, Infants, and Children (WIC) program and food stamps. That these programs improve health and growth is no secret. What is surprising is how fast they work. Mayan mothers in the United States tell me that even their babies are bigger and healthier than the babies they raised in Guatemala, and hospital statistics bear them out. These women must be enjoying a level of health so improved from that of their lives in Guatemala that their babies are growing faster in the womb. Of course, plasticity means that such changes are dependent on external conditions, and unfortunately the rising height—and health—of the Maya is in danger from political forces that are attempting to cut funding for food stamps and the WIC program. If that funding is cut, the negative impact on the lives of poor Americans, including the Mayan refugees, will be as dramatic as were the former positive effects.

Height is only the most obvious example of plasticity's power; there are others to be found everywhere you look. The Andes-dwelling Quechua people of Peru are well-adapted to their high-altitude homes. Their large, barrel-shaped chests house big lungs that inspire huge amounts of air with each breath, and they manage to survive on the lower pressure of oxygen they breathe with an unusually high level of red blood cells. Yet these secrets of mountain living are not hereditary. Instead the bodies of young Quechua adapt as they grow in their particular environment, just as those of European children do when they live at high altitudes.

Plasticity may also have a hand in determining our risks for developing a number of diseases. For example, scientists have long been searching for a cause for Parkinson's disease. Because Parkinson's tends to run in families, it is natural to think there is a genetic cause. But while a genetic mutation linked to some types of Parkinson's disease was reported in mid-1997, the gene accounts for only a fraction of people with the disease. Many more people with Parkinson's do not have the gene, and not all people with the mutated gene develop the disease.

Ralph Garruto, a medical researcher and biological anthropologist at the National Institutes of Health, is investigating the role of the environment and human plasticity not only in Parkinson's but in Lou Gehrig's disease as well. Garruto and his team traveled to the islands of Guam and New Guinea, where rates of both diseases are 50 to 100 times higher than in the United States. Among the native Chamorro people of Guam these diseases kill one person out of every five over the age of 25. The scientists found that both diseases are linked to a shortage of calcium in the diet. This shortage sets off a cascade of events that result in the digestive system's absorbing too much of the aluminum present in the diet. The aluminum wreaks havoc on various parts of the body, including the brain, where it destroys neurons and eventually causes paralysis and death.

The most amazing discovery made by Garruto's team is that up to 70 percent of the people they studied in Guam had some brain damage, but only 20 percent progressed all the way to Parkinson's or Lou Gehrig's disease. Genes and plasticity seem to be working hand in hand to produce these lower-than-expected rates of disease. There is a certain amount of genetic variation in the ability that all people have in coping with calcium shortages—some can function better than others. But thanks to plasticity, it's also possible for people's bodies to gradually develop ways to protect themselves against aluminum poisoning. Some people develop biochemical barriers to the aluminum they eat, while others develop ways to prevent the aluminum from reaching the brain.

An appreciation of plasticity may temper some of our fears about these diseases and even offer some hope. For if Parkinson's and Lou Gehrig's diseases can be prevented among the Chamorro by plasticity, then maybe medical researchers can figure out a way to produce the same sort of plastic changes in you and me. Maybe Lou Gehrig's disease and Parkinson's disease—as well as many other, including some cancers—aren't our genetic doom but a product of our development, just like variations in human height. And maybe their danger will in time prove as illusory as the notion that the Tutsi are giants, or the Maya pygmies—or Americans still the tallest of the tall.

Critical Thinking

1. What is meant by "plasticity" and why does it make "evolutionary good sense"?

2. What is "lactose intolerance" and why is this not an example of plasticity?

3. What are two other kinds of adaptation, pointed out by Lasker, that are examples of plasticity?

4. Why are humans among the most variable of species?

5. How have Americans and the Dutch changed in height since 1850 and why?

172

6. What happens to humans from the fetus to adulthood in a harsh environment, and why?

7. What do studies of monozygotic twins tell us about "reprogramming"?

8. What similarities and differences occurred in the United States and the Netherlands with regard to health care, and what has been the result?

9. Explain the "durable myth" of the Tutsi.

10. What has happened to the Tutsi and other Africans who have migrated to Western Europe or North America?

11. How do various Pygmy groups tell a similar story?

12. How do the Mayans of Guatemala contrast with those in the United States and why?

13. What has been surprising with regard to U.S. programs to improve health? What will happen if such funding is cut?

14. How do the Quechua illustrate plasticity and why?

15. What indications are there that Parkinson's and Lou Gherig's diseases exhibit plasticity?

BARRY BOGIN is a professor of anthropology at the University of Michigan in Dearborn and the author of *Patterns of Human Growth*.

Dead Men Do Tell Tales

The strange and fascinating cases of a forensic anthropologist.

WILLIAM R. MAPLES

"Empty vessel, garment cast,
We that wore you long shall last.
—Another night, another day."
So my bones within me say.

Therefore they shall do my will
To-day while I am master still,
And flesh and soul, now both are strong,
Shall hale the sullen slaves along,

Before this fire of sense decay,
This smoke of thought blow clean away,
And leave with ancient night alone
The stedfast and enduring bone.

—A. E. Housman,
The Immortal Part

As I write these lines, it is a windy, bright spring day in early March in Gainesville. The live oaks have cast their leaves, and the dogwoods and azaleas are beginning to bloom. Eager young students are bicycling across campus, browsing in Goering's bookstore, studying their textbooks on sunlit lawns near dormitories.

But I am not thinking of them. I am thinking of ghosts.

I am recalling five young students, four from the University of Florida, one from nearby Santa Fe Community College, who were tortured, mutilated and murdered with demonic cruelty in August 1990. In all, the five victims suffered sixty-one stab wounds, cuts or other disfigurements. One was beheaded, and her head was placed at eye level on a bookshelf near the door of her apartment. Four of the victims were female: Sonja Larson eighteen, of Deerfield Beach; Christi Powell, seventeen, of Jacksonville; Christa Hoyt, eighteen, of Gainesville; and Tracy Paules, twenty-three, of Miami. One was male: Manny Taboada, twenty-three, of Miami. The horror these murders aroused at the time was so keen that thousands of students literally fled Gainesville, in fear of their lives.

Today, in early March, immured in a lamplit courtroom within the Alachua County Courthouse, a jury has finished staring at pictures of these five young people, taken after their bodies were

discovered. Black tape was placed over parts of the pictures considered so grisly they would have been prejudicial to the jury's reaching an impartial verdict. I can well understand these selective blackouts. In my long career I have seldom seen crime-scene photographs possessed of such sheer depravity.

In the same room with the jury, as they pondered these ghastly photographs, was the author of these terrors: the self-confessed murderer himself, Danny Harold Rolling, a drifter from Shreveport, Louisiana. Rolling claimed he was driven to kill because of abuse suffered as a child—it is a common excuse nowadays. He was arrested almost immediately on another charge after the quintuple murders (which were all committed within forty-eight hours), and only became a suspect in this case two months later, on November 2, 1990. As the prosecutor waved the horrible photographs before the jury, Rolling turned pale and appeared ill. "I've got to get out of here," he whispered at one point.

The jury was tasked with deciding his punishment: life in prison or death in the electric chair. It deliberated through one afternoon, into the evening, and reconvened the next morning, before reaching a verdict. The jury recommended death for Danny Rolling.

I remember how, in the years following his arrest, Rolling toyed with the investigators from prison, admitting nothing. He thought he had been too clever for the police. He thought he had removed all traces of his guilt from the crime scenes. He gathered up all but one piece of the duct tape he used to bind his victims. He washed two of their bodies with detergent after they were dead. He posed the bodies of the slaughtered young women in various lewd positions. Unfortunately for him, he left traces of his semen at the scene, and this identified him by means of DNA "fingerprinting."

Because of my background with weapons and wounds to bone, I was asked to be present at the autopsies, which were conducted by Dr. William Hamilton, the District 8 medical examiner. Hamilton is a quiet man of supreme competence. Unlike some of his brethren, he rigorously shuns the media limelight and works in silence. We have known each other for years, but from the first Hamilton struck me as remarkable and rare: a man who prefers to seek out the truth and to serve the people of his state with deeds of value, rather than chase the will-o'-the-wisp of fame. It is largely because of Hamilton's meticulous work that a close-meshed net of scientific evidence was drawn about Rolling. My own role in this case was minor. But I like to think that, wherever Rolling goes, I gave him one small nudge toward punishment and perdition.

My work centered around the murder weapon, and I was assisted by one of my best students, Dana Austin-Smith. Bones can reveal more about a murder weapon than skin and soft tissue, because they are not as elastic. Skin can stretch, distort, relax and finally deliquesce during decomposition. Bones, though more elastic than you might suppose, nevertheless can take and hold an impression from a murder weapon far longer, and far more accurately. By now I need not tell you that the pattern of the human skeleton is as familiar to me as the rooms of my house.

A large knife had been used in the murders. Its hilt left an imprint on one victim's back, and the point exited her chest on the opposite side, a distance of eight inches, during which the knife was fully sheathed, its entire length buried in the unfortunate girl's body. But allowing for compression of the rib cage from the force and fury of the blow, the blade length might have been somewhat shorter: say seven to eight inches, to be safe.

After preparing specimens of the damaged bones, I began to examine the knife marks under a low-power stereo-microscope. I found sharp cuts from the blade, marks both sharp and dull from the back of the blade, a point mark from the knife sunk in the body of a vertebra, and an array of bone wounds that gave me the width of the blade itself, from its cutting edge to its back.

I summarized the characteristics. Length: 7–8 inches. Width: 1.25–1.5 inches. A sharp, smooth, nonserrated cutting edge. A false edge resulting from the back of the blade being sharpened behind the tip. A certain shape of hilt where the blade joined the handle. A blade whose cross-section resembled an elongated pentagon. All in all, I concluded, this was a sturdy knife, like a military weapon. It was not a thin blade like a kitchen knife. This formidable weapon had cut through thick bone without any evidence of "blade chattering," a technical term describing the distinctive cutting pattern, which a thin blade makes when it jumps slightly from side to side during use.

On the afternoon of September 7, 1990, I was at the state attorney's office in Orlando on another case. I received a telephone call, asking me to join Dr. Hamilton and the leaders of the Gainesville Homicide Task Force for a meeting. It was a fast, hundred-mile drive for me, but I arrived around 4 P.M.

We were asked about the murder weapon. Could it have been an Air Force survival knife? I said no. That knife has a sawlike, ripping design on the back of the blade, which is only five inches long—far too short to match the weapon used in these murders. Then someone asked if it might be a Marine Corps utility knife, known as a Ka-Bar. I replied that it very well might.

After the meeting I pondered the question further. I knew the general shape of the Ka-Bar but wanted to be absolutely sure. That weekend I visited a knife shop in a nearby mall, where Ka-Bars were sold. I carefully examined one, measuring it with the one-meter tape measure I always carry with me. It fit exactly the dimensions of the wounds! The clerk regarded me with some curiosity. Why, he asked finally, was I making so many measurements? I made a vague reply, but as Margaret and I were walking back to the car, I told her what I thought. The weapon used in these ghastly murders had almost certainly been a Ka-Bar.

As I have said earlier, Rolling was in custody on an unrelated charge at this point. He had not yet been focused on as a suspect in the Gainesville murders. Over three years would pass before I learned that Rolling had indeed purchased a Ka-Bar at an Army-Navy store in Tallahassee on July 17, 1990, some weeks before the killings.

The police scanned many likely areas with metal detectors, but the actual murder weapon has not surfaced to this day. On the Thursday before Rolling was scheduled to go to trial, there was a crucial evidentiary hearing, one that changed the complexion of the case completely.

State Attorney Rod Smith won the court's approval to introduce into evidence a "replica weapon," a duplicate of the lost Ka-Bar we believed had been used to commit the crimes. Not only that: the *actual skeletal remains of the victims,* taken from their bodies during the autopsies, and bearing the atrocious nicks, slashes, scorings and gougings, which the knife had caused, and which had enabled me to measure its deadly dimensions with such exactitude, were going to be allowed into evidence as well. Thus, not only the blade, but the bones themselves would be placed before the jury's gaze.

"On the Thursday prior to the beginning of the trial," a court memorandum I have before me reads, "in closed discussions before the judge, part of the discussion was about the replica knife and the accurate work which Dr. Maples had done with the wounds. Also discussed were the skeletal remnants . . . "

The judge ruled that all these things would be allowed into evidence. The memorandum continues:

"It was obvious that Rolling didn't want to face the photographs, let alone the remnants . . . That was the evening the defense came to Mr. Smith and offered the first of a series of plea deals."

The murderer's resolve was crumbling in the face of these fearful resurrections. The knife he imagined was hidden forever was coming back to haunt him in court. The bones of his victims were ready to return from beyond death, to rise up and smite him. The trial would begin in ninety-six hours.

Rolling quailed. On February 15, 1994, as jury selection began in his trial, the accused man suddenly pleaded guilty to five counts of murder and three counts of rape.

"I've been running all my life," he declared. "And there are some things you can't run from anymore."

There began the punishment phase of the case, during which the jury had to decide whether Rolling deserved the death penalty or life in prison. Prosecutor Smith showed the jurors the replica knife, the twin of the Ka-Bar I had identified as the murder weapon. The bones were mercifully withheld from the jurors' sight. The dark blade danced back and forth before their eyes. Together with the hood Rolling wore, and the photographs of his victims, the knife must have made an overwhelming impression on the panel. Their verdict: Death. Rolling received five death sentences from Judge Stan Morris.

"Five years! You're going to go down in five years! You understand that? In less than five years!" screamed Mario Taboada, the brother of the slain Manuel Taboada. He was predicting that Rolling would exhaust all his appeals and be executed by 1999. The judge ordered Taboada ejected from the courtroom. Gradually the din subsided. One of the darkest chapters in Gainesville's history was closed.

All in all, the Rolling case was a significant victory for the science of forensic anthropology in Florida, one that saved the taxpayer the immense cost of a full-blown trial, and the victims' relatives the terrible pain of hearing in a public courtroom exactly how these innocent young people had died. It remains one of the most extraordinary cases in my experience, one that amply demonstrated the sheer power possessed by human bones: the power to bear witness to the truth beyond death; the power to avenge the innocent; the power to terrify the guilty.

Today, at the side of 34th Street in Gainesville, near the crest of a hill, there is a brilliantly painted section of wall dedicated to student graffiti and free speech. Everyone in Gainesville knows it simply as "The Wall." It runs beneath a fence draped with kudzu vine at the boundary of the campus golf course, and its shape rather reminds you of a railroad cutting, revealing all sorts of multicolored minerals, some of them precious, some of them fool's gold.

Anyone is welcome to paint a message on this wall, which is by now a local landmark and a University of Florida tradition. Most of the messages are cheery, or silly, or affectionate, or whimsical. But amid the valentines, the happy birthday wishes and the pleas to save the rain forest is a single dark panel in the wall at the very top of the hill. It contains the names of the five murder victims, neatly lettered against a black background, accompanied by the single word: REMEMBER. If this panel fades or is accidentally defaced, someone always renews it and repaints the names. I pass it twice a day, and I do indeed remember.

I have purposely kept this account of the Gainesville murders for last, not because they struck so close to home—Rolling could have killed anywhere, in any town—but because I believe there is a moral to this melancholy tale. It is simply that the lamp of science, properly grasped and directed, can shine its rays into the very heart of darkness. It can seek out and snare the most artful evildoer in a bright, unequivocal beam of truth. It cannot raise the dead, but it can make them speak, accuse and identify the agent of death. With the capture and punishment of the criminal responsible, the families and relatives of those slain can win a small measure of peace amid their infinite sorrow. With each solved case, with every confession, we extend our knowledge of the criminal mind and its methods, and we render the threat of capture and punishment all the more real and credible.

Yet as I look back on my life, and ahead to the future, I am given pause by the vast amount of work that still needs to be done. Mine is a small field, and it is always going to be a small field; but there is no excuse for its being as small as it is today. Cases now throng in daily to the C. A. Pound Human Identification Laboratory, in such jostling multitudes that I cannot address them all and must focus only on the most serious ones. When the telephone rings, my heartbeat quickens. I know that it is most likely the police, and I know what they will say, for I have heard it hundreds of times now:

"Doc, we've got a problem . . . "

And the problem is always a body, or what is left of one. They tell me they've set up security around the remains. They tell me police officers are guarding and preserving the scene. They ask: can I come immediately? Because I no longer have an undergraduate class load, I am able to break free more often than not. If I am rescued by a murder from a dull and dismal faculty meeting, so much the better! In the case of the three shotgunned drug dealers found in a pit near La Belle, I enlisted the aid of an archaeologist colleague and we both managed to be in Fort Myers, 230 miles away, by dark. By 8 A.M. the next morning we were in the death pit, hard at work.

With crime moving to the forefront of the American domestic political agenda, it would appear likely that investigators such as myself can look forward to busy years and full employment. But against this must be weighed the fact that few universities are willing to underwrite programs like mine, which combine pure academic research with applications in the "real world," and the fact that few state law enforcement agencies have the money or

inclination to avail themselves of the services of a trained forensic anthropologist.

So we fall between two stools. We are regarded by our fellow academics almost as common laborers with dirty hands, who traffic in mundane, workaday police matters, instead of devoting ourselves to pure research. On the other hand the police tend to regard us as woolgatherers and cloud-dwellers from the ivory tower, with no experience of the dark side of life. When I am visiting a new law enforcement agency for the first time, I often assume the persona of the innocent, fuddy-duddy professor who has to have everything pointed out to him. This role-playing won't win me any Oscars, but it humors the police, does no harm and gets results far more quickly than would an attitude of haughty, know-it-all, intellectual arrogance.

Yet sometimes I am prey to doubts. Who will replace me, and others like me? Who will hire the students I train? I cannot say. The need is there. It cries out to heaven. As I compose these lines, there are forty-eight charred corpses left over from the fiery explosion at the Branch Davidian compound outside Waco, awaiting identification. My colleague, Clyde Snow, is in Chiapas, Mexico, looking at the bodies of slain Zapatista revolutionaries, to see if they were murdered by the Mexican army after they surrendered. Remains of MIAs from the Korean War are being returned to America, and their names are a riddle as yet unsolved. The mass graves in Bosnia shout to the skies for discovery and vengeance. Yet programs in forensic anthropology languish, and well-trained young scholars go begging for work.

In my lifetime I have seen programs rise and fall like shooting stars. Once upon a time, at the University of Kansas, three of the gods of forensic anthropology—Tom McKern, Ellis Kerley and Bill Bass—were all on the faculty *at the same time.* They attracted and taught scores of students, many of whom are among the leading people in our field today. Then, almost overnight, they were scattered to the four winds. Bass left one year, McKern and Kerley the next. The university hired a human geneticist, rather than anyone in bone. The same melancholy story is about to be repeated at the University of Arizona, where Walt Birkby has built up a fantastic program. Birkby's students are probably the best-trained of any in the United States. But Walt is retiring in a couple of years, and the university has already announced he will not be replaced. Therefore he has closed admission to his program. He takes no new students.

Bill Bass has just retired from Tennessee. The university is going to replace him with an assistant professor, but without Bill's active guidance that program will undoubtedly change. I will retire myself in a few years and, even though University of Florida President John Lombardi has worked miracles in other areas, I seriously doubt whether the C. A. Pound Human Identification Laboratory will survive my departure.

If these memoirs have demonstrated anything, I would hope that it is that forensic anthropology is a discipline useful to society. Had I the power to command it, I should decree that each state have at least one forensic anthropologist working in its crime laboratory. Climate and crime rates have to be taken into consideration of course. A forensic anthropologist would probably starve to death in a cold state like Maine or Minnesota—bodies last forever in those arctic regions! He might find little to do in a state like New Hampshire, where there are only a couple of dozen murders in a year. But here in the sunny, homicidal South there are plenty of bodies to go around, and plenty of bugs to feast on them. Decomposition is swift and sure, and nameless skeletons accumulate in thousands, each beseeching us silently for identification.

Larger states, such as Texas, California, New York, Florida and the like, could easily employ several scientists like me, and none would be idle, I assure you. I know from long experience that I can't begin to look at all the cases demanding my attention in the state of Florida. A handful of states, those having a single medical examiner with statewide responsibility, have appointed forensic anthropologists to that office, but they are few and far between. As our elected officials bay like bloodhounds over the crime issue, as our state budgets allocate large sums for prisons, police training and equipment, parole officers, boot camps for teenagers and heaven knows what else, they overlook utterly the need to fund research by universities to develop new scientific techniques necessary to apprehend criminals. The Forensic Sciences Foundation has started a small grant program to provide funds, largely supported by donations from members of the American Academy of Forensic Scientists. But none of us is a Croesus or a Rockefeller. Our little fund is growing painfully slowly. It can only provide a few modest grants each year.

Seldom does a week go by without my receiving a visit or a telephone call from some young person eager to go into forensic anthropology. Will I accept him or her as a student? Alas, I don't have the money to support large numbers of students, nor the space in which to teach and train them, nor the time to give them all the attention they deserve. Even if I were to take them in, where would they go when they left me, having won their doctorates? Where would they get jobs? No doubt a handful of them would, as I did, work their way into a university system and slowly establish a practice. Most wouldn't. That is the bitter truth.

The murder and suicide rate in the state of Florida could easily furnish cases for six full-time forensic anthropologists. In my daydreams I locate them on a mind-map of the state with stickpins: there would be one in the Panhandle, another in Gainesville, another in Orlando, one in southwest Florida and one, perhaps two, in Miami. Miami, as we all know, is a very special place: the deadliest city in the most crime-ridden state in the Union. Forensic anthropologists would find plenty to do there. They would be useful to state medical examiners in skeletonized cases, cases involving burn victims, decomposed bodies and the like. We could even help identify fresh bodies belonging to the nameless and the homeless, who are flocking to Florida—and to Florida's morgues—in ever increasing numbers nowadays. Some medical examiners' offices perform over three thousand autopsies each year.

I can't be everywhere. I have been under as many as four separate subpoenas, to testify in four separate cities, all on the same day. One prosecutor, jokingly I hope, actually threatened to throw me in jail if I did not testify for him, rather than in another case scheduled for that day! Ours is a very large state. If a decomposed body is found in the Florida Keys, there is no way I can be on the scene immediately. Sometimes the remains are shipped to me, if I cannot go to them. Federal Express won't transport human remains, including cremains, but the U. S. Post Office has no such qualms,

as long as the remains are identified as "evidence" or "specimens." But if we had a forensic anthropologist stationed in Miami, these cases could be attended to on the spot.

Such are the thoughts that sometimes visit me at night. But "sufficient unto the day is the evil thereof," as the Bible says. Whenever I am beset by doubts over the future of my discipline, or the career opportunities for my students, or the fate of my laboratory after I am gone, I look at the filing cabinets filled with case reports. Here at least is solid, measurable progress. Here I can claim to have made a difference.

In days when people knew more Latin than they do now, someone composed a deeply moving inscription that can still be read over the lintel of the New York City medical examiner's office:

Taceant Colloquia. Effugiat Risus. Hic Locus Est Ubi Mors Gaudet Succurrere Vitae.

[Let idle talk be silenced. Let laughter be banished. Here is the place where Death delights to succour Life.]

I have no room over my laboratory door lintel for an engraved inscription, but if I did I would choose the last words of the explorer, Robert Falcon Scott, who perished in the frozen wastes of Antarctica in 1912, of hunger and exposure, in a place that was only a few miles from food and safety. The last entry in his diary read:

Had we lived, I should have had a tale to tell of the hardihood, endurance and courage of my companions, that would have stirred the heart of every Englishman. These rough notes and our dead bodies must tell the tale.

That's how I feel about the skeletons here in my laboratory. They have tales to tell us, even though they are dead. It is up to me, the forensic anthropologist, to catch their mute cries and whispers, and to interpret them for the living, as long as I am able.

Critical Thinking

1. Why is it that bones can reveal more about a murder weapon than skin and soft tissue?

2. In what sense did the bones of the victims and the knife used to kill them come back to haunt Danny Harold Rolling at his murder trial?

3. Why does the author consider the Rolling case a "significant victory" for the science of forensic anthropology?

4. What is the "moral to this melancholy tale," according to the author?

5. Why is the field of forensic anthropology so small even though there is a great need?

6. How are forensic anthropologists regarded by their fellow academics? By the police?

7. To what doubts is the author sometimes prey to?

8. In what regions of the United States does the author see the greatest need and why?

UNIT 7
Living with the Past

Unit Selections

Learning Outcomes

After reading this Unit, you will be able to:

- Explain how mental disorders may have passed the Darwinian fitness test in our evolutionary past.

- List ways to prevent epidemics in the human species.

- Determine whether the concept of natural selection has any relevance to the treatment of disease and defend your answer.

- Describe some healthful habits we can learn by studying hunter-gatherers.

- Identify the traditional Inuit (Eskimo) practices that are important for their survival in the circumstances they live in and contrast them with the values professed by the society you live in.

- Explain why Tay-Sachs disease is so common among East European Jews.

- Explain why a deadly disease such as hemochromatosis would be bred into our genetic code.

- Explain the difference between "wrongful life" and "wrongful birth."

- Explain the advantages and disadvantages of consanguineous marriages.

Student Website
www.mhhe.com/cls

Internet References

Evolution and Medicine Network
    http://evmedreview.com
The Paleolithic Diet Page
    www.paleodiet.com

Anthropology continues to evolve as a discipline, not only with respect to the tools and techniques of the trade, but also in the application of whatever knowledge we stand to gain about ourselves. Sometimes an awareness of our biological and behavioral past may help us to better understand the present. For instance, in showing how our evolutionary past may make a difference in bodily health, Patricia Gadsby (in "The Inuit Paradox") deals with the question of how traditional hunters, such as the Inuit, gorged themselves on fat, rarely saw a vegetable, and were still healthier than we are. Jared Diamond, in "Curse and Blessing of the Ghetto" and Sharon Moalem in "Ironing It Out" show that, while many deleterious genes do get weeded out of the population by means of natural selection, there are other harmful ones that may actually have a good side to them and will therefore be perpetuated.

As we reflect upon where we have been and how we came to be as we are in the evolutionary sense, the inevitable question arises as to what will happen next. This is the most difficult issue of all, because our biological future depends so much on long-range environmental trends that no one seems to be able to predict. Take, for example, the sweeping effects of ecological change upon the viruses of the world, which in turn seem to be paving the way for new waves of human epidemics. There is no better example of this problem than the recent explosion of new diseases, as described in "The Viral Superhighway" by George Armelagos. As we gain a better understanding of the processes of mutation and natural selection, and their relevance to human beings, we might even gain some control over the evolutionary direction of our species. However, the issue of what is a beneficial application of scientific knowledge becomes a subject for debate. Who will have the final word as to how these technological breakthroughs are to be employed in the future? Even with the best of intentions, how can we be certain of the long-range consequences of our actions in such a complicated field?

Knowledge in itself, of course, is neutral—its potential for good or ill being determined by those who happen to be in the position to use it. Consider, for example, that some men may be dying from a genetically caused overabundance of iron in their

© Library of Congress Prints and Photographs Division [LC-USZ62-135995]

blood systems in a trade-off that allows some women to absorb sufficient amounts of the element to guarantee their own survival. The question of whether we should eliminate such a gene that brings about this situation would seem to depend on which sex we decide should reap the benefit.

As we read the essays in this unit and contemplate the significance of "Darwinian medicine" for human evolution, we can hope that a better understanding of the diseases that afflict our species will lead to a reduction of human suffering. At the same time, we must remain aware that someone, at some time, may actually use the same knowledge to increase rather than reduce the misery that exists in the world.

Because it has been our conscious decision making (and not the genetically predetermined behavior that characterizes some species) that has gotten us into this mess, then it is the conscious will of our generation and future generations that will get us out of it. But, can we wait much longer for humanity to collectively come to its senses? Or is it too late already?

Different Minds

**Could mental illness have been the making of our species?
Kate Ravilious considers a controversial idea.**

**Misfit minds gave our ancestors the edge. Conditions such as
schizophrenia, autism and bipolar disorder may be so prevalent
today because they helped our forebears conquer the world.**

KATE RAVILIOUS

My dad hears voices inside his head. "Tiddles" interrupts conversations with cheerful interjections and the odd profanity. "The Bloodbeast" is more sinister, shouting at dad and instructing him to do inappropriate and socially unacceptable things. For most of his life these voices have plagued him and prevented him from living an ordinary life. I know how debilitating and stigmatising mental illness can be, so I must declare an interest in what follows.

In the industrialised world, roughly 1 person in every 25 has severe mental disorder, and nearly half of us will experience some kind of mental illness during our lives. Many conditions, including schizophrenia and bipolar disorder, as well as developmental conditions like autism, are at least in part inherited from our parents. If they affect people's chance of survival you would expect natural selection to have eliminated them, but instead they persist at high levels.

Some argue that these genes bring benefits—mental illness and genius have a long-standing link—but archaeologist Penny Spikins at the University of York, UK, goes further. She believes that mental illness and conditions such as autism persist at such high levels because in the past they were advantageous to humanity. "I think that part of the reason *Homo sapiens* were so successful is because they were willing to include people with different minds in their society—people with autism or schizophrenia, for example."

According to Spikins, human tolerance allowed the genes associated with different kinds of brain development and mental illness to flourish, kick-starting a revolution. "At some point our ancestors began to develop very complex emotions such as compassion, gratitude and admiration," she says. "These helped them accept and tolerate people with different minds." By embracing the unique skills and attributes that came with unusual ways of thinking, early humans became more inventive and adaptable, and eventually out-competed all other hominins, she says.

The archaeological evidence is circumstantial, but new findings in genetics are helping to bolster Spikins's idea. It turns out that some genes associated with mental illness proliferated at just the time when human society was flowering and confer attributes that other hominins may not have shared. All of this raises the interesting issue of whether, in the modern world, we should place more value on people like my father. So, when did our ancestors start to value different minds? Spikins sees the answer in some radical changes in the archaeological record (*Cambridge Archaeological Journal*, vol 19, p 179). Consider stone tool technology. Emerging around 2.6 million years ago, the first stone tools were crude and developments slow. For hundreds of thousands of years our ancestors made do with an array of hand axes, scrapers and thrusting spears. Then, around 100,000 years ago, there was a technological revolution, with many new and sophisticated implements appearing. "We see a sudden change in the archaeological record to more standardised tools that are more precisely made and more technologically focused," says Spikins. The invention of spear throwers, bows and arrows, fishing harpoons, traps and snares, for example, allowed hunters to distance themselves from their prey and so hunt more aggressive animals.

Autistic Advantage

Spikins argues that this technological tool revolution may have been triggered by a greater tolerance for people with traits on the autism spectrum. "I'm not saying that someone who isn't autistic wouldn't understand this technology, but that the innovation is more likely to come from someone who is systematic and has that unique focus on precision," she says. Spikins also notes that other hominins, including Neanderthals, show few signs of tool innovation and never reached the level of sophistication achieved by our ancestors.

At around the same time as the tool revolution, archaeologists see a burst of artistic creativity. This begins with things like shell and bead necklaces and decorations on bone and ochre, and later carved figurines and simple musical instruments. By about 35,000 years ago modern humans were painting stunning lifelike animals and people on cave walls. The striking similarity between these and the drawings produced by some autistic people with savant-like abilities has been noted by Nicholas Humphrey at the London School of Economics (*Cambridge Archaeological Journal*, vol 8, p 165). "This emergence of very realistic art, which is drawn with incredible precision, could be linked to the tolerance of autistic people, who had those special skills," says Spikins.

Evidence of religion and spirituality also appear during this period. It has been argued that shamans were responsible for painting the more metaphorical and dream-like cave art, and Spikins believes they would have had a big impact on society. "I think that they helped to bind people together, by helping them to make sense of their world, through myths, ritual and a belief in a spirit world," she says. In modern hunter-gatherer societies shamans tend to be unusual and creative people, who sometimes go into trances. Some also express traits associated with schizophrenia, such as hearing voices, and other mental disorders. "Using modern criteria to diagnose mental illness, I think we would say that most shamans appear to have had mood disorders—most probably bipolar disorder," says David Whitley, author of *Cave Paintings and the Human Spirit* (Prometheus, 2009).

Anthropologist Henry Harpending at the University of Utah in Salt Lake City says Spikins's idea is plausible. "The points she makes about standardised tool types and the detail in art certainly ring true." But would mental disorders have passed the "survival of the fittest" test? "People with bipolar disorder might very well bind communities together, but first they have to survive and reproduce themselves," he says. "In the case of schizophrenia, we have data in contemporary industrial societies and we know it causes a big fitness reduction." Different minds may have contributed to our evolutionary success, says Catriona Pickard from the University of Edinburgh, UK, but mental illness is more likely to be an unfortunate by-product of evolving a highly developed brain (*Cambridge Archaeological Journal*, vol 21, p 357).

Others argue that modern society is not a good analogue for the past. "Eccentricity is much more accepted in small scale hunter-gatherer societies, as everyone has a role to play," says Benjamin Campbell, an anthropologist at the University of Wisconsin-Milwaukee. He is supportive of Spikins's idea and agrees that complex emotions such as compassion set us apart from other species. "Modern humans understand that someone else has different thoughts, and we have developed this ability to a tremendous extent," he says. For sure, the archaeological evidence is circumstantial, but genetic studies are starting to put the theory on firmer ground. Last year's sequencing of the Neanderthal genome showed that around 99.8 per cent of the genes were the same as those of modern humans (*Science*, vol 328, p 710). That is hardly surprising, given that we shared an ancestor within the past 500,000 years. But David Reich at Harvard Medical School in Boston points to some key differences. "We found that Neanderthals carried subtly different forms of the AUTS2, CADPS2 and NRG3 genes compared with modern humans," he says.

AUTS2 and CADPS2 are associated with autism and NRG3 with schizophrenia. However, Reich adds, it is not clear whether these differences influenced the way our ancestors thought.

Neanderthals became extinct around 30,000 years ago, and Spikins is not alone in thinking that superior adaptability helped early modern humans outcompete them. Whether our ancestors were aided by having genes associated with mental illness is another matter, but the fact is that humans are the only hominin that survives to this day. What's more, in recent years it has become clear that our ancestors had more contemporaries than had previously been thought. Around 80,000 years ago, there were at least five species of hominin roaming the planet, says Chris Stringer from the Natural History Museum in London. While *H. sapiens* predominated in Africa and Neanderthals were dominant in western Eurasia, descendants of *H. erectus* probably still survived in Indonesia, *H. floresiensis* (aka "the Hobbit") resided on the Indonesian island of Flores and the newly discovered Denisovans seem to have ranged across a swathe of Asia (*New Scientist*, 2 August, p 34). We don't yet know whether early modern humans had more genes associated with mental illness than these other species, but we may not have to wait long to find out, given the speed with which ancient DNA sequencing is progressing.

What we do know is that inherited mental illness is extremely rare among living primates. Klaus-Peter Lesch at the University of Würzburg, Germany, and colleagues looked at the gene responsible for the serotonin transporter protein, SERT, which has been implicated in several inherited disorders. Responsible for regulating the movement of serotonin—a neurotransmitter crucial to mood, among other things—the gene comes in a "long" and "short" form. Every human carries a combination of two of these. People with the long/long combination appear to be protected from very low mood, whereas those with the short/short or short/long variants are more susceptible to depression. Lesch and colleagues looked at the gene in 12 species of primate and found that the short version is found only in humans and one other primate, rhesus monkeys (*Molecular Psychiatry*, DOI: 10.1038/sj.mp.4001157). "Carrying one of the short variants of the SERT gene seems to expose humans and rhesus monkeys to emotional dysregulation commonly associated with emotional disorders, which we don't see in other species," says Lesch.

Double-edged Sword

But it can also confer advantages. "The short variant appears to be linked with emotional responsivity. In a stressful environment this seems to increase vulnerability to depression, but in a good and nurturing environment people with this variant are often highly successful, with excellent communication and social skills." And the benefits may extend even further. "One trait that humans and rhesus monkeys share is their ability to live almost anywhere," say Lesch. Noting that other primates thrive only in very specific niches, he speculates that behavioural traits connected with the short versions of the gene for SERT may have helped both humans and rhesus monkeys adapt to new and challenging environments.

Such adaptability would have been crucial in the past 50,000 years as our ancestors migrated around the world, and it turns out

Beautiful Minds?

With advances in genetic selection we may be able to screen the genetic make-up of embryos and reduce the prevalence of conditions such as schizophrenia and autism. Could this in fact be a retrograde step? Simon Baron-Cohen, director of the Autism Research Centre at the University of Cambridge thinks so, and not just because he considers it a form of eugenics. He believes it could also deprive humanity of some crucial attributes.

Recently, Baron-Cohen and his colleagues reported that people living and working in Eindhoven—a major information technology and industry hub in Holland—are more than twice as likely to have children with autism than those living in Haarlem and Utrecht, similar-sized Dutch cities that lack the focus on technology-based industries (*New Scientist*, 22 June).

"Our work suggests that parents of children with autism—and who therefore carry some of the genes for autism—have talents in systemising, which has been responsible for innovation in fields like science, mathematics, music, technology, art and engineering," he says.

Similarly, several studies have shown an apparent link between the genes associated with schizophrenia and creative ability. And in 2005, Daniel Nettle from Newcastle University, UK, showed that professional poets and artists commonly possess several of the traits used to diagnose schizophrenia such as delusions, hallucinations, moodiness and difficulties concentrating (*Journal of Research in Personality*, DOI: 10.1016/j.jrp.2005.09.004).

Such findings help explain why many scientists are equivocal when it comes to the possibility of genetic screening. "If we start selecting against the outer margins on any set of attributes, we may be losing something valuable for our culture," says Robert Cook-Deegan, director of the Center for Genome Ethics, Law and Policy at Duke University in North Carolina. "And yet the stories of pain and suffering of those who live out on those extremes are quite real too."

---

that the gene responsible for SERT is among many that evolved rapidly during this period (see *The 10,000 Year Explosion* by Henry Harpending and Gregory Cochran, Basic Books, 2009). The genetic analysis that revealed this dramatic acceleration in human evolution also exposed the rise of another gene variant linked with mental disorder—this time one that helps regulate dopamine, the neurotransmitter associated with pleasure and reward. Harpending and colleagues found that a particular variant of the gene that codes for the D4 dopamine receptor has increased very rapidly in frequency in humans. People with this variant, known as DRD4-7R, tend to have very high energy levels and an increased risk of attention-deficit hyperactivity disorder (ADHD). Yet the prevalence of the variant among certain groups—it is found in 80 per cent of lowland Amazonian Indians, for example—indicates that extra energy has its advantages. "Previously these traits have been highly regarded in some societies," says Lesch.

"We see a higher percentage of ADHD-associated traits in migratory people, for example." Like the SERT gene, DRD4-7R can be both a boon and a bane. Some researchers describe such genes as "orchid genes": nurture them and the carrier thrives, neglect them and a maladaptive personality trait appears. If Spikins is correct, many other genes associated with developmental conditions and mental illness should possess such Jekyll-and-Hyde characteristics. Our ancestors may have benefited from this, but modern societies tend instead to view different minds as a major impediment. "Nowadays, being 'mad' is bad," says Whitley. "In the west, we continue to pathologise difference, and lose its potential adaptive advantage."

Instead of ostracising people with maverick minds, perhaps we would do better to cherish them (see box "Beautiful minds?"). My dad, for one, has always maintained that having schizophrenia is beneficial in some ways. If the special talents possessed by some people like him have helped to get us this far, we may need their different ways of thinking to see us through the next few thousand years. If the past teaches us anything, it's that humanity thrives by being adaptable.

Critical Thinking

1. Why was the development of such emotions as compassion, gratitude, and admiration important to human inventiveness and adaptability, according to archeologist Penny Spikins?

2. How does the genetic and archeological evidence support such a notion?

3. How does Spikins interpret the burst of artistic creativity at the same time as the tool revolution?

4. How did religion and spirituality have a big impact on society?

5. Discuss the issue as to whether or not mental disorders could have passed the "survival of the fittest" test.

6. What is the connection between the serotonin transporter protein, SERT and mental illness and communication and social skills?

7. What is the significance of the association between adaptability and the SERT gene? adaptability and the DRD4-7R gene?

8. What is the association between ADHD–associated traits and migration?

9. Why are such genes referred to as the "orchid genes"?

10. How should we be treating people with "maverick minds," according to the author?

11. Might genetic screening for conditions such as schizophrenia and autism be a "retrograde step"? Explain, in the light of current research findings.

From *New Scientist Magazine*, November 15, 2011, pp. 34–37. Copyright © 2011 by Reed Business Information, Ltd, UK. Reprinted by permission via Tribune Media Services.

The Viral Superhighway

Environmental disruptions and international travel have brought on a new era in human illness, one marked by diabolical new diseases.

GEORGE J. ARMELAGOS

So the Lord sent a pestilence upon Israel from the morning until the appointed time; and there died of the people from Dan to Beer-sheba seventy thousand men.

—2 Sam. 24:15

Swarms of crop-destroying locusts, rivers fouled with blood, lion-headed horses breathing fire and sulfur: the Bible presents a lurid assortment of plagues, described as acts of retribution by a vengeful God. Indeed, real-life epidemics—such as the influenza outbreak of 1918, which killed 21 million people in a matter of months—can be so sudden and deadly that it is easy, even for nonbelievers, to view them as angry messages from the beyond.

How reassuring it was, then, when the march of technology began to give people some control over the scourges of the past. In the 1950s the Salk vaccine, and later, the Sabin vaccine, dramatically reduced the incidence of polio. And by 1980 a determined effort by health workers worldwide eradicated smallpox, a disease that had afflicted humankind since earliest times with blindness, disfigurement and death, killing nearly 300 million people in the twentieth century alone.

But those optimistic years in the second half of our century now seem, with hindsight, to have been an era of inflated expectations, even arrogance. In 1967 the surgeon general of the United States, William H. Stewart, announced that victory over infectious diseases was imminent—a victory that would close the book on modern plagues. Sadly, we now know differently. Not only have deadly and previously unimagined new illnesses such as AIDS and Legionnaires' disease emerged in recent years, but historical diseases that just a few decades ago seemed to have been tamed are returning in virulent, drug-resistant varieties. Tuberculosis, the ancient lung disease that haunted nineteenth-century Europe, afflicting, among others, Chopin, Dostoyevski and Keats, is aggressively mutating into strains that defy the standard medicines; as a result, modern TB victims must undergo a daily drug regimen so elaborate that health-department workers often have to personally monitor patients to make sure they comply [see "A Plague Returns," by Mark Earnest and John A. Sbarbaro, September/October 1993]. Meanwhile, bacteria and viruses in foods from chicken to strawberries to alfalfa sprouts are sickening as many as 80 million Americans each year.

And those are only symptoms of a much more general threat. Deaths from infectious diseases in the United States rose 58 percent between 1980 and 1992. Twenty-nine new diseases have been reported in the past twenty-five years, a few of them so bloodcurdling and bizarre that descriptions of them bring to mind tacky horror movies. Ebola virus, for instance, can in just a few days reduce a healthy person to a bag of teeming flesh spilling blood and organ parts from every orifice. Creutzfeldt-Jakob disease, which killed the choreographer George Balanchine in 1983, eats away at its victims' brains until they resemble wet sponges. Never slow to fan mass hysteria, Hollywood has capitalized on the phenomenon with films such as *Outbreak,* in which a monkey carrying a deadly new virus from central Africa infects unwitting Californians and starts an epidemic that threatens to annihilate the human race.

The reality about infectious disease is less sensational but alarming nonetheless. Gruesome new pathogens such as Ebola are unlikely to cause a widespread epidemic because they sicken and kill so quickly that victims can be easily identified and isolated; on the other hand, the seemingly innocuous practice of overprescribing antibiotics for bad colds could ultimately lead to untold deaths, as familiar germs evolve to become untreatable. We are living in the twilight of the antibiotic era: within our lifetimes, scraped knees and cut fingers may return to the realm of fatal conditions.

Through international travel, global commerce and the accelerating destruction of ecosystems worldwide, people are inadvertently exposing themselves to a Pandora's box of emerging microbial threats. And the recent rumblings of biological terrorism from Iraq highlight the appalling potential of disease organisms for being manipulated to vile ends. But although it may appear that the apocalypse has arrived, the truth is that people today are not facing a unique predicament. Emerging diseases have long loomed like a shadow over the human race.

People and pathogens have a long history together. Infections have been detected in the bones of human ancestors more than a million years old, and evidence from the mummy of the Egyptian pharaoh Ramses V suggests that he may have died from smallpox more than 3,000 years ago. Widespread outbreaks of disease are also well documented. Between 1347 and 1351 roughly a third of the population of medieval Europe was wiped out by bubonic plague, which is carried by fleas that live on rodents. In 1793, 10 percent of the population of Philadelphia succumbed to yellow fever, which is spread by mosquitoes. And in 1875 the son of a Fiji chief came down with measles after a ceremonial trip to Australia. Within four months more than 20,000 Fijians were dead from the imported disease, which spreads through the air when its victims cough or sneeze.

According to conventional wisdom in biology, people and invading microorganisms evolve together: people gradually become more resistant, and the microorganisms become less virulent. The result is either mutualism, in which the relation benefits both species, or commensalism, in which one species benefits without harming the other. Chicken pox and measles, once fatal afflictions, now exist in more benign forms. Logic would suggest, after all, that the best interests of an organism are not served if it kills its host; doing so would be like picking a fight with the person who signs your paycheck.

But recently it has become clear to epidemiologists that the reverse of that cooperative paradigm of illness can also be true: microorganisms and their hosts sometimes exhaust their energies devising increasingly powerful weaponry and defenses. For example, several variants of human immunodeficiency virus (HIV) may compete for dominance within a person's body, placing the immune system under ever-greater siege. As long as a virus has an effective mechanism for jumping from one person to another, it can afford to kill its victims [see "The Deadliest Virus," by Cynthia Mills, January/February 1997].

If the competition were merely a question of size, humans would surely win: the average person is 10^{17} times the size of the average bacterium. But human beings, after all, constitute only one species, which must compete with 5,000 kinds of viruses and more than 300,000 species of bacteria. Moreover, in the twenty years it takes humans to produce a new generation, bacteria can reproduce a half-million times. That disparity enables pathogens to evolve ever more virulent adaptations that quickly outstrip human responses to them. The scenario is governed by what the English zoologist Richard Dawkins of the University of Oxford and a colleague have called the "Red Queen Principle." In Lewis Carroll's *Through the Looking Glass* the Red Queen tells Alice she will need to run faster and faster just to stay in the same place. Staving off illness can be equally elusive.

The Centers For Disease Control and Prevention (CDC) in Atlanta, Georgia, has compiled a list of the most recent emerging pathogens. They include:

- *Campylobacter,* a bacterium widely found in chickens because of the commercial practice of raising them in cramped, unhealthy conditions. It causes between two

million and eight million cases of food poisoning a year in the United States and between 200 and 800 deaths.
- *Escherichia coli* 0157:H7, a dangerously mutated version of an often harmless bacterium. Hamburger meat from Jack in the Box fast-food restaurants that was contaminated with this bug led to the deaths of at least four people in 1993.
- Hantaviruses, a genus of fast-acting, lethal viruses, often carried by rodents, that kill by causing the capillaries to leak blood. A new hantavirus known as *sin nombre* (Spanish for "nameless") surfaced in 1993 in the southwestern United States, causing the sudden and mysterious deaths of thirty-two people.
- HIV, the deadly virus that causes AIDS (acquired immunodeficiency syndrome). Although it was first observed in people as recently as 1981, it has spread like wildfire and is now a global scourge, affecting more than 30 million people worldwide.
- The strange new infectious agent that causes bovine spongiform encephalopathy, or mad cow disease, which recently threw the British meat industry and consumers into a panic. This bizarre agent, known as a prion, or "proteinaceous infectious particle," is also responsible for Creutzfeldt-Jakob disease, the brain-eater I mentioned earlier. A Nobel Prize was awarded last year to the biochemist Stanley B. Prusiner of the University of California, San Francisco, for his discovery of the prion.
- *Legionella pneumophila,* the bacterium that causes Legionnaires' disease. The microorganism thrives in wet environments; when it lodges in air-conditioning systems or the mist machines in supermarket produce sections, it can be expelled into the air, reaching people's lungs. In 1976 thirty-four participants at an American Legion convention in Philadelphia died—the incident that led to the discovery and naming of the disease.
- *Borrelia burgdorferi,* the bacterium that causes Lyme disease. It is carried by ticks that live on deer and white-footed mice. Left untreated, it can cause crippling, chronic problems in the nerves, joints and internal organs.

How ironic, given such a rogues' gallery of nasty characters, that just a quarter-century ago the Egyptian demographer Abdel R. Omran could observe that in many modern industrial nations the major killers were no longer infectious diseases. Death, he noted, now came not from outside but rather from within the body, the result of gradual deterioration. Omran traced the change to the middle of the nineteenth century, when the industrial revolution took hold in the United States and parts of Europe. Thanks to better nutrition, improved public-health measures and medical advances such as mass immunization and the introduction of antibiotics, microorganisms were brought under control. As people began living longer, their aging bodies succumbed to "diseases of civilization": cancer, clogged arteries, diabetes, obesity and osteoporosis. Omran was the first to formally recognize that shift in the disease environment. He called it an "epidemiological transition."

Like other anthropologists of my generation, I learned of Omran's theory early in my career, and it soon became a basic tenet—a comforting one, too, implying as it did an end to the supremacy of microorganisms. Then, three years ago, I began working with the anthropologist Kathleen C. Barnes of Johns Hopkins University in Baltimore, Maryland, to formulate an expansion of Omran's ideas. It occurred to us that his epidemiological transition had not been a unique event. Throughout history human populations have undergone shifts in their relations with disease—shifts, we noted, that are always linked to major changes in the way people interact with the environment. Barnes and I, along with James Lin, a master's student at Johns Hopkins University School of Hygiene and Public Health, have since developed a new theory: that there have been not one but three major epidemiological transitions; that each one has been sparked by human activities; and that we are living through the third one right now.

The first epidemiological transition took place some 10,000 years ago, when people abandoned their nomadic existence and began farming. That profoundly new way of life disrupted ecosystems and created denser living conditions that led, as I will soon detail, to new diseases. The second epidemiological transition was the salutary one Omran singled out in 1971, when the war against infectious diseases seemed to have been won. And in the past two decades the emergence of illnesses such as hepatitis C, cat scratch disease (caused by the bacterium *Bartonella henselae*), Ebola and others on CDC's list has created a third epidemiological transition, a disheartening set of changes that in many ways have reversed the effects of the second transition and coincide with the shift to globalism. Burgeoning population growth and urbanization, widespread environmental degradation, including global warming and tropical deforestation, and radically improved methods of transportation have given rise to new ways of contracting and spreading disease.

We are, quite literally, making ourselves sick.

When early human ancestors moved from African forests onto the savanna millions of years ago, a few diseases came along for the ride. Those "heirloom" species—thus designated by the Australian parasitologist J. F. A. Sprent because they had afflicted earlier primates—included head and body lice; parasitic worms such as pinworms, tapeworms and liver flukes; and possibly herpes virus and malaria.

For 99.8 percent of the five million years of human existence, hunting and gathering was the primary mode of subsistence. Our ancestors lived in small groups and relied on wild animals and plants for their survival. In their foraging rounds, early humans would occasionally have contracted new kinds of illnesses through insect bites or by butchering and eating disease-ridden animals. Such events would not have led to widespread epidemics, however, because groups of people were so sparse and widely dispersed.

About 10,000 years ago, at the end of the last ice age, many groups began to abandon their nomadic lifestyles for a more efficient and secure way of life. The agricultural revolution first appeared in the Middle East; later, farming centers developed independently in China and Central America. Permanent villages grew up, and people turned their attention to crafts such as toolmaking and pottery. Thus when people took to cultivating wheat and barley, they planted the seeds of civilization as well.

With the new ways, however, came certain costs. As wild habitats were transformed into urban settings, the farmers who brought in the harvest with their flint-bladed sickles were assailed by grim new ailments. Among the most common was scrub typhus, which is carried by mites that live in tall grasses, and causes a potentially lethal fever. Clearing vegetation to create arable fields brought farmers frequently into mite-infested terrain.

Irrigation brought further hazards. Standing thigh-deep in watery canals, farm workers were prey to the worms that cause schistosomiasis. After living within aquatic snails during their larval stage, those worms emerge in a free-swimming form that can penetrate human skin, lodge in the intestine or urinary tract, and cause bloody urine and other serious maladies. Schistosomiasis was well known in ancient Egypt, where outlying fields were irrigated with water from the Nile River; descriptions of its symptoms and remedies are preserved in contemporary medical papyruses.

The domestication of sheep, goats and other animals cleared another pathway for microorganisms. With pigs in their yards and chickens roaming the streets, people in agricultural societies were constantly vulnerable to pathogens that could cross interspecies barriers. Many such organisms had long since reached commensalism with their animal hosts, but they were highly dangerous to humans. Milk from infected cattle could transmit tuberculosis, a slow killer that eats away at the lungs and causes its victims to cough blood and pus. Wool and skins were loaded with anthrax, which can be fatal when inhaled and, in modern times, has been developed by several nations as a potential agent of biological warfare. Blood from infected cattle, injected into people by biting insects such as the tsetse fly, spread sleeping sickness, an often-fatal disease marked by tremors and protracted lethargy.

A second major effect of agriculture was to spur population growth and, perhaps more important, density. Cities with populations as high as 50,000 had developed in the Near East by 3000 B.C. Scavenger species such as rats, mice and sparrows, which congregate wherever large groups of people live, exposed city dwellers to bubonic plague, typhus and rabies. And now that people were crowded together, a new pathogen could quickly start an epidemic. Larger populations also enabled diseases such as measles, mumps, chicken pox and smallpox to persist in an endemic form—always present, afflicting part of the population while sparing those with acquired immunity.

Thus the birth of agriculture launched humanity on a trajectory that has again and again brought people into contact with new pathogens. Tilling soil and raising livestock led to more energy-intensive ways of extracting resources from the earth—to lumbering, coal mining, oil drilling. New resources led to increasingly complex social organization, and to new and more frequent contacts between various societies. Loggers today who venture into the rain forest disturb previously untouched creatures and give them, for the first time, the chance to attack humans. But there is nothing new about this drama; only the players have changed. Some 2,000 years ago the introduction of iron tools to sub-Saharan Africa led to a slash-and-burn style of agriculture that brought people into contact with *Anopheles gambiae,* a mosquito that transmits malaria.

Improved transportation methods also help diseases extend their reach: microorganisms cannot travel far on their own, but they are expert hitchhikers. When the Spanish invaded Mexico in the early 1500s, for instance, they brought with them diseases that quickly raged through Tenochtitlán, the stately, temple-filled capital of the Aztec Empire. Smallpox, measles and influenza wiped out millions of Central America's original inhabitants, becoming the invisible weapon in the European conquest.

In the past three decades people and their inventions have drilled, polluted, engineered, paved, planted and deforested at soaring rates, changing the biosphere faster than ever before. The combined effects can, without hyperbole, be called a global revolution. After all, many of them have worldwide repercussions: the widespread chemical contamination of waterways, the thinning of the ozone layer, the loss of species diversity. And such global human actions have put people at risk for infectious diseases in newly complex and devastating ways. Global warming, for instance, could expose millions of people for the first time to malaria, sleeping sickness and other insect-borne illnesses; in the United States, a slight overall temperature increase would allow the mosquitoes that carry dengue fever to survive as far north as New York City.

Global Warming could allow the mosquitoes that carry dengue fever to survive as far north as New York City.

Major changes to the landscape that have become possible in the past quarter-century have also triggered new diseases. After the construction of the Aswan Dam in 1970, for instance, Rift Valley fever infected 200,000 people in Egypt, killing 600. The disease had been known to affect livestock, but it was not a major problem in people until the vast quantities of dammed water became a breeding ground for mosquitoes. The insects bit both cattle and humans, helping the virus jump the interspecies barrier.

In the eastern United States, suburbanization, another relatively recent phenomenon, is a dominant factor in the emergence of Lyme disease—10,000 cases of which are reported annually. Thanks to modern earth-moving equipment, a soaring economy and population pressures, many Americans have built homes in formerly remote, wooded areas. Nourished by lawns and gardens and unchecked by wolves, which were exterminated by settlers long ago, the deer population has exploded, exposing people to the ticks that carry Lyme disease.

Meanwhile, widespread pollution has made the oceans a breeding ground for microorganisms. Epidemiologists have suggested that toxic algal blooms—fed by the sewage, fertilizers and other contaminants that wash into the oceans—harbor countless viruses and bacteria. Thrown together into what amounts to a dirty genetic soup, those pathogens can undergo gene-swapping and mutations, engendering newly antibiotic-resistant strains. Nautical traffic can carry ocean pathogens far and wide: a devastating outbreak of cholera hit Latin America in 1991 after a ship from Asia unloaded its contaminated ballast water into the harbor of Callao, Peru. Cholera causes diarrhea so severe its victims can die in a few days from dehydration; in that outbreak more than 300,000 people became ill, and more than 3,000 died.

The modern world is becoming—to paraphrase the words of the microbiologist Stephen S. Morse of Columbia University—a viral superhighway. Everyone is at risk.

Our newly global society is characterized by huge increases in population, international travel and international trade—factors that enable diseases to spread much more readily than ever before from person to person and from continent to continent. By 2020 the world population will have surpassed seven billion, and half those people will be living in urban centers. Beleaguered third-world nations are already hard-pressed to provide sewers, plumbing and other infrastructure; in the future, clean water and adequate sanitation could become increasingly rare. Meanwhile, political upheavals regularly cause millions of people to flee their homelands and gather in refugee camps, which become petri dishes for germs.

More than 500 million people cross international borders each year on commercial flights. Not only does that traffic volume dramatically increase the chance a sick person will infect the inhabitants of a distant area when she reaches her destination; it also exposes the sick person's fellow passengers to the disease, because of poor air circulation on planes. Many of those passengers can, in turn, pass the disease on to others when they disembark.

The global economy that has arisen in the past two decades has established a myriad of connections between far-flung places. Not too long ago bananas and oranges were rare treats in northern climes. Now you can walk into your neighborhood market and find food that has been flown and trucked in from all over the world: oranges from Israel, apples from New Zealand, avocados from California. Consumers in affluent nations expect to be able to buy whatever they want whenever they want it. What people do not generally realize, however, is that this global network of food production and delivery provides countless pathways for pathogens. Raspberries from Guatemala, carrots from Peru and coconut milk from Thailand have been responsible for recent outbreaks of food poisoning in the United States. And the problem cuts both ways: contaminated radish seeds and frozen beef from the United States have ended up in Japan and South Korea.

Finally, the widespread and often indiscriminate use of antibiotics has played a key role in spurring disease. Forty million pounds of antibiotics are manufactured annually in the United States, an eightyfold increase since 1954. Dangerous microorganisms have evolved accordingly, often developing antibiotic-resistant strains. Physicians are now faced with penicillin-resistant gonorrhea, multiple-drug-resistant tuberculosis and E. coli variants such as 0157:H7. And frighteningly, some enterococcus bacteria have become resistant to all known antibiotics. Enterococcus infections are rare, but staphylococcus infections are not, and many strains of staph bacteria now respond to just one antibiotic, vancomycin. How long will it be before run-of-the-mill staph infections—in a boil, for instance, or in a surgical incision—become untreatable?

Although civilization can expose people to new pathogens, cultural progress also has an obvious countervailing effect: it can provide tools—medicines, sensible city planning, educational campaigns about sexually transmitted diseases—to fight the encroachments of disease. Moreover, since biology seems to side with microorganisms anyway, people have little choice but to depend on protective cultural practices to keep pace: vaccinations, for instance, to confer immunity, combined with practices such as hand-washing by physicians between patient visits, to limit contact between people and pathogens.

All too often, though, obvious protective measures such as using only clean hypodermic needles or treating urban drinking water with chlorine are neglected, whether out of ignorance or a wrongheaded emphasis on the short-term financial costs. The worldwide disparity in wealth is also to blame: not surprisingly, the advances made during the second epidemiological transition were limited largely to the affluent of the industrial world.

Such lapses are now beginning to teach the bitter lesson that the delicate balance between humans and invasive microorganisms can tip the other way again. Overconfidence—the legacy of the second epidemiological transition—has made us especially vulnerable to emerging and reemerging diseases. Evolutionary principles can provide this useful corrective: in spite of all our medical and technological hubris, there is no quick fix. If human beings are to overcome the current crisis, it will be through sensible changes in behavior, such as increased condom use and improved sanitation, combined with a commitment to stop disturbing the ecological balance of the planet.

The Bible, in short, was not far from wrong: We do bring plagues upon ourselves—not by sinning, but by refusing to heed our own alarms, our own best judgment. The price of peace—or at least peaceful coexistence—with the microorganisms on this planet is eternal vigilance.

Critical Thinking

1. Why were the 1950s and 1960s years of optimism with regard to eradicating disease? Why do we now know differently?

2. Why is the reality about infectious diseases less sensational but alarming nonetheless? Is this a unique predicament?

3. Why does the author say "people and pathologies have a long history together"?

4. What is the "conventional wisdom" and what does logic suggest in this regard? How can the reverse also happen?

5. How does the author characterize the nature of "the competition"? What is the "Red Queen Principle"?

6. Why was the view of Abdel R. Omran so ironic? What did he mean by an "epidemiological transition"?

7. What is the author's new theory regarding such transitions? How does he explain each transition?

8. What are the "heirloom" species? Why were there no epidemics for most of human existence?

9. What kinds of diseases came with farming? irrigation? domestication of animals? population density?

10. How did iron tools and improved transportation methods help the spread of disease?

11. How might global warming increase disease? Dammed water?

12. Why has Lyme disease been on the increase?

13. How might further population increase and political upheavals increase the spread of disease?

14. Why would a global network of food production help increase disease?

15. What role does the widespread and indiscriminate use of antibiotics play?

16. Why are protective measures not always taken?

17. What do we need to do to overcome the current crisis?

George J. Armelagos is a professor of anthropology at Emory University in Atlanta, Georgia. He has coedited two books on the evolution of human disease: *Paleopathology at the Origins of Agriculture,* which deals with prehistoric populations, and *Disease in Populations in Transition,* which focuses on contemporary societies.

From *The Sciences,* January/February 1998, pp. 24–29. Copyright © 1998 by The New York Academy of Sciences. www.nyas.org. Reprinted by permission of Blackwell Publishing, Ltd. For subscription, email: publicationse@nyas.org.

The Perfect Plague

The next killer germ could burst from the African rain forest—or from your family pet.

JARED DIAMOND AND NATHAN WOLFE

Shortly after one of us (Jared Diamond) boarded a flight from Hong Kong back to Los Angeles, the passenger in the next seat sneezed. She sneezed again—and again—and then she began coughing. Finally she gagged, pulled out the vomit bag from the seat back in front of her, threw up into the bag, stood up, squeezed past, and lurched to the toilet at the front of the plane. The woman was obviously miserable, but sympathy for her pain was not what I felt. Instead I was frightened and asked the flight attendant to move me to a seat as far from her as possible.

All I could think of was another sick person, a man from Guangdong province in southern China, who spent the night of February 21, 2003, at the Metropole Hotel in Hong Kong, an upscale establishment with a swimming pool, fitness center, restaurants, a bar, and all kinds of areas where visitors could socialize and connect. The man stayed a single night in room 911. Unfortunately for him and for many other people, he had picked up severe acute respiratory syndrome, or SARS—perhaps directly from an infected bat or from a small, arboreal mammal called a civet, common in one of Guangdong's famous "wet markets" that sell wild animals for food, or else from a person or chain of people ultimately infected from one of those animal sources.

In the course of his brief stay, the man initiated a SARS "super spreader" event that led to at least 16 more SARS cases among the hotel's guests and visitors and then to hundreds of other cases throughout Asia, Europe, and North America as those guests and visitors continued on their travels—just as my neighbor was now traveling to L.A. The infectiousness of room 911's guest can be gauged from the fact that three months later, the carpet right outside the door and near the hotel elevator yielded genetic evidence of the SARS virus, presumably spewed out in his own sneezing, coughing, or vomiting.

I didn't end up with SARS, but my experience drives home the terrifying prospect of a novel, unstoppable infectious disease. Globalization, changing climate, and the threat of drug resistance have conspired to set the stage for that perfect microbial storm: a situation in which an emerging pathogen—another HIV or smallpox, perhaps—might burst on the scene and kill millions before we can respond.

Pathogen Paradox

To grasp the risk, we first must understand why *any* microbe would evolve to sicken or kill us. In evolutionary terms, how does destroying its host help a microbe to survive?

Think of your body as a potential "habitat" for tiny microbes, just as a forest provides a habitat for bigger creatures like birds and squirrels. The species living in the forests of our bodies include lice, worms, bacteria, viruses, and amoebas. Many of those denizens are benign and cause us no harm. But some microbes seem to go out of their way to make us sick—either mildly sick, as in the case of the common cold, or else sick to the point of killing us, as in the case of smallpox.

Killer microbes have long posed a paradox for evolutionary biologists. Why would a microbe evolve to devastate the very habitat on which it depends? By analogy, you might reason that there should be no squirrels that destroy the forest they live in, because such a species would quickly go extinct.

The answer stems from the fact that in order to survive over the long haul, any microbe restricted to humans must be able to spread from one victim to the next. There is a simple mathematical requirement here: On average, the germ must infect at least one new victim for every old one who either dies or recovers and purges himself of the microbe. If the average number of new victims per old drops to fewer than one, then the spread of the microbe is doomed.

A microbe can't walk or fly from one host to the next. Instead it must resort to a range of nefarious tricks. What from our point of view is simply a disease symptom can, from the bug's perspective, be an all-important means of enlisting our help to move around. Common microbe tricks are to make us cough or sneeze, suffer from diarrhea, or develop open sores on our skin. Respectively, these symptoms spread the microbe into our exhaled breath, into the local water supply via our feces, and onto the skin of those who touch us, explaining why a microbe might want to induce unpleasant symptoms in its victims.

Evolutionary biologists reason that keeping us alive and pumping out new microbes would be an excellent strategy for such a bug, which might therefore evolve to be less, not more, virulent over time. An example comes from the history of syphilis. When it first appeared in Europe in 1495, it caused severe and painful symptoms within a few months, but by 1546 it had begun evolving into the slowly progressing disease that we know today.

Yet if keeping us alive is strategically sound, why do some pathogens go so far as to actually kill us?

Sometimes a microbe's deadly rampage through a human population stems from an accident of nature. For instance, the microbe could be comfortably adapted to some animal host that it routinely inhabits without deadly consequences, but it could be maladapted to the human environment. The microbe may rarely infect people, but when it does, it may kill the human host, who becomes a literal dead end for the virus as well.

A microbe's deadly rampage through humans might stem from an accident of nature.

But what of those killer microbes that target humans, making us their primary host? Their survival strategy, evolutionary biologists now realize, differs from that of a disease like syphilis but works just as well. Take the cholera bacterium that gives us diarrhea or the smallpox virus that makes us develop skin sores; both of these can kill us in days to weeks. Such virulence may be evolutionary favored if, in the brief time between our becoming infected and dying, the fatal symptoms spread trillions of microbes to potential new victims. The fact that we may die is unfortunate for us but an acceptable cost for the microbe. In the world of evolution and natural selection, anything that the microbe does to us is fair—just as long as at least one new victim gets infected for each old one.

Hence the recipe for a killer disease is for the microbe to achieve a balance between two things: the probability of its killing us quickly once we become infected and its efficiency in leading our bodies to transmit the microbe to new victims.

Humanity's greatest predators can be seen only with the aid of a microscope. The virus responsible for AIDS; the SARS virus; *Vibrio cholerae* bacteria, responsible for cholera; and spores of anthrax.

Those two things are connected. The greater its efficiency in inducing lethal, bug-spreading syndromes (good for the microbe), the faster the microbe kills us (bad for the microbe). Following this logic, a pathogen may end up killing lots of people by one of two routes. In the style of HIV, it can keep the disease carrier alive for a long time, infecting new victims over the course of months or years. Or in the style of smallpox and cholera, it might kill quickly with explosive symptoms that can spread an infection to dozens of new victims within a day.

Searching for the Source

For epidemiologists hoping to stanch such outbreaks, tracking killer germs to the source is key. Do deadly pandemics arise spontaneously in human populations? Or are they "gifts" from other species, mutating and then crossing over to make us ill? Which ecosystems are spawning them, and can we catch them at the start, before they cause too much damage?

Some answers can be found in the history of yellow fever, a virus spread by mosquitoes. The cause of devastating human epidemics throughout history, yellow fever is still rife in tropical South America and Africa. Biologists now understand that yellow fever arose in tropical African monkeys, which, through the mosquito vector, infected (and continue to infect) tropical African people, some of whom unintentionally carried yellow fever with them on slave ships several hundred years ago to South America.

Mosquitoes bit the infected slaves and in turn carried the virus to South American monkeys. In due course, mosquitoes bit infected monkeys and transmitted yellow fever right back to the human population there.

In Venezuela today, the Ministry of Health keeps a lookout for the appearance of unusual numbers of dead wild monkeys, such as howler monkeys. Because the monkeys are so susceptible to yellow fever and can act as a reservoir from which the virus leaps to the human population, an explosion of monkey deaths serves as an advance warning system, signaling the need to vaccinate humans in the vicinity.

This pattern of cross-infection from animals to humans is par for the course in emerging infectious disease. In fact, the big killer diseases of history all came to us from microbes living in other species, overwhelmingly from other warm-blooded mammals and, to a lesser extent, from birds.

On reflection, this all makes sense. Each new animal host to which a microbe adapts represents a new habitat. It is easiest for a microbe to jump between closely related habitats, from an animal species with one sort of body chemistry to a closely related animal species with very similar body chemistry.

In the tropics, disease sources have included a host of wild animals, most notably the nonhuman primates. We can thank our primate cousins not just for yellow fever but also for HIV, dengue fever, hepatitis B, and vivax malaria. Other wild animal disease donors include rats, the source of the plague and typhus.

In temperate regions like the United States, meanwhile, ticks in suburban neighborhoods and domestic livestock living in proximity to humans have posed threats. Mammalian reservoirs like mice and chipmunks carry Lyme disease and tularemia; ticks transmit these diseases to humans. Cattle probably gave rise to the measles and tuberculosis. Smallpox is likely to have come from camels, biologists say, and flu from pigs and ducks.

The Next Wave

Today, with fewer people tending farms and more living in the suburbs, things have certainly changed. The principles of infectious disease are the same as they have always been, but modern conditions, including life in proximity to pets and mammal-filled woods, are exposing us to new pathogen reservoirs and new modes of transmitting disease.

One of us (Nathan Wolfe) has spent much of the last six years in the tropical African country of Cameroon, studying the kinds of interspecies jumps that such conditions might spawn. To examine the mechanisms, I worked with rural hunters who butchered wild animals for food. I collected blood samples from the hunters, from other people in their community, and from their animal prey. By testing all those samples, I identified microbes inhabiting the animal reservoirs and focused on those that showed up in the hunters' blood, making them candidates for firing up human disease.

Three strains of influenza virus, including H5N1, better known as the avian flu virus. The influenza virus frequently mutates, creating new strains. This makes it difficult to produce vaccines and opens the door to another global influenza pandemic, such as the one that struck in 1918 and eventually killed more than 20 million people.

One evening I asked a group of hunters if they had ever cut themselves while butchering wild monkeys or apes. The response was incredulous laughter: "You don't know the answer to that?" Of course, they said. All of them had cut themselves once or more, thereby giving themselves ample opportunity to get infected from animal blood.

On reflection, I shouldn't have been surprised. I can't count all the times I have cut myself while chopping onions. The difference is that onions aren't closely related to us humans, and an onion virus has far less chance of taking hold in us than does a monkey virus.

The statistics are telling. Researchers like Mark Woolhouse, professor of infectious disease epidemiology at the University of Edinburgh in Scotland, have found at least 868 human pathogens that infect both animals and humans, although some are not as fearsome as they seem.

Overhyped microbes include anthrax (famous for the U.S. mail attacks in 2000), the Ebola and Marburg viruses (which can cause dramatic bleeding and high fever in their victims), and the prion agent of mad cow disease (otherwise known as bovine spongiform encephalopathy, or BSE), which kills people by making their nervous systems degenerate. These bugs arouse terror because they kill so many of their victims. For example, in the 2000 Ebola outbreak, which struck the Gulu district of Uganda, 53 percent of the 425 people who contracted the disease died. The case fatality rate for BSE is 100 percent.

Although spectacularly lethal, these pathogens generally kill just a few hundred people at a time and then burn themselves out. They transmit from human to human too inefficiently to spread very widely; 100 percent of a small number of victims is still a small number of fatalities.

There are many reasons why an agent leaping from animals to humans might not affect more individuals. For example, humans do not normally bite, scratch, hunt, or eat each other. This surely contributes to the rarity or nonexistence of human-to-human transmission of rabies (acquired by the bite of an infected dog or bat); cat-scratch disease (which causes skin lesions and swollen lymph nodes); tularemia (a disease, often acquired when hunting and cutting up an infected rabbit, that can cause skin ulcers, swollen lymph nodes, and fever); and BSE (probably acquired by eating the nervous system tissue of infected cows).

Some outbreaks, once recognized, are relatively easy to control. Anthrax is treatable with antibiotics; after an initial malaria-like stage, the rapid onset and severity of Ebola and Marburg symptoms have made identification and containment straightforward.

In fact, within the last 40 years, only HIV (derived from chimpanzees) has taken off to cause a pandemic.

Back to the Future

If not anthrax or Ebola, which pathogens might spawn the next deadly pandemic in our midst?

New pandemics are most likely to be triggered by mutant strains of familiar microbe species, especially those that have caused plagues by churning out mutant strains in the past. For example, the highest known epidemic death toll in history was caused by a new strain of influenza virus that killed more than 20 million people in 1918 and 1919. Unfairly named Spanish influenza, it apparently emerged in Kansas during World War I, was carried by American troops to Europe, and then spread around the world in three waves before ebbing in outbreaks of declining virulence in the 1920s. Mutant strains of influenza or cholera remain prime candidates for another deadly outbreak. Both can persist in animal reservoirs or the environment, and both are adept at spawning new strains. Both pathogens also transmit efficiently, and it is possible that these two important diseases of the past could become important diseases of the future.

A future pandemic could also come from tuberculosis. New mutants have already arisen through the mechanism of drug resistance. And the disease lives on in the human population, especially among those with weakened immunity, including patients with HIV.

Also of concern are emerging sexually transmitted diseases, which, once introduced, may be difficult to control because it is hard to persuade humans to change sexual behavior or to abstain from sex. HIV offers a grim warning: Despite its huge global impact, the AIDS epidemic would have been far worse if the sexual transmissibility of HIV (which is actually rather modest) had equaled that of some other sexually transmitted agents, such as human papilloma virus (HPV). While the probability of HIV transmission varies with the stage of the disease and the type of sexual contact, it appears to pass from infected to uninfected individuals in less than 1 percent of acts of unprotected heterosexual intercourse, while the corresponding probability of HPV transmission is thought to be higher than 5 percent—probably much higher.

Similarly, it could be difficult to control emerging pathogens transmitted by pets, which increasingly include exotic species along with traditional domestic animals like dogs and cats. Already we are at risk of catching rabies from our dogs, toxoplasmosis and cat-scratch disease from our cats, and psittacosis from our parrots. Most people now accept the need to cull millions of farmyard animals in the face of epidemics like mad cow disease, but it is hard to imagine killing beloved puppies, bunnies, and kittens, even if those pets do turn out to offer a pathway for a dangerous new disease.

Have Plague, Will Travel

Once a killer disease has emerged, modern societies offer new ways for it to flourish and spread. Global travel, the close quarters of the urban environment, climate change, the evolution of drug-resistant microbes, and increasing numbers of the elderly or antibiotic-treated immunosuppressed could all aid the next great plague.

For example, rapid urbanization in Africa could transform yellow fever, Chikungunya fever (which causes severe joint pain and fever), and other rural African arboviruses (viruses, including yellow fever, spread by bloodsucking insects) into plagues of African cities, as has already happened with dengue hemorrhagic fever. One of us (Wolfe) theorizes that this might follow increasing demand in those cities for bush meat. Like urban people everywhere, urban Africans love to eat the foods enjoyed by their village-dwelling ancestors, and in tropical Africa this means bush meat. In that respect it's similar to the smoked fish and bagels that I eat in the United States, which give me some comforting memory of my Eastern European roots. But there's an important difference: The wild game that I see served in fancy restaurants in the capital of Cameroon is much more likely to transmit a dangerous virus to the person who hunted and butchered it, or to the cook who prepared it, or to the restaurant patron who ate the meat undercooked, than is my brunch of smoked fish and bagels.

By connecting distant places, meanwhile, globalization permits the long-distance transfer of microbes along with their insect vectors and their human victims, as evidenced not only by the spread of HIV around the world, but also by North American cases of cholera and SARS brought by infected passengers on jet flights from South America and Asia, respectively. Indeed, when a flight from Buenos Aires to Los Angeles stopped in Lima in 1992, it picked up some seafood infected with the cholera then making the rounds in Peru. As a result, dozens of passengers who arrived in Los Angeles, some of whom then changed planes

and flew on to Nevada and even as far as Japan, found that they had contracted cholera. Within days that single airplane spread cholera 10,000 miles around the whole rim of the Pacific Basin.

The tuberculosis bacterium, *Mycobacterium tuberculosis,* has developed a resistance to antibiotics in many regions of the world, fueling a resurgence of this disease.

Consider as well those diseases thought of as "just" tropical because they are transmitted by tropical vectors: malaria transmitted by mosquitoes, sleeping sickness spread by tsetse flies, and Chagas' disease (associated with edema, fever, and heart disease) spread by kissing bugs. How will we feel about those tropical diseases if global warming enables their vectors to spread into temperate zones? While microbe and vector movement can be difficult to detect, modeling suggests that global warming will expand the reach of malaria to higher latitudes and into tropical mountain regions.

The transmission of emerging diseases has also been enhanced by a host of modern practices and technologies. The commercial bush meat trade has introduced retroviruses into human populations. Ecotourism has exposed first-world tourists to cutaneous leishmaniasis and other third-world diseases. Underequipped rural hospitals have facilitated Ebola virus outbreaks in Africa. Air conditioners and water circulation systems have spread Legionnaires' disease. Industrial food production was responsible in Europe for the spread of BSE. And intravenous drug use and blood transfusion have both spread HIV and hepatitis B and C.

We have the potential to avert the next HIV, saving millions of lives and billions of dollars.

All this shows that disease prevention and treatment need to be supplemented by a new effort: disease forecasting. This refers to the early detection of potential pandemics at a stage when we might still be able to localize them, before they have had the opportunity to infect a high percentage of the local population and thereby spread around the world, as happened with HIV. Already one of us (Wolfe) is working through a new initiative, the Global Viral Forecasting Initiative (GVFI), to do just that. GVFI works in countries throughout the world to monitor the entry and movement of new agents before they become pandemics. By studying emerging agents at the interface between humans and animals, GVFI hopes to stop new epidemics before they explode. Monitoring for the emergence of both new sexually transmitted diseases and pet-associated diseases would be good investments.

The predictions here are admittedly educated guesses—but they are educated by some of the best science available. The time to act is now. If we don't, then we will continue to be like the cardiologists of the 1950s, waiting for their patients' heart attacks and doing little to prevent them. If we do act, we have the potential to avert the next HIV, saving millions of lives and billions of dollars. The choice seems obvious.

Critical Thinking

1. How did the author's (Jared Diamond) airline experience illustrate the possible spread of a novel, unstoppable infectious disease?

2. What must a microbe be able to do to survive if it kills its host?

3. What are some of the "microbe tricks" designed to allow it to spread from one victim to the next?

4. Under what circumstance would keeping us alive be an excellent strategy?

5. When would virulence be evolutionarily favored?

6. In what sense does a recipe for a killer disease involve a balance between two things?

7. By what two routes may a pathogen end up killing lots of people?

8. Discuss the cross-infection from animals to humans as the explanation for the big killer disease of history and why this could easily happen.

9. What are the modern conditions exposing us to new pathogen reservoirs?

10. What is a principle way in which African hunters become exposed to infectious microbes?

11. Where are new pandemics likely to come from and why?

12. How have modern societies offered new ways for killer disease to flourish and spread?

13. What is "disease forecasting" and why is it important?

The Human Vector

WENDY ORENT

"How do you make preparedness sexy?" Dave Daigle asks. A communications expert in disaster readiness at the Centers for Disease Control and Prevention in Atlanta, Daigle created last year's cheeky Zombie Apocalypse campaign, designed to teach the social media generation how to survive natural disasters and uncontained infectious outbreaks. He never expected the associated Twitter campaign to crash his server and ultimately garner three billion hits. The whole initiative, the most successful in CDC public-relations history, cost taxpayers all of $87—for clip art.

The Zombie Apocalypse campaign instructs you how to prepare for pandemics and catastrophes like hurricanes, tornadoes, and floods. You need a plan. You need flashlights, an all-weather radio, bottled water. You need food you can stock, like peanut butter, canned tuna, and crackers. You need first-aid supplies like bandages, antiseptics, and soap. And you need somewhere safe to stay—a basement room, preferably windowless, where you can hole up for several days until the danger is past.

That style of preparation also resonates with the plots of popular disease-disaster movies, like the recent "Contagion". The film presents a fictional virus, a construct devised by Columbia University epidemiologist Ian Lipkin, vectoring its way across the planet, killing millions of the fecklessly unprepared and leaving social havoc and innumerable bodies in its wake. The CDC campaign and the film spring from the same conviction: Since nature can always turn on us, we had better be ready for the consequences.

This kind of preparedness for natural catastrophes makes sense, but for pandemics the idea rings false; unlike the scenario in "Contagion," pandemics don't spring on us like hurricanes. Instead, they are overwhelmingly social phenomena. Mother Nature doesn't create them; human beings do. We create the settings that allow new, deadly diseases to evolve and invade. Understanding those settings, which can be thought of as disease factories, and taking steps to disrupt them are far better preparation than sending families down to huddle in the basement.

The term pandemic almost always refers to waves of acute infectious disease across a wide geographical area. In A.D. 542, during the savage Plague of Justinian, the citizens of Constantinople buried their dead in towers along the city walls and, when there was no more room, in massive pits into which corpses were flung like carrion. That epidemic, almost certainly bubonic plague, rimmed the entire Mediterranean at least as far west as Marseille and killed millions. The Black Death—caused by a variant of the same germ, *Yersinia pestis*—swept into Europe from central Asia in 1347 and killed between a quarter and a third of Europe. And plague was not done with Europe yet. Londoners of the 17th century watched additional waves of disease come in by ship from Holland. In a matter of weeks, they too were infected, nailed up in their houses, and left to die. The bodies, stacked like logs on gravediggers' wagons, were carted through the streets and dumped in mass graves, which you can still see in London today.

Blaming pestilence on God's wrath goes back to Homer's *Iliad*. In the opening pages, a priest asks Apollo to avenge his daughter, who has been taken by the Greek leader, Agamemnon, as a spoil of war. Apollo complies with a rain of arrows, and the Greeks begin to die. The same image of plague as God's punishment crops up during the Plague of Justinian and the Black Death, and something of it remains today, though in the modern narrative it is no longer God but nature that we have offended. Since the publication of Laurie Garrett's influential 1994 book, *The Coming Plague,* people commonly talk about pandemics as nature's retribution: something sprung on us as a penalty for disturbing the world's innate balance, for penetrating too deeply into forests and jungles, for disrupting the order of the Earth's precarious ecosystems. It is our version of God's punishment, and it is just as false.

The idea that new diseases come from human invasions of pristine environments probably stems from HIV, the virus causing AIDS. HIV originated as a simian virus and most likely crossed the species line around 1930. Yet AIDS did not turn into a human pandemic until sexual activity transformed a sluggish disease into an explosive and probably more virulent one, contends evolutionary biologist Paul Ewald of the University of Louisville. It was not just the spark of infection, but what happened to that infection when it entered human society, that converted a simian retrovirus into HIV and then into the deadly pandemic that is AIDS.

This is why pandemics are necessarily social phenomena. Each human pandemic exists because social conditions have allowed it to evolve. Some diseases move across species lines and yet harm us not at all. An example is Ebola-Reston, a virus deadly to monkeys. It infected four people at an animal facility in Reston, Virginia, in November 1989, but no one fell ill; the infections were detectable only through blood tests. At the same time, other, related Ebola viruses ravage the human body. Some particularly notorious strains almost always kill.

What most new diseases, including Ebola, don't do very well is spread from person to person. Without such spread there is no pandemic. There isn't even a new, self-sustaining human disease. If we are looking for the real engine for infection—the driver of the disease factory, if you like—we have to understand what human-to-human transmission is, and how it turns an animal disease into a human one.

To be transmitted, a germ has to be shed from one human host and picked up by another. Some germs, like cholera, make their hosts produce copious diarrhea. If there is poor sanitation or people are crowded together, those germs are likely to infect other hosts. Respiratory infections are shed into the air or onto surfaces. If someone sneezes into her hand and touches a doorknob that you touch afterwards, you may catch her infection. Some germs float through the air and you breathe them in. Measles and tuberculosis spread this way. These germs have to keep their hosts mobile. If you are knocked off your feet right away by an infection and you don't walk around sneezing or coughing, it is harder for the germ to find another person to infect.

But manipulating the host into producing diarrhea or a germ-filled sneeze is not a trivial task. Highly virulent H5N1 avian flu, which many experts thought would trigger a deadly pandemic between 2004 and 2007, has so far been unable to convert from a chicken flu to a human one. On the vast chicken farms of Asia, where millions of birds are crowded under disease-factory conditions, H5N1 gained tremendous virulence, becoming a sophisticated chicken-killing machine. When people are exposed to high doses of this virus, they can succumb as well. But H5N1, well adapted to the higher temperatures and particular cell receptors found in chickens, does not spread from person to person. In its present form, therefore, it has shown no capacity to turn from a well-adapted chicken disease to a human one.

Experts have warned that H5N1 could recombine with a human virus at any moment, mutating so it becomes transmissible. But transmission doesn't just happen; it evolves. It would take a whole series of mutations, and they would have to happen in the bodies of a chain of human beings, not chickens. Nor would a single recombination event be likely to spawn a fully transmissible human disease. Instead, you would have to start with a huge dose of virus, says flu virologist Earl Brown of the University of Ottawa. A huge dose would be more likely to contain many diverse strains. Then you would have to expose those strains to a chain of human hosts. As the virus moved from person to person (assuming it could), the strains that are most easily transmitted would be selected over the others. Eventually you would get a human-adapted virus, though what that virus would look like is anybody's guess. To produce a truly lethal human flu or other virus, you would need the same sort of conditions that produced virulent chicken flu. You would need a disease factory for people.

Yet in 2005 scientists were so terrified of a lethal avian flu pandemic that they devised all sorts of preparations, which surely helped inspire the CDC's Zombie Apocalypse campaign. Tamiflu, an antiviral drug, was stockpiled in enormous quantities, even though the late influenza virologist Edwin Kibourne noted that it is useless for prophylaxis. The drug also has dangerous side effects—and there are practical limits for how long you could keep people on it, anyway. Governments and drug companies developed candidates for anti-pandemic vaccines, and some experts called for mass prophylactic vaccination, even though no human H5N1 virus existed. Government agencies urged people to stockpile water and peanut butter and tuna fish in preparation for what Michael Osterholm, director of the Center for Infectious Disease Research and Policy at the University of Minnesota, told the press would be "three years of a given hell. . . . I can't think of any other risk, terrorism or Mother Nature included, that could potentially pose any greater risk to society than this."

We never got three years of hell, but we did get a new pandemic influenza. While experts were fixated on birds in Asia, this strain came from pigs in Mexico. Packing pigs into cramped quarters produces another kind of disease factory. In the winter of 2009, people living near a giant industrial pig farm in La Gloria, Mexico, reportedly became ill with a severe respiratory virus. No one except local reporters and a few health officials paid attention.

Then the virus began to spread. By the time the supposed "index case"—a 5-year-old La Gloria child named Edgar Hernandez—was identified, the so-called swine flu had been transmitted widely across Mexico. Within days it landed across the border, and in just weeks it spread across the world. Pigs and people, both mammals, pass flu back and forth quite easily; a pig is more like a person than a chicken when it comes to temperature and cell receptors. Pigs were always more likely to produce a pandemic flu than chickens. But most people weren't looking.

Enormous animal farms remain a source of danger, a far greater danger to people than new viruses emerging straight out of nature. Virologist Brown warns that we have to find new ways to raise animals that don't pack them so closely together in huge industrial farms. Under such crowded conditions, even the most innocuous germs can rapidly evolve virulence. The deadly Escherichia coli outbreak in Germany last year, which sickened more than 4,000 people and killed more than 50, may be traceable to modern factory farming, which uses massive doses of antibiotics to curb animal infections, likely converting a normally benign microbe into an antibiotic-resistant killer.

Hospitals also encourage the emergence of lethal human microbes. Paul Ewald points out that any conditions allowing germs to be transported from a person immobilized by serious illness to new human hosts can produce deadly infections. Ironically, hospitals turn out to be highly efficient disease factories. They allow the proliferation and spread of dangerous germs among patients, and the evolution of those germs to extreme levels of virulence. The last decades have seen the evolution of virulent, antibiotic-resistant staphylococcus germs (MRSA), now spread worldwide, along with potentially lethal strains of Clostridium difficile, a usually benign intestinal infection. And the normally innocuous soil bacterium Acinetobacter baumannii has plagued veterans' hospitals, evolving intense virulence and antibiotic resistance and afflicting wounded soldiers returning from Afghanistan and Iraq.

The CDC's Zombie Apocalypse program is well intentioned, and for natural disasters it gives great advice. But preparing for a pandemic has almost nothing to do with personal supplies of crackers and duct tape. It lies in understanding the real engines of infection: the giant industrial farms and crowded hospitals with insufficient hygiene.

Many European hospitals have reduced their rates of MRSA transmission by screening patients with nasal swabs prior to admission, and some American hospitals are following suit. Shutting down industrial farming should probably come next. These germ incubators need to be replaced with less intensive farms that raise fewer animals on more land. Switching to grass-fed cattle, which live on the open range, would help as well. The price, including the end of cheap chicken, pork, or beef, might be more than we are willing to pay, even at risk to our health. But as long as there are industrial farms, the possibility of pandemics arising from them persists.

Critical Thinking

1. What is the Zombie Apocalypse campaign? Why does it "ring false" for pandemics?

2. Why is it that blaming pestilence on God's wrath or on nature's retribution are equally false?

3. Using specific examples, show how pandemics are necessarily social phenomena.

4. What is it that most new diseases do not do very well?

5. What must germs do to be transmitted?

6. Why has the H5N1 avian flu not shown a capacity to turn from a well-adapted chicken disease to a human one?

7. What are the necessary conditions to produce a truly lethal human flu from a chicken flu virus?

8. What were the measures taken in anticipation of an avian flu epidemic? Where did the new pandemic influenza actually come from and why?

9. Why must we find new ways to raise animals in order to prevent virulence? How was the Escherichia coli outbreak in Germany a good example of modern factory farming?

10. How do hospitals encourage the emergence of lethal human microbes?

11. What measures does the author suggest we take in order to prevent pandemics?

The Inuit Paradox

How can people who gorge on fat and rarely see a vegetable be healthier than we are?

PATRICIA GADSBY

Patricia Cochran, an Inupiat from Northwestern Alaska, is talking about the native foods of her childhood: "We pretty much had a subsistence way of life. Our food supply was right outside our front door. We did our hunting and foraging on the Seward Peninsula and along the Bering Sea."

"Our meat was seal and walrus, marine mammals that live in cold water and have lots of fat. We used seal oil for our cooking and as a dipping sauce for food. We had moose, caribou, and reindeer. We hunted ducks, geese, and little land birds like quail, called ptarmigan. We caught crab and lots of fish—salmon, whitefish, tomcod, pike, and char. Our fish were cooked, dried, smoked, or frozen. We ate frozen raw whitefish, sliced thin. The elders liked stinkfish, fish buried in seal bags or cans in the tundra and left to ferment. And fermented seal flipper, they liked that too."

Cochran's family also received shipments of whale meat from kin living farther north, near Barrow. Beluga was one she liked; raw muktuk, which is whale skin with its underlying blubber, she definitely did not. "To me it has a chew-on-a-tire consistency," she says, "but to many people it's a mainstay." In the short subarctic summers, the family searched for roots and greens and, best of all from a child's point of view, wild blueberries, crowberries, or salmonberries, which her aunts would mix with whipped fat to make a special treat called *akutuq*—in colloquial English, Eskimo ice cream.

Now Cochran directs the Alaska Native Science Commission, which promotes research on native cultures and the health and environmental issues that affect them. She sits at her keyboard in Anchorage, a bustling city offering fare from Taco Bell to French cuisine. But at home Cochran keeps a freezer filled with fish, seal, walrus, reindeer, and whale meat, sent by her family up north, and she and her husband fish and go berry picking—"sometimes a challenge in Anchorage," she adds, laughing. "I eat fifty-fifty," she explains, half traditional, half regular American.

No one, not even residents of the northernmost villages on Earth, eats an entirely traditional northern diet anymore. Even the groups we came to know as Eskimo—which include the Inupiat and the Yupiks of Alaska, the Canadian Inuit and Inuvialuit, Inuit Greenlanders, and the Siberian Yupiks—have probably seen more changes in their diet in a lifetime than their ancestors did over thousands of years. The closer people live to towns and the more access they have to stores and cash-paying jobs, the more likely they are to have westernized their eating. And with westernization, at least on the North American continent, comes processed foods and cheap carbohydrates—Crisco, Tang, soda, cookies, chips, pizza, fries. "The young and urbanized," says Harriet Kuhnlein, director of the Centre for Indigenous Peoples' Nutrition and Environment at McGill University in Montreal, "are increasingly into fast food." So much so that type 2 diabetes, obesity, and other diseases of Western civilization are becoming causes for concern there too.

Today, when diet books top the best-seller list and nobody seems sure of what to eat to stay healthy, it's surprising to learn how well the Eskimo did on a high-protein, high-fat diet. Shaped by glacial temperatures, stark landscapes, and protracted winters, the traditional Eskimo diet had little in the way of plant food, no agricultural or dairy products, and was unusually low in carbohydrates. Mostly people subsisted on what they hunted and fished. Inland dwellers took advantage of caribou feeding on tundra mosses, lichens, and plants too tough for humans to stomach (though predigested vegetation in the animals' paunches became dinner as well). Coastal people exploited the sea. The main nutritional challenge was avoiding starvation in late winter if primary meat sources became too scarce or lean.

These foods hardly make up the "balanced" diet most of us grew up with, and they look nothing like the mix of grains, fruits, vegetables, meat, eggs, and dairy we're accustomed to seeing in conventional food pyramid diagrams. How could such a diet possibly be adequate? How did people get along on little else but fat and animal protein?

The diet of the far north shows that there are no essential foods—only essential nutrients.

What the diet of the Far North illustrates, says Harold Draper, a biochemist and expert in Eskimo nutrition, is that there are no essential foods—only essential nutrients. And humans can get those nutrients from diverse and eye-opening sources.

One might, for instance, imagine gross vitamin deficiencies arising from a diet with scarcely any fruits and vegetables. What furnishes vitamin A, vital for eyes and bones? We derive much of ours from colorful plant foods, constructing it from pigmented plant precursors called carotenoids (as in carrots). But vitamin A, which is oil soluble, is also plentiful in the oils of cold-water fishes and sea mammals, as well as in the animals' livers, where fat is processed. These dietary staples also provide vitamin D, another oil-soluble vitamin needed for bones. Those of us living in temperate and tropical climates, on the other hand, usually make vitamin D indirectly by exposing skin to strong sun—hardly an option in the Arctic winter—and by consuming fortified cow's milk, to which the indigenous northern groups had little access until recent decades and often don't tolerate all that well.

As for vitamin C, the source in the Eskimo diet was long a mystery. Most animals can synthesize their own vitamin C, or ascorbic acid, in their livers, but humans are among the exceptions, along with other primates and oddballs like guinea pigs and bats. If we don't ingest enough of it, we fall apart from scurvy, a gruesome connective-tissue disease. In the United States today we can get ample supplies from orange juice, citrus fruits, and fresh vegetables. But vitamin C oxidizes with time; getting enough from a ship's provisions was tricky for early 18th- and 19th-century voyagers to the polar regions. Scurvy—joint pain, rotting gums, leaky blood vessels, physical and mental degeneration—plagued European and U.S. expeditions even in the 20th century. However, Arctic peoples living on fresh fish and meat were free of the disease.

Impressed, the explorer Vilhjalmur Stefansson adopted an Eskimo-style diet for five years during the two Arctic expeditions he led between 1908 and 1918. "The thing to do is to find your antiscorbutics where you are," he wrote. "Pick them up as you go." In 1928, to convince skeptics, he and a young colleague spent a year on an Americanized version of the diet under medical supervision at Bellevue Hospital in New York City. The pair ate steaks, chops, organ meats like brain and liver, poultry, fish, and fat with gusto. "If you have

some fresh meat in your diet every day and don't overcook it," Stefansson declared triumphantly, "there will be enough C from that source alone to prevent scurvy."

In fact, all it takes to ward off scurvy is a daily dose of 10 milligrams, says Karen Fediuk, a consulting dietitian and former graduate student of Harriet Kuhnlein's who did her master's thesis on vitamin C. (That's far less than the U.S. recommended daily allowance of 75 to 90 milligrams—75 for women, 90 for men.) Native foods easily supply those 10 milligrams of scurvy prevention, especially when organ meats—preferably raw—are on the menu. For a study published with Kuhnlein in 2002, Fediuk compared the vitamin C content of 100-gram (3.55-ounce) samples of foods eaten by Inuit women living in the Canadian Arctic: Raw caribou liver supplied almost 24 milligrams, seal brain close to 15 milligrams, and raw kelp more than 28 milligrams. Still higher levels were found in whale skin and muktuk.

As you might guess from its antiscorbutic role, vitamin C is crucial for the synthesis of connective tissue, including the matrix of skin. "Wherever collagen's made, you can expect vitamin C," says Kuhnlein. Thick skinned, chewy, and collagen rich, raw muktuk can serve up an impressive 36 milligrams in a 100-gram piece, according to Fediuk's analyses. "Weight for weight, it's as good as orange juice," she says. Traditional Inuit practices like freezing meat and fish and frequently eating them raw, she notes, conserve vitamin C, which is easily cooked off and lost in food processing.

Hunter-gatherer diets like those eaten by these northern groups and other traditional diets based on nomadic herding or subsistence farming are among the older approaches to human eating. Some of these eating plans might seem strange to us— diets centered around milk, meat, and blood among the East African pastoralists, enthusiastic tuber eating by the Quechua living in the High Andes, the staple use of the mongongo nut in the southern African !Kung—but all proved resourceful adaptations to particular eco-niches. No people, though, may have been forced to push the nutritional envelope further than those living at Earth's frozen extremes. The unusual makeup of the far-northern diet led Loren Cordain, a professor of evolutionary nutrition at Colorado State University at Fort Collins, to make an intriguing observation.

Four years ago, Cordain reviewed the macronutrient content (protein, carbohydrates, fat) in the diets of 229 hunter-gatherer groups listed in a series of journal articles collectively known as the Ethnographic Atlas. These are some of the oldest surviving human diets. In general, hunter-gatherers tend to eat more animal protein than we do in our standard Western diet, with its reliance on agriculture and carbohydrates derived from grains and starchy plants. Lowest of all in carbohydrate, and highest in combined fat and protein, are the diets of peoples living in the Far North, where they make up for fewer plant foods with extra fish. What's equally striking, though, says Cordain, is that these meat-and-fish diets also exhibit a natural "protein ceiling." Protein accounts for no more than 35 to 40 percent of their total calories, which suggests to him that's all the protein humans can comfortably handle.

Wild-animal fats are different from other fats. Farm animals typically have lots of highly saturated fat.

This ceiling, Cordain thinks, could be imposed by the way we process protein for energy. The simplest, fastest way to make energy is to convert carbohydrates into glucose, our body's primary fuel. But if the body is out of carbs, it can burn fat, or if necessary, break down protein. The name given to the convoluted business of making glucose from protein is gluconeogenesis. It takes place in the liver, uses a dizzying slew of enzymes, and creates nitrogen waste that has to be converted into urea and disposed of through the kidneys. On a truly traditional diet, says Draper, recalling his studies in the 1970s, Arctic people had plenty of protein but little carbohydrate, so they often relied on gluconeogenesis. Not only did they have bigger livers to handle the additional work but their urine volumes were also typically larger to get rid of the extra urea. Nonetheless, there appears to be a limit on how much protein the human liver can safely cope with: Too much overwhelms the liver's waste-disposal system, leading to protein poisoning—nausea, diarrhea, wasting, and death.

Whatever the metabolic reason for this syndrome, says John Speth, an archaeologist at the University of Michigan's Museum of Anthropology, plenty of evidence shows that hunters through the ages avoided protein excesses, discarding fat-depleted animals even when food was scarce. Early pioneers and trappers in North America encountered what looks like a similar affliction, sometimes referred to as rabbit starvation because rabbit meat is notoriously lean. Forced to subsist on fat-deficient meat, the men would gorge themselves, yet wither away. Protein can't be the sole source of energy for humans, concludes Cordain. Anyone eating a meaty diet that is low in carbohydrates must have fat as well.

Stefansson had arrived at this conclusion, too, while living among the Copper Eskimo. He recalled how he and his Eskimo companions had become quite ill after weeks of eating "caribou so skinny that there was no appreciable fat behind the eyes or in the marrow." Later he agreed to repeat the miserable experience at Bellevue Hospital, for science's sake, and for a while ate nothing but defatted meat. "The symptoms brought on at Bellevue by an incomplete meat diet [lean without fat] were exactly the same as in the Arctic

. . . diarrhea and a feeling of general baffling discomfort," he wrote. He was restored with a fat fix but "had lost considerable weight." For the remainder of his year on meat, Stefansson tucked into his rations of chops and steaks with fat intact. "A normal meat diet is not a high-protein diet," he pronounced. "We were really getting three-quarters of our calories from fat." (Fat is more than twice as calorie dense as protein or carbohydrate, but even so, that's a lot of lard. A typical U.S diet provides about 35 percent of its calories from fat.)

Stefansson dropped 10 pounds on his meat-and-fat regimen and remarked on its "slenderizing" aspect, so perhaps it's no surprise he's been co-opted as a posthumous poster boy for Atkins-type diets. No discussion about diet these days can avoid Atkins. Even some researchers interviewed for this article couldn't resist referring to the Inuit way of eating as the "original Atkins." "Superficially, at a macronutrient level, the two diets certainly look similar," allows Samuel Klein, a nutrition researcher at Washington University in St. Louis, who's attempting to study how Atkins stacks up against conventional weight-loss diets. Like the Inuit diet, Atkins is low in carbohydrates and very high in fat. But numerous researchers, including Klein, point out that there are profound differences between the two diets, beginning with the type of meat and fat eaten.

Fats have been demonized in the United States, says Eric Dewailly, a professor of preventive medicine at Laval University in Quebec. But all fats are not created equal. This lies at the heart of a paradox—the Inuit paradox, if you will. In the Nunavik villages in northern Quebec, adults over 40 get almost half their calories from native foods, says Dewailly, and they don't die of heart attacks at nearly the same rates as other Canadians or Americans. Their cardiac death rate is about half of ours, he says. As someone who looks for links between diet and cardiovascular health, he's intrigued by that reduced risk. Because the traditional Inuit diet is "so restricted," he says, it's easier to study than the famously heart-healthy Mediterranean diet, with its cornucopia of vegetables, fruits, grains, herbs, spices, olive oil, and red wine.

A key difference in the typical Nunavik Inuit's diet is that more than 50 percent of the calories in Inuit native foods come from fats. Much more important, the fats come from wild animals.

Wild-animal fats are different from both farm-animal fats and processed fats, says Dewailly. Farm animals, cooped up and stuffed with agricultural grains (carbohydrates) typically have lots of solid, highly saturated fat. Much of our processed food is also riddled with solid fats, or so-called trans fats, such as the reengineered vegetable oils and shortenings cached in baked goods and snacks. "A lot of the packaged food on supermarket shelves contains them. So do commercial french fries," Dewailly adds.

Trans fats are polyunsaturated vegetable oils tricked up to make them more solid at room temperature. Manufacturers do this by hydrogenating the oils—adding extra hydrogen atoms to their molecular structures—which "twists" their shapes. Dewailly makes twisting sound less like a chemical transformation than a perversion, an act of public-health sabotage: "These man-made fats are dangerous, even worse for the heart than saturated fats." They not only lower high-density lipoprotein cholesterol (HDL, the "good" cholesterol) but they also raise low-density lipoprotein cholesterol (LDL, the "bad" cholesterol) and triglycerides, he says. In the process, trans fats set the stage for heart attacks because they lead to the increase of fatty buildup in artery walls.

Wild animals that range freely and eat what nature intended, says Dewailly, have fat that is far more healthful. Less of their fat is saturated, and more of it is in the monounsaturated form (like olive oil). What's more, cold-water fishes and sea mammals are particularly rich in polyunsaturated fats called n-3 fatty acids or omega-3 fatty acids. These fats appear to benefit the heart and vascular system. But the polyunsaturated fats in most Americans' diets are the omega-6 fatty acids supplied by vegetable oils. By contrast, whale blubber consists of 70 percent monounsaturated fat and close to 30 percent omega-3s, says Dewailly.

Dieting is the price we pay for too little exercise and too much mass-produced food.

Omega-3s evidently help raise HDL cholesterol, lower triglycerides, and are known for anticlotting effects. (Ethnographers have remarked on an Eskimo propensity for nosebleeds.) These fatty acids are believed to protect the heart from life-threatening arrhythmias that can lead to sudden cardiac death. And like a "natural aspirin," adds Dewailly, omega-3 polyunsaturated fats help put a damper on runaway inflammatory processes, which play a part in atherosclerosis, arthritis, diabetes, and other so-called diseases of civilization.

You can be sure, however, that Atkins devotees aren't routinely eating seal and whale blubber. Besides the acquired taste problem, their commerce is extremely restricted in the United States by the Marine Mammal Protection Act, says Bruce Holub, a nutritional biochemist in the department of human biology and nutritional sciences at the University of Guelph in Ontario.

"In heartland America it's probable they're not eating in an Eskimo-like way," says Gary Foster, clinical director of the Weight and Eating Disorders Program at the Pennsylvania School of Medicine. Foster, who describes himself as open-minded about Atkins, says he'd nonetheless worry if people saw the diet as a green light to eat all the butter and bacon—saturated fats—they want. Just before rumors

surfaced that Robert Atkins had heart and weight problems when he died, Atkins officials themselves were stressing saturated fat should account for no more than 20 percent of dieters' calories. This seems to be a clear retreat from the diet's original don't-count-the-calories approach to bacon and butter and its happy exhortations to "plow into those prime ribs." Furthermore, 20 percent of calories from saturated fats is *double* what most nutritionists advise. Before plowing into those prime ribs, readers of a recent edition of the *Dr. Atkins' New Diet Revolution* are urged to take omega-3 pills to help protect their hearts. "If you watch carefully," says Holub wryly, "you'll see many popular U.S. diets have quietly added omega-3 pills, in the form of fish oil or flaxseed capsules, as supplements."

Needless to say, the subsistence diets of the Far North are not "dieting." Dieting is the price we pay for too little exercise and too much mass-produced food. Northern diets were a way of life in places too cold for agriculture, where food, whether hunted, fished, or foraged, could not be taken for granted. They were about keeping weight on.

This is not to say that people in the Far North were fat: Subsistence living requires exercise—hard physical work. Indeed, among the good reasons for native people to maintain their old way of eating, as far as it's possible today, is that it provides a hedge against obesity, type 2 diabetes, and heart disease. Unfortunately, no place on Earth is immune to the spreading taint of growth and development. The very well-being of the northern food chain is coming under threat from global warming, land development, and industrial pollutants in the marine environment. "I'm a pragmatist," says Cochran, whose organization is involved in pollution monitoring and disseminating food-safety information to native villages. "Global warming we don't have control over. But we can, for example, do cleanups of military sites in Alaska or of communication cables leaching lead into fish-spawning areas. We can help communities make informed food choices. A young woman of childbearing age may choose not to eat certain organ meats that concentrate contaminants. As individuals, we do have options. And eating our salmon and our seal is still a heck of a better option than pulling something processed that's full of additives off a store shelf."

Not often in our industrial society do we hear someone speak so familiarly about "our" food animals. We don't talk of "our pig" and "our beef." We've lost that creature feeling, that sense of kinship with food sources. "You're taught to think in boxes," says Cochran. "In our culture the connectivity between humans, animals, plants, the land they live on, and the air they share is ingrained in us from birth.

"You truthfully can't separate the way we get our food from the way we live," she says. "How we get our food is intrinsic to our culture. It's how we pass on our values and knowledge to the young. When you go out with your aunts and uncles to hunt or to gather, you learn to smell the air, watch the wind, understand the way the ice moves, know the land. You get to know where to pick which plant and what animal to take."

"It's part, too, of your development as a person. You share food with your community. You show respect to your elders by offering them the first catch. You give thanks to the animal that gave up its life for your sustenance. So you get all the physical activity of harvesting your own food, all the social activity of sharing and preparing it, and all the spiritual aspects as well," says Cochran. "You certainly don't get all that, do you, when you buy prepackaged food from a store."

"That's why some of us here in Anchorage are working to protect what's ours, so that others can continue to live back home in the villages," she adds. "Because if we don't take care of our food, it won't be there for us in the future. And if we lose our foods, we lose who we are." The word Inupiat means "the real people." "That's who we are," says Cochran.

Critical Thinking

1. What kinds of diseases are on the increase among the Inuit and why?

2. Discuss the traditional high-protein, high-fat diet. How does this compare with the "balanced diet" most of us grew up with? What does this mean, according to Harold Draper?

3. Discuss the contrasting sources of vitamins A, D, and C between our diet and the diet of the Inuit. What is the advantage of eating meat and fish raw?

4. What is a "protein ceiling" and why? How did hunter-gatherers cope with the problem?

5. Where do the more healthful fats (monounsaturated and omega-3 fatty acids) come from? What are their benefits?

6. Why is it that Atkins-dieters are not really eating in an "Eskimo-like way"?

7. What are the differences between the subsistence diets of the Far North and "dieting"?

8. Were people of the Far North fat? Why not? In what ways did the old way of eating protect them?

9. How is the northern food chain threatened?

10. In what sense is there a kinship with food sources in the Far North that our industrial societies does not have and why? Why is it also a part of one's development as a person?

Curse and Blessing of the Ghetto

Tay-Sachs disease is a choosy killer, one that for centuries targeted Eastern European Jews above all others. By decoding its lethal logic, we can learn a lot about how genetic diseases evolve—and how they can be conquered.

JARED DIAMOND

Marie and I hated her at first sight, even though she was trying hard to be helpful. As our obstetrician's genetics counselor, she was just doing her job, explaining to us the unpleasant results that might come out of the genetic tests we were about to have performed. As a scientist, though, I already knew all I wanted to know about Tay-Sachs disease, and I didn't need to be reminded that the baby sentenced to death by it could be my own.

Fortunately, the tests would reveal that my wife and I were not carriers of the Tay-Sachs gene, and our preparenthood fears on that matter at least could be put to rest. But at the time I didn't yet know that. As I glared angrily at that poor genetics counselor, so strong was my anxiety that now, four years later, I can still clearly remember what was going through my mind: If I were an evil deity, I thought, trying to devise exquisite tortures for babies and their parents, I would be proud to have designed Tay-Sachs disease.

Tay-Sachs is completely incurable, unpreventable, and preprogrammed in the genes. A Tay-Sachs infant usually appears normal for the first few months after birth, just long enough for the parents to grow to love him. An exaggerated "startle reaction" to sounds is the first ominous sign. At about six months the baby starts to lose control of his head and can't roll over or sit without support. Later he begins to drool, breaks out into unmotivated bouts of laughter, and suffers convulsions. Then his head grows abnormally large, and he becomes blind. Perhaps what's most frightening for the parents is that their baby loses all contact with his environment and becomes virtually a vegetable. By the child's third birthday, if he's still alive, his skin will turn yellow and his hands pudgy. Most likely he will die before he's four years old.

My wife and I were tested for the Tay-Sachs gene because at the time we rated as high-risk candidates, for two reasons. First, Marie was carrying twins, so we had double the usual chance to bear a Tay-Sachs baby. Second, both she and I are of Eastern European Jewish ancestry, the population with by far the world's highest Tay-Sachs frequency.

In peoples around the world Tay-Sachs appears once in every 400,000 births. But it appears a hundred times more frequently—about once in 3,600 births—among descendants of Eastern European Jews, people known as Ashkenazim. For descendants of most other groups of Jews—Oriental Jews, chiefly from the Middle East, or Sephardic Jews, from Spain and other Mediterranean countries—the frequency of Tay-Sachs disease is no higher than in non-Jews. Faced with such a clear correlation, one cannot help but wonder: What is it about this one group of people that produces such an extraordinarily high risk of this disease?

Finding the answer to this question concerns all of us, regardless of our ancestry. Every human population is especially susceptible to certain diseases, not only because of its life-style but also because of its genetic inheritance. For example, genes put European whites at high risk for cystic fibrosis, African blacks for sickle-cell disease, Pacific Islanders for diabetes—and Eastern European Jews for ten different diseases, including Tay-Sachs. It's not that Jews are notably susceptible to genetic diseases in general; but a combination of historical factors has led to Jews' being intensively studied, and so their susceptibilities are far better known than those of, say, Pacific Islanders.

Tay-Sachs exemplifies how we can deal with such diseases; it has been the object of the most successful screening program to date. Moreover, Tay-Sachs is helping us understand how ethnic diseases evolve. Within the past couple of years discoveries by molecular biologists have provided tantalizing clues to precisely how a deadly gene can persist and spread over the centuries. Tay-Sachs may be primarily a disease of Eastern European Jews, but through this affliction of one group of people, we gain a window on how our genes simultaneously curse and bless us all.

The disease's hyphenated name comes from the two physicians—British ophthalmologist W. Tay and New York neurologist B. Sachs—who independently first recognized the disease, in 1881 and 1887, respectively. By 1896 Sachs had seen enough cases to realize that the disease was most common among Jewish children.

Not until 1962, however, were researchers able to trace the cause of the affliction to a single biochemical abnormality: the excessive accumulation in nerve cells of a fatty substance called G_{M2} ganglioside. Normally G_{M2} ganglioside is present at only modest levels in cell membranes, because it is constantly being broken down as well as synthesized. The breakdown depends on the enzyme hexosaminidase A, which is found in the tiny structures within our cells known as lysosomes. In the unfortunate Tay-Sachs victims this enzyme is lacking, and without it the ganglioside piles up and produces all the symptoms of the disease.

We have two copies of the gene that programs our supply of hexosaminidase A, one inherited from our father, the other from our mother; each of our parents, in turn, has two copies derived from their own parents. As long as we have one good copy of the gene, we can produce enough hexosaminidase A to prevent a buildup of G_{M2} ganglioside and we won't get Tay-Sachs. This genetic disease is of the sort termed recessive rather than dominant—meaning that to get it, a child must inherit a defective gene not just from one parent but from both of them. Clearly, each parent must have had one good copy of the gene along with the defective copy—if either had had two defective genes, he or she would have died of the disease long before reaching the age of reproduction. In genetic terms the diseased child is homozygous for the defective gene and both parents are heterozygous for it.

None of this yet gives any hint as to why the Tay-Sachs gene should be most common among Eastern European Jews. To come to grips with that question, we must take a short detour into history.

From their biblical home of ancient Israel, Jews spread peacefully to other Mediterranean lands, Yemen, and India. They were also dispersed violently through conquest by Assyrians, Babylonians, and Romans. Under the Carolingian kings of the eighth and ninth centuries Jews were invited to settle in France and Germany as traders and financiers. In subsequent centuries, however, persecutions triggered by the Crusades gradually drove Jews out of Western Europe; the process culminated in their total expulsion from Spain in 1492. Those Spanish Jews—called Sephardim—fled to other lands around the Mediterranean. Jews of France and Germany—the Ashkenazim—fled east to Poland and from there to Lithuania and western Russia, where they settled mostly in towns, as businessmen engaged in whatever pursuit they were allowed.

There the Jews stayed for centuries, through periods of both tolerance and oppression. But toward the end of the nineteenth century and the beginning of the twentieth, waves of murderous anti-Semitic attacks drove millions of Jews out of Eastern Europe, with most of them heading for the United States. My mother's parents, for example, fled to New York from Lithuanian pogroms of the 1880s, while my father's parents fled from the Ukrainian pogroms of 1903–6. The more modern history of Jewish migration is probably well known to you all: most Jews who remained in Eastern Europe were exterminated during World War II, while most of the survivors immigrated to the United States and Israel. Of the 13 million Jews alive today, more than three-quarters are Ashkenazim, the descendants of the Eastern European Jews and the people most at risk for Tay-Sachs.

Have these Jews maintained their genetic distinctness through the thousands of years of wandering? Some scholars claim that there has been so much intermarriage and conversion that Ashkenazic Jews are now just Eastern Europeans who adopted Jewish culture. However, modern genetic studies refute that speculation.

First of all, there are those ten genetic diseases that the Ashkenazim have somehow acquired, by which they differ both from other Jews and from Eastern European non-Jews. In addition, many Ashkenazic genes turn out to be ones typical of Palestinian Arabs and other peoples of the Eastern Mediterranean areas where Jews originated. (In fact, by genetic standards the current Arab-Israeli conflict is an internecine civil war.) Other Ashkenazic genes have indeed diverged from Mediterranean ones (including genes of Sephardic and Oriental Jews) and have evolved to converge on genes of Eastern European non-Jews subject to the same local forces of natural selection. But the degree to which Ashkenazim prove to differ genetically from Eastern European non-Jews implies an intermarriage rate of only about 15 percent.

Can history help explain why the Tay-Sachs gene in particular is so much more common in Ashkenazim than in their non-Jewish neighbors or in other Jews? At the risk of spoiling a mystery, I'll tell you now that the answer is yes, but to appreciate it, you'll have to understand the four possible explanations for the persistence of the Tay-Sachs gene.

First, new copies of the gene might be arising by mutation as fast as existing copies disappear with the death of Tay-Sachs children. That's the most likely explanation for the gene's persistence in most of the world, where the disease frequency is only one in 400,000 births—that frequency reflects a typical human mutation rate. But for this explanation to apply to the Ashkenazim would require a mutation rate of at least one per 3,600 births—far above the frequency observed for any human gene. Furthermore, there would be no precedent for one particular gene mutating so much more often in one human population than in others.

As a second possibility, the Ashkenazim might have acquired the Tay-Sachs gene from some other people who already had the gene at high frequency. Arthur Koestler's controversial book *The Thirteenth Tribe,* for example, popularized the view that the Ashkenazim are really not a Semitic people but are instead descended from the Khazar, a Turkic tribe whose rulers converted to Judaism in the eighth century. Could the Khazar have brought the Tay-Sachs gene to Eastern Europe? This speculation makes good romantic reading, but there is no good evidence to support it. Moreover, it fails to explain why deaths of Tay-Sachs children didn't eliminate the gene by natural selection in the past 1,200 years, nor how the Khazar acquired high frequencies of the gene in the first place.

The third hypothesis was the one preferred by a good many geneticists until recently. It invokes two genetic processes, termed the founder effect and genetic drift, that may operate in small populations. To understand these concepts, imagine that 100 couples settle in a new land and found a population that then increases. Imagine further that one parent among those original 100 couples happens to have some rare gene, one, say, that normally occurs at a frequency of one in a million. The gene's frequency in the new population will now be one in 200 as a result of the accidental presence of that rare founder.

Or suppose again that 100 couples found a population, but that one of the 100 men happens to have lots of kids by his wife or that he is exceptionally popular with other women, while the other 99 men are childless or have few kids or are simply less popular. That one man may thereby father 10 percent rather than a more representative one percent of the next generation's babies, and their genes will disproportionately reflect that man's genes. In other words, gene frequencies will have drifted between the first and second generation.

Through these two types of genetic accidents a rare gene may occur with an unusually high frequency in a small expanding population. Eventually, if the gene is harmful, natural selection will bring its frequency back to normal by killing off gene bearers. But if the resultant disease is recessive—if heterozygous individuals don't get the disease and only the rare, homozygous individuals die of it—the gene's high frequency may persist for many generations.

These accidents do in fact account for the astonishingly high Tay-Sachs gene frequency found in one group of Pennsylvania Dutch: out of the 333 people in this group, 98 proved to carry the Tay-Sachs gene. Those 333 are all descended from one couple who settled in the United States in the eighteenth century and had 13 children. Clearly, one of that founding couple must have carried the gene. A similar accident may explain why Tay-Sachs is also relatively common among French Canadians, who number 5 million today but are descended from fewer than 6,000 French immigrants who arrived in the New World between 1638 and 1759. In the two or three centuries since both these founding events, the high Tay-Sachs gene frequency among Pennsylvania Dutch and French Canadians has not yet had enough time to decline to normal levels.

The same mechanisms were one proposed to explain the high rate of Tay-Sachs disease among the Ashkenazim. Perhaps, the reasoning went, the gene just happened to be overrepresented in the founding Jewish population that settled in Germany or Eastern Europe. Perhaps the gene just happened to drift up in frequency in the Jewish populations scattered among the isolated towns of Eastern Europe.

But geneticists have long questioned whether the Ashkenazim population's history was really suitable for these genetic accidents to have been significant. Remember, the founder effect and genetic drift become significant only in small populations, and the founding populations of Ashkenazim may have been quite large. Moreover, Ashkenazic communities were considerably widespread; drift would have sent gene frequencies up in some towns but down in others. And, finally, natural selection has by now had a thousand years to restore gene frequencies to normal.

Granted, those doubts are based on historical data, which are not always as precise or reliable as one might want. But within the past several years the case against those accidental explanations for Tay-Sachs disease in the Ashkenazim has been bolstered by discoveries by molecular biologists.

Like all proteins, the enzyme absent in Tay-Sachs children is coded for by a piece of our DNA. Along that particular stretch of DNA there are thousands of different sites where a mutation could occur that would result in no enzyme and hence in the same set of symptoms. If molecular biologists had discovered that all cases of Tay-Sachs in Ashkenazim involved damage to DNA at the same site, that would have been strong evidence that in Ashkenazim the disease stems from a single mutation that has been multiplied by the founder effect or genetic drift—in other words, the high incidence of Tay-Sachs among Eastern European Jews is accidental.

In reality, though, several different mutations along this stretch of DNA have been identified in Ashkenazim, and two of them occur much more frequently than in non-Ashkenazim populations. It seems unlikely that genetic accidents would have pumped up the frequency of the same gene not once but twice in the same population.

It seems unlikely that genetic accidents would have pumped up the frequency of the same gene not once but twice in the same population.

And that's not the sole unlikely coincidence arguing against accidental explanations. Recall that Tay-Sachs is caused by the excessive accumulation of one fatty substance, G_{M2} ganglioside, from a defect in one enzyme, hexosaminidase A. But Tay-Sachs is one of ten genetic diseases characteristic of Ashkenazim. Among those other nine, two—Gaucher's disease and Niemann-Pick disease—result from the accumulation of two other fatty substances similar to G_{M2} ganglioside, as a result of defects in two other enzymes similar to hexosaminidase A. Yet our bodies contain thousands of different enzymes. It would have been an incredible roll of the genetic dice if, by nothing more than chance, Ashkenazim had independently acquired mutations in three closely related enzymes—and had acquired mutations in one of those enzymes twice.

All these facts bring us to the fourth possible explanation of why the Tay-Sachs gene is so prevalent among Ashkenazim: namely, that something about them favored accumulation of G_{M2} ganglioside and related fats.

For comparison, suppose that a friend doubles her money on one stock while you are getting wiped out with your investments. Taken alone, that could just mean she was lucky on that one occasion. But suppose that she doubles her money on each of two different stocks and at the same time rings up big profits in real estate while also making a killing in bonds. That implies more than lady luck; it suggests that something about your friend—like shrewd judgment—favors financial success.

What could be the blessings of fat accumulation in Eastern European Jews? At first this question sounds weird. After all, that fat accumulation was noticed only because of the curses it bestows: Tay-Sachs, Gaucher's, or Niemann-Pick disease. But many of our common genetic diseases may persist because they bring both blessings and curses (see "The Cruel Logic of Our Genes," *Discover,* November 1989). They kill or impair individuals who inherit two copies of the faulty gene, but they help those who receive only one defective gene by protecting them against other diseases. The best understood example is the sickle-cell gene of African blacks, which often kills homozygotes but protects heterozygotes against malaria. Natural selection sustains such genes because more heterozygotes than normal individuals survive to pass on their genes, and those extra gene copies offset the copies lost through the deaths of homozygotes.

So let us refine our question and ask, What blessing could the Tay-Sachs gene bring to those individuals who are heterozygous for it? A clue first emerged back in 1972, with the publication of the results of a questionnaire that had asked U.S. Ashkenzaic parents of Tay-Sachs children what their own Eastern European-born parents had died of. Keep in mind that since these unfortunate children had to be homozygotes, with two copies of the Tay-Sachs gene, all their parents had to be heterozygotes, with one copy, and half of the parents' parents also had to be heterozygotes.

As it turned out, most of those Tay-Sachs grandparents had died of the usual causes: heart disease, stroke, cancer, and diabetes. But strikingly, only one of the 306 grandparents had died of tuberculosis, even though TB was generally one of the big killers in these grandparents' time. Indeed, among the general population of large Eastern European cities in the early twentieth century, TB caused up to 20 percent of all deaths.

This big discrepancy suggested that Tay-Sachs heterozygotes might somehow have been protected against TB. Interestingly, it was already well known that Ashkenazim in general had some such protection: even when Jews and non-Jews were compared within the same European city, class, and occupational group (for example, Warsaw garment workers), Jews had only half the TB death rate of non-Jews, despite their being equally susceptible to infection. Perhaps, one could reason, the Tay-Sachs gene furnished part of that well-established Jewish resistance.

A second clue to a heterozygote advantage conveyed by the Tay-Sachs gene emerged in 1983, with a fresh look at the data concerning the distributions of TB and the Tay-Sachs gene within Europe. The statistics showed that the Tay-Sachs gene was nearly three times more frequent among Jews originating from Austria, Hungary, and Czechoslovakia—areas where an amazing 9 to 10 percent of the population were heterozygotes— than among Jews from Poland, Russia, and Germany. At the same time records from an old Jewish TB sanatorium in Denver in 1904 showed that among patients born in Europe between 1860 and 1910, Jews from Austria and Hungary were overrepresented.

Initially, in putting together these two pieces of information, you might be tempted to conclude that because the highest frequency of the Tay-Sachs gene appeared in the same geographic region that produced the most cases of TB, the gene in fact offers no protection whatsoever. Indeed, this was precisely the mistaken conclusion of many researchers who had looked at these data before. But you have to pay careful attention to the numbers here: even at its highest frequency the Tay-Sachs gene was carried by far fewer people than would be infected by TB. What the statistics really indicate is that where TB is the biggest threat, natural selection produces the biggest response.

Think of it this way: You arrive at an island where you find that all the inhabitants of the north end wear suits of armor, while all the inhabitants of the south end wear only cloth shirts. You'd be pretty safe in assuming that warfare is more prevalent in the north—and that war-related injuries account for far more deaths there than in the south. Thus, if the Tay-Sachs gene does indeed lend heterozygotes some protection against TB, you would expect to find the gene most often precisely where you find TB most often. Similarly, the sickle-cell gene reaches its highest frequencies in those parts of Africa where malaria is the biggest risk.

But you may believe there's still a hole in the argument: If Tay-Sachs heterozygotes are protected against TB, you may be asking, why is the gene common just in the Ashkenazim? Why did it not become common in the non-Jewish populations also exposed to TB in Austria, Hungary, and Czechoslovakia?

At this point we must recall the peculiar circumstances in which the Jews of Eastern Europe were forced to live. They were unique among the world's ethnic groups in having been virtually confined to towns for most of the past 2,000 years. Being forbidden to own land, Eastern European Jews were not peasant farmers living in the countryside, but businesspeople forced to live in crowded ghettos, in an environment where tuberculosis thrived.

Of course, until recent improvements in sanitation, these towns were not very healthy places for non-Jews either. Indeed, their populations couldn't sustain themselves: deaths exceeded births, and the number of dead had to be balanced by continued emigration from the countryside. For non-Jews, therefore, there was no genetically distinct urban population. For ghetto-bound Jews, however, there could be no emigration from the countryside; thus the Jewish population was under the strongest selection to evolve genetic resistance to TB.

Those are the conditions that probably led to Jewish TB resistance, whatever particular genetic factors prove to underlie it. I'd speculate that G_{M2} and related fats accumulate at slightly higher-than-normal levels in heterozygotes, although not at the lethal levels seen in homozygotes. (The fat accumulation in heterozygotes probably takes place in the cell membrane, the cell's "armor.") I'd also speculate that the accumulation provides heterozygotes with some protection against TB, and that that's why the genes for Tay-Sachs, Gaucher's, and Niemann-Pick disease reached high frequencies in the Ashkenazim.

Having thus stated the case, let me make clear that I don't want to overstate it. The evidence is still speculative. Depending on how you do the calculation, the low frequency of TB deaths in Tay-Sachs grandparents either barely reaches or doesn't quite reach the level of proof that statisticians require to accept an effect as real rather than as one that's arisen by chance. Moreover, we have no idea of the biochemical mechanism by which fat accumulation might confer resistance against TB. For the moment, I'd say that the evidence points to some selective advantage of Tay-Sachs heterozygotes among the Ashkenazim, and that TB resistance is the only plausible hypothesis yet proposed.

For now Tay-Sachs remains a speculative model for the evolution of ethnic diseases. But it's already a proven model of what to do about them. Twenty years ago a test was developed to identify Tay-Sachs heterozygotes, based on their lower-than-normal levels of hexosaminidase A. The test is simple, cheap, and accurate: all I did was to donate a small sample of my blood, pay $35, and wait a few days to receive the results.

If that test shows that at least one member of a couple is not a Tay-Sachs heterozygote, then any child of theirs can't be a Tay-Sachs homozygote. If both parents prove to be heterozygotes, there's a one-in-four chance of their child being a homozygote; that can then be determined by other tests performed on the mother early in pregnancy. If the results are positive, it's early enough for her to abort, should she choose to. That critical bit of knowledge has enabled parents who had gone through the agony of bearing a Tay-Sachs baby and watching him die to find the courage to try again.

The Tay-Sachs screening program launched in the United States in 1971 was targeted at the high-risk population: Ashkenazic Jewish couples of childbearing age. So successful has this approach been that the number of Tay-Sachs babies born each year in this country has declined tenfold. Today, in fact, more Tay-Sachs cases appear here in non-Jews than in Jews, because only the latter couples are routinely tested. Thus, what used to be the classic genetic disease of Jews is so no longer.

There's also a broader message to the Tay-Sachs story. We commonly refer to the United States as a melting pot, and in many ways that metaphor is apt. But in other ways we're not a melting pot, and we won't be for a long time. Each ethnic group has some characteristic genes of its own, a legacy of its distinct history. Tuberculosis and malaria are not major causes of death in the United States, but the genes that some of us evolved to protect ourselves against them are still frequent. Those genes are frequent only in certain ethnic groups, though, and they'll be slow to melt through the population.

We're not a melting pot, and we won't be for a long time. Each ethnic group has some characteristic genes of its own, a legacy of its distinct history.

With modern advances in molecular genetics, we can expect to see more, not less, ethnically targeted practice of medicine. Genetic screening for cystic fibrosis in European whites, for example, is one program that has been much discussed recently; when it comes, it will surely be based on the Tay-Sachs experience. Of course, what that may mean someday is more anxiety-ridden parents-to-be glowering at more dedicated genetics counselors. It will also mean fewer babies doomed to the agonies of diseases we may understand but that we'll never be able to accept.

Critical Thinking

1. How does the author describe Tay-Sachs disease?

2. What is the world-wide frequency of the disease? Who is most at risk and what is their frequency?

3. Are Jews more susceptible to genetic diseases than other human populations? Explain.

4. Discuss the genetic basis of the disease. (Do not bother with the chemical aspect.)

5. What evidence is there that Eastern European Jews have maintained a degree of genetic distinctness?

6. Discuss and evaluate the first three hypotheses on the origins of Tay-Sachs among the Ashkenazim. Note in particular the evidence for the founder effect among the Pennsylvania Dutch and the French Canadians.

7. Discuss the fourth hypothesis and the evidence for it. Why must we still call this a "speculative model"?

8. Describe the diagnostic possibilities of the Tay-Sachs story. What can we expect in the future with regard to genetic screening?

Contributing editor **JARED DIAMOND** is a professor of physiology at the UCLA School of Medicine.

From *Discover*, March 1991, pp. 60–65. Copyright © 1991 by Jared Diamond. Reprinted by permission of the author.

Ironing It Out

SHARON MOALEM

Aran Gordon is a born competitor. He's a top financial executive, a competitive swimmer since he was six years old, and a natural long-distance runner. A little more than a dozen years after he ran his first marathon in 1984 he set his sights on the Mount Everest of marathons—the Marathon des Sables, a 150-mile race across the Sahara Desert, all brutal heat and endlesss sand that test endurance runners like nothing else.

As he began to train he experienced something he'd never really had to deal with before—physical difficulty. He was tired all the time. His joints hurt. His heart seemed to skip a funny beat. He told his running partner he wasn't sure he could go on with training, with running at all. And he went to the doctor.

Actually, he went to *doctors*. Doctor after doctor—they couldn't account for his symptoms, or they drew the wrong conclusion. When his illness left him depressed, they told him it was stress and recommended he talk to a therapist. When blood tests revealed a liver problem, they told him he was drinking too much. Finally, after three years, his doctors uncovered the real problem. New tests revealed massive amounts of iron in his blood and liver—off-the-charts amounts of iron.

Aran Gordon was rusting to death.

Hemochromatosis is a hereditary disease that disrupts the way the body metabolizes iron. Normally, when your body detects that it has sufficient iron in the blood, it reduces the amount of iron absorbed by your intestines from the food you eat. So even if you stuffed yourself with iron supplements you wouldn't load up with excess iron. Once your body is satisfied with the amount of iron it has, the excess will pass through you instead of being absorbed. But in a person who has hemochromatosis, the body always thinks that it doesn't have enough iron and continues to absorb iron unabated. This iron loading has deadly consequences over time. The excess iron is deposited throughout the body, ultimately damaging the joints, the major organs, and overall body chemistry. Unchecked, hemochromatosis can lead to liver failure, heart failure, diabetes, arthritis, infertility, psychiatric disorders, and even cancer. Unchecked, hemochromatosis will lead to death.

For more than 125 years after Armand Trousseau first described it in 1865, hemochromatosis was thought to be extremely rare. Then, in 1996, the primary gene that causes the condition was isolated for the first time. Since then, we've discovered that the gene for hemochromatosis is the most common genetic variant in people of Western European descent. If your ancestors are Western European, the odds are about one in three, or one in four, that you carry at least one copy of the hemochromatosis gene. Yet only one in two hundred people of Western European ancestry actually have hemochromatosis disease with all of its assorted symptoms. In genetics parlance, the degree that a given gene manifests itself in an individual is called penetrance. If a single gene means everyone who carries it will have dimples, that gene has very high or complete penetrance. On the other hand, a gene that requires a host of other circumstances to really manifest, like the gene for hemochromatosis, is considered to have low penetrance.

Aran Gordon had hemochromatosis. His body had been accumulating iron for more than thirty years. If it were untreated, doctors told him, it would kill him in another five. Fortunately for Aran, one of the oldest medical therapies known to man would soon enter his life and help him manage his iron-loading problem. But to get there, we have to go back.

Why would a disease so deadly be bred into our genetic code? You see, hemochromatosis isn't an infectious disease like malaria, related to bad habits like lung cancer caused by smoking, or a viral invader like smallpox. Hemochromatosis is inherited—and the gene for it is very common in certain populations. In evolutionary terms, that means we asked for it.

Remember how natural selection works. If a given genetic trait makes you stronger—especially if it makes you stronger before you have children—then you're more likely to survive, reproduce, and pass that trait on. If a given trait makes you weaker, you're less likely to survive, reproduce, and pass that trait on. Over time, species "select" those traits that make them stronger and eliminate those traits that make them weaker.

So why is a natural-born killer like hemochromatosis swimming in our gene pool? To answer that, we have to examine the relationship between life—not just human life, but pretty much all life—and iron. But before we do, think about this—why would you take a drug that is guaranteed to kill you in forty years? One reason, right? It's the only thing that will stop you from dying tomorrow.

Just about every form of life has a thing for iron. Humans need iron for nearly every function of our metabolism. Iron carries oxygen from our lungs through the bloodstream and releases it in the body where it's needed. Iron is built into the enzymes that do most of the chemical heavy lifting in our bodies, where it helps us to detoxify poisons and to convert sugars into energy. Iron-poor diets and other iron deficiencies are the most common cause of anemia, a lack of red blood cells that can cause fatigue, shortness of breath, and even heart failure. (As many as 20 percent of menstruating women may have iron-related anemia because their monthly blood loss produces an iron deficiency. That may be the case in as much as half of all pregnant women as well—they're not menstruating, but the passenger they're carrying is hungry for iron too!) Without enough iron our immune system functions poorly, the skin gets pale, and people can feel confused, dizzy, cold, and extremely fatigued.

Iron even explains why some areas of the world's ocean are crystal clear blue and almost devoid of life, while others are bright green and teeming with it. It turns out that oceans can be seeded with iron when dust from land is blown across them. Oceans, like parts of the Pacific, that aren't in the path of these iron-bearing winds develop smaller communities of phytoplankton, the single-celled creatures at the bottom of the ocean's food chain. No phytoplankton, no zooplankton. No zooplankton, no anchovies. No anchovies, no tuna. But an ocean area like the North Atlantic, straight in the path of iron-rich dust from the Sahara Desert, is a green-hued aquatic metropolis. (This has even given rise to an idea to fight global warming that its originator calls the Geritol Solution. The notion is basically this— dumping billions of tons of iron solution into the ocean will stimulate massive plant growth that will suck enough carbon dioxide out of the atmosphere to counter the effects of all the CO_2 humans are releasing into the atmosphere by burning fossil fuels. A test of the theory in 1995 transformed a patch of ocean near the Galápagos Islands from sparkling blue to murky green overnight, as the iron triggered the growth of massive amounts of phytoplankton.)

Because iron is so important, most medical research has focused on populations who don't get enough iron. Some doctors and nutritionists have operated under the assumption that more iron can only be better. The food industry currently supplements everything from flour to breakfast cereal to baby formula with iron.

You know what they say about too much of a good thing?

Our relationship with iron is much more complex than it's been considered traditionally. It's essential—but it also provides a proverbial leg up to just about every biological threat to our lives. With very few exceptions in the form of a few bacteria that use other metals in its place, almost all life on earth needs iron to survive. Parasites hunt us for our iron; cancer cells thrive on

our iron. Finding, controlling, and using iron is the game of life. For bacteria, fungi, and protozoa, human blood and tissue are an iron gold mine. Add too much iron to the human system and you may just be loading up the buffet table.

In 1952, Eugene D. Weinberg was a gifted microbial researcher with a healthy curiosity and a sick wife. Diagnosed with a mild infection, his wife was prescribed tetracycline, an antibiotic. Professor Weinberg wondered whether anything in her diet could interfere with the effectiveness of the antibiotic. We've only scratched the surface of our understanding of bacterial interactions today; in 1952, medical science had only scratched the surface of the scratch. Weinberg knew how little we knew, and he knew how unpredictable bacteria could be, so he wanted to test how the antibiotic would react to the presence or absence of specific chemicals that his wife was adding to her system by eating.

In his lab, at Indiana University, he directed his assistant to load up dozens of petri dishes with three compounds: tetracycline, bacteria, and a third organic or elemental nutrient, which varied from dish to dish. A few days later, one dish was so loaded with bacteria that Professor Weinberg's assistant assumed she had forgotten to add the antibiotic to that dish. She repeated the test for that nutrient and got the same result—massive bacteria growth. The nutrient in this sample was providing so much booster fuel to the bacteria that it effectively neutralized the antibiotic. You guessed it—it was iron.

Weinberg went on to prove that access to iron helps nearly all bacteria multiply almost unimpeded. From that point on, he dedicated his life's work to understanding the negative effect that the ingestion of excess iron can have on humans and the relationship other life-forms have to it.

Human iron regulation is a complex system that involves virtually every part of the body. A healthy adult usually has between three and four grams of iron in his or her body. Most of this iron is in the bloodstream within hemoglobin, distributing oxygen, but iron can also be found throughout the body. Given that iron is not only crucial to our survival but can be a potentially deadly liability, it shouldn't be surprising that we have iron-related defense mechanisms as well.

We're most vulnerable to infection where infection has a gateway to our bodies. In an adult without wounds or broken skin, that means our mouths, eyes, noses, ears, and genitals. And because infectious agents need iron to survive, all those openings have been declared iron no-fly-zones by our bodies. On top of that, those openings are patrolled by chelators—proteins that lock up iron molecules and prevent them from being used. Everything from tears to saliva to mucus—all the fluids found in those bodily entry points—are rich with chelators.

There's more to our iron defense system. When we're first beset by illness, our immune system kicks into high gear and fights back with what is called the *acute phase response*. The bloodstream is flooded with illness-fighting proteins, and, at the same time, iron is locked away to prevent biological invaders from using it against us. It's the biological equivalent of a prison lockdown—flood the halls with guards and secure the guns.

A similar response appears to occur when cells become cancerous and begin to spread without control. Cancer cells require iron to grow, so the body attempts to limit its availability. New pharmaceutical research is exploring ways to mimic this response by developing drugs to treat cancer and infections by limiting their access to iron.

Even some folk cures have regained respect as our understanding of bacteria's reliance on iron has grown. People used to cover wounds with egg-white-soaked straw to protect them from infection. It turns out that wasn't such a bad idea—preventing infection is what egg whites are made for. Egg shells are porous so that the chick embryo inside can "breathe." The problem with a porous shell, of course, is that air isn't the only thing that can get through it—so can all sorts of nasty microbes. The egg white's there to stop them. Egg whites are chock-full of chelators (those iron locking proteins that patrol our bodies' entry points) like ovoferrin in order to protect the developing chicken embryo—the yolk—from infection.

The relationship between iron and infection also explains one of the ways breast-feeding helps to prevent infections in newborns. Mother's milk contains lactoferrin—a chelating protein that binds with iron and prevents bacteria from feeding on it.

Before we return to Aran Gordon and hemochromatosis, we need to take a side trip, this time to Europe in the middle of the fourteenth century—not the best time to visit.

From 1347 through the next few years, the bubonic plague swept across Europe, leaving death, death, and more death in its wake. Somewhere between one-third and one-half of the population was killed—more than 25 million people. No recorded pandemic, before or since, has come close to touching the plague's record. We hope none ever will.

It was a gruesome disease. In its most common form the bacterium that's thought to have caused the plague (*Yersinia pestis,* named after Alexander Yersin, one of the bacteriologists who first isolated it in 1894) finds a home in the body's lymphatic system, painfully swelling the lymph nodes in the armpits and groin until those swollen lymph nodes literally burst through the skin. Untreated, the survival rate is about one in three. (And that's just the bubonic form, which infects the lymphatic system; when *Y. pestis* makes it into the lungs and becomes airborne, it kills nine out of ten—and not only is it more lethal when it's airborne, it's more contagious!)

The most likely origin of the European outbreak is thought to be a fleet of Genoese trading ships that docked in Messina, Italy, in the fall of 1347. By the time the ships reached port, most of the crews were already dead or dying. Some of the ships never even made it to port, running aground along the coast after the last of their crew became too sick to steer the ship. Looters preyed on the wrecks and got a lot more than they bargained for—and so did just about everyone they encountered as they carried the plague to land.

In 1348 a Sicilian notary named Gabriele de' Mussi tells of how the disease spread from ships to the coastal populations and then inward across the continent:

Alas! Our ships enter the port, but of a thousand sailors hardly ten are spared. We reach our homes; our kindred . . . come from all parts to visit us. Woe to us for we cast at them the darts of death! . . . Going back to their homes, they in turn soon infected their whole families, who in three days succumbed, and were buried in one common grave.

Panic rose as the disease spread from town to town. Prayer vigils were held, bonfires were lighted, churches were filled with throngs. Inevitably, people looked for someone to blame. First it was Jews, and then it was witches. But rounding them up and burning them alive did nothing to stop the plague's deadly march.

Interestingly, it's possible that practices related to the observance of Passover helped to protect Jewish neighborhoods from the plague. Passover is a week-long holiday commemorating Jews' escape from slavery in Egypt. As part of its observance, Jews do not eat leavened bread and remove all traces of it from their homes. In many parts of the world, especially Europe, wheat, grain, and even legumes are also forbidden during Passover. Dr. Martin J. Blaser, a professor of internal medicine at New York University Medical Center, thinks this "spring cleaning" of grain stores may have helped to protect Jews from the plague, by decreasing their exposure to rats hunting for food—rats that carried the plague.

Victims and physicians alike had little idea what was causing the disease. Communities were overwhelmed simply by the volume of bodies that needed burying. And that, of course, contributed to the spread of the disease as rats fed on infected corpses, fleas fed on infected rats, and additional humans caught the disease from infected fleas. In 1348 a Sienese named Agnolo di Tura wrote:

Father abandoned child, wife husband, one brother another, for this illness seemed to strike through the breath and sight. And so they died. And none could be found to bury the dead for money or friendship. Members of a household brought their dead to a ditch as best they could, without priest, without divine offices . . . great pits were dug and piled deep with the multitude of dead. And they died by the hundreds both day and night. . . . And as soon as those ditches were filled more were dug. . . . And I, Agnolo di Tura, called the Fat, buried my five children with my own hands. And there were also those who were so sparsely covered with earth that the dogs dragged them forth and devoured many bodies throughout the city. There was no one who wept for any death, for all awaited death. And so many died that all believed it was the end of the world.

As it turned out, it wasn't the end of the world, and it didn't kill everyone on earth or even in Europe. It didn't even kill everyone it infected. Why? Why did some people die and others survive?

The emerging answer may be found in the same place Aran Gordon finally found the answer to his health problem—iron. New research indicates that the more iron in a given population, the more vulnerable that population is to the plague. In the past, healthy adult men were at greater risk than anybody else—children and the elderly tended to be malnourished, with corresponding iron deficiencies, and adult women are regularly iron depleted by menstruation, pregnancy, and breast-feeding. It might be that, as Stephen Ell, a professor at the University of Iowa, wrote, "Iron status mirror[ed] mortality. Adult males were at highest risk on this basis, with women [who lose iron through menstruation], children, and the elderly relatively spared."

There aren't any highly reliable mortality records from the fourteenth century, but many scholars believe that men in their prime were the most vulnerable. More recent—but still long ago—outbreaks of bubonic plague, for which there are reliable mortality records, demonstrate that the perception of heightened vulnerability in healthy adult men is very real. A study of plague in St. Botolph's Parish in 1625 indicates that men between fifteen and forty-four killed by the disease outnumbered women of the same age by a factor of two to one.

So let's get back to hemochromatosis. With all this iron in their systems, people with hemochromatosis should be magnets for infection in general and the plague in particular, right?

Wrong.

Remember the iron-locking response of the body at the onset of illness? It turns out that people who have hemochromatosis have a form of iron locking going on as a permanent condition. The excess iron that the body takes on is distributed throughout the body—but it isn't distributed *everywhere* throughout the body. And while most cells end up with too much iron, one particular type of cell ends up with much *less* iron than normal. The cells that hemochromatosis is stingy with when it comes to iron are a type of white blood cell called *macrophages*. Macrophages are the police wagons of the immune system. They circle our systems looking for trouble; when they find it, they surround it, try to subdue or kill it, and bring it back to the station in our lymph nodes.

In a nonhemochromatic person, macrophages have plenty of iron. Many infectious agents, like tuberculosis, can use that iron within the microphage to feed and multiply (which is exactly what the body is trying to prevent through the iron-locking response). So when a normal macrophage gathers up certain infectious agents to protect the body, it inadvertently is giving those infectious agents a Trojan horse access to the iron they need to grow stronger. By the time those macrophages get to the lymph node, the invaders in the wagon are armed and dangerous and can use the lymphatic system to travel throughout the body. That's exactly what happens with bubonic plague: the swollen and bursting lymph nodes that characterize it are the direct result of the bacteria's subversion of the body's immune system for its own purposes.

Ultimately, the ability to access iron within our macrophages is what makes some intracellular infections deadly and others benign. The longer our immune system is able to prevent an infection from spreading by containing it, the better it can develop other means, like antibodies, to overwhelm it. If your macrophages lack iron, as they do in people who have hemochromatosis, those macrophages have an additional advantage—not only do they isolate infectious agents and cordon them off from the rest of the body, they also starve those infectious agents to death.

New research has demonstrated that iron-deficient macrophages are indeed the Bruce Lees of the immune system. In one set of experiments, macrophages from people who had hemochromatosis and macrophages from people who did not were matched against bacteria in separate dishes to test their killing ability. The hemochromatic macrophages crushed the bacteria—they are thought to be significantly better at combating bacteria by limiting the availability of iron than the nonhemochromatic macrophages.

Which brings us full circle. Why would you take a pill that was guaranteed to kill you in forty years? Because it will save you tomorrow. Why would we select for a gene that will kill us through iron loading by the time we reach what is now middle age? Because it will protect us from a disease that is killing everyone else long before that.

Hemochromatosis is caused by a genetic mutation. It predates the plague, of course. Recent research has suggested that it originated with the Vikings and was spread throughout Northern Europe as the Vikings colonized the European coastline. It may have originally evolved as a mechanism to minimize iron deficiencies in poorly nourished populations living in harsh environments. (If this was the case, you'd expect to find hemochromatosis in all populations living in iron-deficient environments, but you don't.) Some researchers have speculated that women who had hemochromatosis might have benefited from the additional iron absorbed through their diet because it prevented anemia caused by menstruation. This, in turn, led them to have more children, who also carried the hemochromatosis mutation. Even more speculative theories have suggested that Viking men may have offset the negative effects of hemochromatosis because their warrior culture resulted in frequent blood loss.

As the Vikings settled the European coast, the mutation may have grown in frequency through what geneticists call the founder effect. When small populations establish colonies in unpopulated or secluded areas, there is significant inbreeding for generations. This inbreeding virtually guarantees that any mutations that aren't fatal at a very early age will be maintained in large portions of the population.

Then, in 1347, the plague begins its march across Europe. People who have the hemochromatosis mutation are especially resistant to infection because of their iron-starved macrophages. So, though it will kill them decades later, they are much more likely than people without hemochromatosis to survive the plague, reproduce, and pass the mutation on to their children. In a population where most people don't survive until middle age, a genetic trait that will kill you when you get there but increases your chance of arriving is—well, something to ask for.

The pandemic known as the Black Death is the most famous—and deadly—outbreak of bubonic plague, but historians and scientists believe there were recurring outbreaks in

Europe virtually every generation until the eighteenth or nineteenth century. If hemochromatosis helped that first generation of carriers to survive the plague, multiplying its frequency across the population as a result, it's likely that these successive outbreaks compounded that effect, further breeding the mutation into the Northern and Western European populations every time the disease resurfaced over the ensuing three hundred years. The growing percentage of hemochromatosis carriers—potentially able to fend off the plague—may also explain why no subsequent epidemic was as deadly as the pandemic of 1347 to 1350.

This new understanding of hemochromatosis, infection, and iron has provoked a reevaluation of two long-established medical treatments—one very old and all but discredited, the other more recent and all but dogma. The first, bleeding, is back; the second, iron dosing, especially for anemics, is being reconsidered in many circumstances.

Bloodletting is one of the oldest medical practices in history, and nothing has a longer or more complicated record. First recorded three thousand years ago in Egypt, it reached its peak in the nineteenth century only to be roundly discredited as almost savage over the last hundred years. There are records of Syrian doctors using leeches for bloodletting more than two thousand years ago and accounts of the great Jewish scholar Maimonides' employing bloodletting as the physician to the royal court of Saladin, sultan of Egypt, in the twelfth century. Doctors and shamans from Asia to Europe to the Americas used instruments as varied as sharpened sticks, shark's teeth, and miniature bows and arrows to bleed their patients.

In Western medicine, the practice was derived from the thinking of the Greek physician Galen, who practiced the theory of the four humours—blood, black bile, yellow bile, and phlegm. According to Galen and his intellectual descendants, all illness resulted from an imbalance of the four humours, and it was the doctor's job to balance those fluids through fasting, purging, and bloodletting.

Volumes of old medical texts are devoted to how and how much blood should be drawn. An illustration from a 1506 book on medicine points to forty-three different places on the human body that should be used for bleeding—fourteen on the head alone.

For centuries in the West, the place to go for bloodletting was the barber shop. In fact, the barber's pole originated as a symbol for bloodletting—the brass bowl at the top represented the bowl where leeches were kept; the one at the bottom represented the bowl for collecting blood. And the red and white spirals have their origins in the medieval practice of hanging bandages on a pole to dry them after they were washed. The bandages would twist in the wind and wrap themselves in spirals around the pole. As to why barbers were the surgeons of the day? Well, they were the guys with the razor blades.

Bloodletting reached its peak in the eighteenth and nineteenth centuries. According to medical texts of the time, if you presented to your doctor with a fever, hypertension, or dropsy, you would be bled. If you had an inflammation, apoplexy, or a nervous disorder, you would be bled. If you suffered from a cough, dizziness, headache, drunkenness, palsy, rheumatism, or shortness of breath, you would be bled. As crazy as it sounds, even if you were hemorrhaging blood you would be bled.

Modern medical science has been skeptical of bloodletting for many reasons—at least some of them deserved. First of all, eighteenth- and nineteenth-century reliance on bleeding as a treatment for just about everything is reasonably suspect.

When George Washington was ill with a throat infection, doctors treating him conducted at least four bleedings in just twenty-four hours. It's unclear today whether Washington actually died from the infection or from shock caused by blood loss. Doctors in the nineteenth century routinely bled patients until they fainted; they took that as a sign they'd removed just the right amount of blood.

After millennia of practice, bloodletting fell into extreme disfavor at the beginning of the twentieth century. The medical community—even the general public—considered bleeding to be the epitome of everything that was barbaric about prescientific medicine. Now, new research indicates that—like so much else—the broad discrediting of bloodletting may have been a rush to judgment.

First of all, it's now absolutely clear that bloodletting—or phlebotomy, as it's known today—is the treatment of choice for hemochromatosis patients. Regular bleeding of hemochromatosis patients reduces the iron in their systems to normal levels and prevents the iron buildup in the body's organs that is so damaging.

It's not just for hemochromatosis, either—doctors and researchers are examining phlebotomy as an aid in combating heart disease, high blood pressure, and pulmonary edema. And even our complete dismissal of historic bloodletting practices is getting another look. New evidence suggests that, in moderation, bloodletting may have had a beneficial effect.

A Canadian physiologist named Norman Kasting discovered that bleeding animals induces the release of the hormone vasopressin; this reduces their fevers and spurs their immune system into higher gear. The connection isn't unequivocally proven in humans, but there is much correlation between bloodletting and fever reduction in the historic record. Bleeding also may have helped to fight infection by reducing the amount of iron available to feed an invader, providing an assist to the body's natural tendency to hide iron when it recognizes an infection.

When you think about it, the notion that humans across the globe continued to practice phlebotomy for thousands of years probably indicates that it produced *some* positive results. If everyone who was treated with bloodletting died, its practitioners would have been out of business pretty quickly.

One thing is clear—an ancient medical practice that "modern" medical science dismissed out of hand is the only effective treatment for a disease that would otherwise destroy the lives of thousands of people. The lesson for medical science is a simple one—there is much more that the scientific community doesn't understand than there is that it does understand.

Iron is good. Iron is good. Iron is good.

Well, now you know that, like just about every other good thing under the sun, when it comes to iron, it's moderation, moderation, moderation. But until recently, current medical thinking didn't recognize that. Iron was thought to be good, so the more iron the better.

A doctor named John Murray was working with his wife in a Somali refugee camp when he noticed that many of the nomads, despite pervasive anemia and repeated exposure to a range of virulent pathogens, including malaria, tuberculosis, and brucellosis, were free of visible infection. He responded to this anomaly by deciding to treat only part of the population with iron at first. Sure enough, he treated some of the nomads for anemia by giving them iron supplements, and suddenly the infections gained the upper hand. The rate of infection in nomads receiving the extra iron skyrocketed. The Somali nomads weren't withstanding these infections *despite* their anemia: they were withstanding these infections *because of* their anemia. It was iron locking in high gear.

Thirty-five years ago, doctors in New Zealand routinely injected Maori babies with iron supplements. They assumed that the Maori (the indigenous people of New Zealand) had a poor diet, lacking iron, and that their babies would be anemic as a result.

The Maori babies injected with iron were seven times as likely to suffer from potentially deadly infections, including septicemias (blood poisoning) and meningitis. Like all of us, babies have isolated strains of potentially harmful bacteria in their systems, but those strains are normally kept under control by their bodies. When the doctors gave these babies iron boosters, they were giving booster fuel to the bacteria, with tragic results.

It's not just iron dosing through injection that can cause this blossoming of infections; iron-supplemented food can be food for bacteria too. Many infants can have botulism spores in their intestines (the spores can be found in honey, and that's one of the reasons parents are warned not to feed honey to babies, especially before they turn one). If the spores germinate, the results can be fatal. A study of sixty-nine cases of infant botulism in California showed one key difference between fatal and nonfatal cases of botulism in babies. Babies who were fed with iron-supplemented formula instead of breast-fed were much younger when they began to get sick and more vulnerable as a result. Of the ten who died, all had been fed with the iron-enhanced formula.

By the way, hemochromatosis and anemia aren't the only hereditary diseases that have gained pride of place in our gene pool by offering protection from another threat, and they're not all related to iron. The second most common genetic disease in Europeans, after hemochromatosis, is cystic fibrosis. It's a terrible, debilitating disease that affects different parts of the body. Most people with cystic fibrosis die young, usually from lung-related illness. Cystic fibrosis is caused by a mutation in a gene called CFTR; it takes two copies of the mutated gene to cause the disease. Somebody with only one copy of the mutated gene is known as a carrier but does not have cystic fibrosis. It's thought that at least 2 percent of people descended from Europeans are carriers, making the mutation very common indeed from a genetic perspective. New research suggests that, sure enough, carrying a copy of the gene that causes cystic fibrosis seems to offer some protection from tuberculosis. Tuberculosis, which has also been called consumption because of the way it seems to consume its victims from the inside out, caused 20 percent of all the deaths in Europe between 1600 and 1900, making it a very deadly disease. And making anything that helped to protect people from it look pretty attractive while lounging in the gene pool.

Aran Gordon first manifested symptoms of hemochromatosis as he began training for the Marathon des Sables—that grueling 150-mile race across the Sahara Desert. But it would take three years of progressive health problems, frustrating tests, and inaccurate conclusions before he finally learned what was wrong with him. When he did, he was told that untreated he had five years to live.

Today, we know that Aran suffered the effects of the most common genetic disorder in people of European descent—hemochromatosis, a disorder that may very well have helped his ancestors to survive the plague.

Today, Aran's health has been restored through bloodletting, one of the oldest medical practices on earth.

Today, we understand much more about the complex interrelationship of our bodies, iron, infection, and conditions like hemochromatosis and anemia.

What doesn't kill us, makes us stronger.

Which is probably some version of what Aran Gordon was thinking when he finished the Marathon des Sables for the second time in April 2006—just a few months after he was supposed to have died.

Critical Thinking

1. What is "hemochromatosis," why does it occur, and what are its consequences? What is its primary cause?

2. Why is iron important to humans?

3. Why does our iron set us up for biological threats?

4. Discuss the ways in which our bodies regulate iron in order to fight disease.

5. Discuss the way in which the bubonic plague killed its victims and why people with hemochromatosis were the more likely survivors.

6. How did hemochromatosis seem to get its start in Europe? How might the "founder effect" have played a role? How might the gene have increased over the centuries?

7. Why was bloodletting favored as a treatment over the millennia, then discounted, and now is back in favor in several respects?

8. What evidence is there that too much iron can be harmful?

9. Why is having two genes for cystic fibrosis harmful? Why is having one gene beneficial?

Children Who Sue for Being Born

Why are more and more people in Israel with genetic disorders filing lawsuits for "wrongful life"?

The case for wrongful life: the children encouraged to sue for being born. Children in Israel are increasingly suing the medical profession for allowing them to be born in the first place.

ANJANA AHUJA

I sraeli children with birth defects are increasingly suing the medical authorities for ever allowing them to be born. The rise in such "wrongful life" lawsuits, which the medical profession estimates at 600 since the first case in 1987, has prompted an investigation by the Israeli government.

According to medical ethicists contacted by *New Scientist,* these cases raise serious ethical questions—not least concerning the value of the lives of disabled people—and raise fears that medical professionals may become overly cautious in their interpretations of diagnostic tests, resulting in terminations of healthy pregnancies. One ethicist also claims that lawyers looking to drum up business are trawling communities with high rates of inbreeding and genetic disease.

"Wrongful birth" cases, in which parents seek compensation for the costs of raising a disabled child, are well documented. Last month, a couple in California won $4.5 million in damages after doctors and sonographers failed to pick up that their son, now aged 3, had no legs and only one arm.

"I find it very difficult to understand how parents can go on the witness stand and tell their children 'it would have been better for you not to have been born'," says Rabbi Avraham Steinberg, a medical ethicist from the Hebrew University-Hadassah Medical School in Jerusalem. "What are the psychological effects on the children?"

The trend in Israel is now for the children themselves to sue for wrongful life, which generally carries a bigger award designed to compensate for a lifetime of suffering. Steinberg sits on the Matza committee—named after the judge chairing it—set up by the government to investigate the issue. He has also been an expert witness in such cases.

One of the first successful wrongful life cases was brought before the California Court of Appeal in 1980, when a child sued for damages for being born with a neurodegenerative condition called Tay-Sachs disease. In Israel the rate of lawsuits

has been rising since a legal precedent was set there in 1987, whereas wrongful life litigation is not accepted in many other countries, including the UK and all but four US states.

The problem is exacerbated in Israel by a very strong pro-science, pro-genetic testing culture. "There is an entire system fuelled by money and the quest for the perfect baby," says Carmel Shalev, a human rights lawyer and bioethicist at the University of Haifa in Israel. "Everyone buys in to it—parents, doctors and labs. Parents want healthy babies, doctors encourage them to get tested, and some genetic tests are being marketed too early. Genetic testing has enormous benefits but it is overused and misused."

The popularity of these tests is in part due to the fact that genetic disorders such as Down's syndrome, deafness and cystic fibrosis are prevalent in Israel because of high rates of consanguineous marriage—unions between second cousins or closer relatives. Many settlements were founded only a few generations ago by a handful of people, and marriage within villages means that couples end up effectively marrying within their extended family (see box "Risky Relationships").

Since we all carry a smattering of defective genes, marrying a blood relative increases the risk of autosomal recessive disorders, in which two healthy partners—each carrying a single faulty copy—produce a child who inherits the double whammy of two defective copies.

A common example within ultra-orthodox Jewish communities is Tay-Sachs disease, which manifests itself in people carrying both faulty copies of the gene. If both parents carry a single copy, children have a 1-in-4 chance of having the disease.

Couples at high risk have the option of being screened before making the decision to marry or try for children. In Israel, in particular, a wide range of prenatal testing is offered by the state. Private genetic testing is also extremely popular with Israeli couples, and it is permissible there to terminate viable pregnancies due to health reasons, with permission from an abortion committee. Asaf Posner, a prominent medical malpractice lawyer in Jerusalem, says he has dealt with families who, despite being very religious, had been given special dispensation by religious elders to abort a fetus suspected of having cystic fibrosis—a decision which would almost certainly have been approved by the committee.

In the past five years, Posner has won wrongful life cases on behalf of children with cystic fibrosis and spina bifida, and says typical payouts are in the region of 4.5 million shekels (£775,000). He reckons a forthcoming ruling on a fragile-X syndrome case could potentially bring in 10 million shekels (£1.7 million).

Following a handful of wrongful life lawsuits in the past year, the Israel Society of Obstetrics and Gynecology advised the country's Supreme Court that not every undetected birth defect should be the basis of a malpractice suit. Extreme learning difficulties or around-the-clock assistance with basic tasks such as eating and going to the toilet, for example, should not be equated with milder impairments such as missing fingers.

Without such distinctions, clinicians and sonographers who fear being sued over the birth of a disabled or diseased baby might become over-cautious in their risk assessments, leading couples to abort healthy fetuses. "Physicians are increasingly practising defensive medicine, and doing a lot of testing," Steinberg says. "But more testing means more false positives—and that means more abortions, because geneticists don't always know if results indicating the possibility of chromosomal abnormalities are meaningful. I'd like to see a study of aborted fetuses to see how many are diseased." The Matza committee will submit its findings in the next few months.

Speaking at a genetics conference in Jerusalem last month, organised by the Anglo-Israel Association charity, Steinberg also voiced concerns that some lawyers are seeking to exploit the high rates of genetic defects in some communities by trawling them for cases. "To go to these villages and look around for people willing to file a claim that it would have been better not to be born is going too far," he said.

Posner, who also sits on the Matza committee, reckons only a small number of cases exist as a result of rogue lawyers targeting villages with high rates of inbreeding. He says most of his own clients are Jewish couples who feel they have been let down by the medical profession following genetic testing.

"Doctors gain a tremendous amount of money from prospective parents paying for private tests, such as ultrasound,"

Risky Relationships

Israel is home to a diverse population of traditional communities with high rates of consanguineous marriage (between second cousins or closer relatives). Among Muslims and Druze, it accounts for around 40 per cent of marriages, among the Bedouin 67 per cent, and among Christians about 20 per cent.

But Israel is not alone: consanguinity is common in the Middle East, India and North Africa. According to Joel Zlotogora of Israel's Ministry of Health, kinship marriage also carries advantages: it strengthens social ties and lowers rates of domestic violence and family breakdown.

Zlotogora, who has documented Bedouin villages with genetic conditions caused by inbreeding, told the Anglo-Israel Association: "Our message is not 'Don't marry your cousin' but 'Marry your cousin and know the risk.'" The ministry offers genetic screening and testing for at-risk communities.

That sentiment is shared by Dian Donnai, a geneticist at the University of Manchester, UK, who has worked with the UK's Pakistani Muslim community, where 55 per cent of marriages are between first cousins. "We are not there to influence people," Donnai says. "We give people the genetic information they need in order to make the right reproductive choices for them," she says.

Posner says. "They shouldn't complain when, if they are negligent, someone comes after them. Without criticism, the medical profession would become corrupt."

Critical Thinking

1. What are "wrongful life" lawsuits? What serious ethical issues do they raise?

2. What are "wrongful birth" cases?

3. What are the differences between the two kinds of lawsuits?

4. How is the problem of wrongful life lawsuits exacerbated in Israel?

5. Why is genetic testing so popular in Israel? What are the dangers of practicing "defensive medicine" with respect to possible birth defects?

6. What are the advantages and disadvantages of consanguineous marriages?

Test-Your-Knowledge Form

We encourage you to photocopy and use this page as a tool to assess how the articles in *Annual Editions* expand on the information in your textbook. By reflecting on the articles you will gain enhanced text information. You can also access this useful form on a product's book support website at www.mhhe.com/cls

NAME: DATE:

_____

TITLE AND NUMBER OF ARTICLE:

_____

BRIEFLY STATE THE MAIN IDEA OF THIS ARTICLE:

_____

LIST THREE IMPORTANT FACTS THAT THE AUTHOR USES TO SUPPORT THE MAIN IDEA:

_____

WHAT INFORMATION OR IDEAS DISCUSSED IN THIS ARTICLE ARE ALSO DISCUSSED IN YOUR TEXTBOOK OR OTHER READINGS THAT YOU HAVE DONE? LIST THE TEXTBOOK CHAPTERS AND PAGE NUMBERS:

_____

LIST ANY EXAMPLES OF BIAS OR FAULTY REASONING THAT YOU FOUND IN THE ARTICLE:

_____

LIST ANY NEW TERMS/CONCEPTS THAT WERE DISCUSSED IN THE ARTICLE, AND WRITE A SHORT DEFINITION:

NOTES

NOTES

NOTES

NOTES

NOTES

NOTES